Bangkok
Through the Looking Glass
A Photographic Exploration

Hae Won Shin

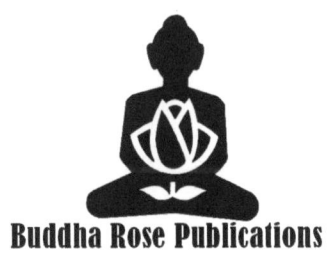
Buddha Rose Publications

Bangkok Through the Looking Glass
Copyright © 2022 by Hae Won Shin
All Rights Reserved

First Edition 2022

No part of this book may be reproduced
in any manner without the expressed
permission of the author or the publishing company.

ISBN: 978-1-949251-83-8

Printed in the United States of America

10 9 8 7 6 5 4 3 2 1

Bangkok
Through the Looking Glass

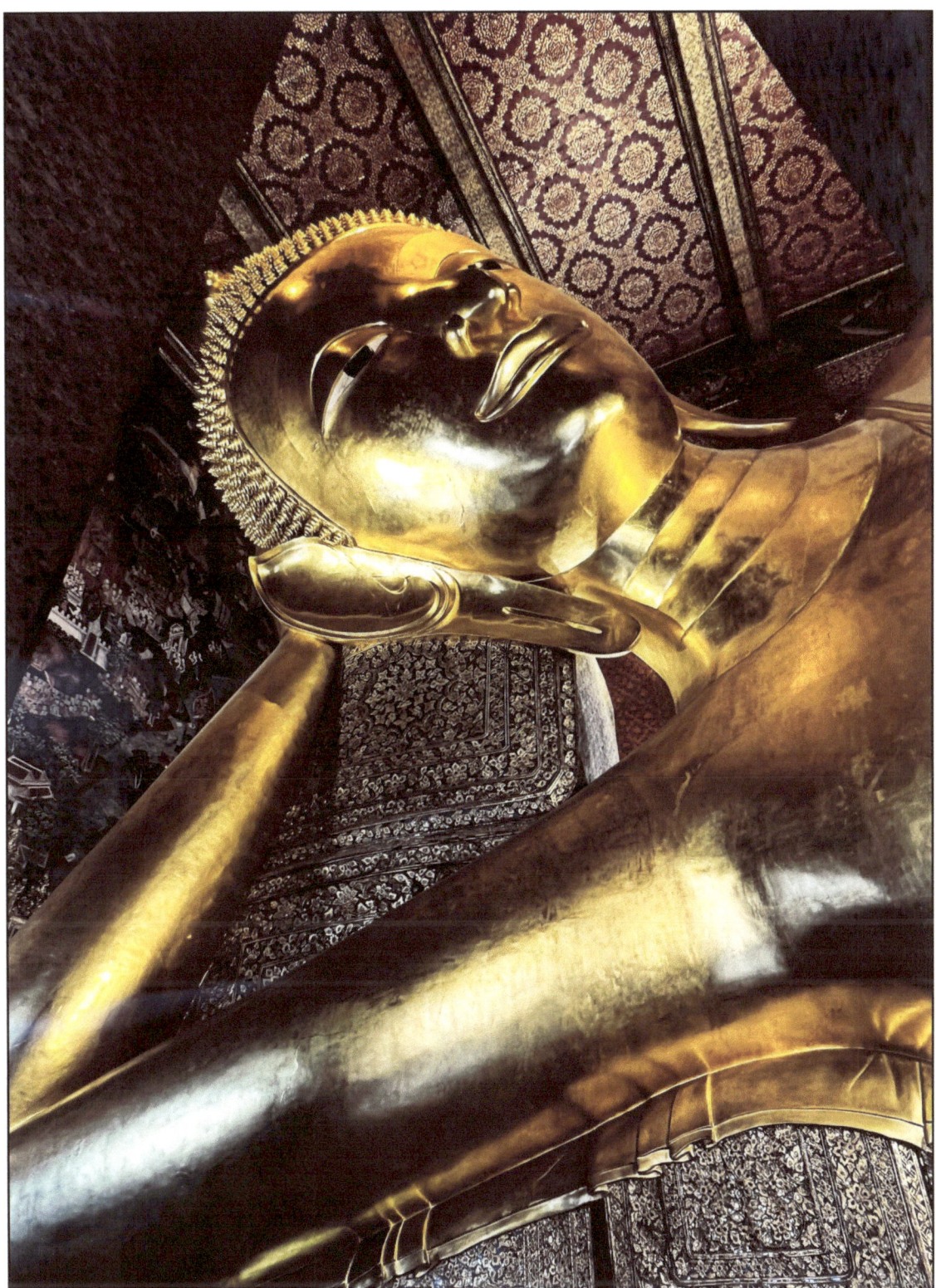

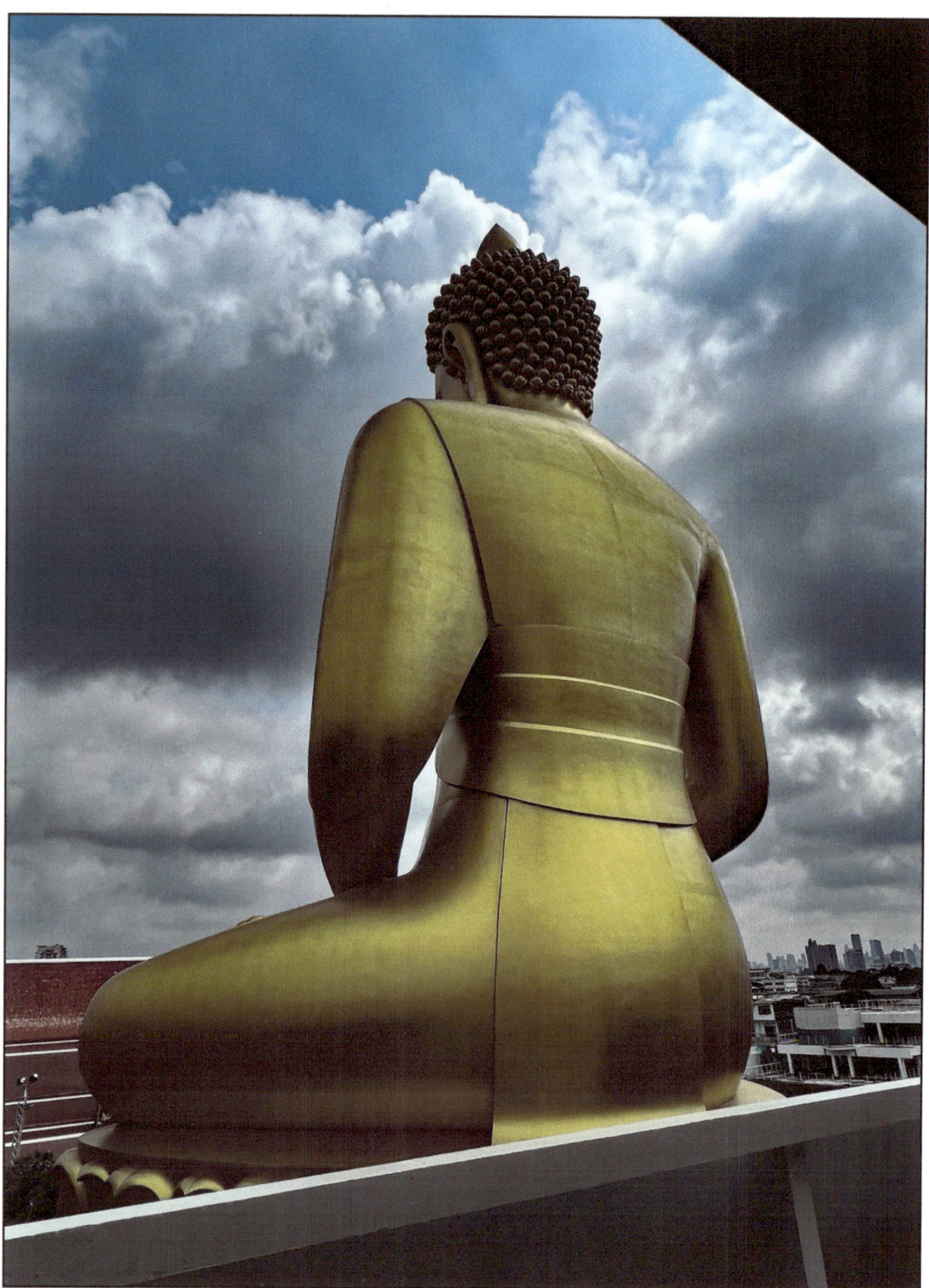

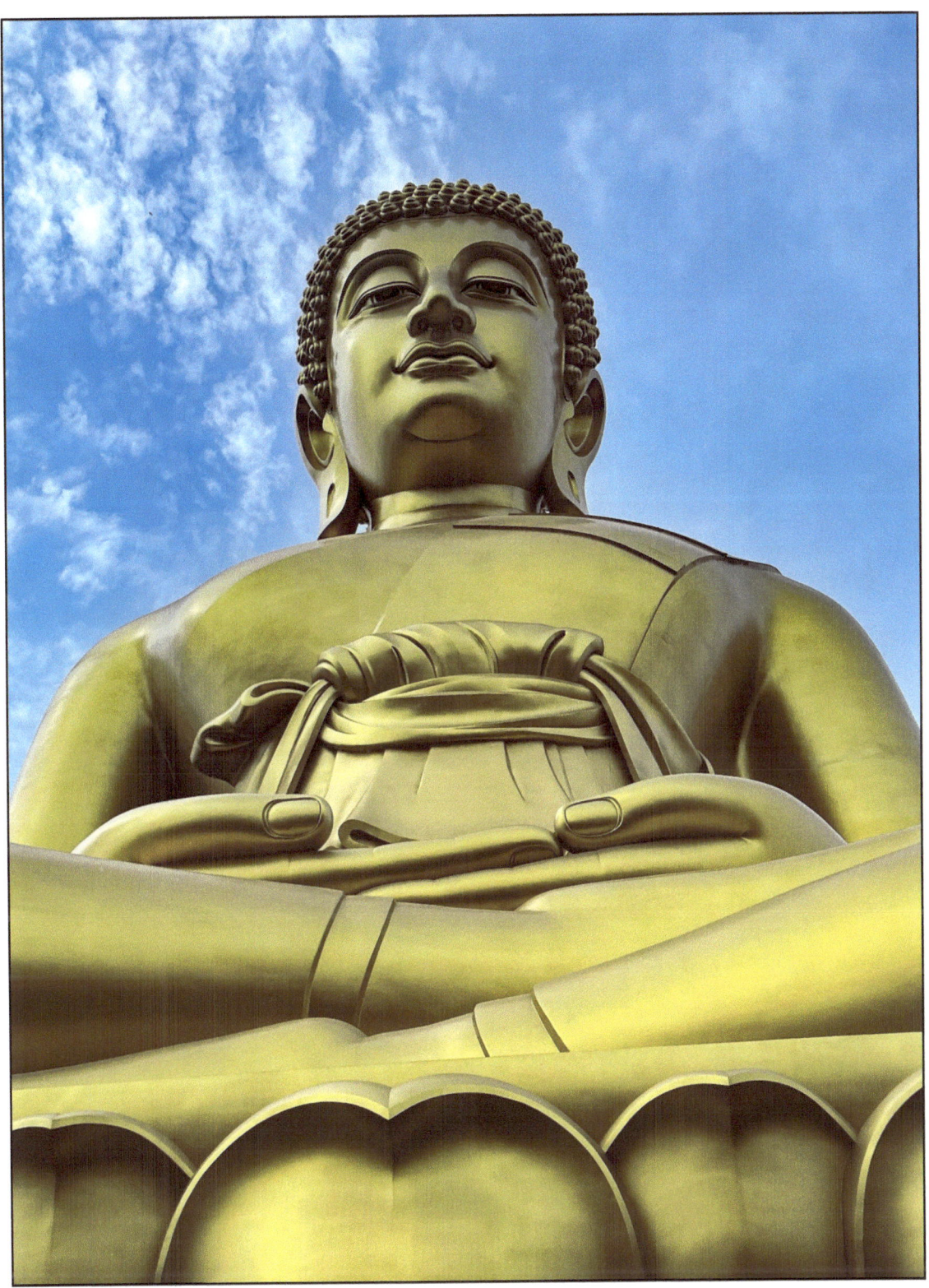

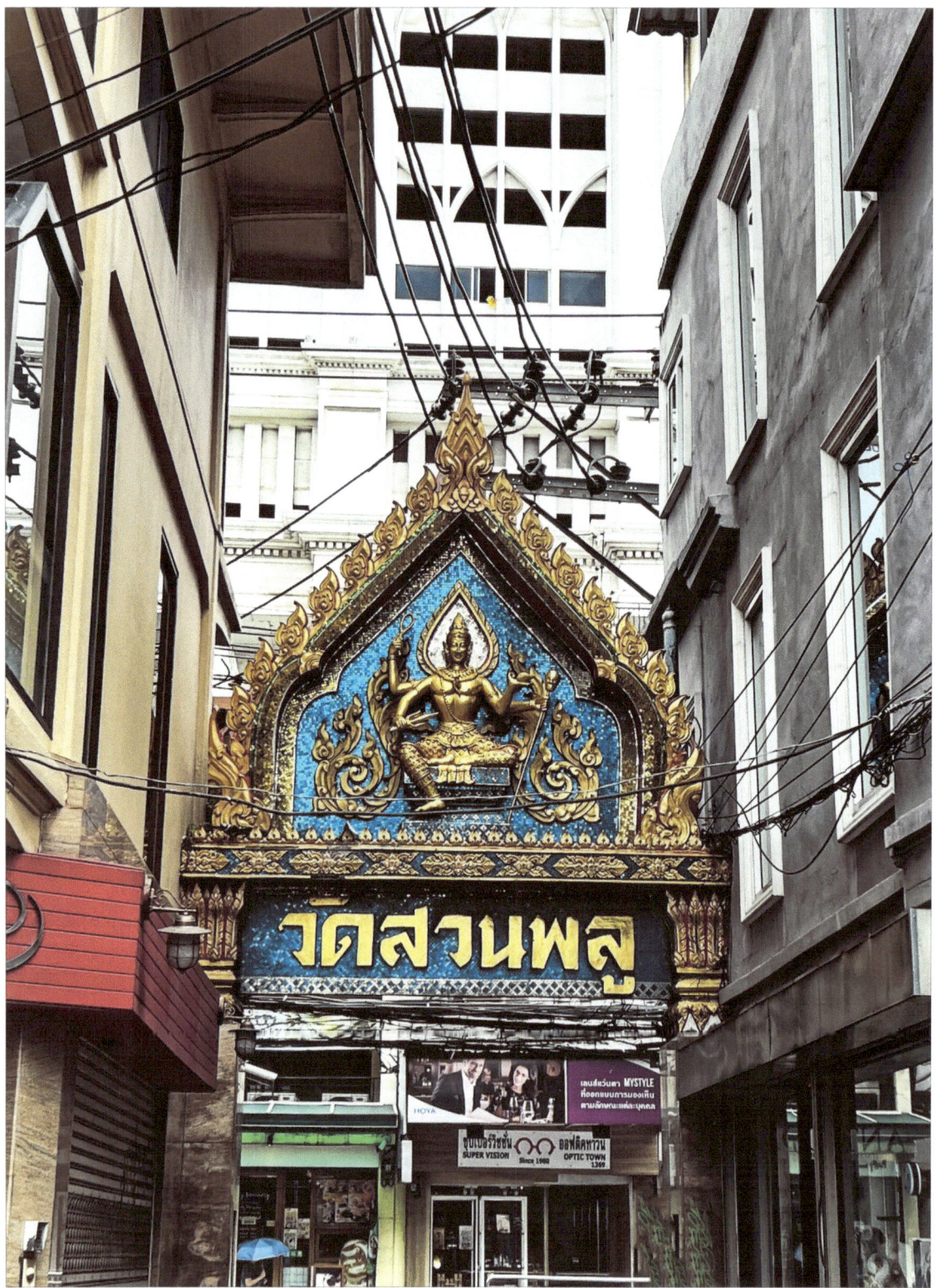

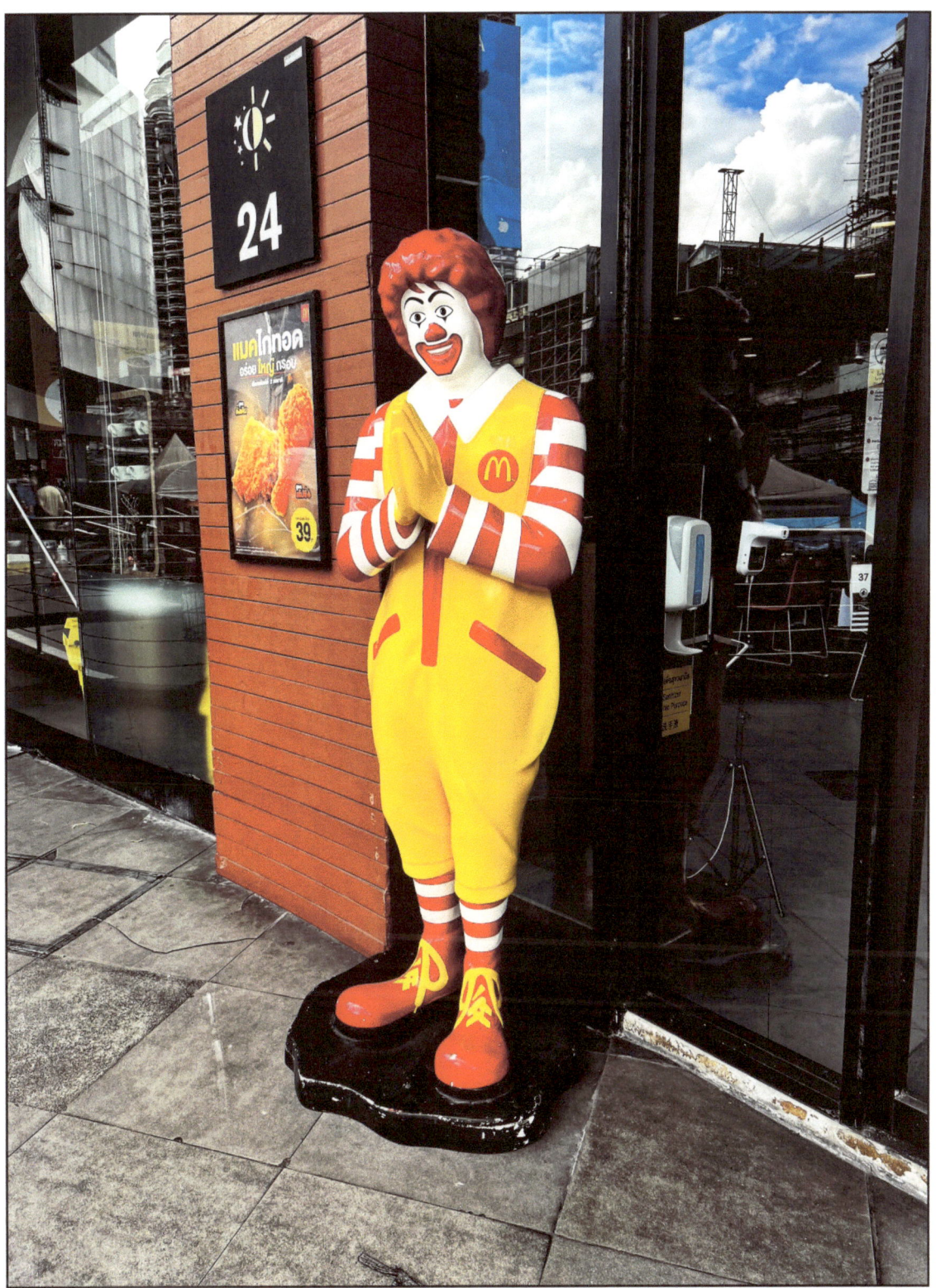

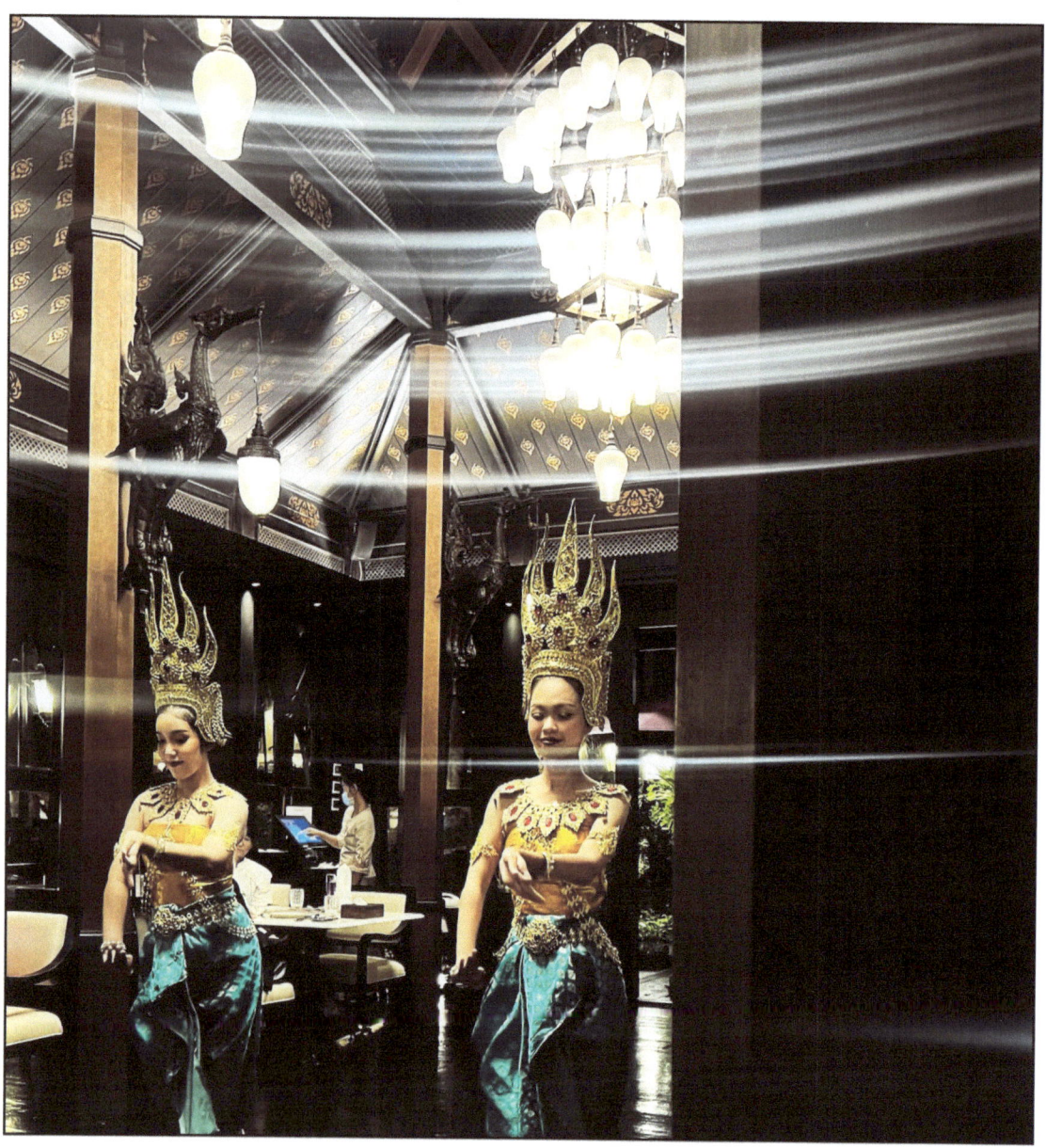

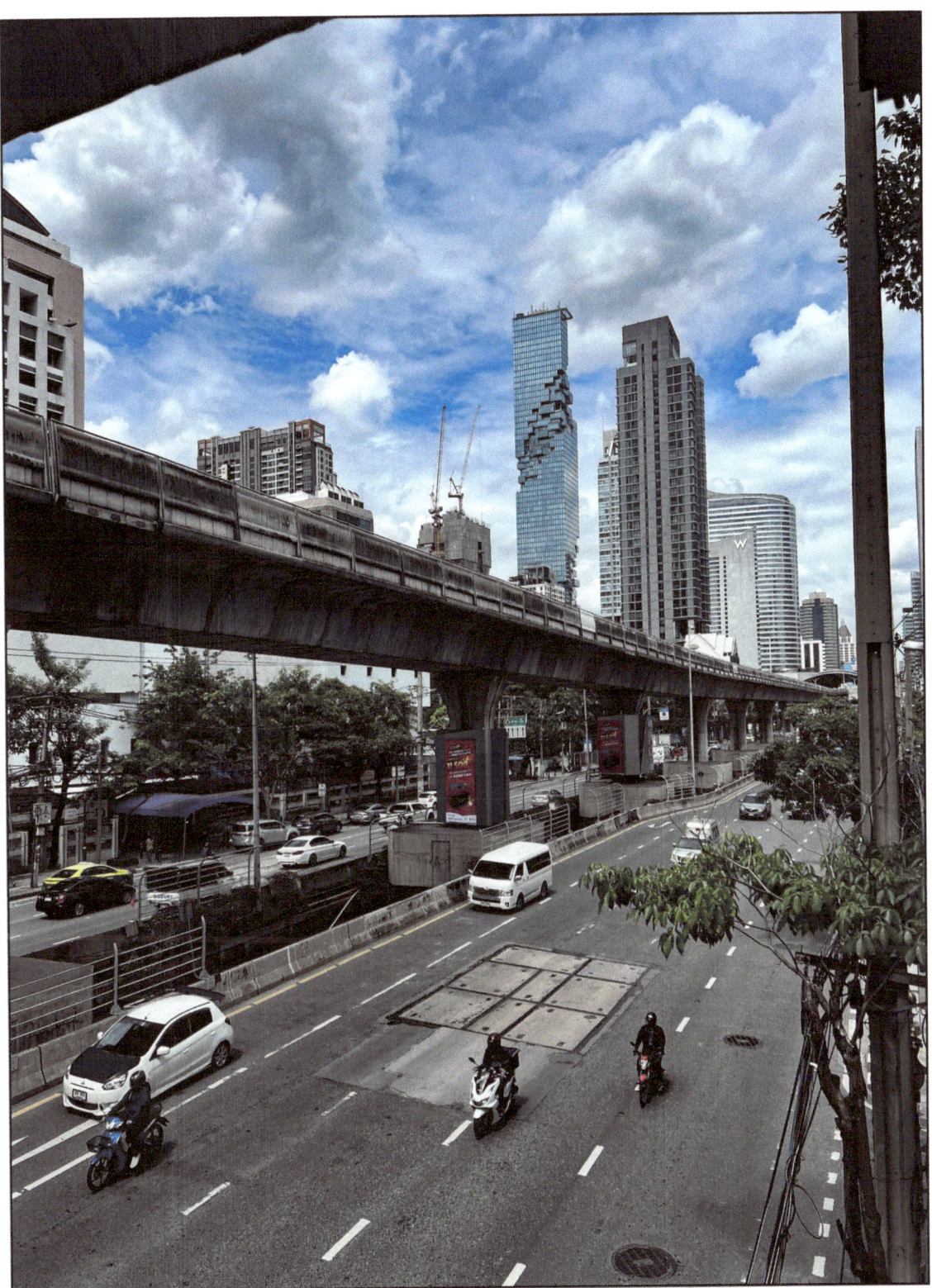

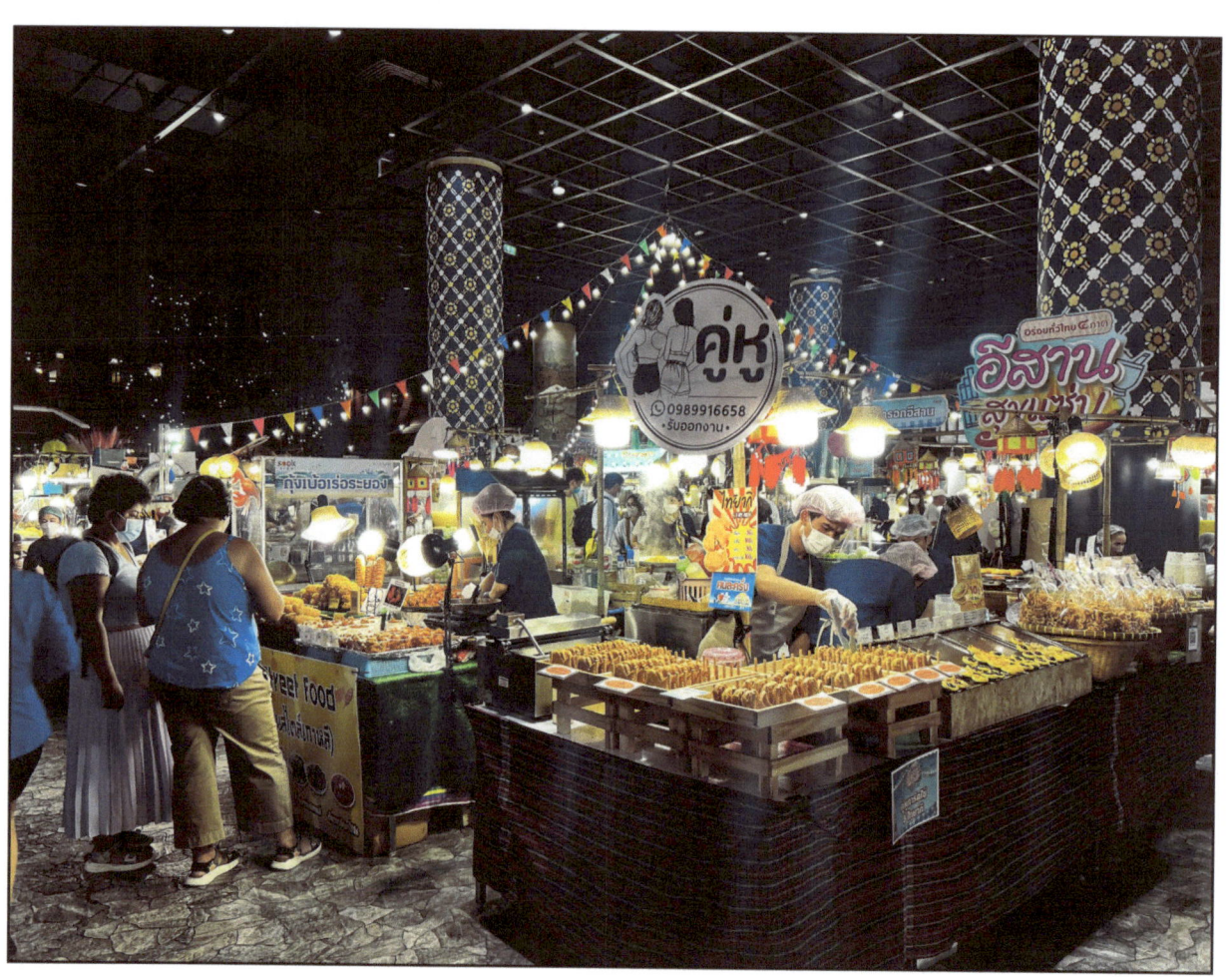

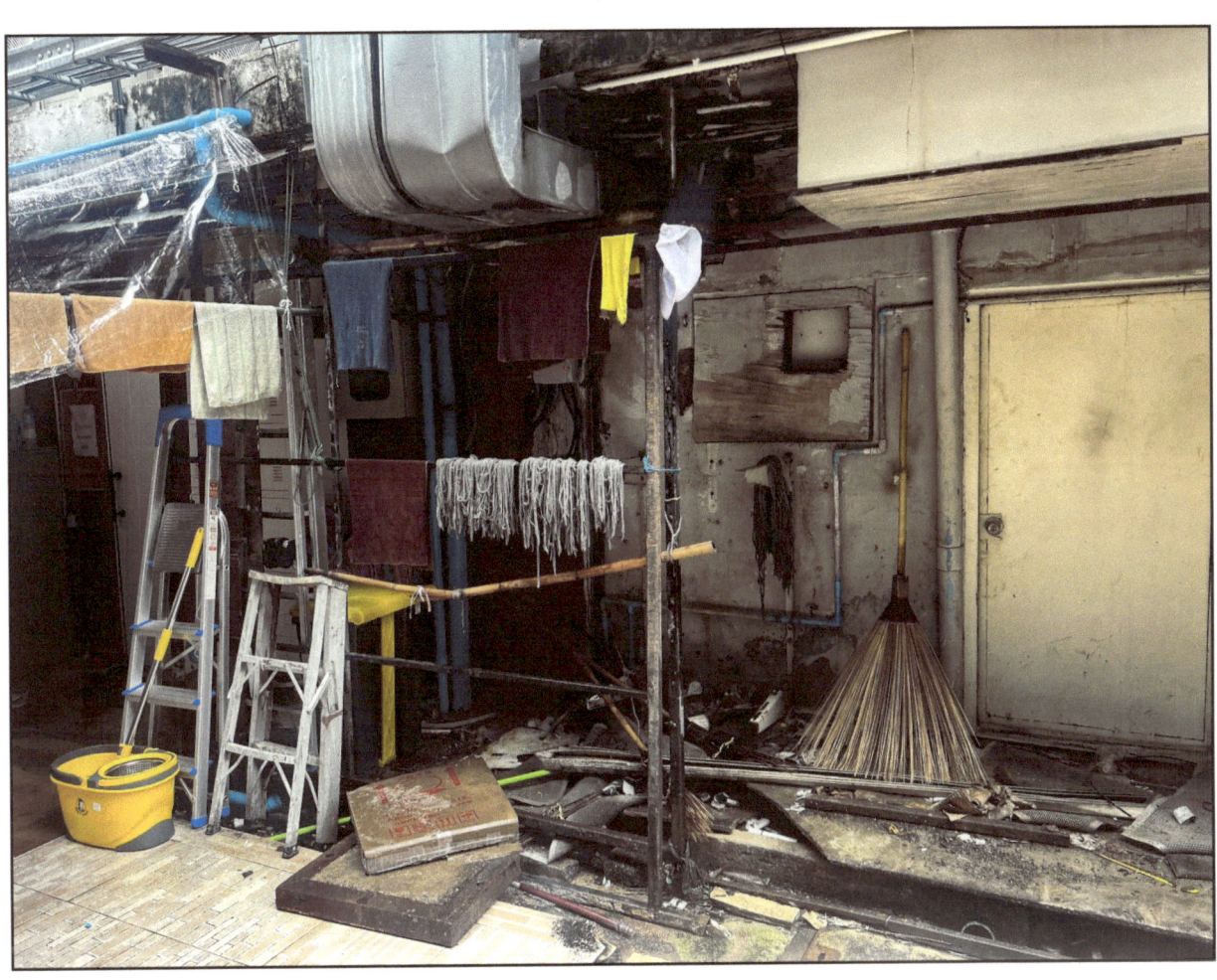

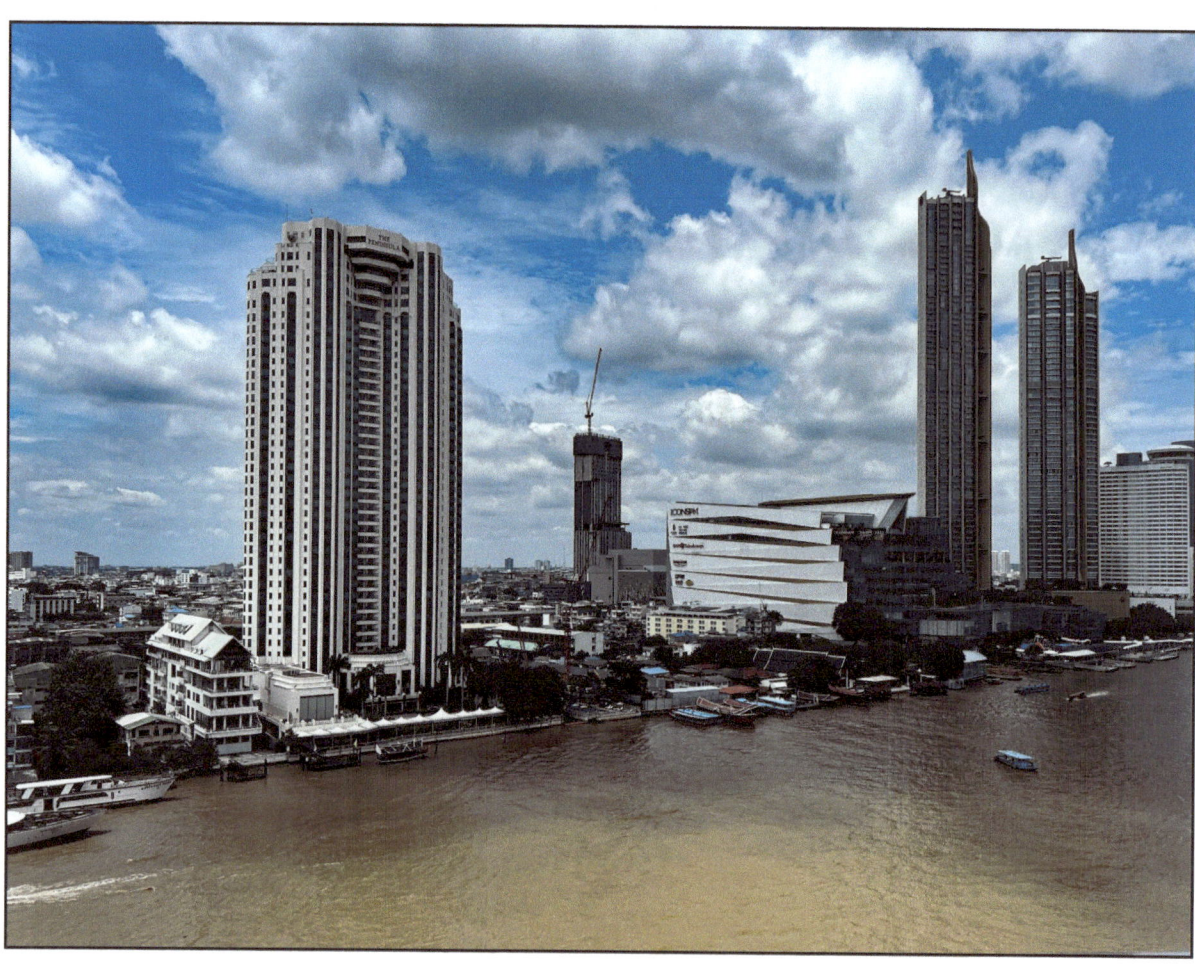

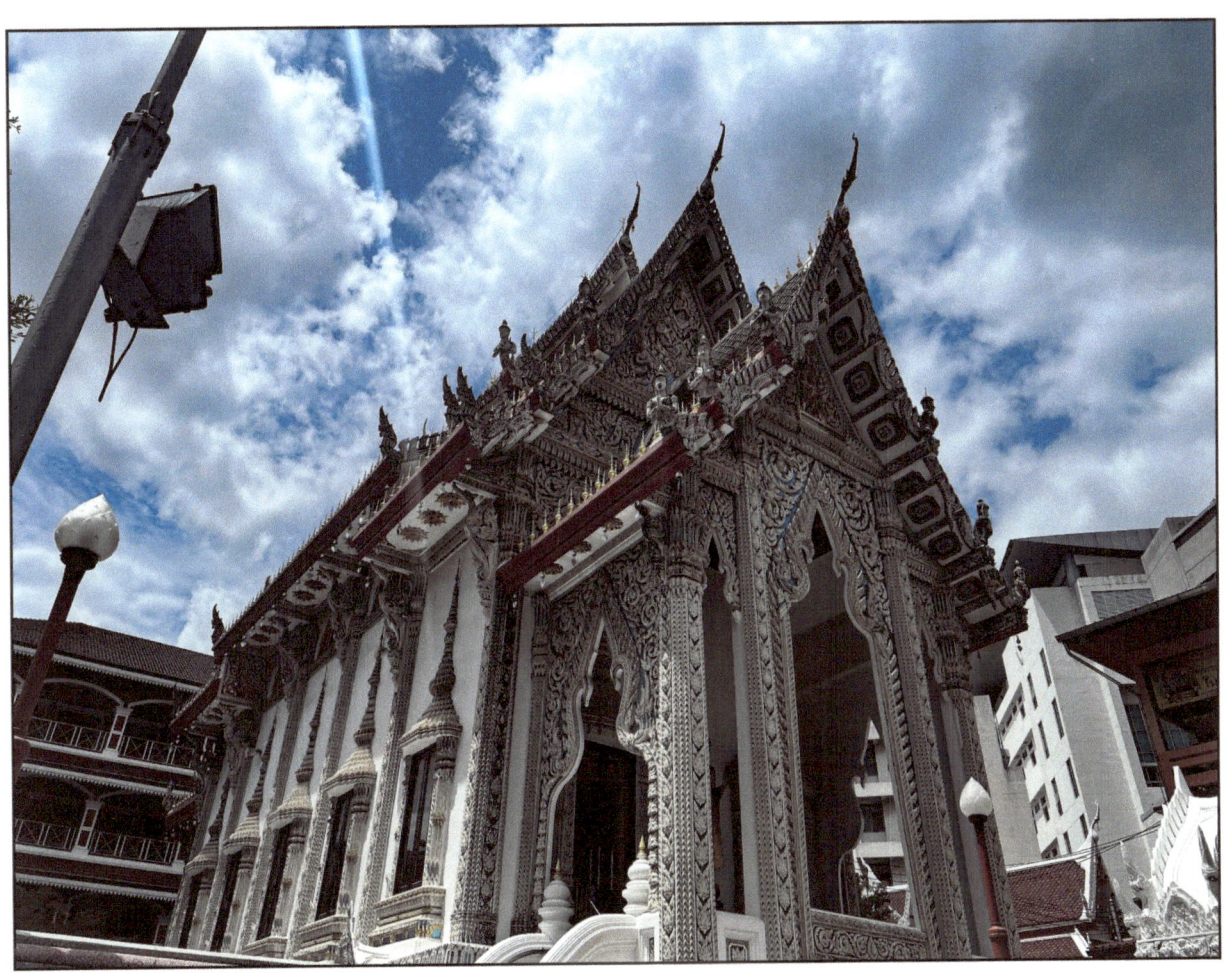

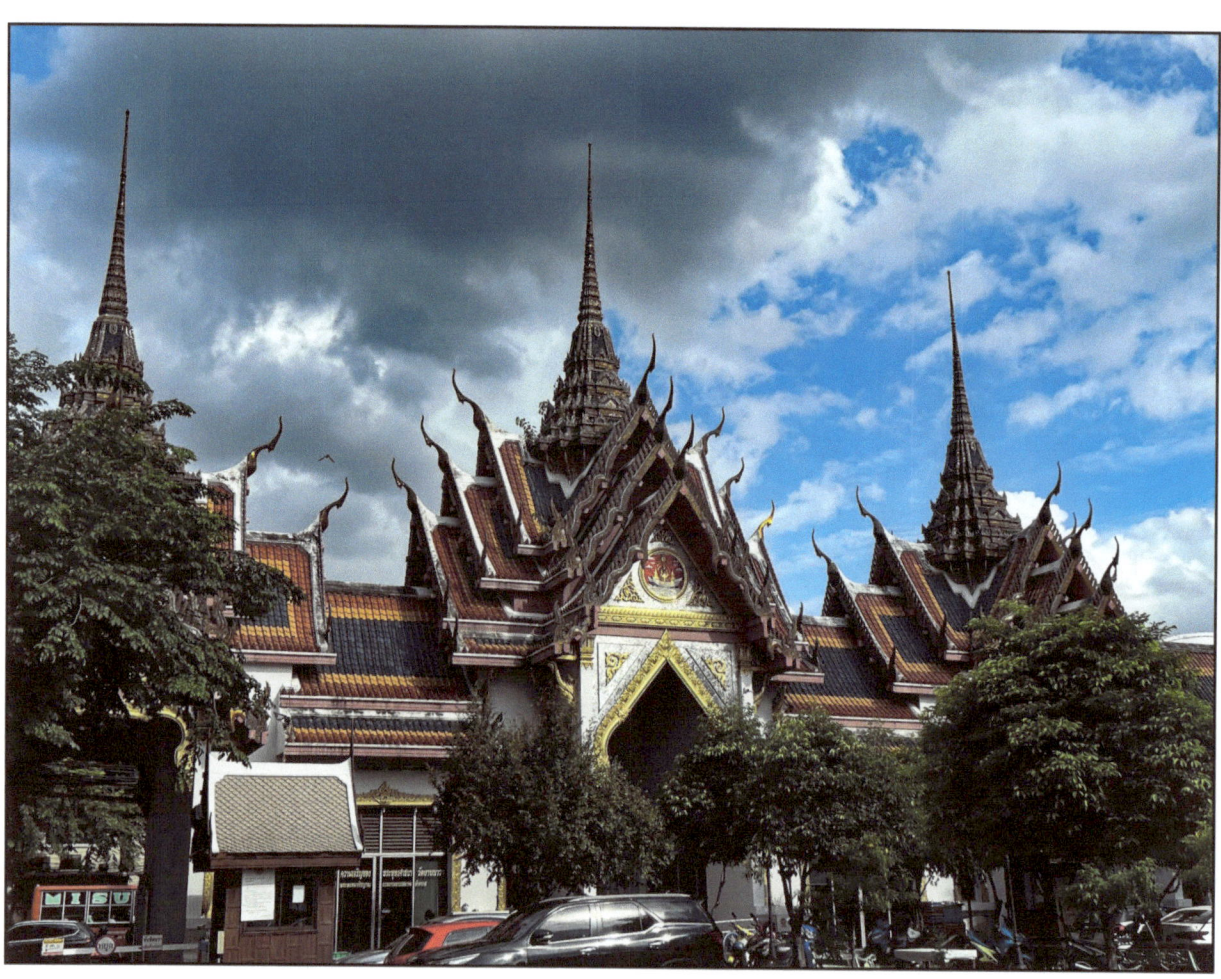

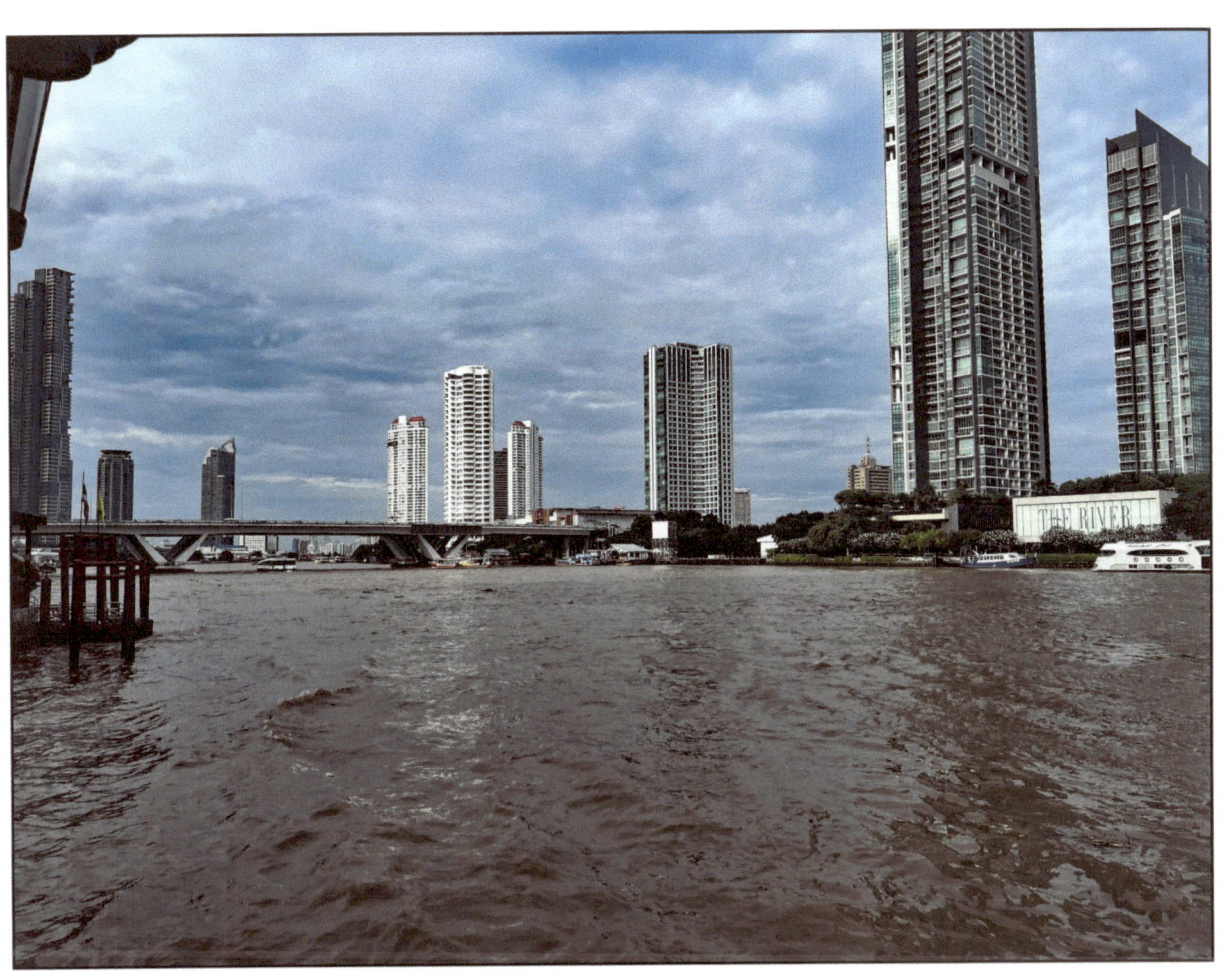

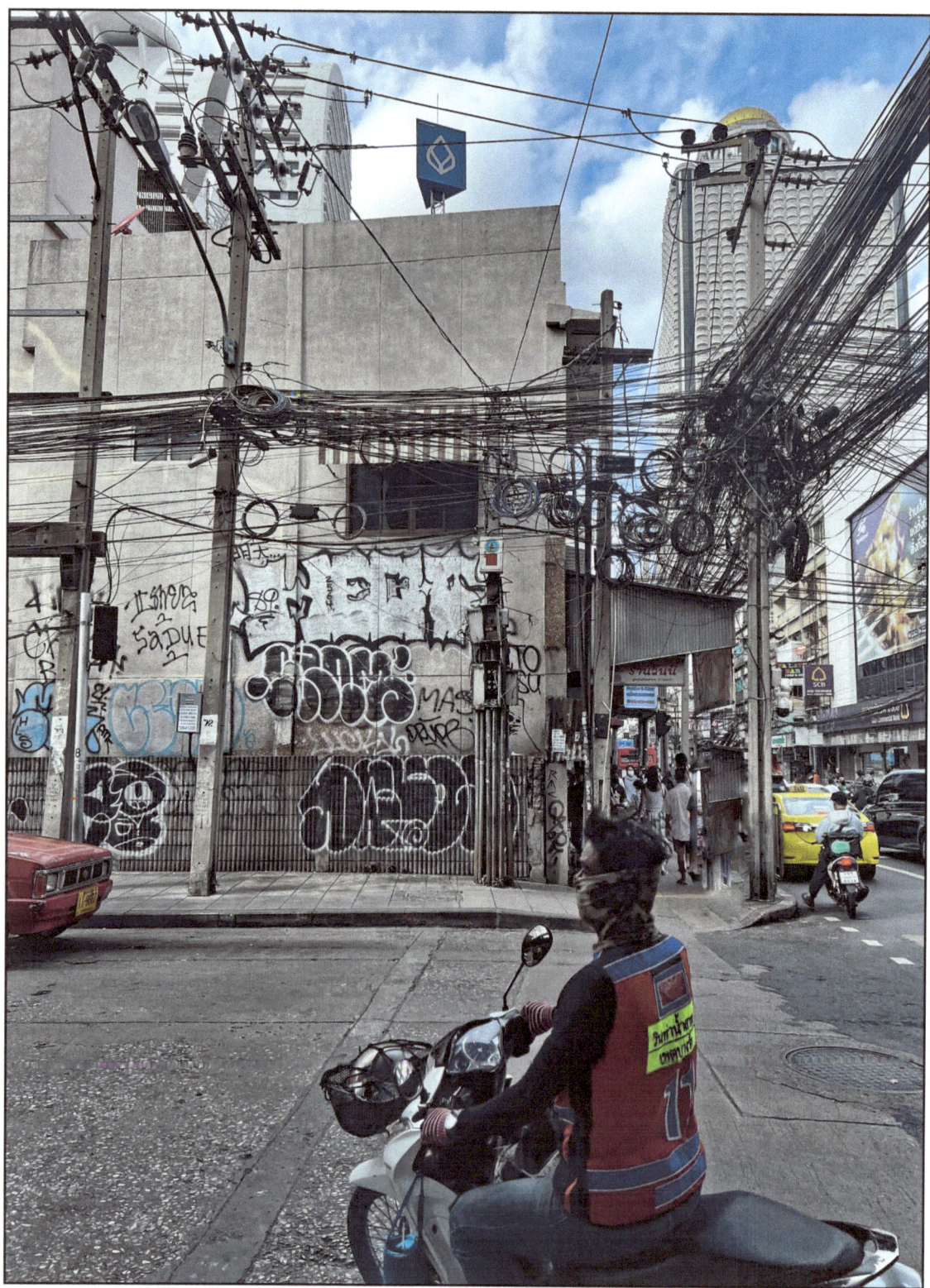

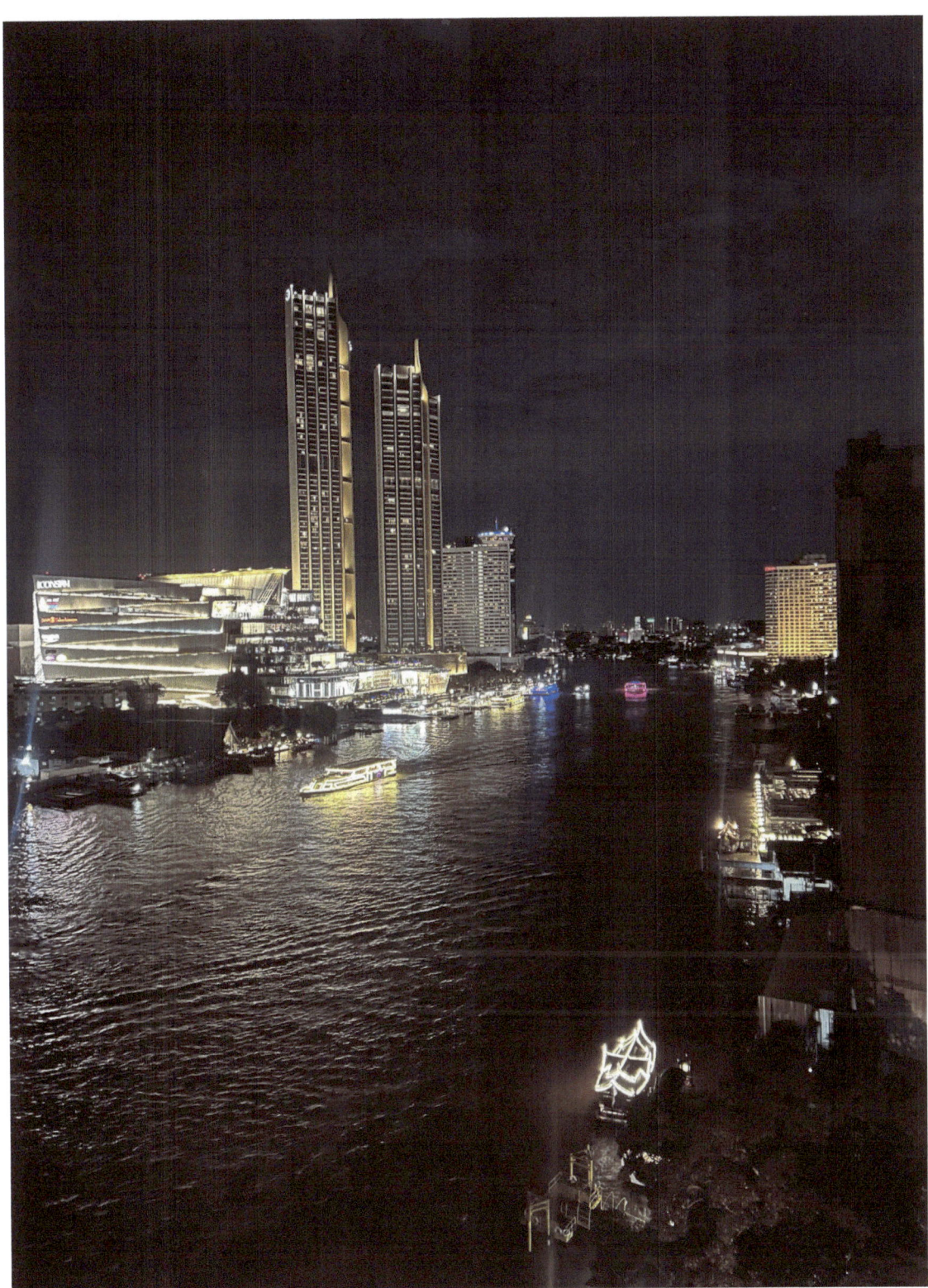

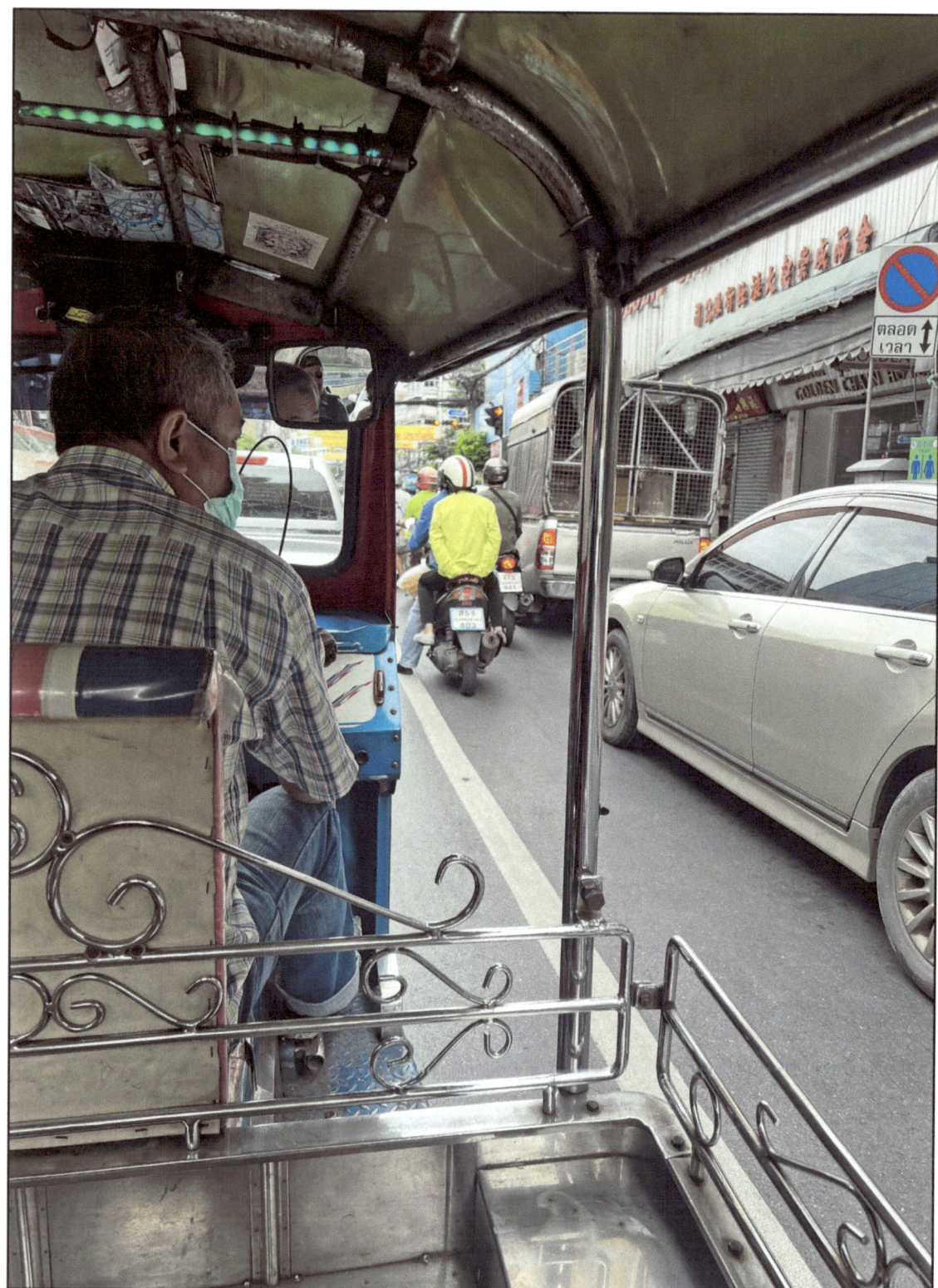

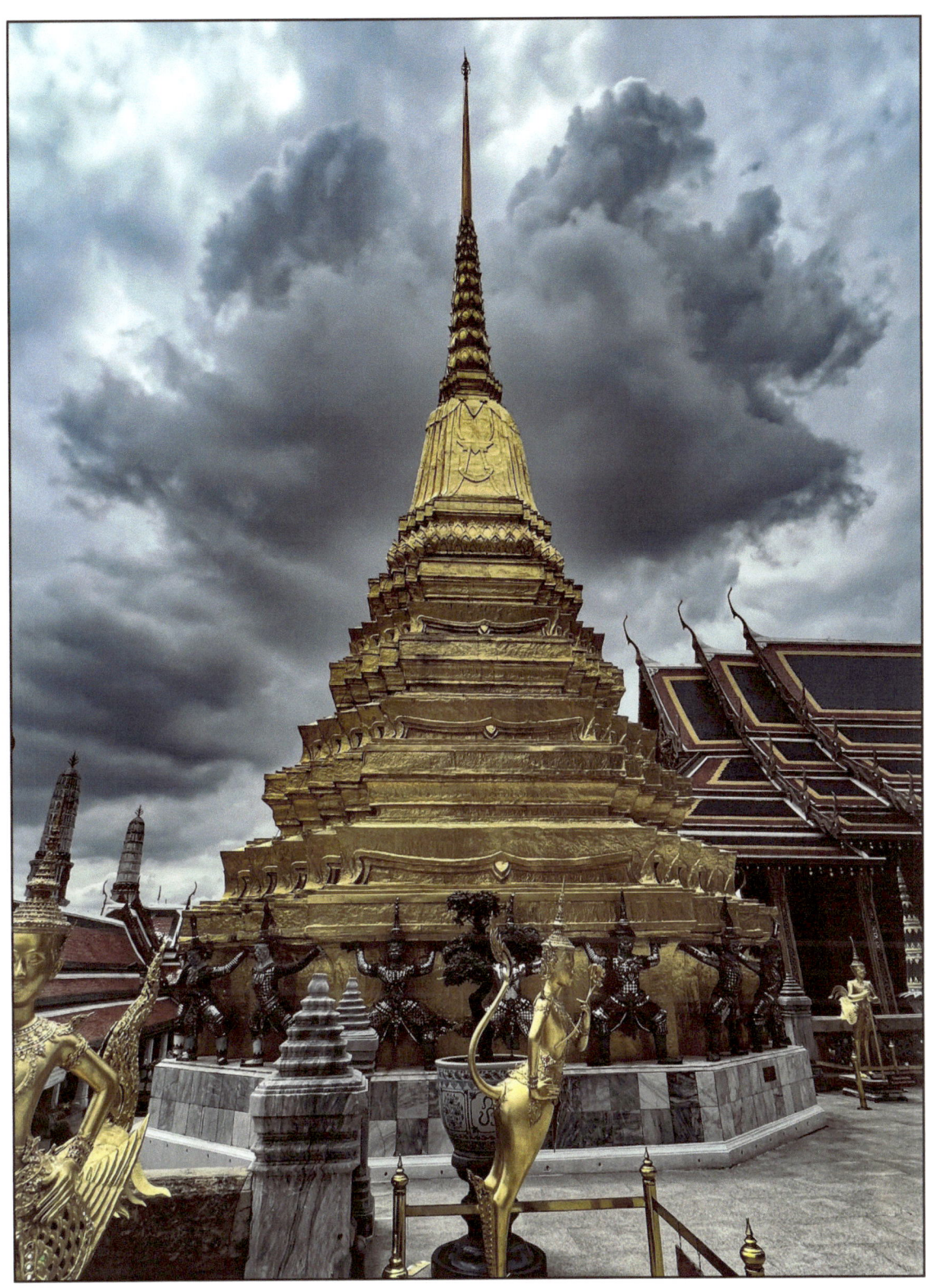

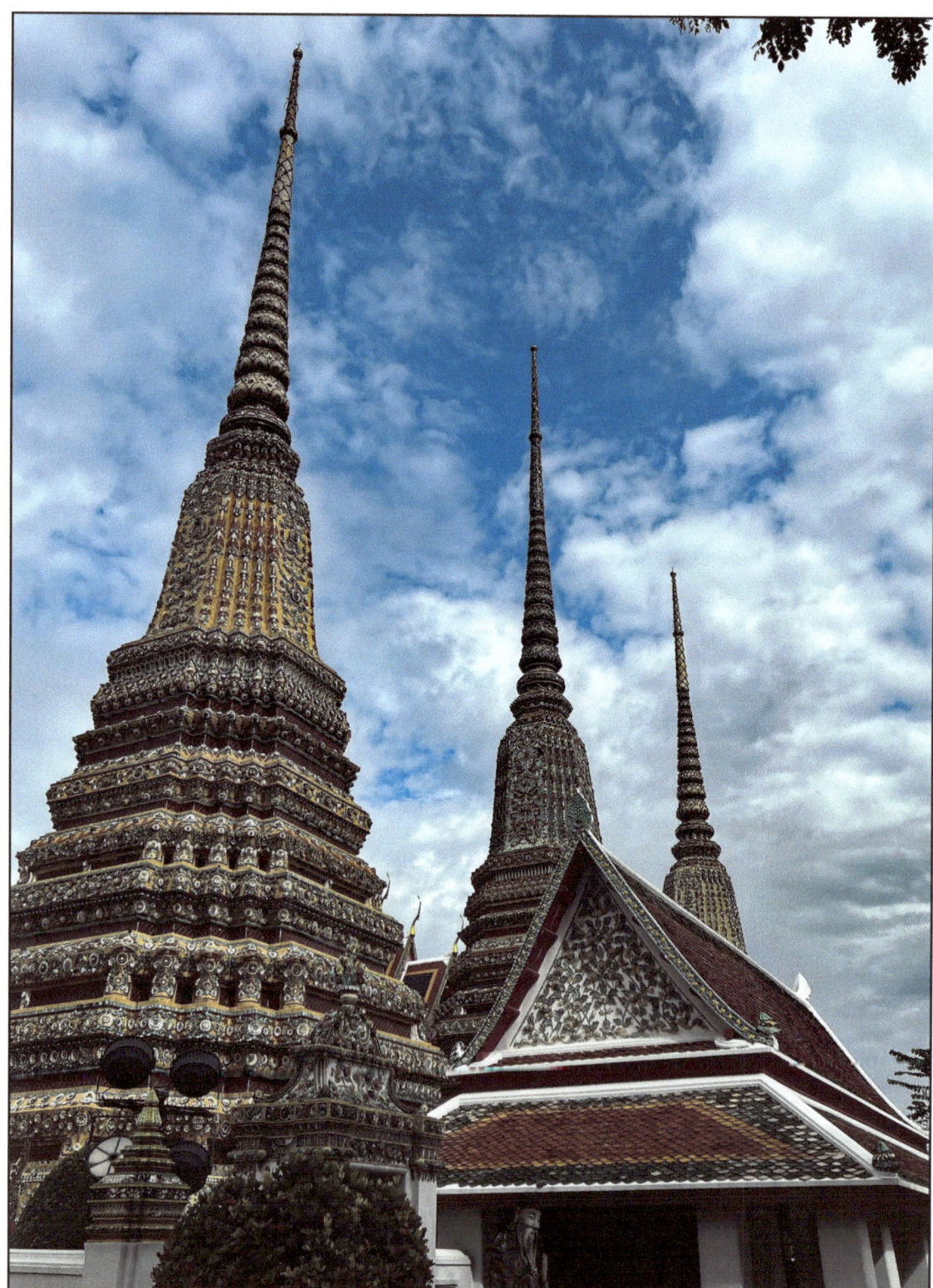

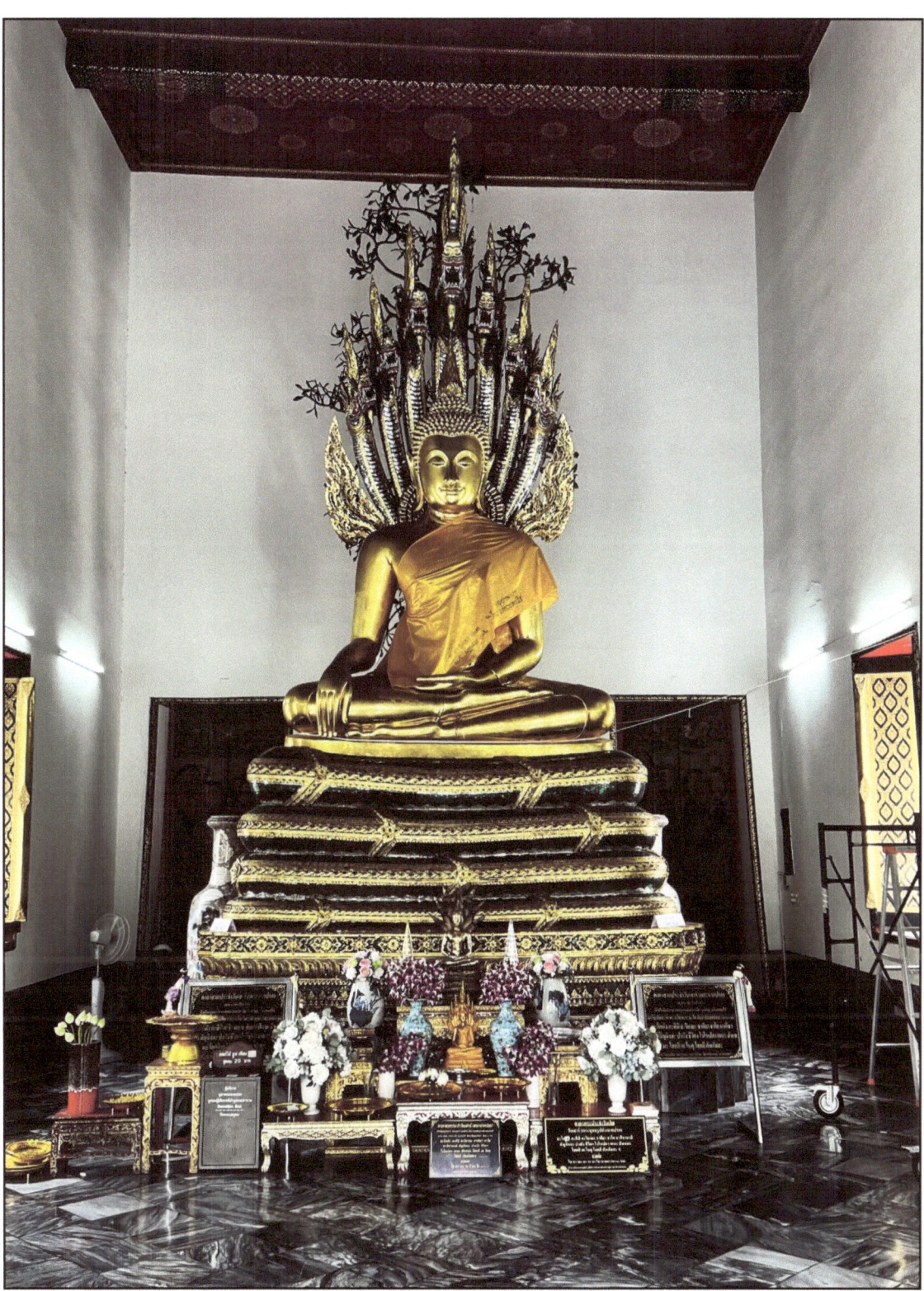

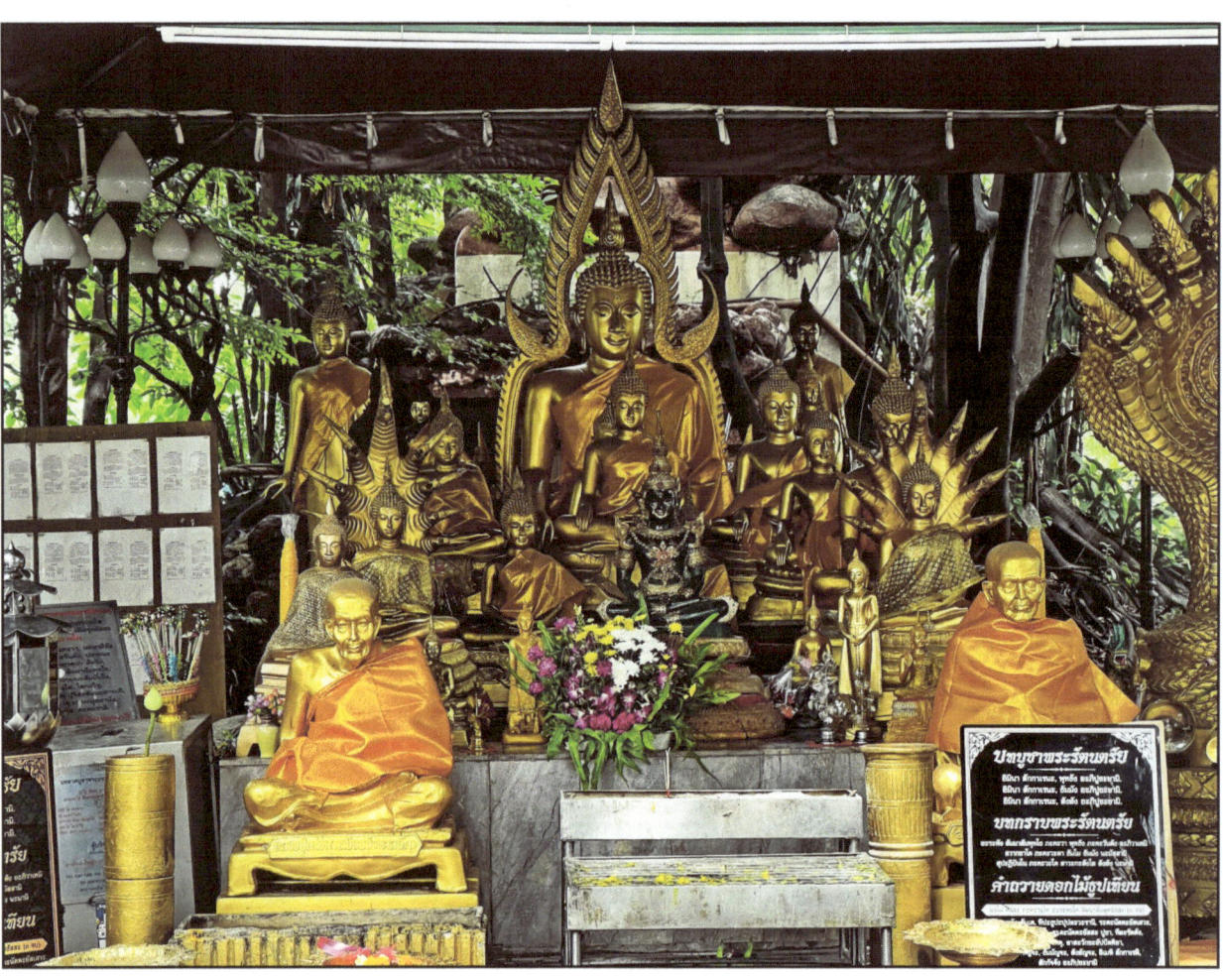

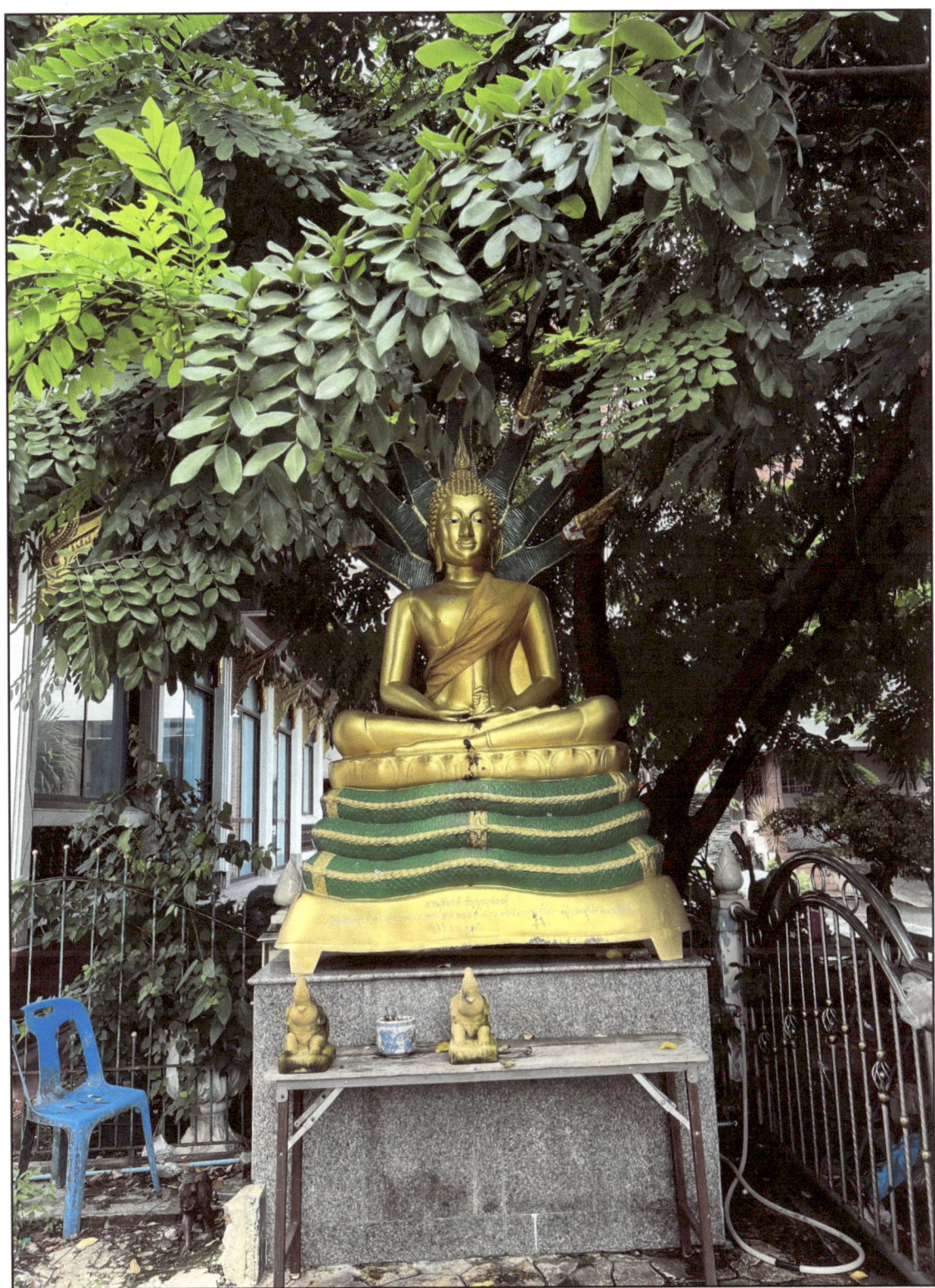

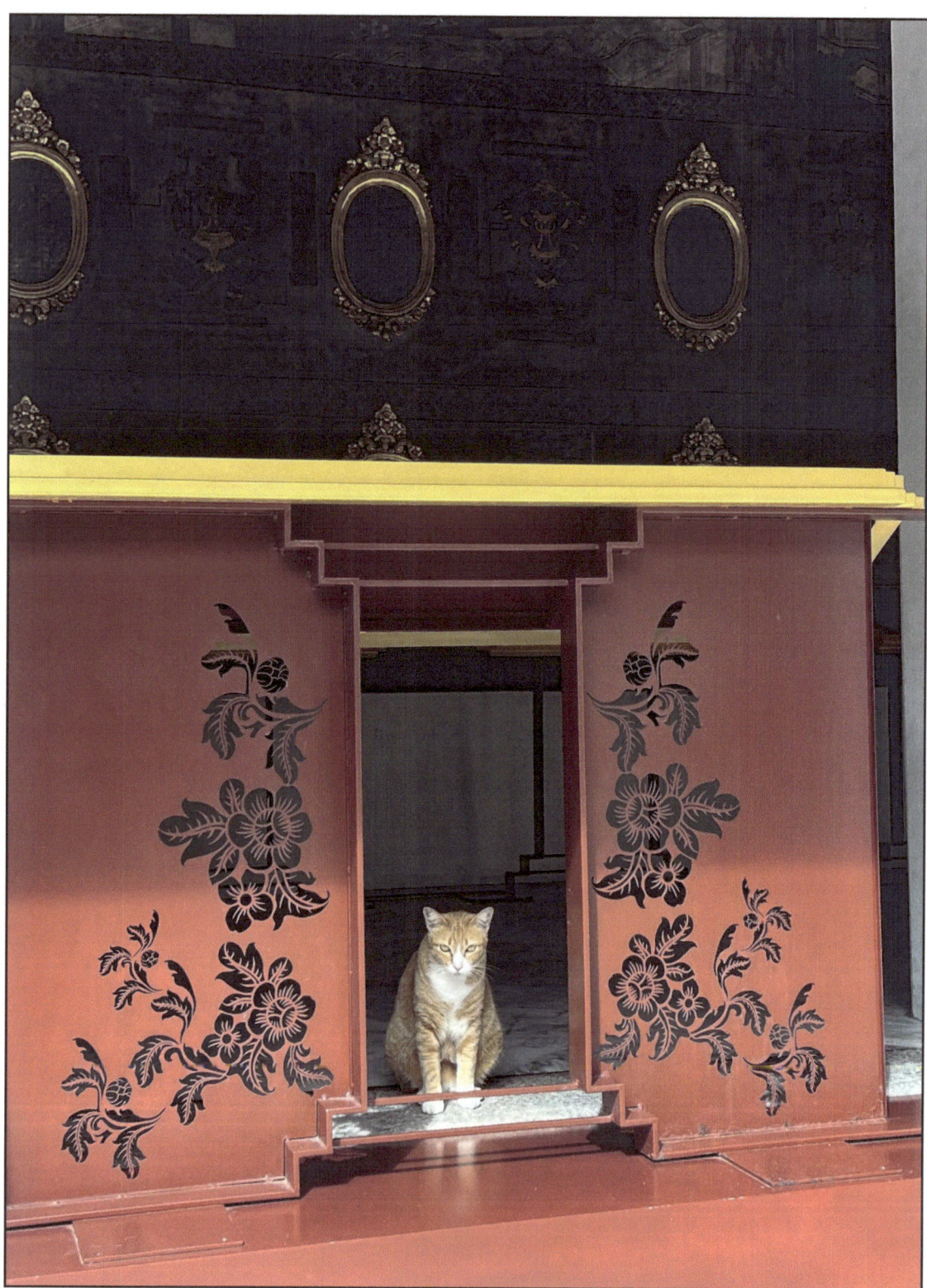

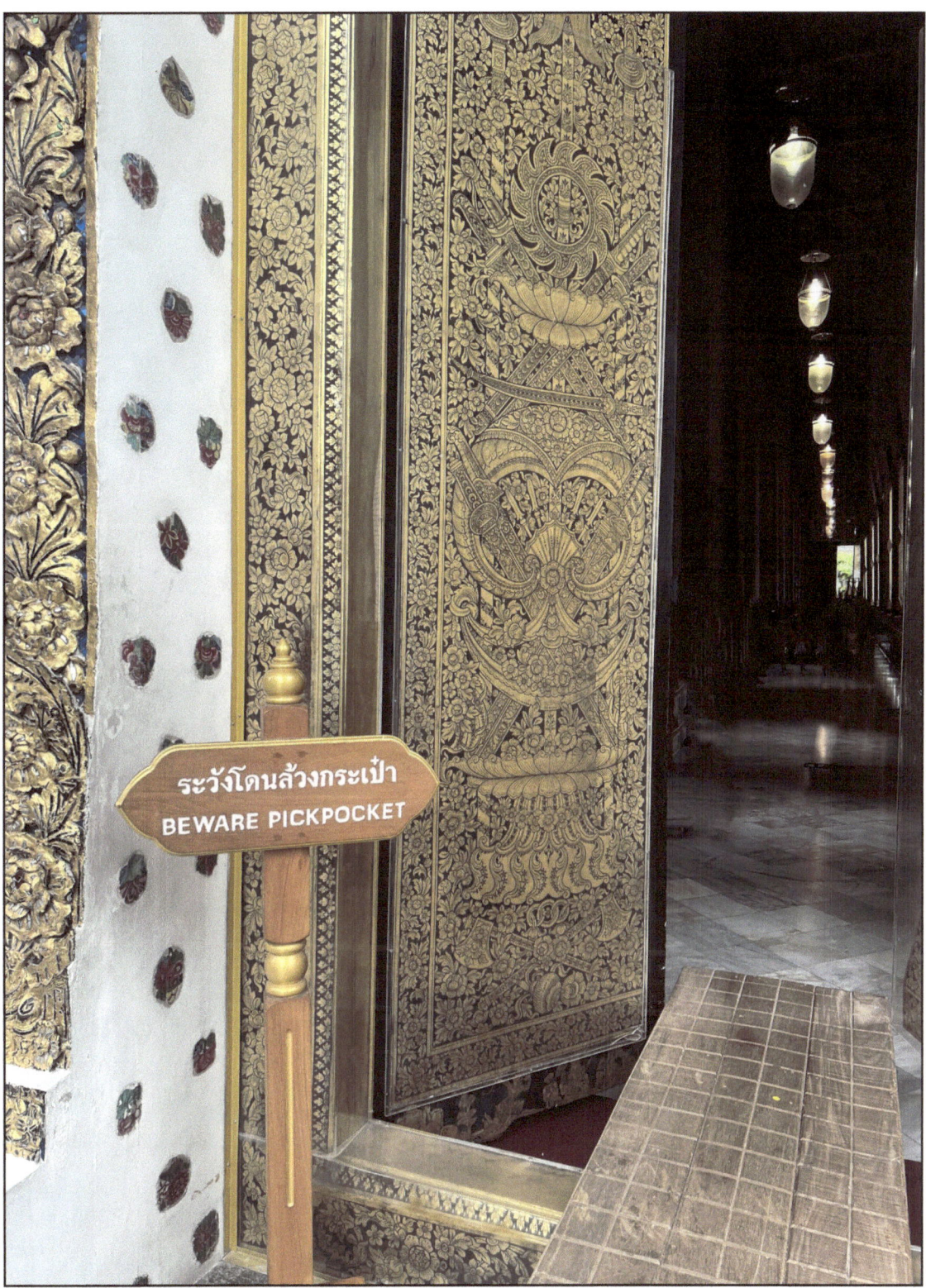

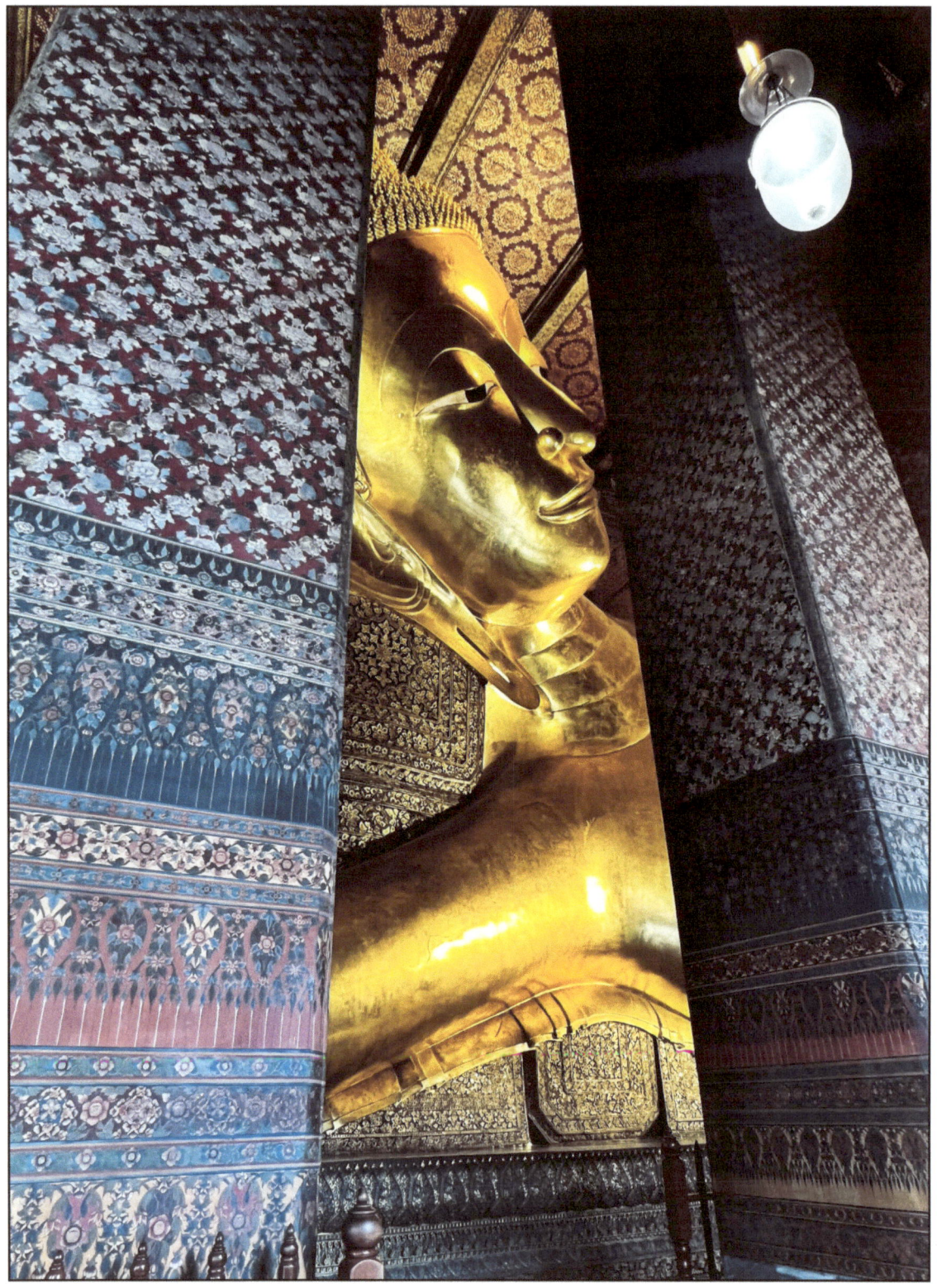

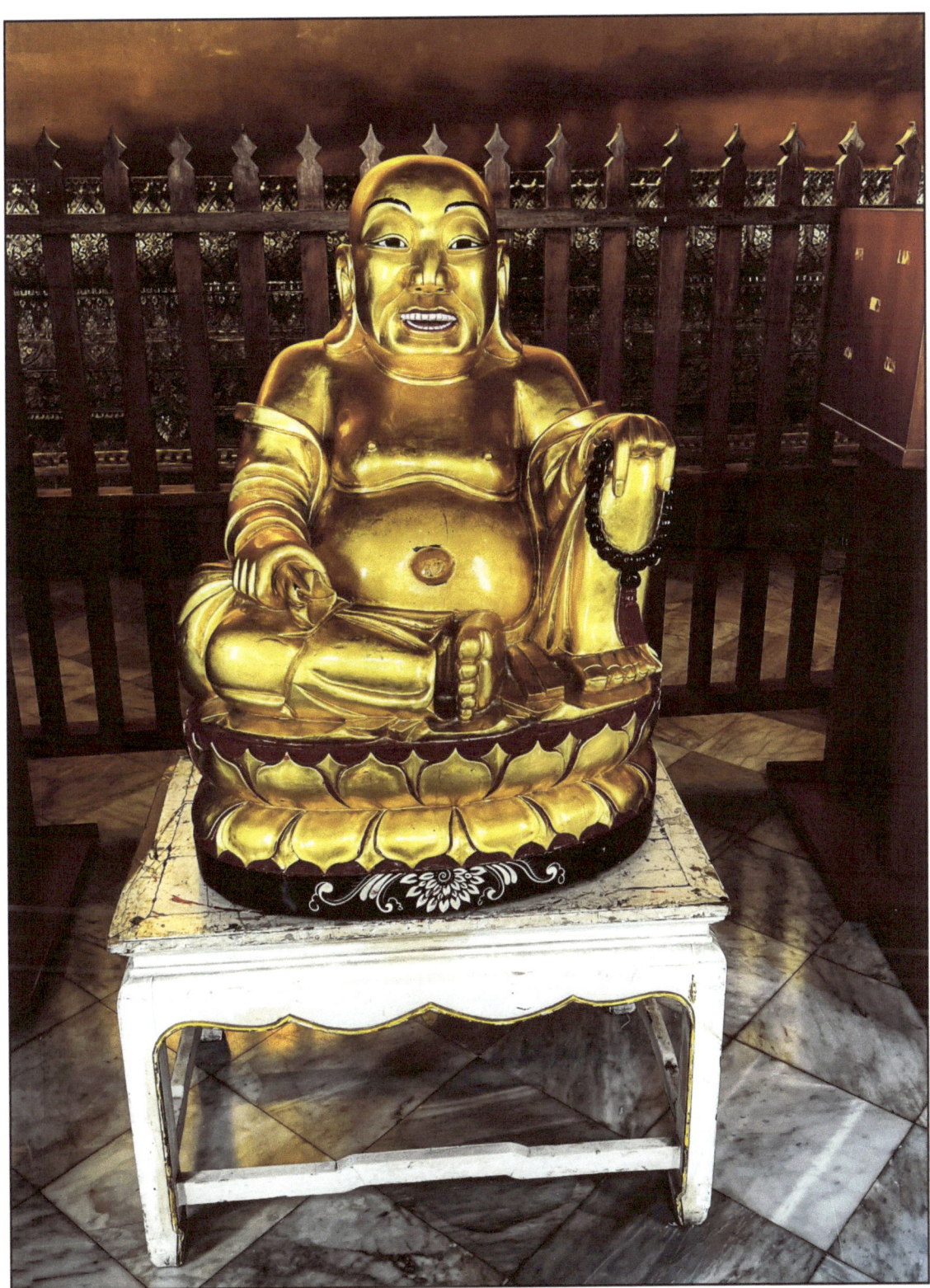

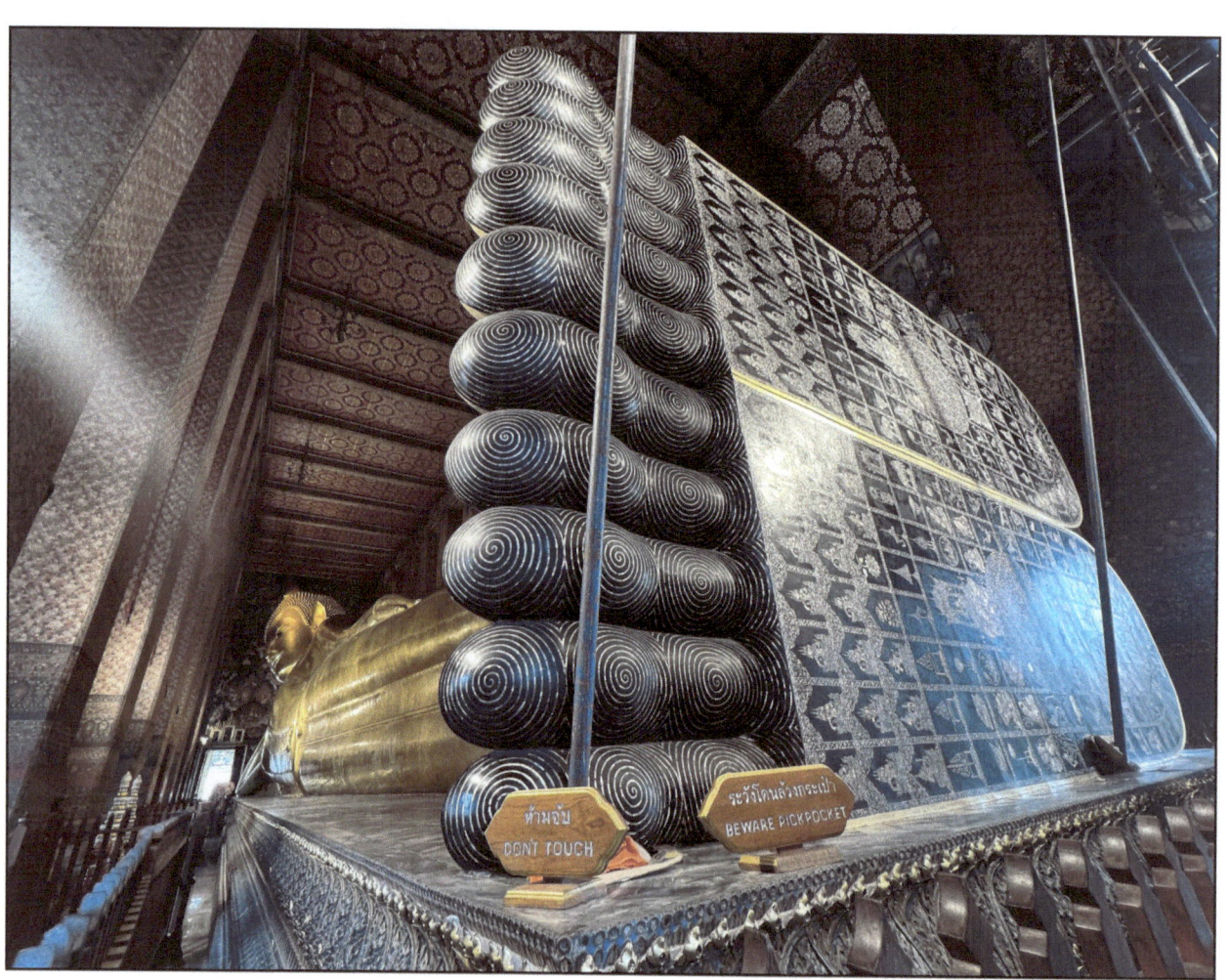

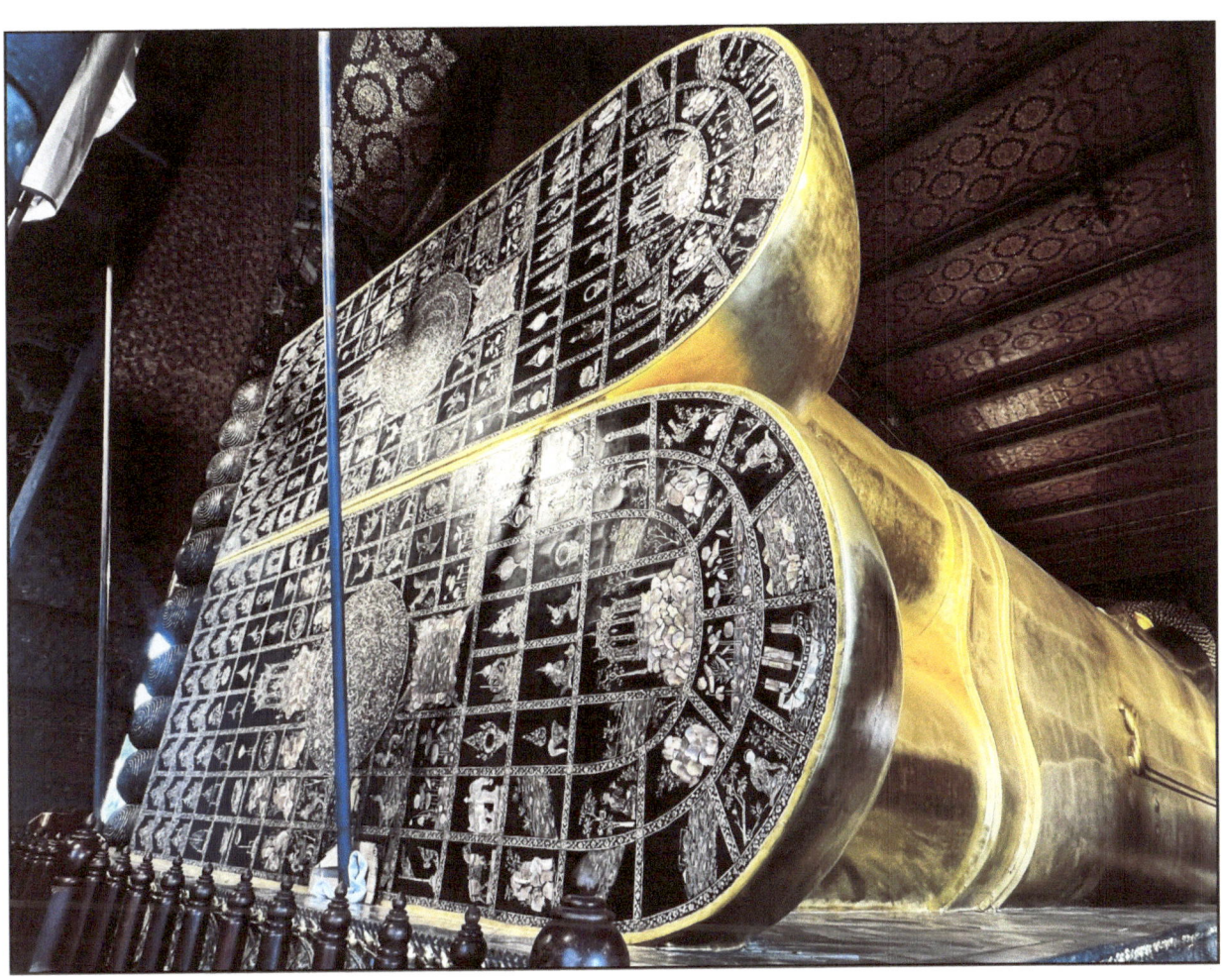

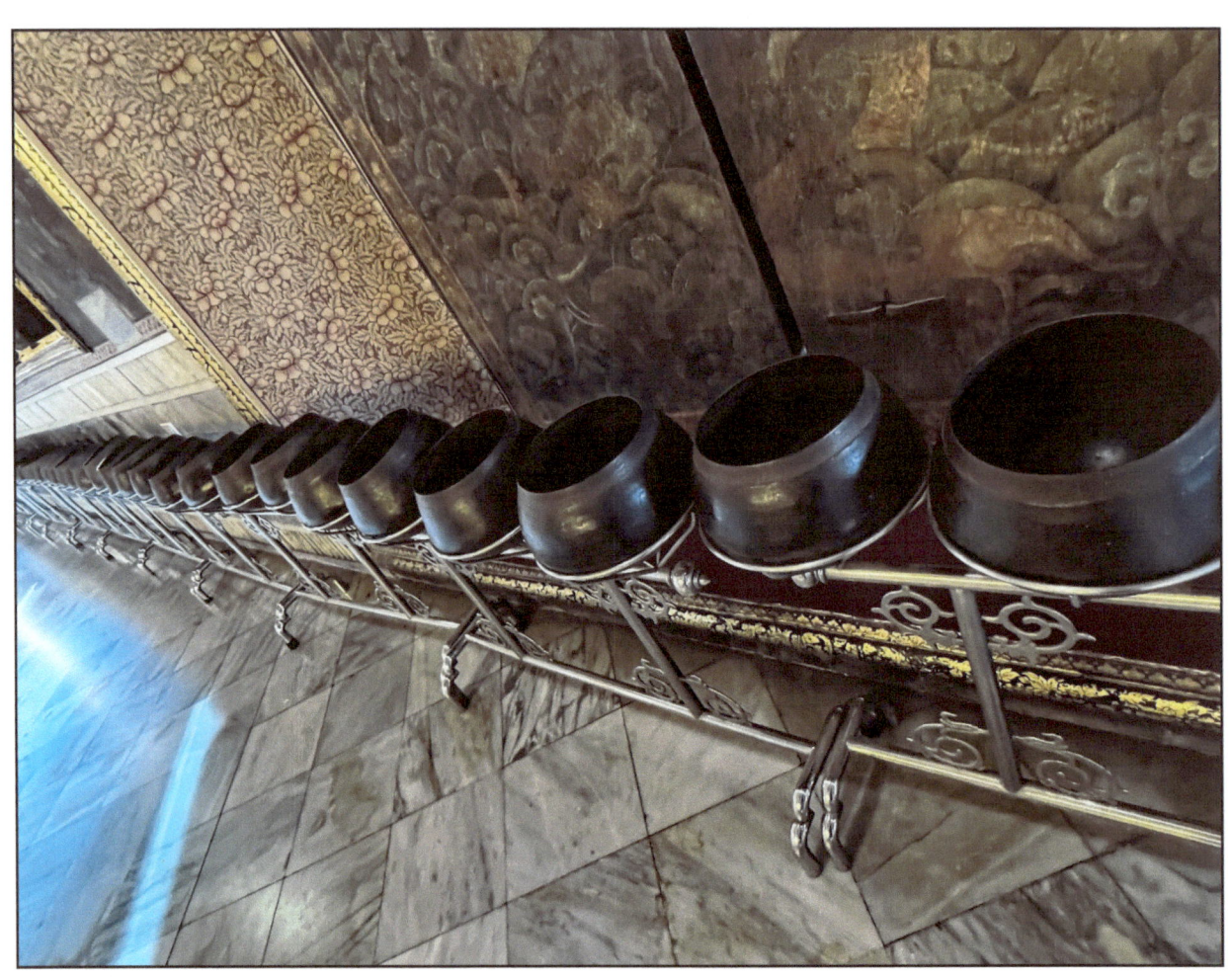

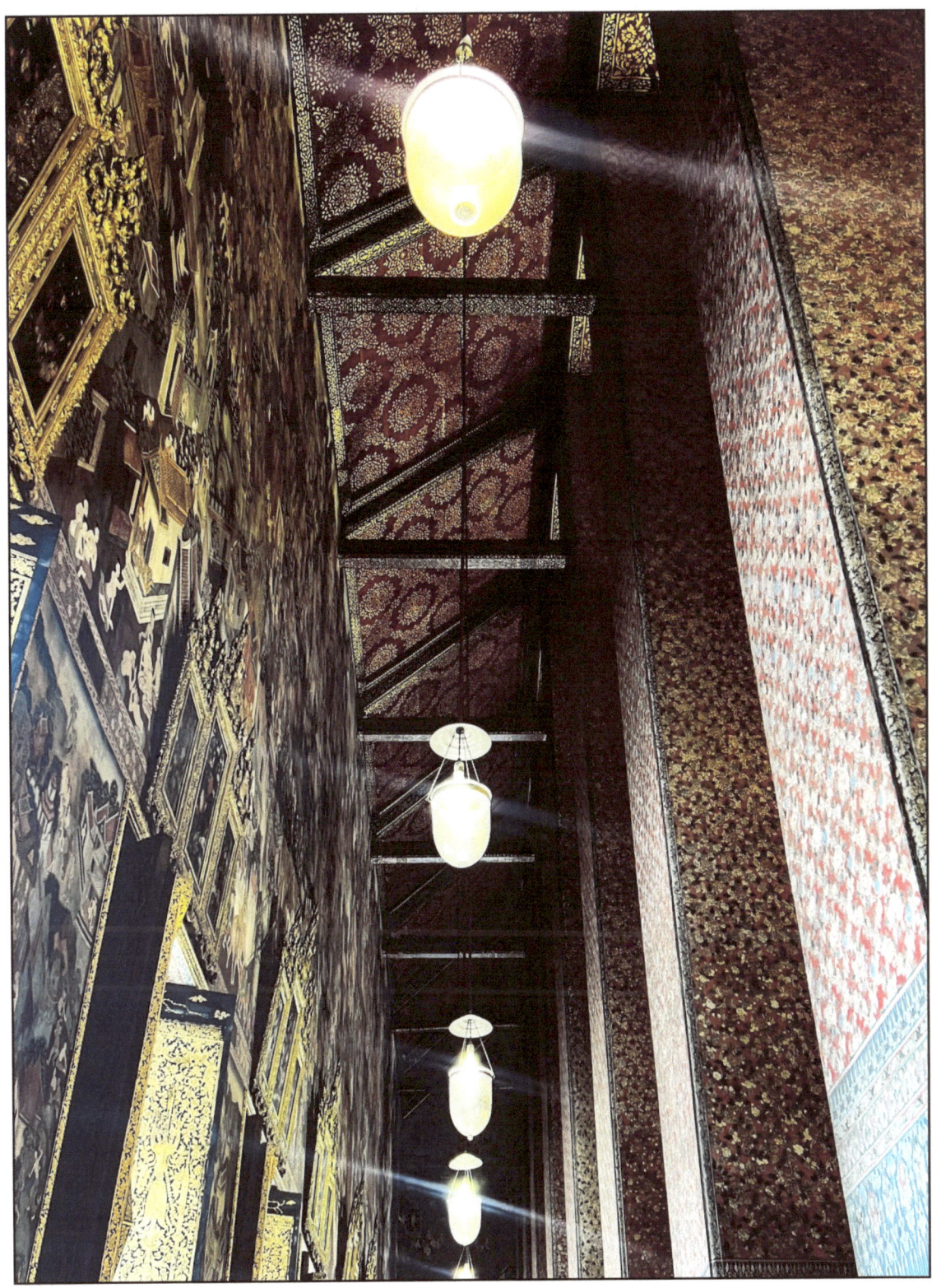

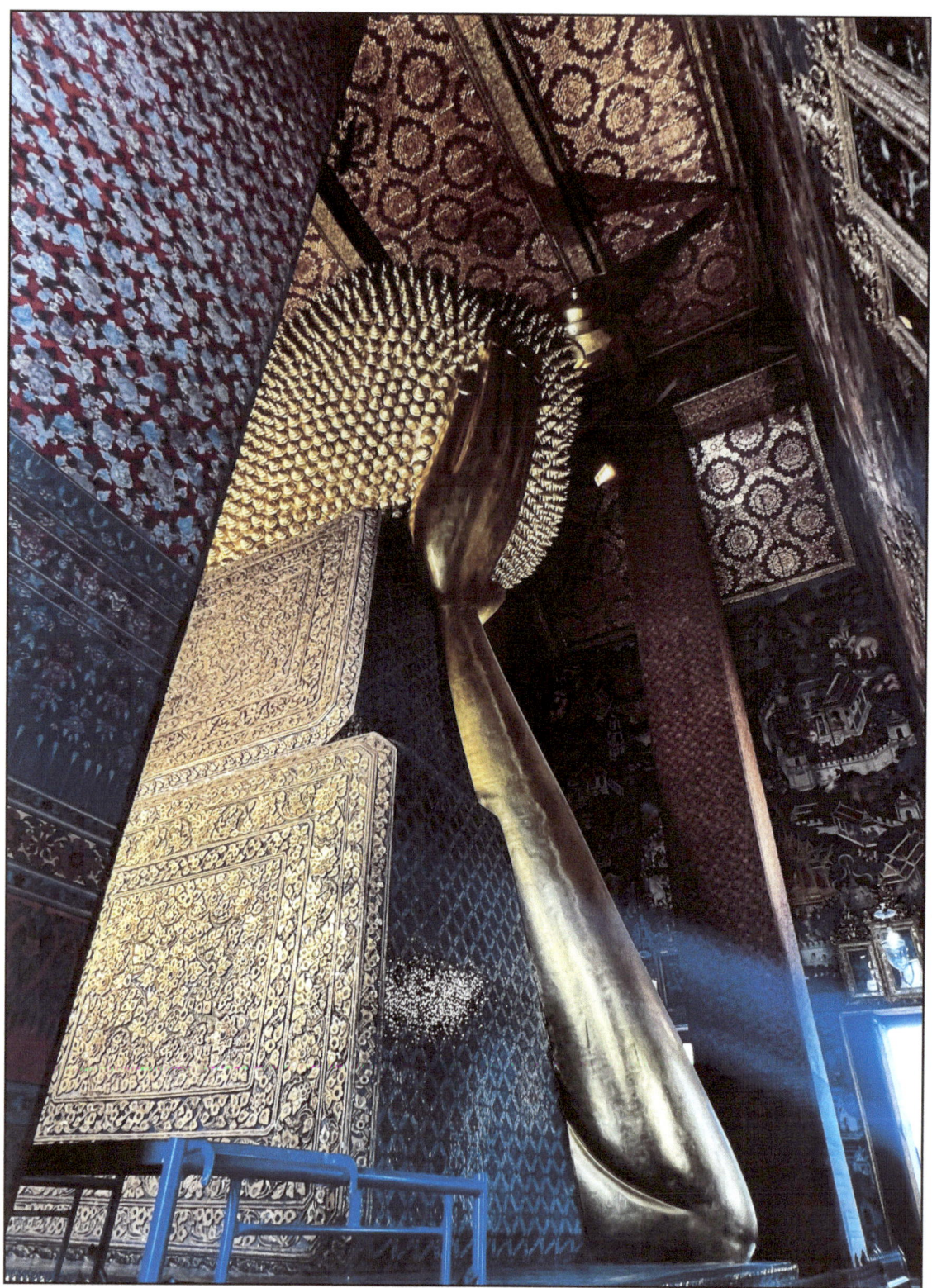

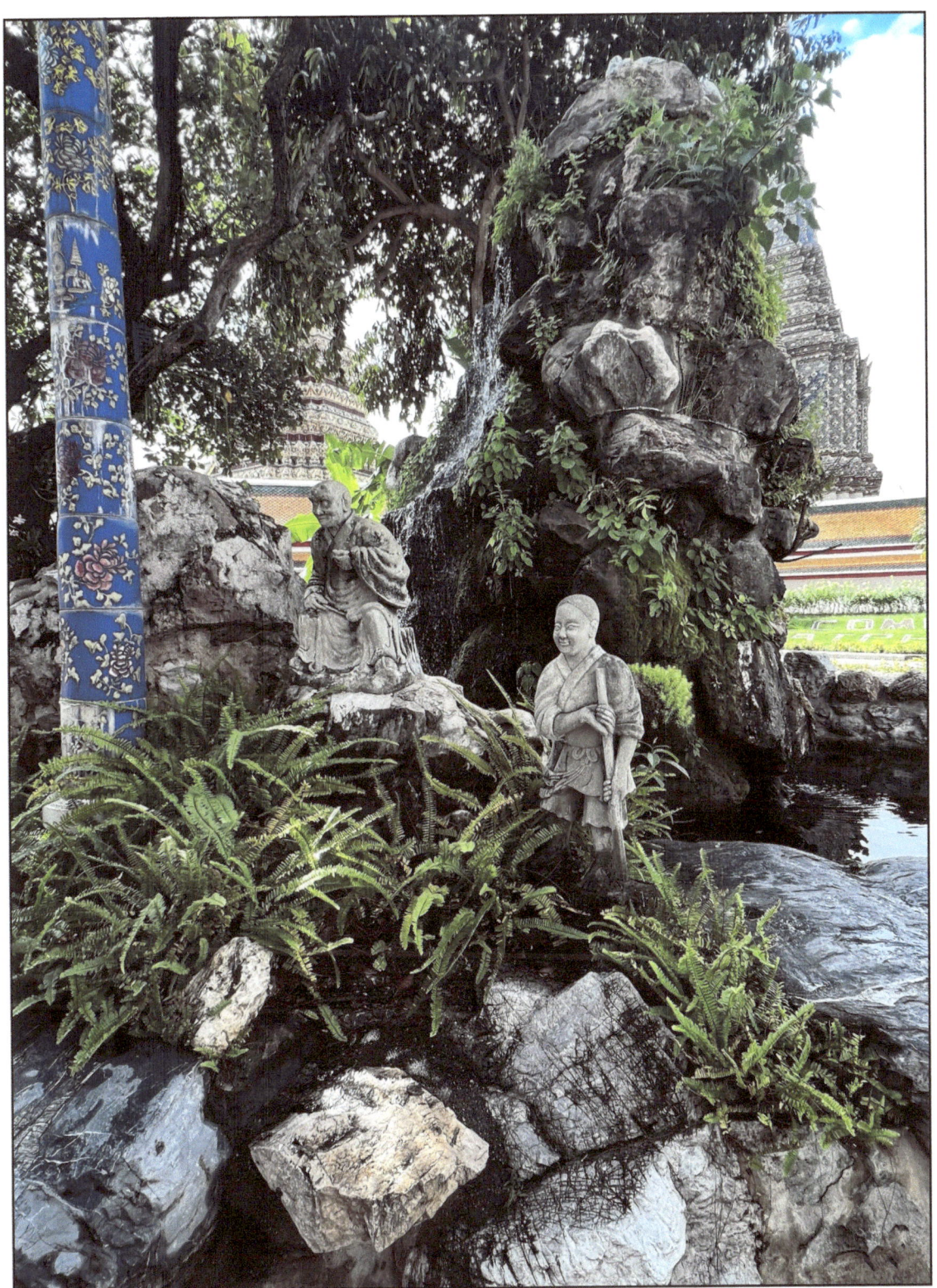

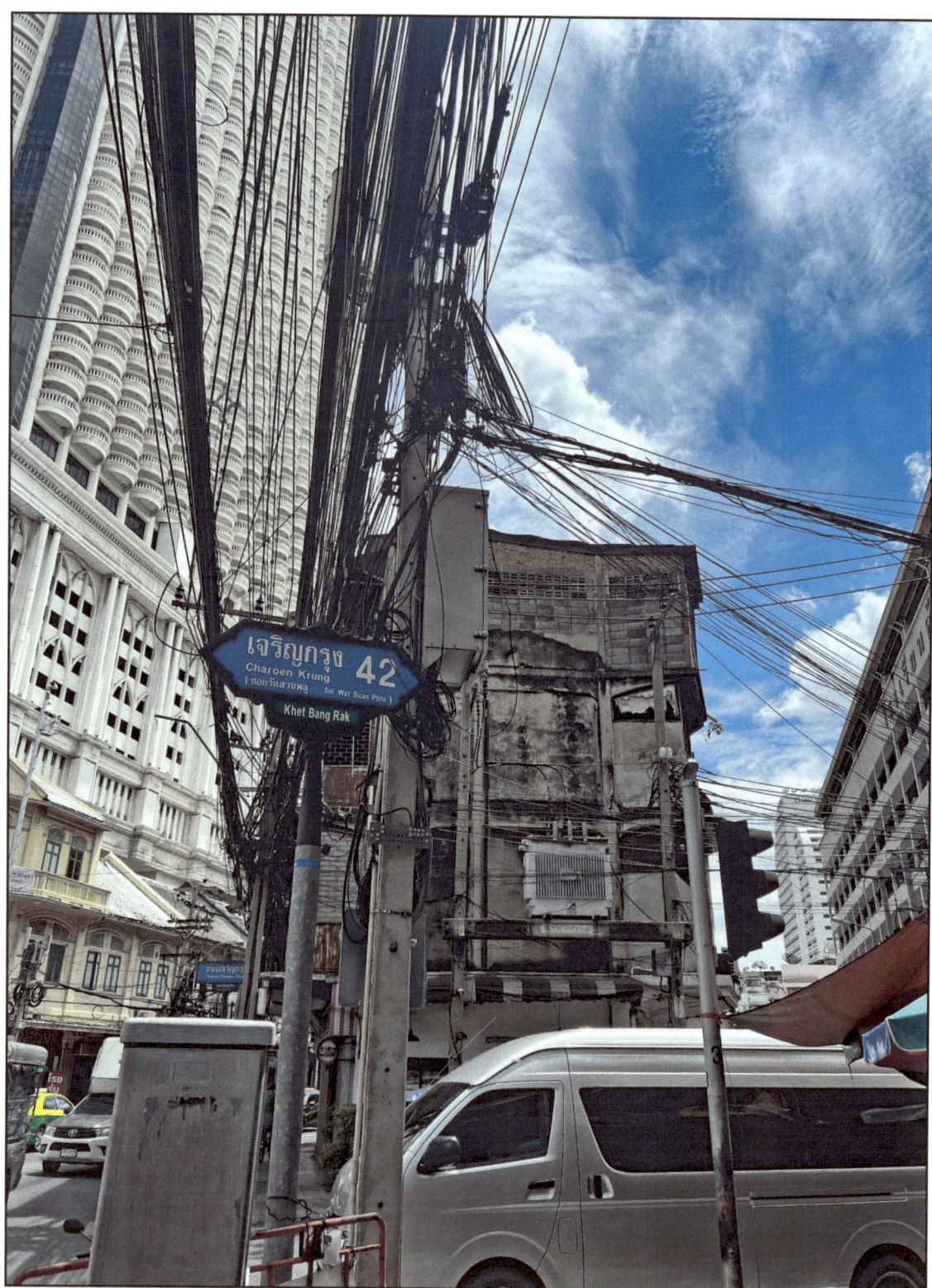

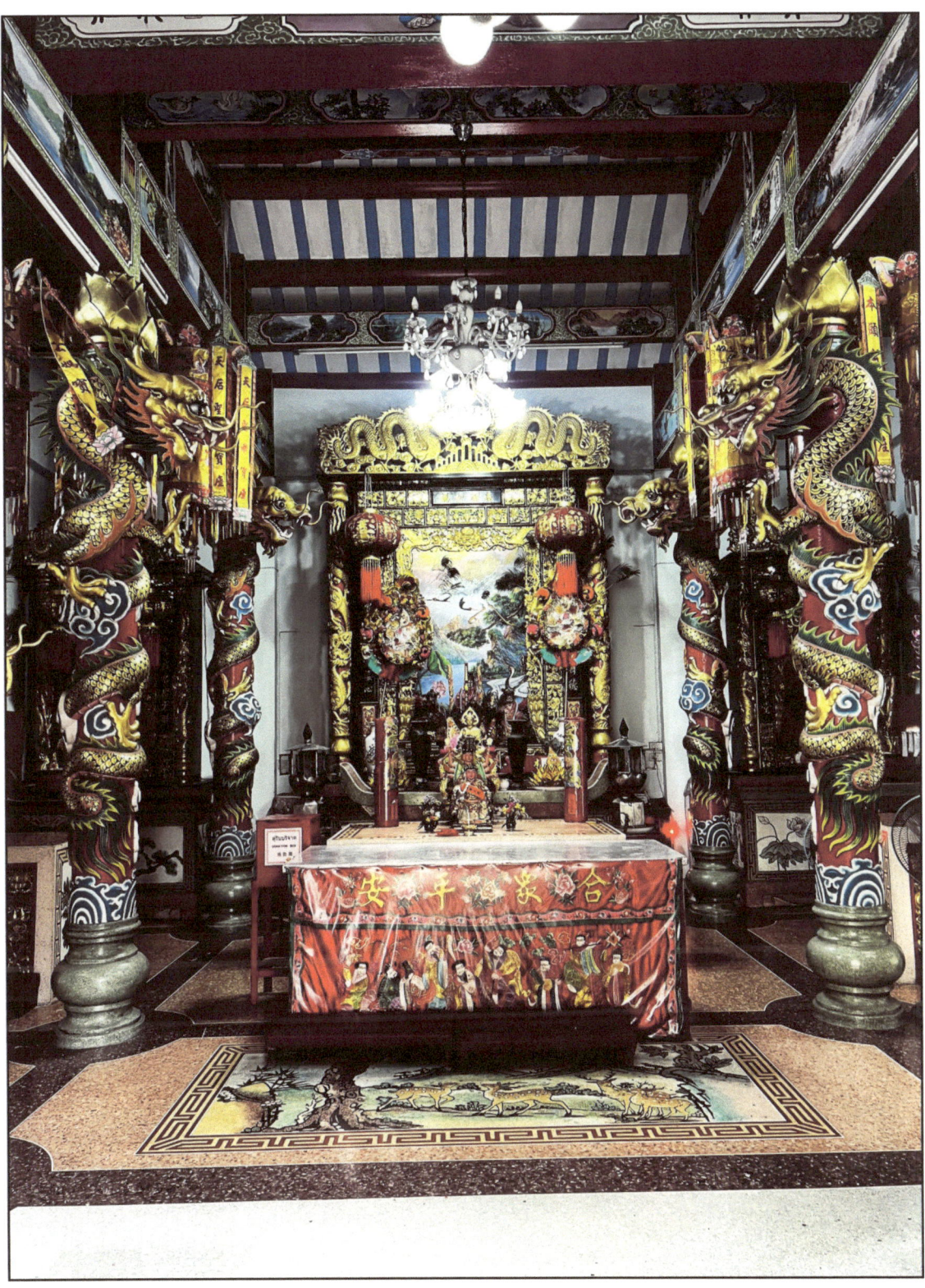

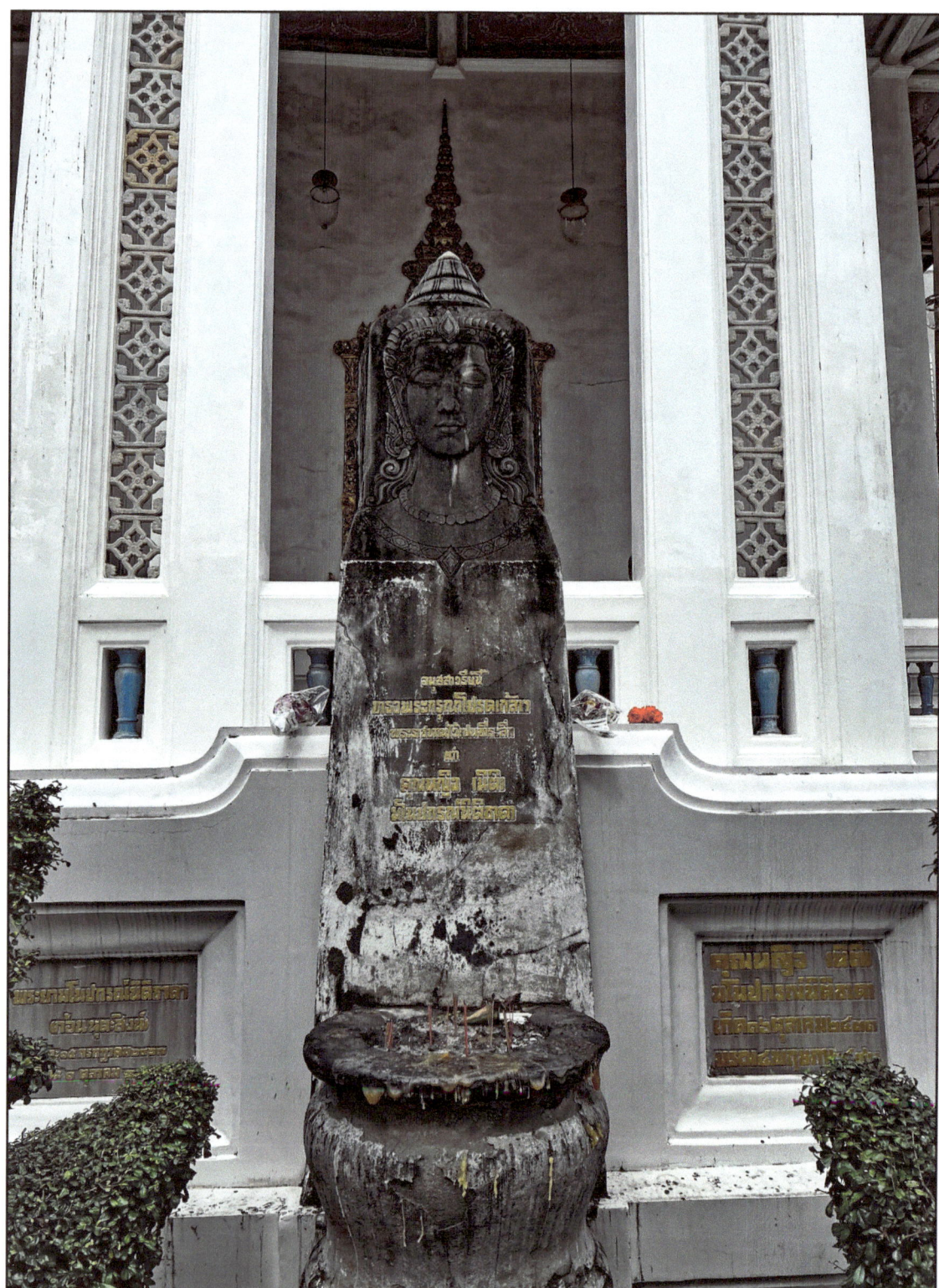

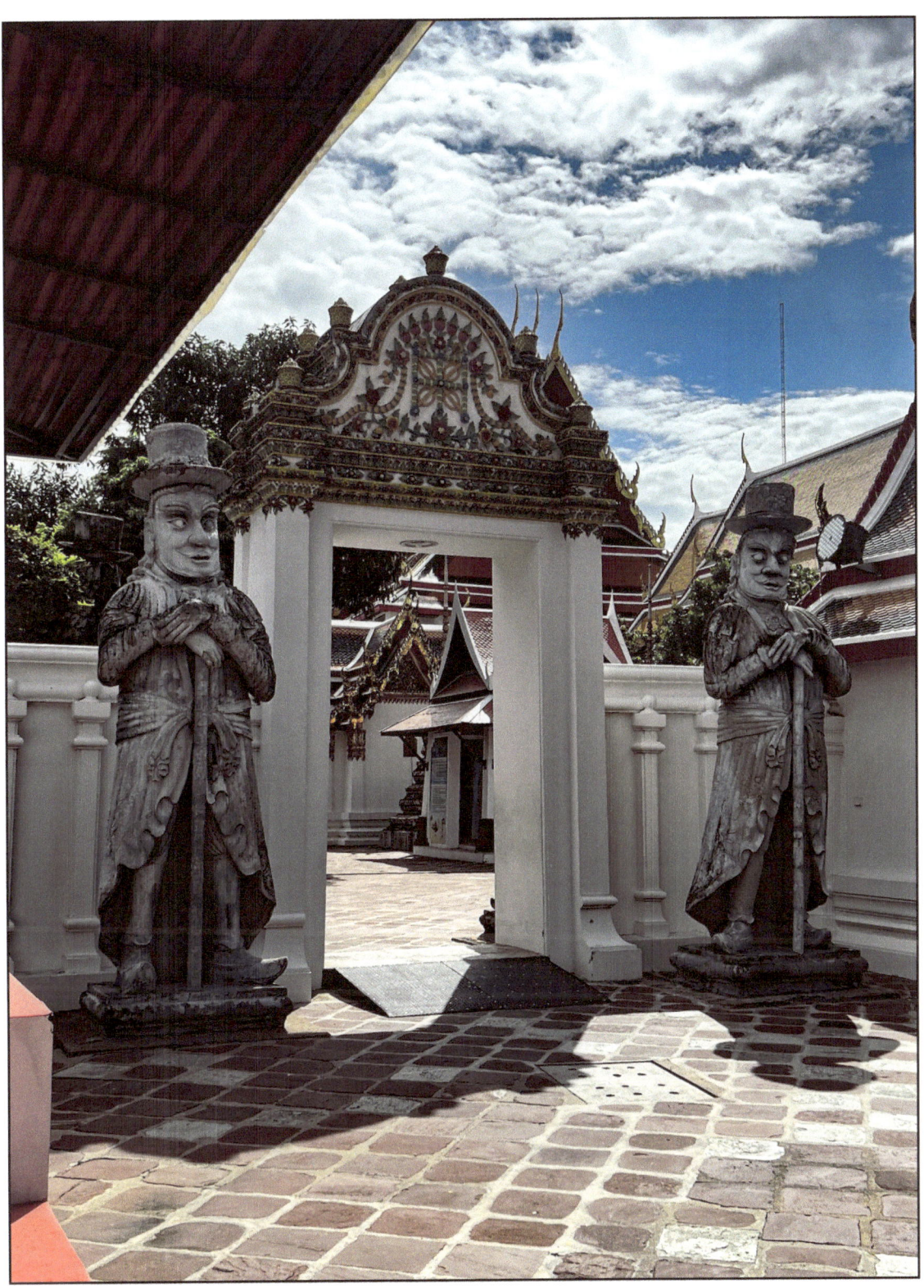

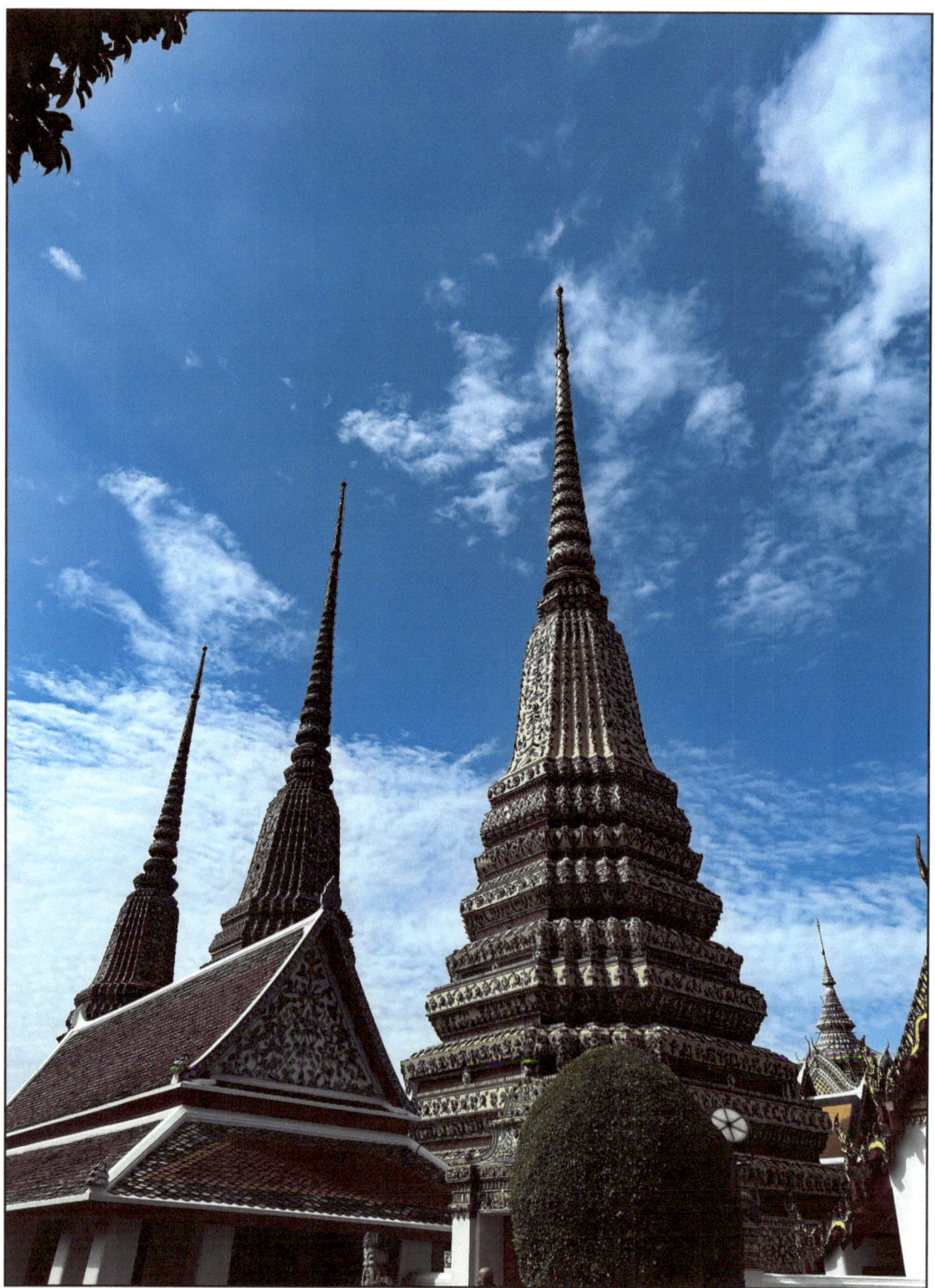

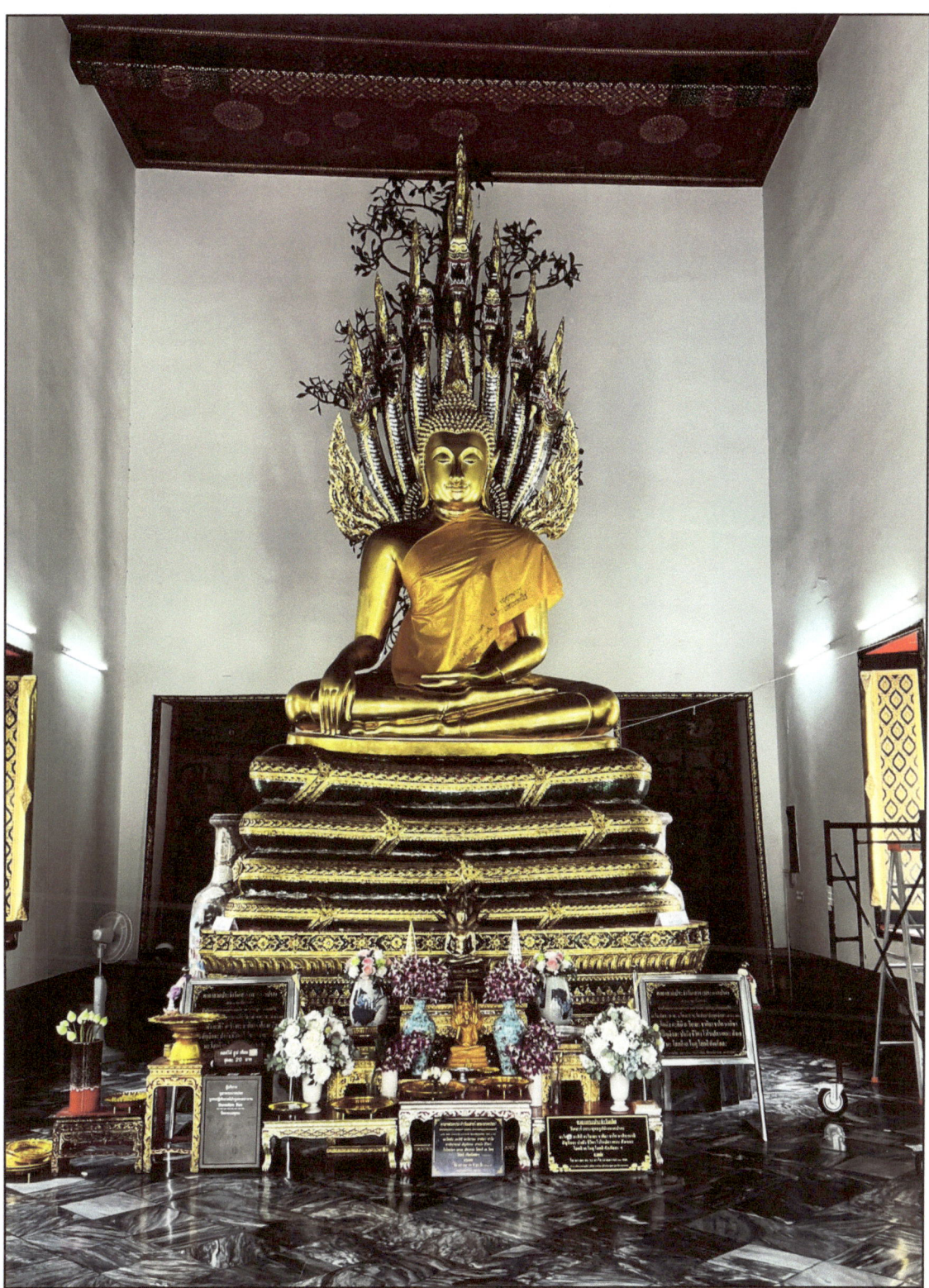

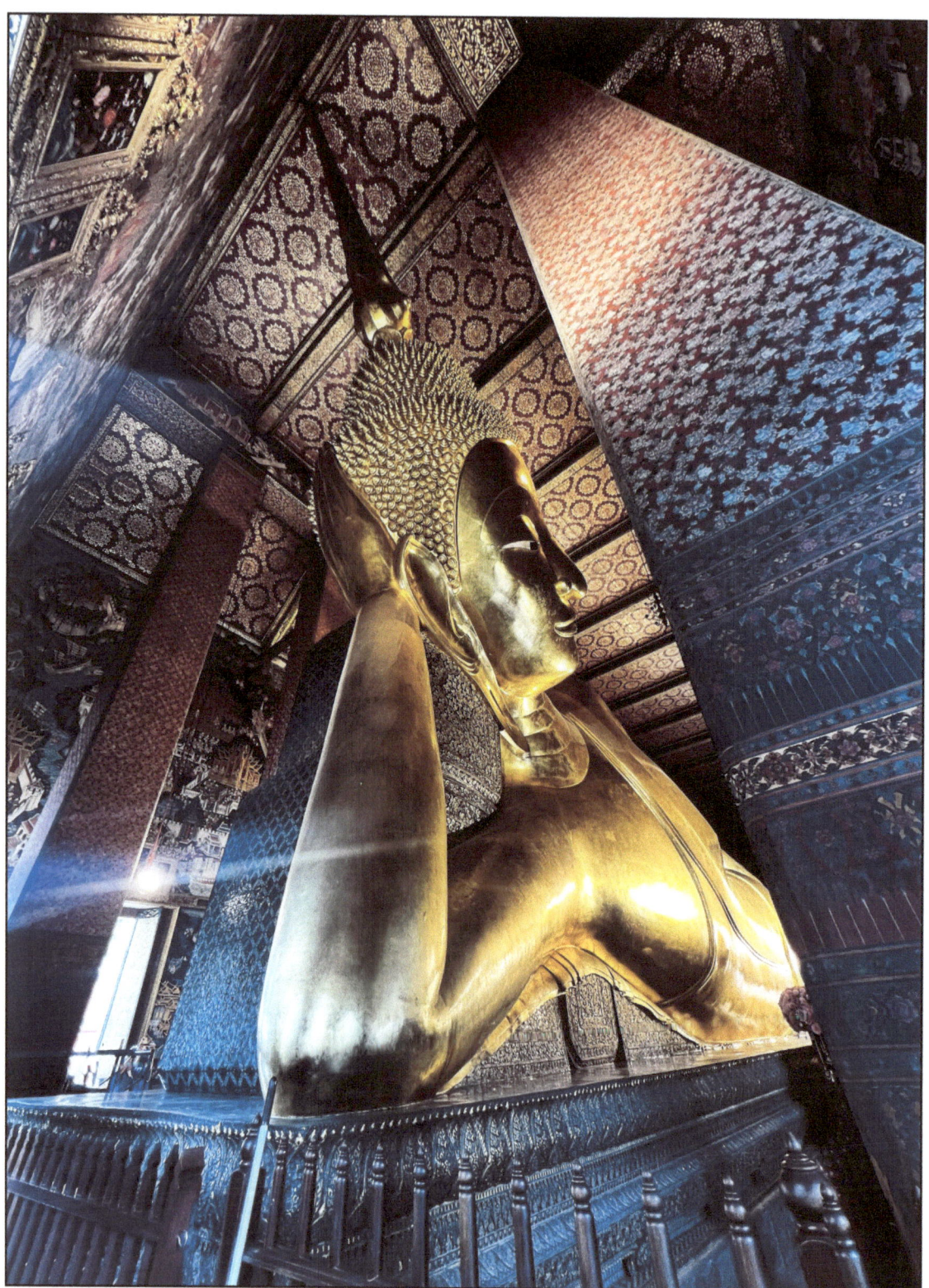

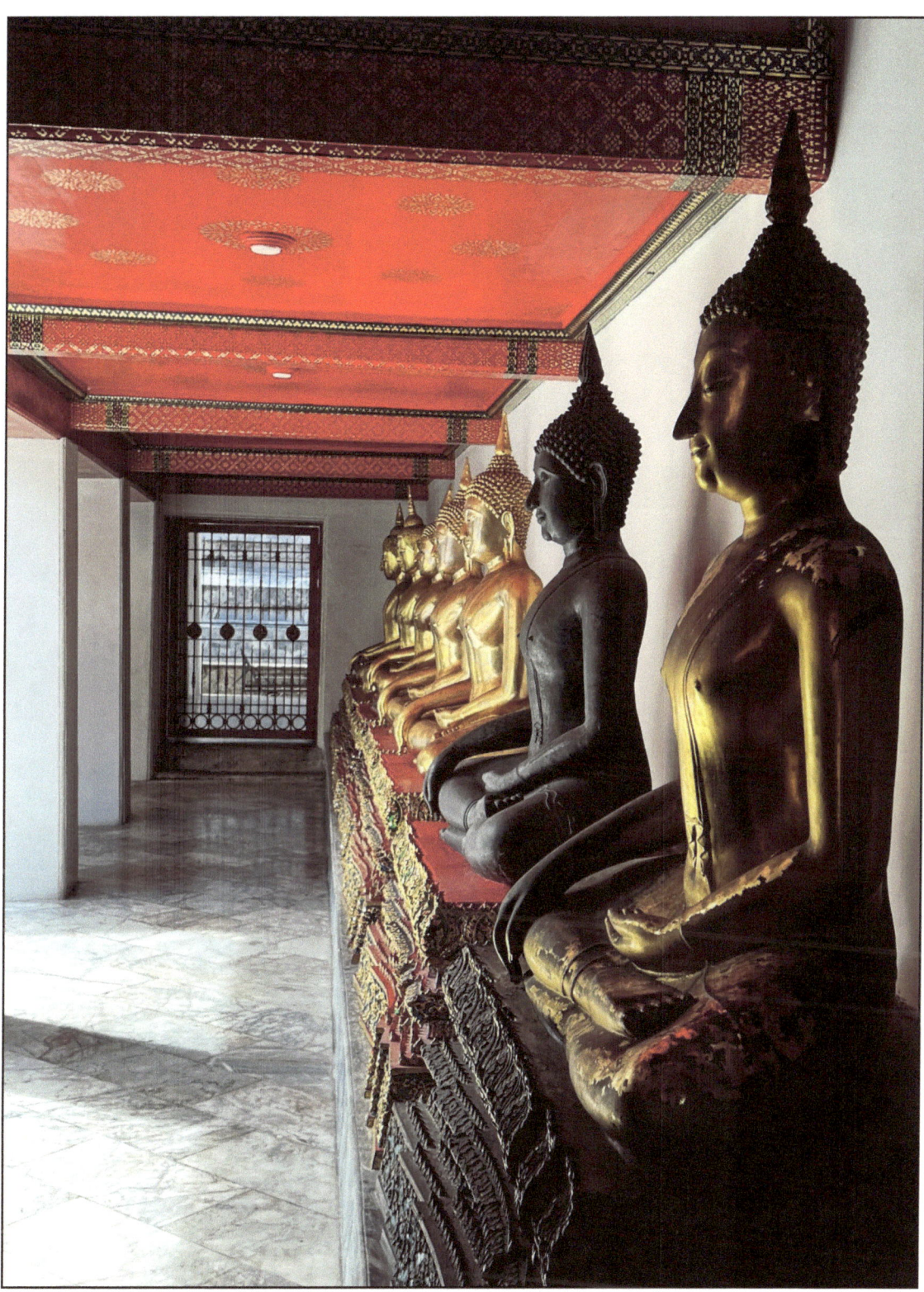

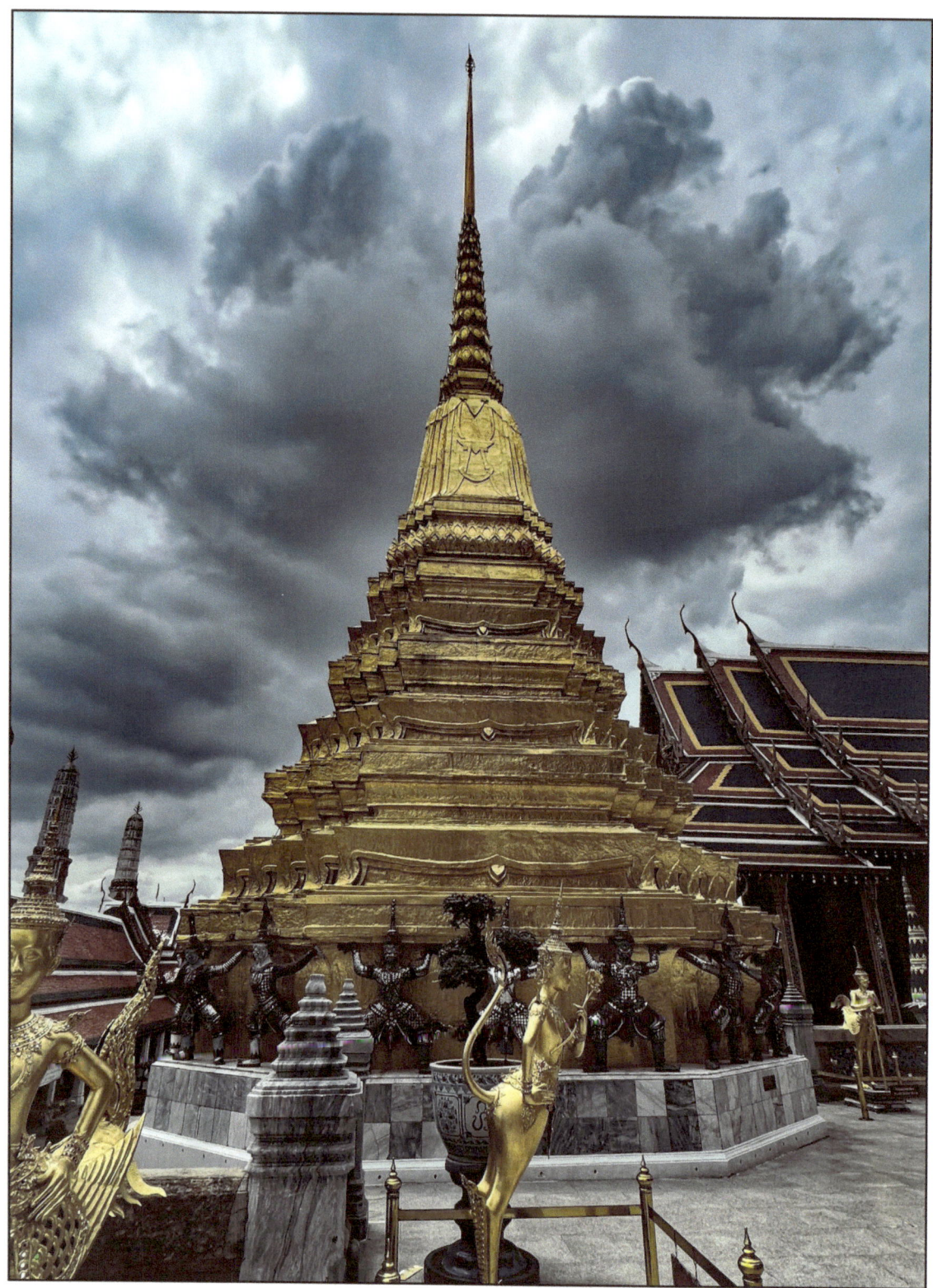

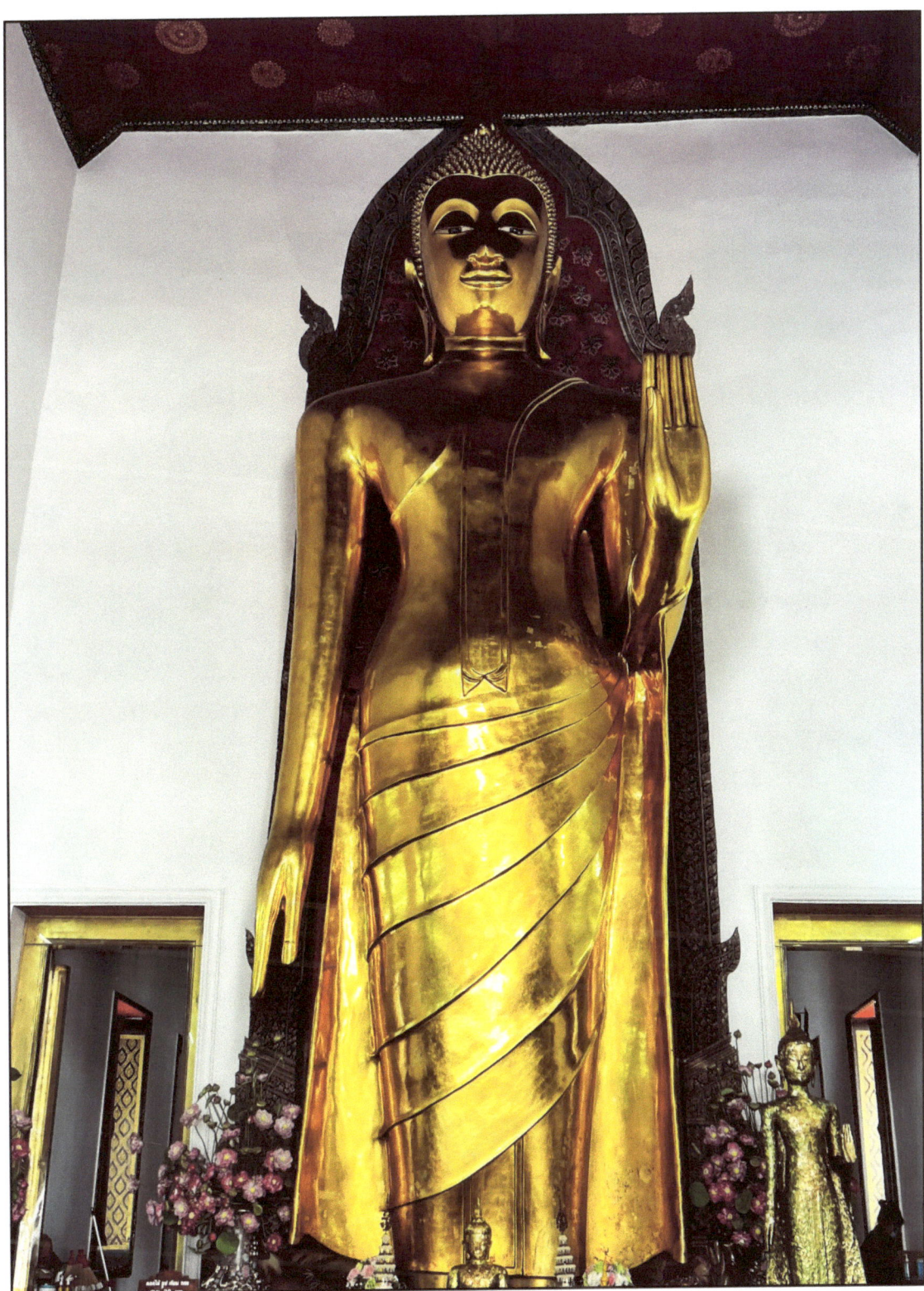

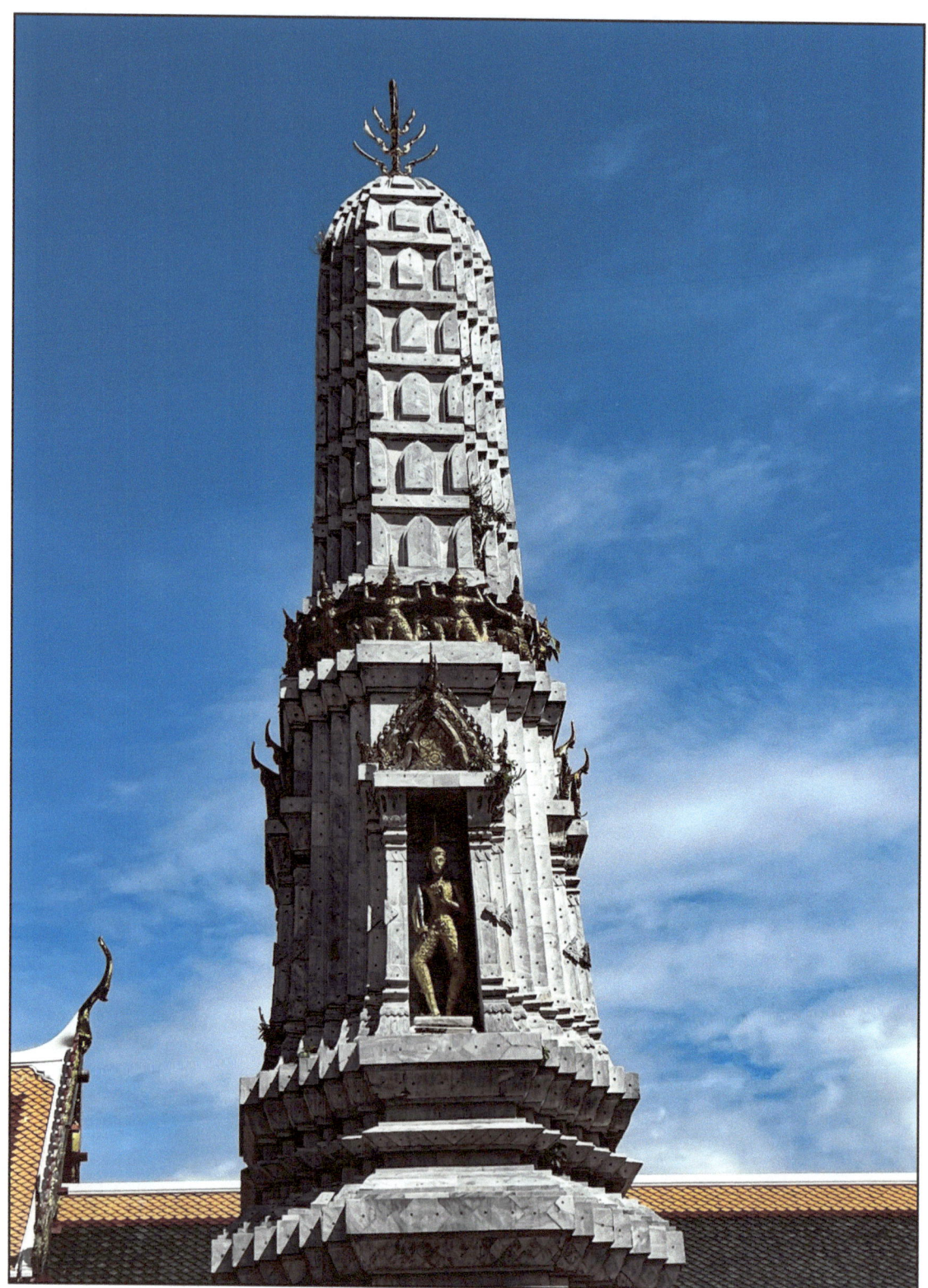

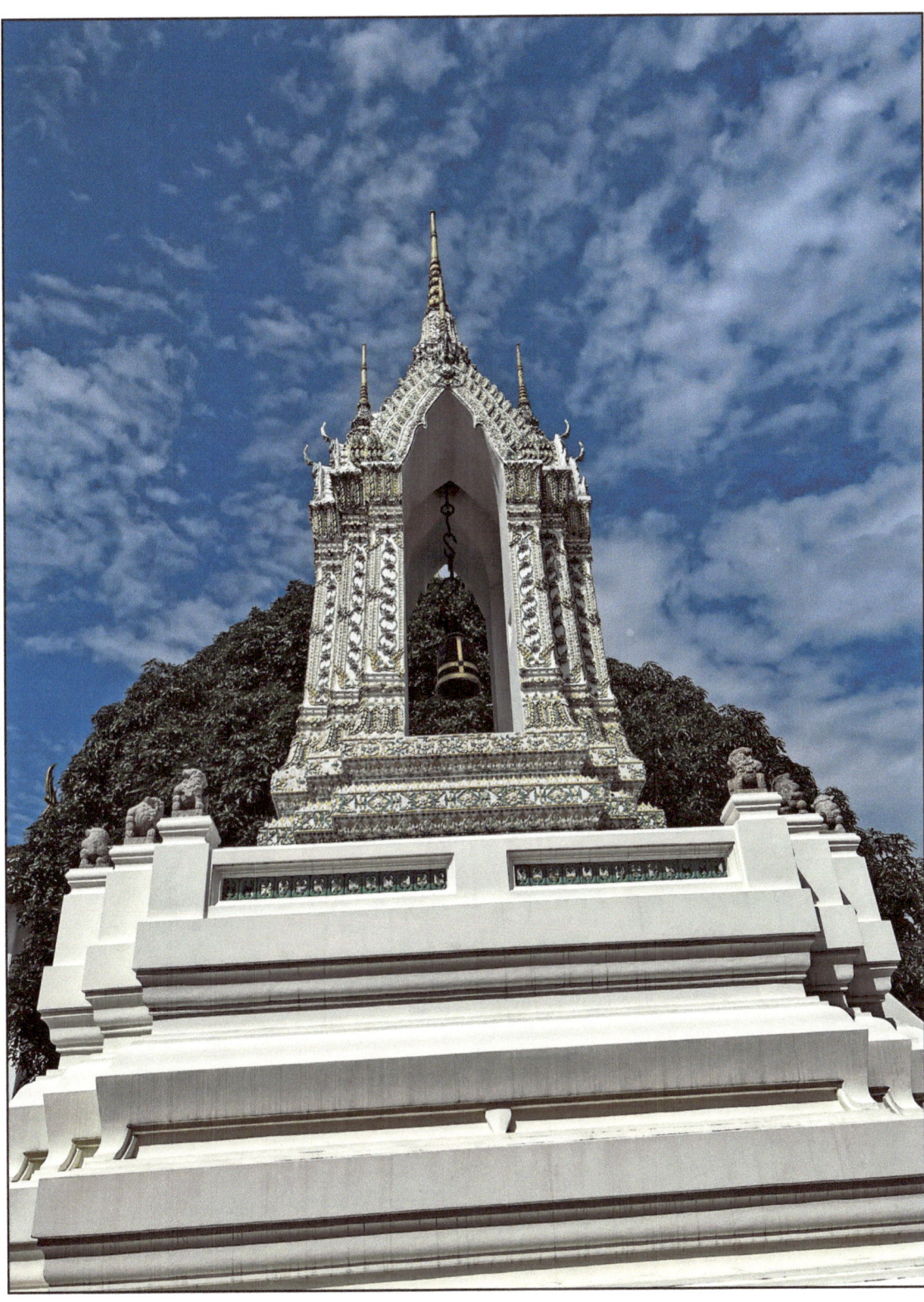

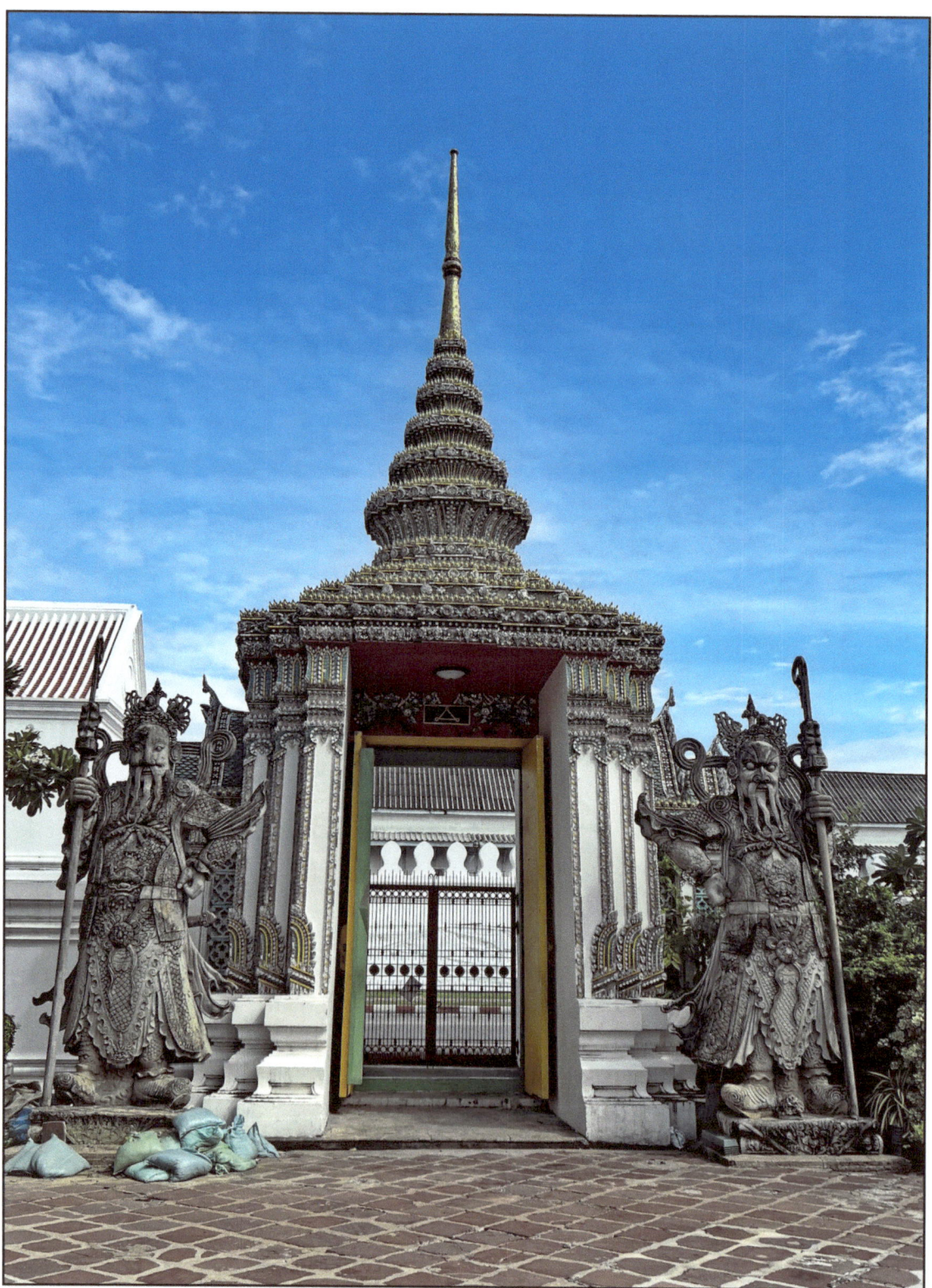

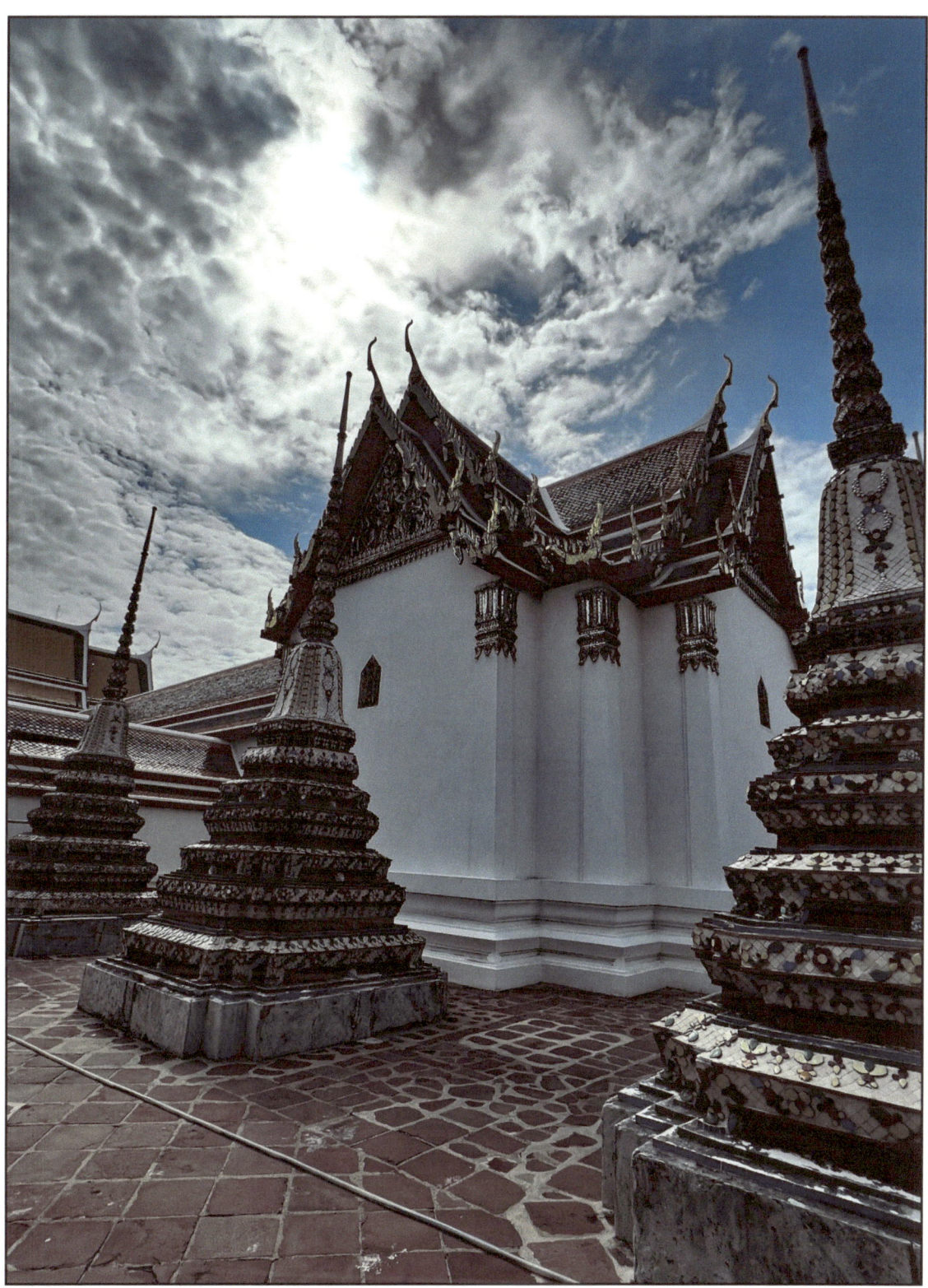

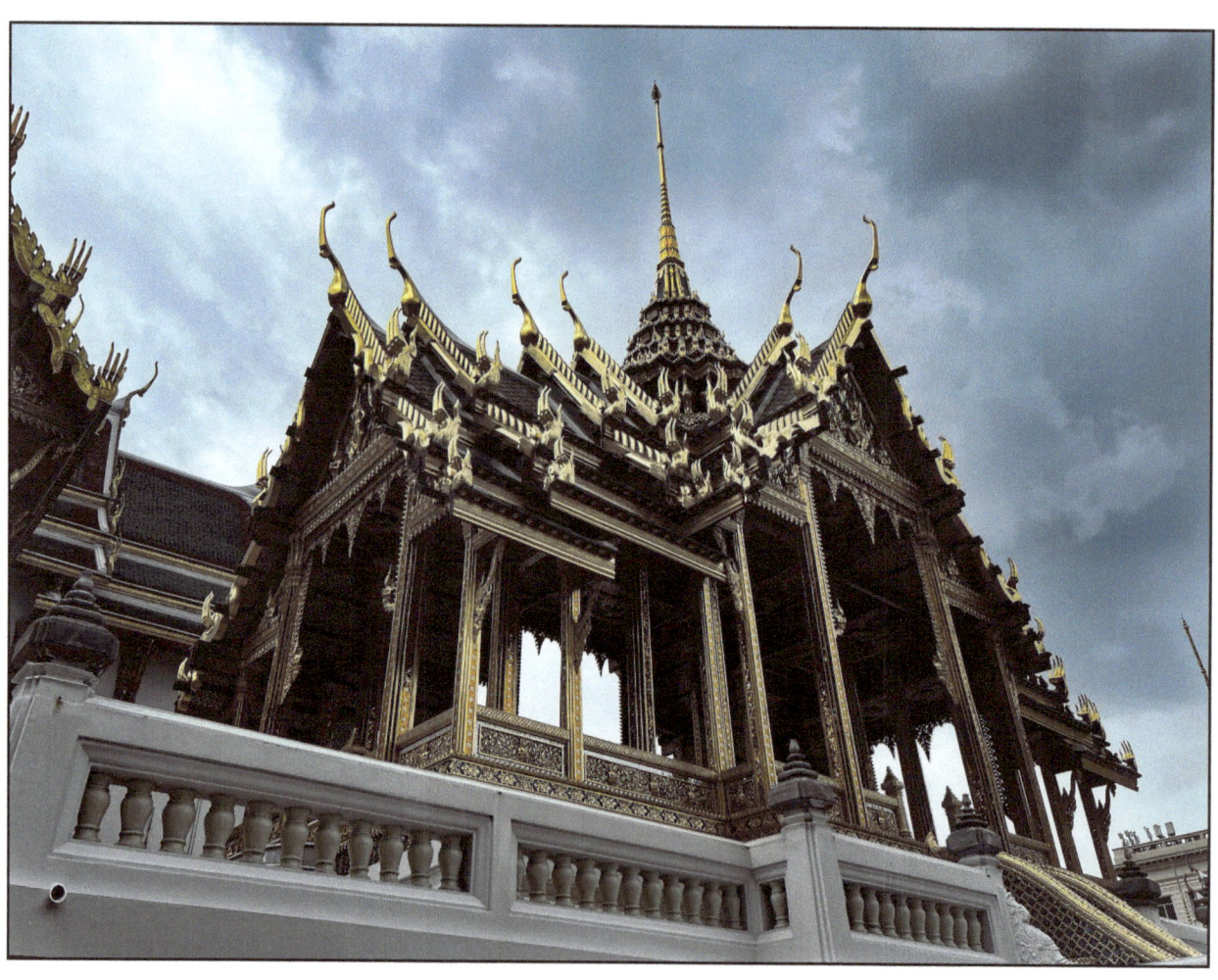

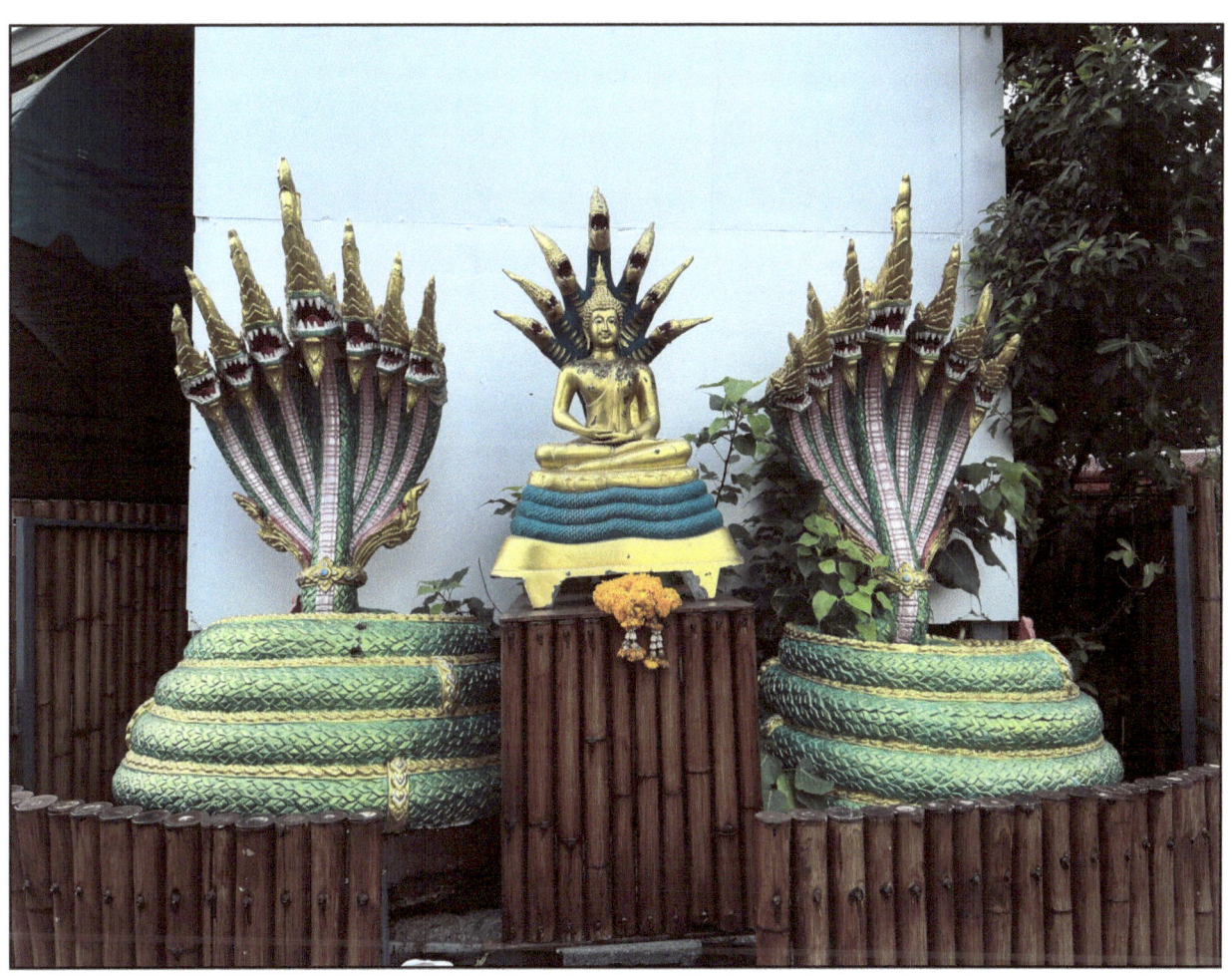

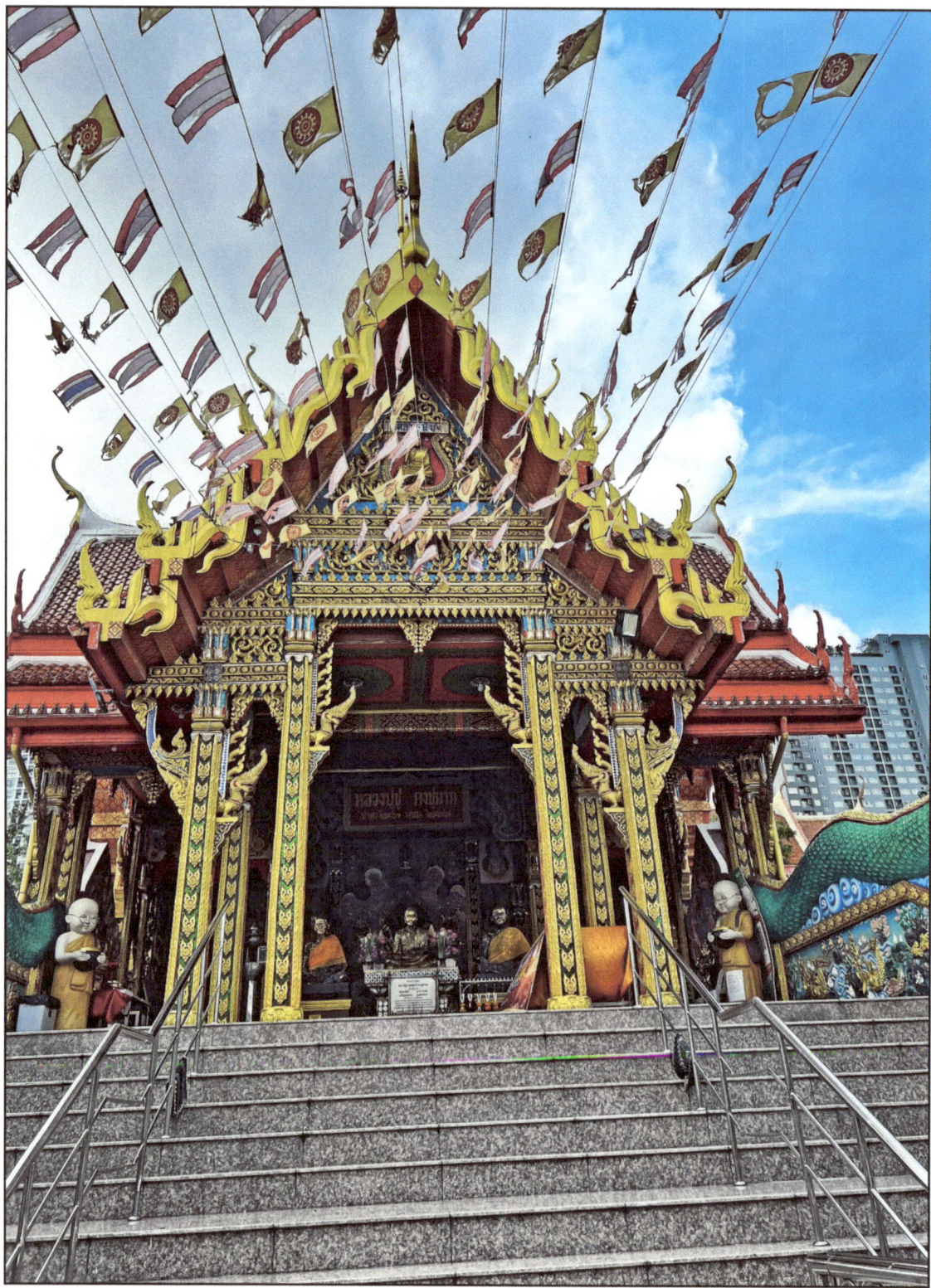

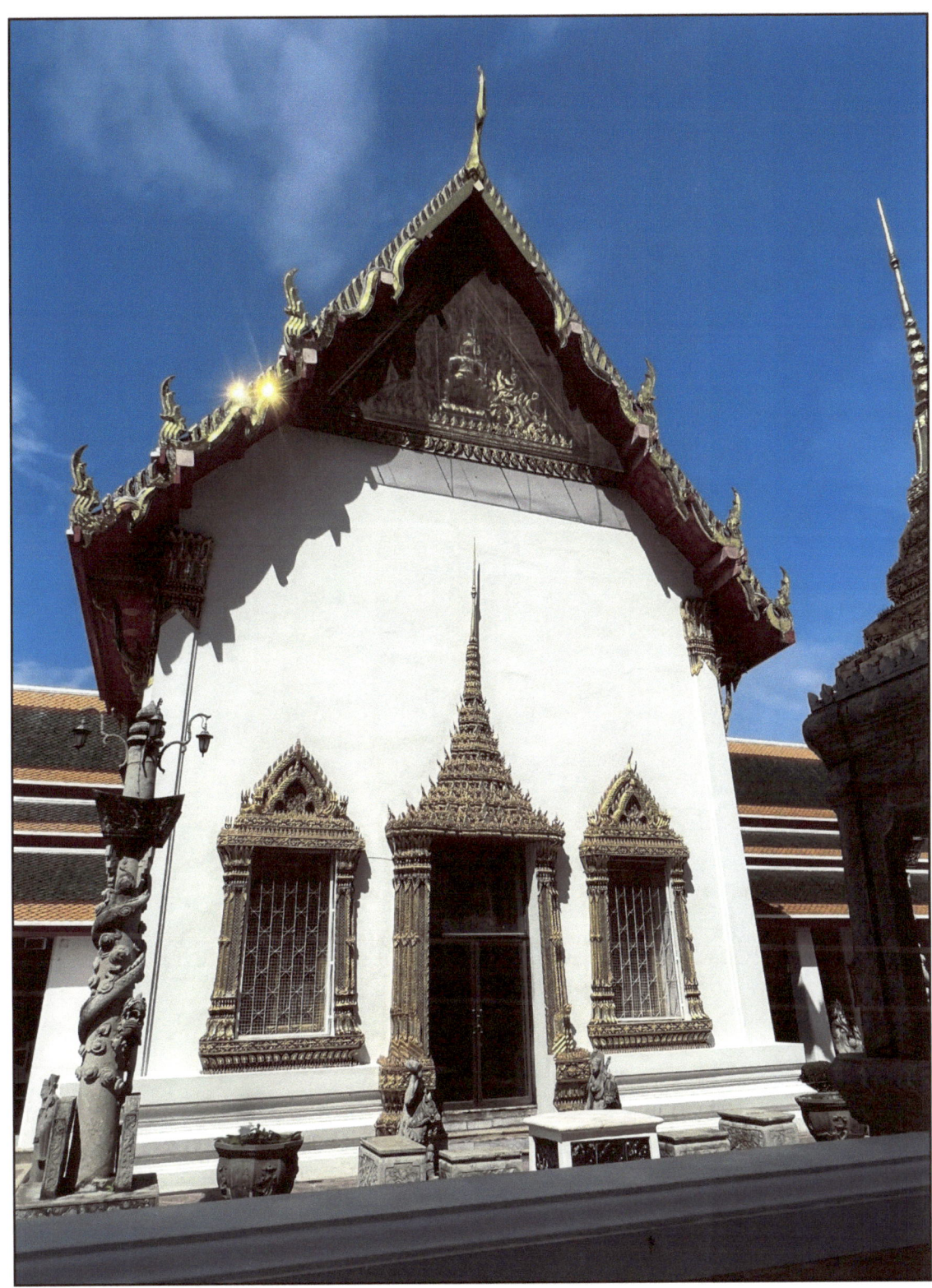

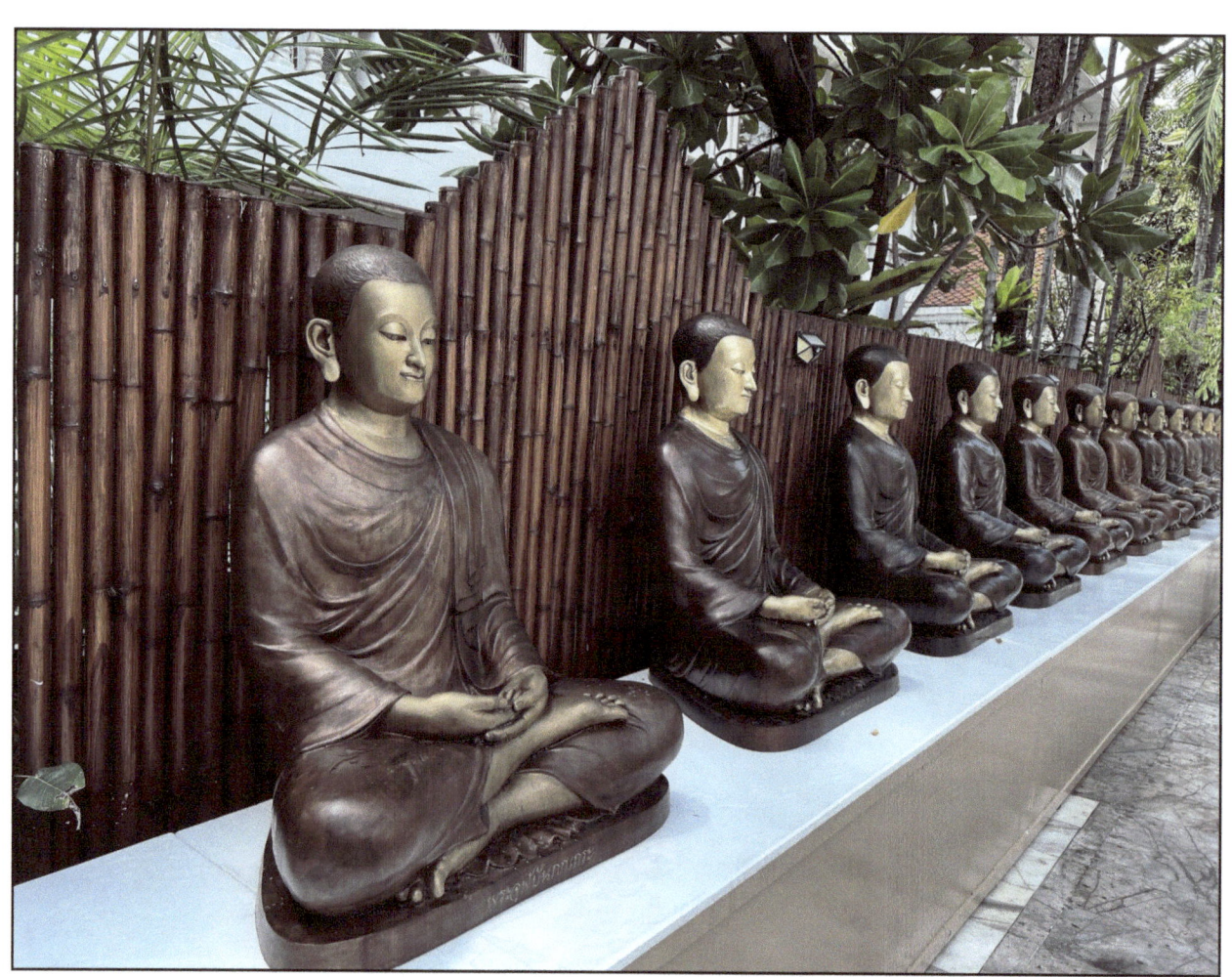

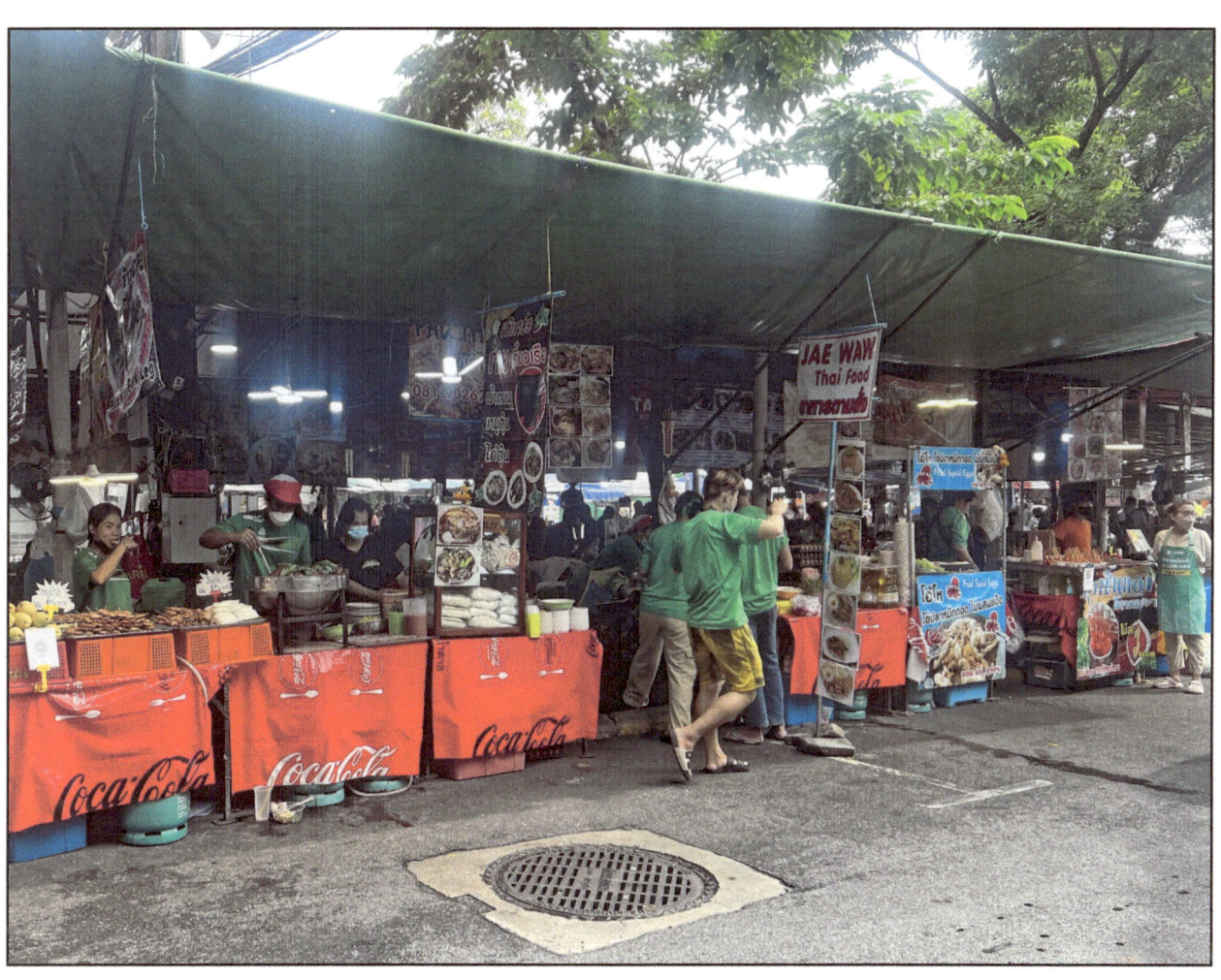

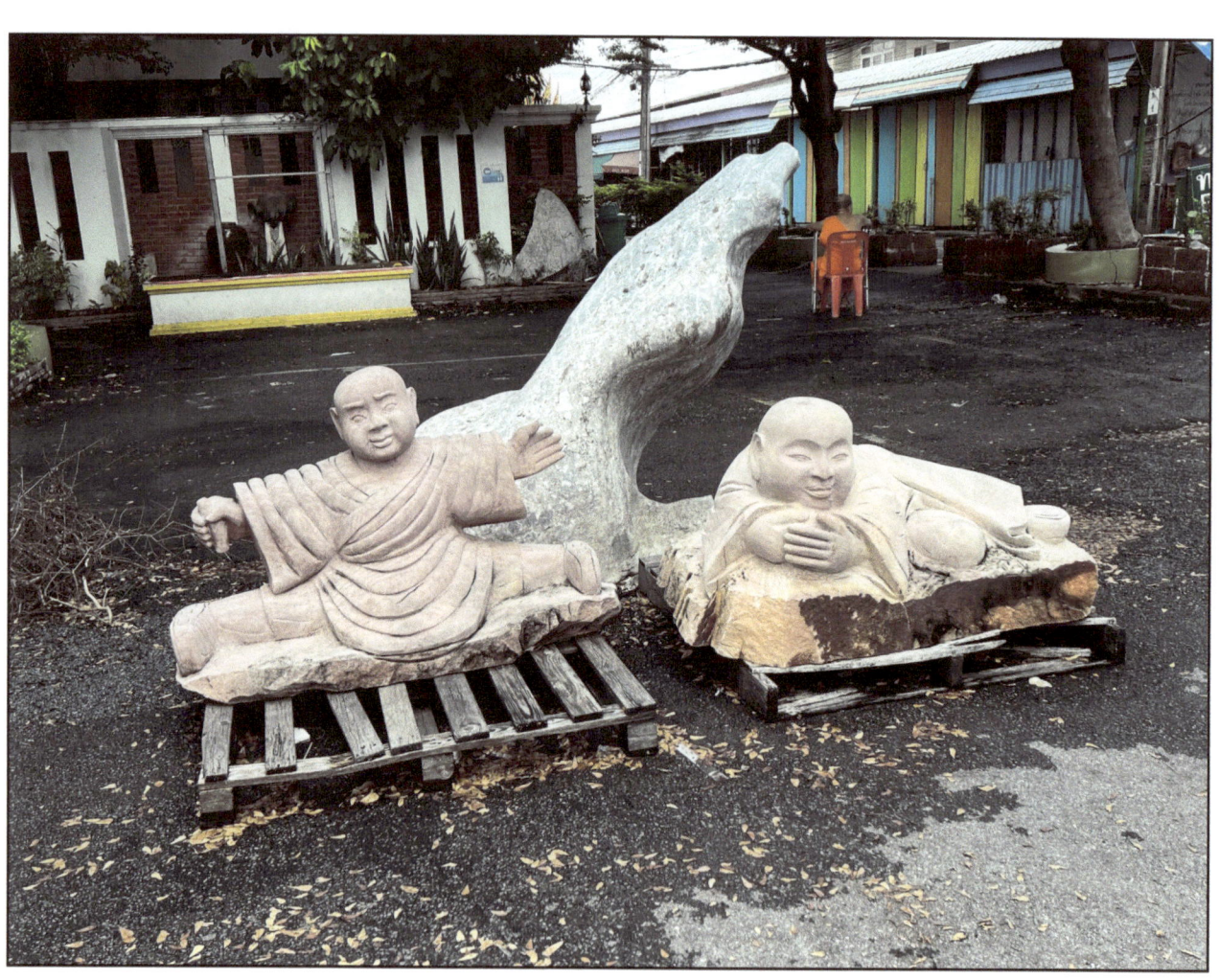

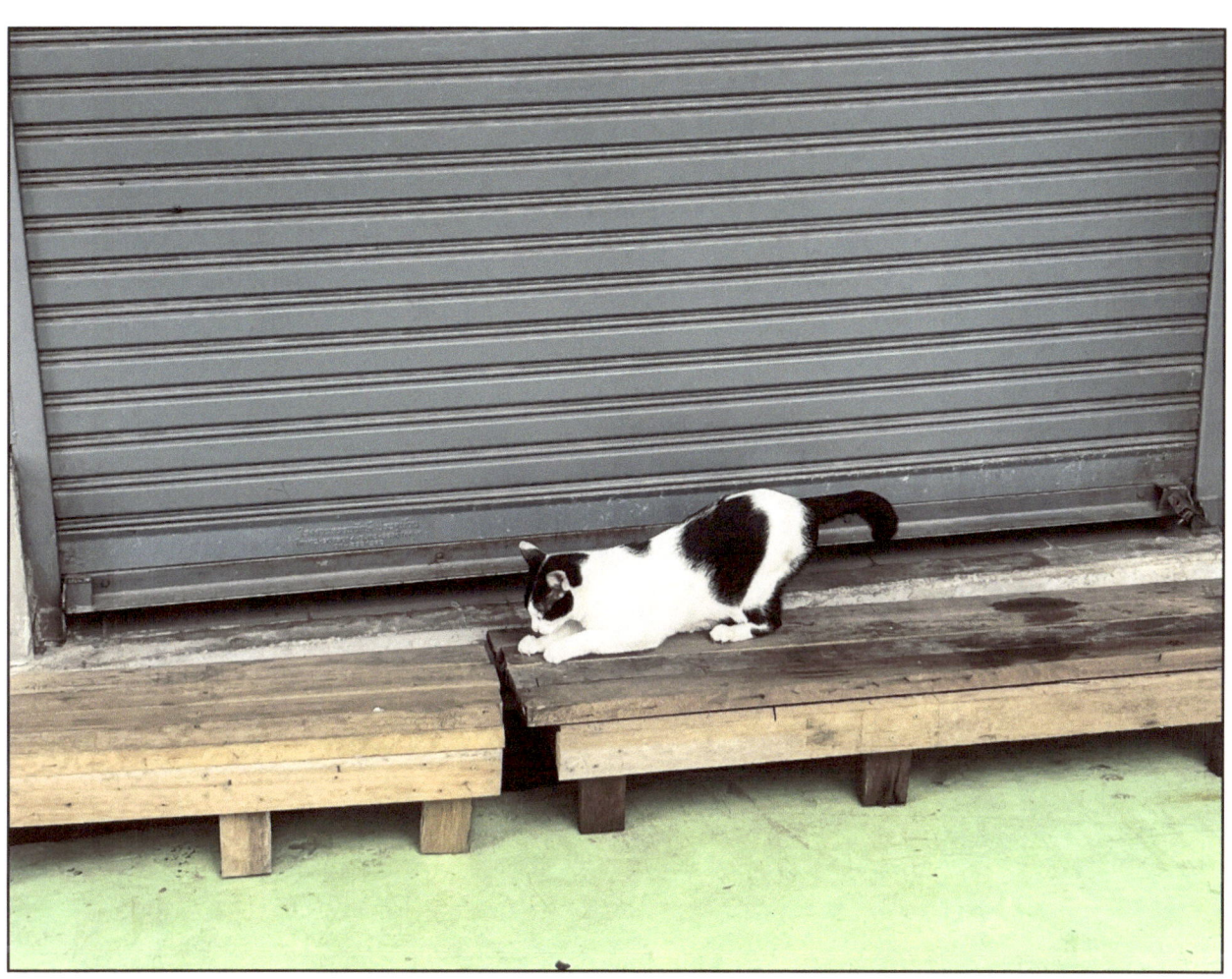

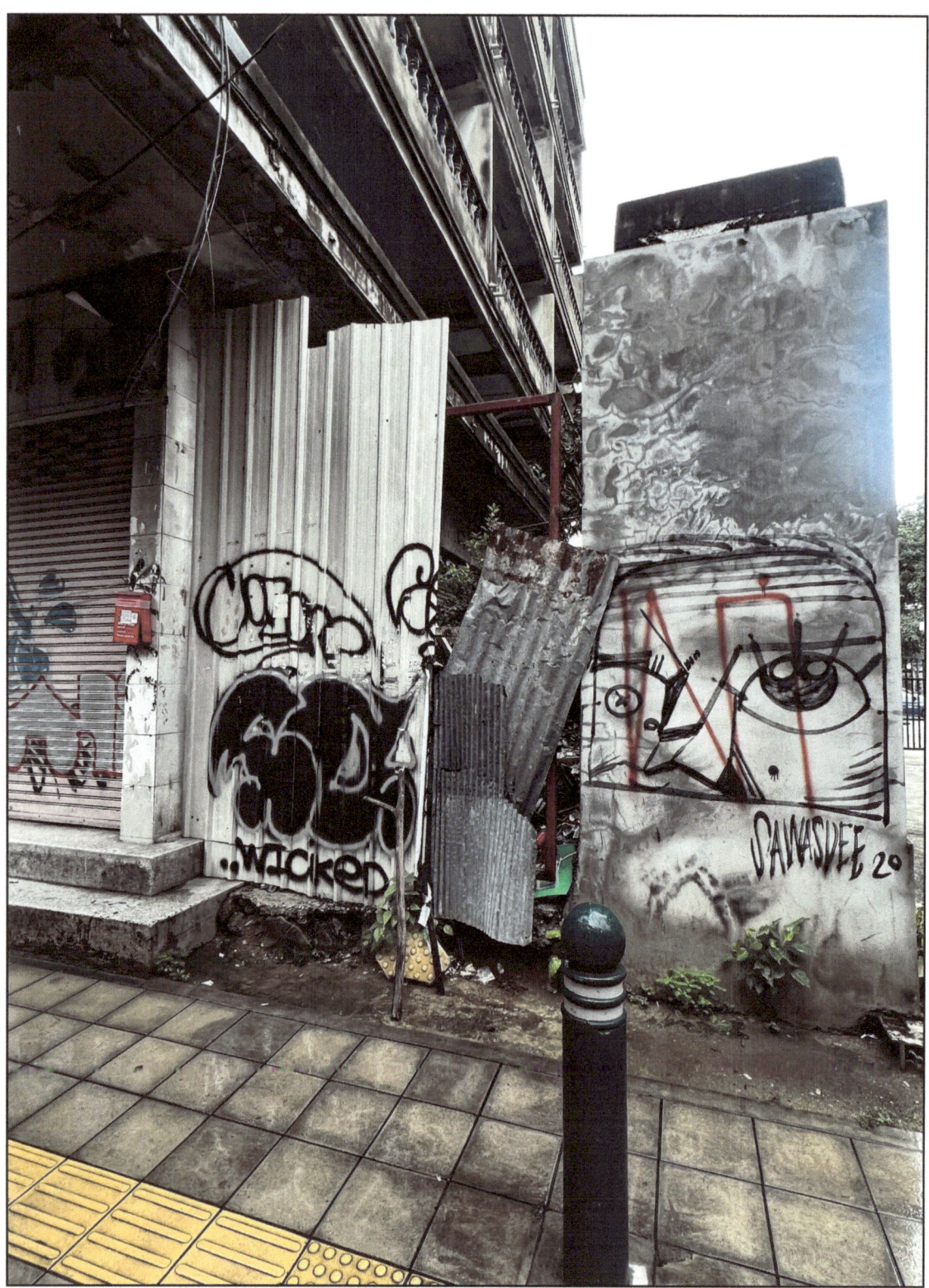

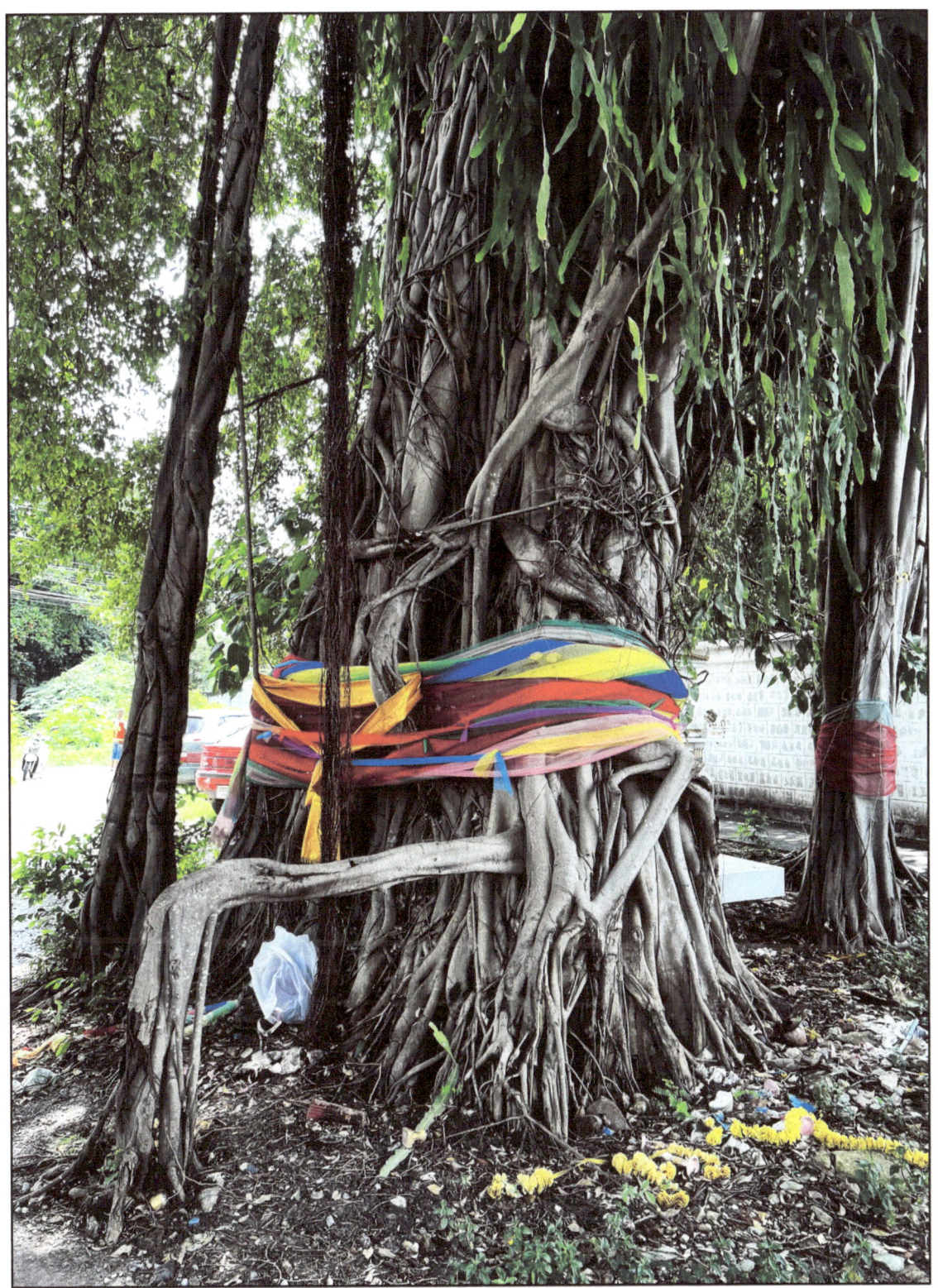

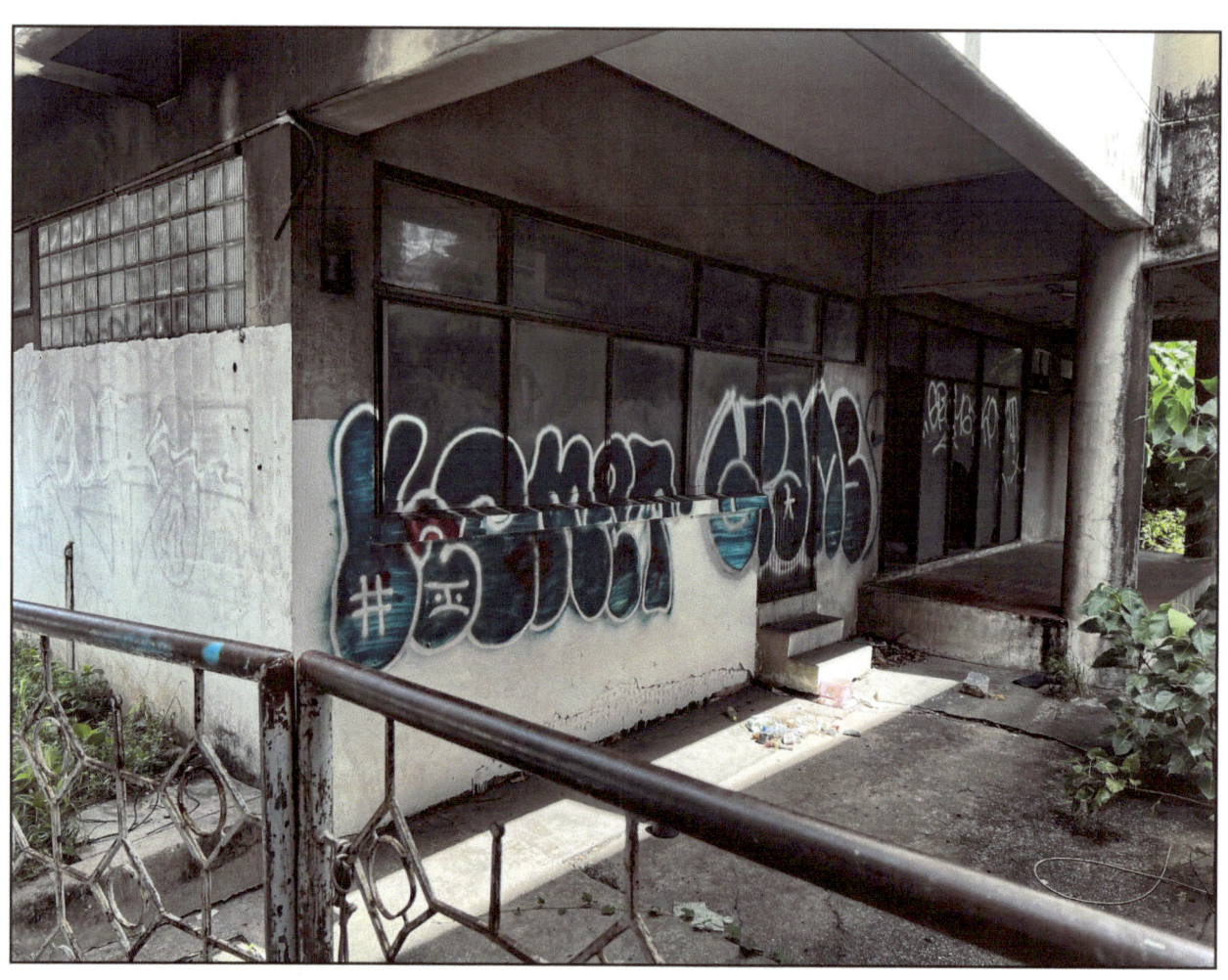

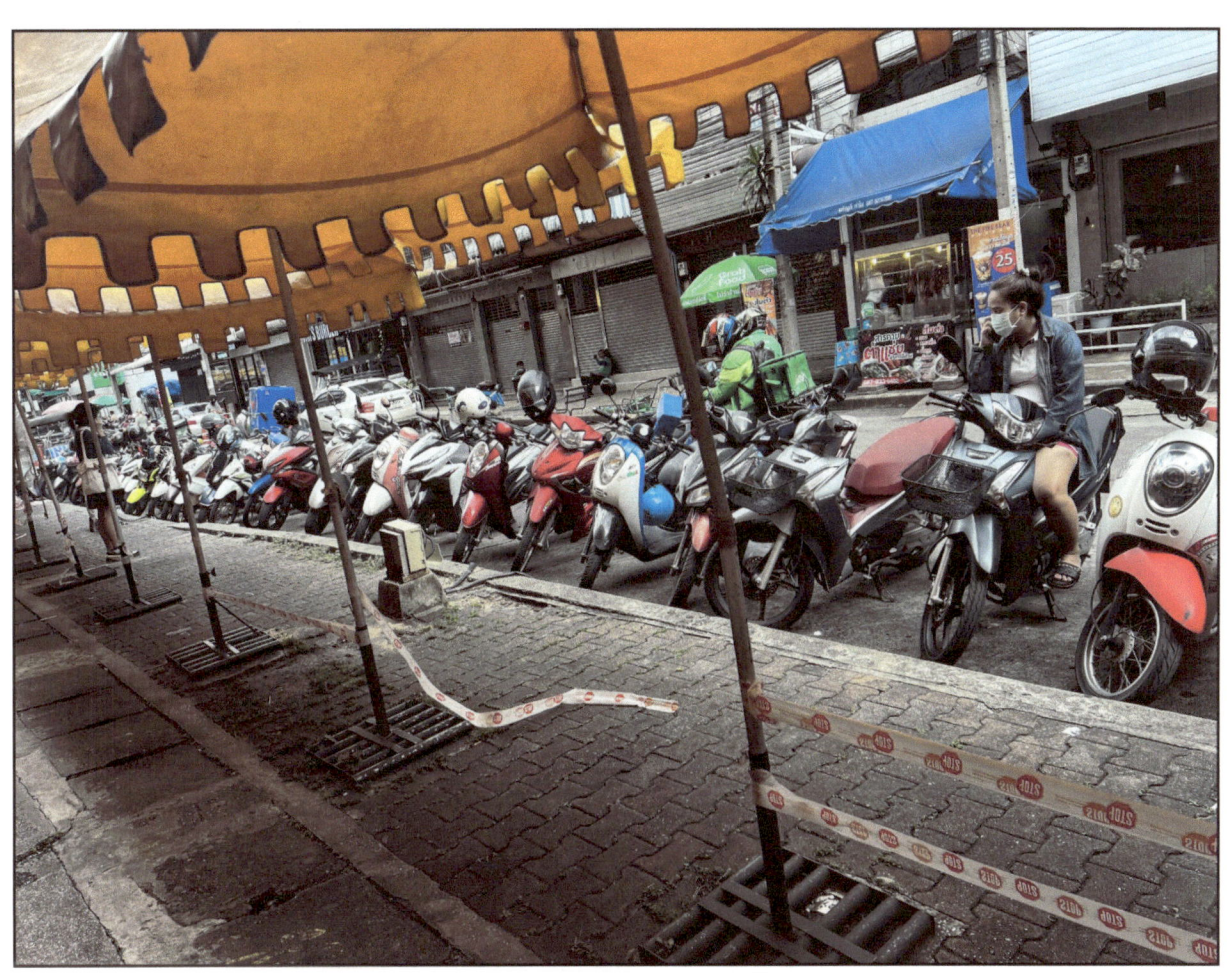

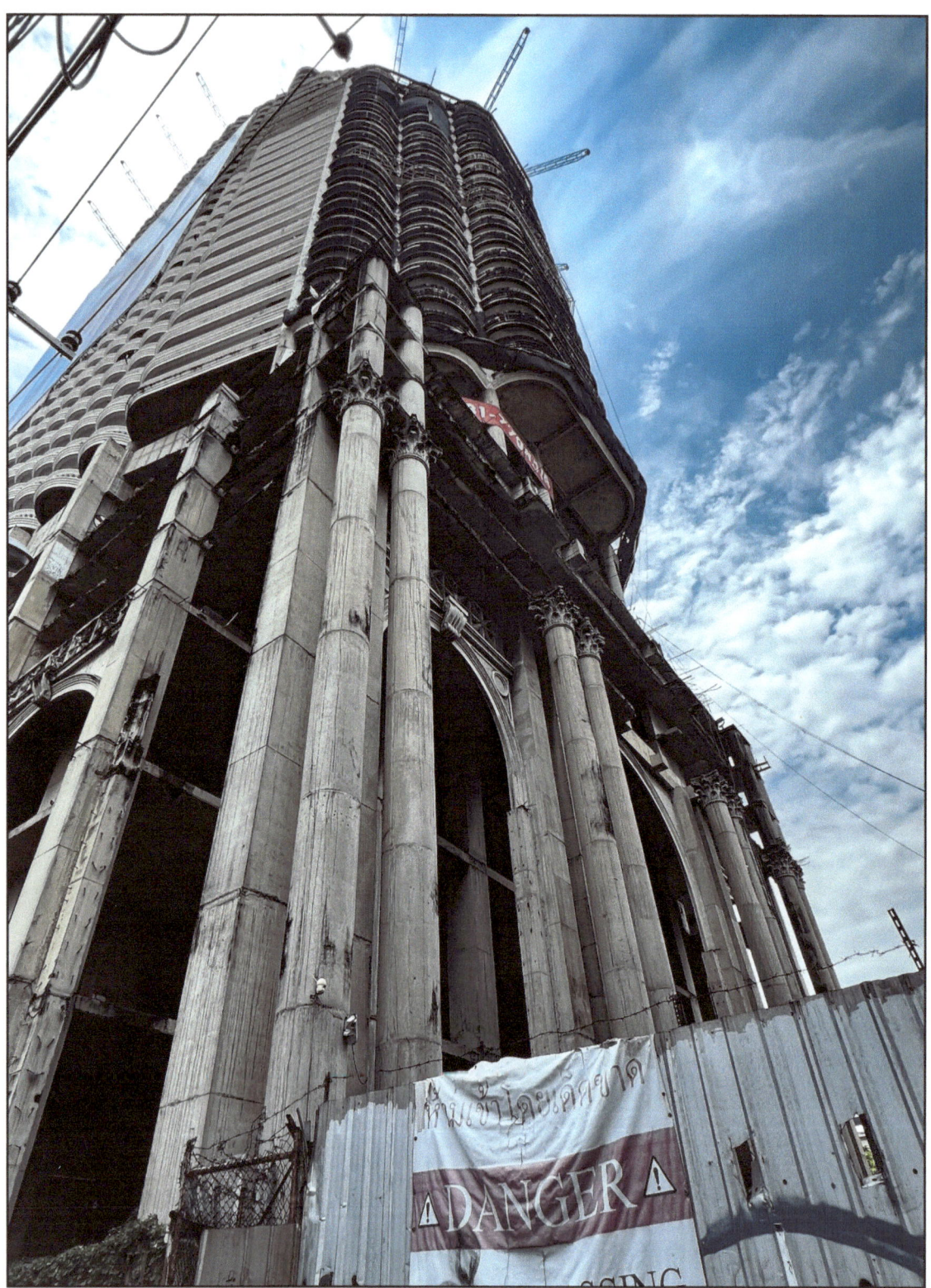

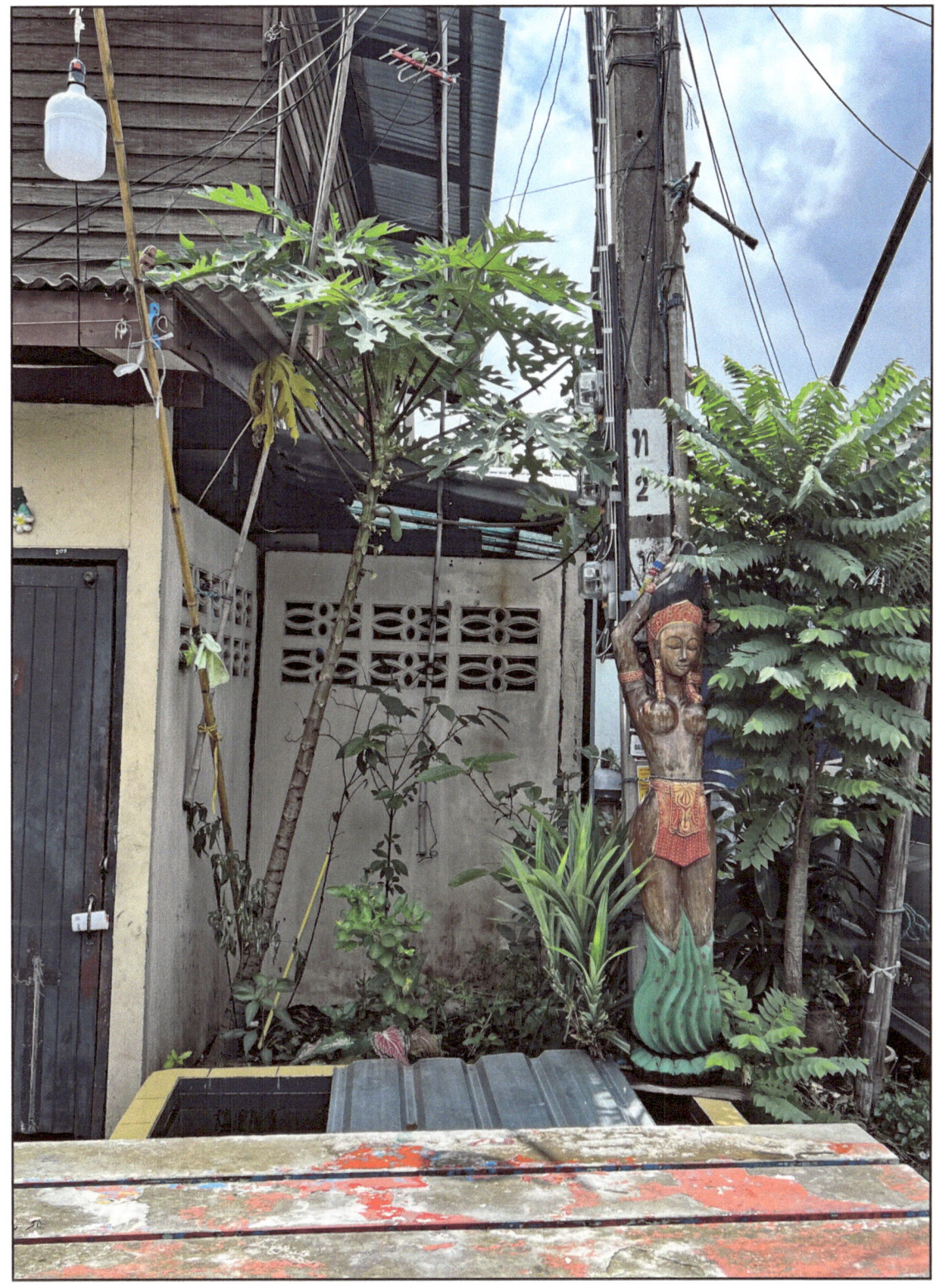

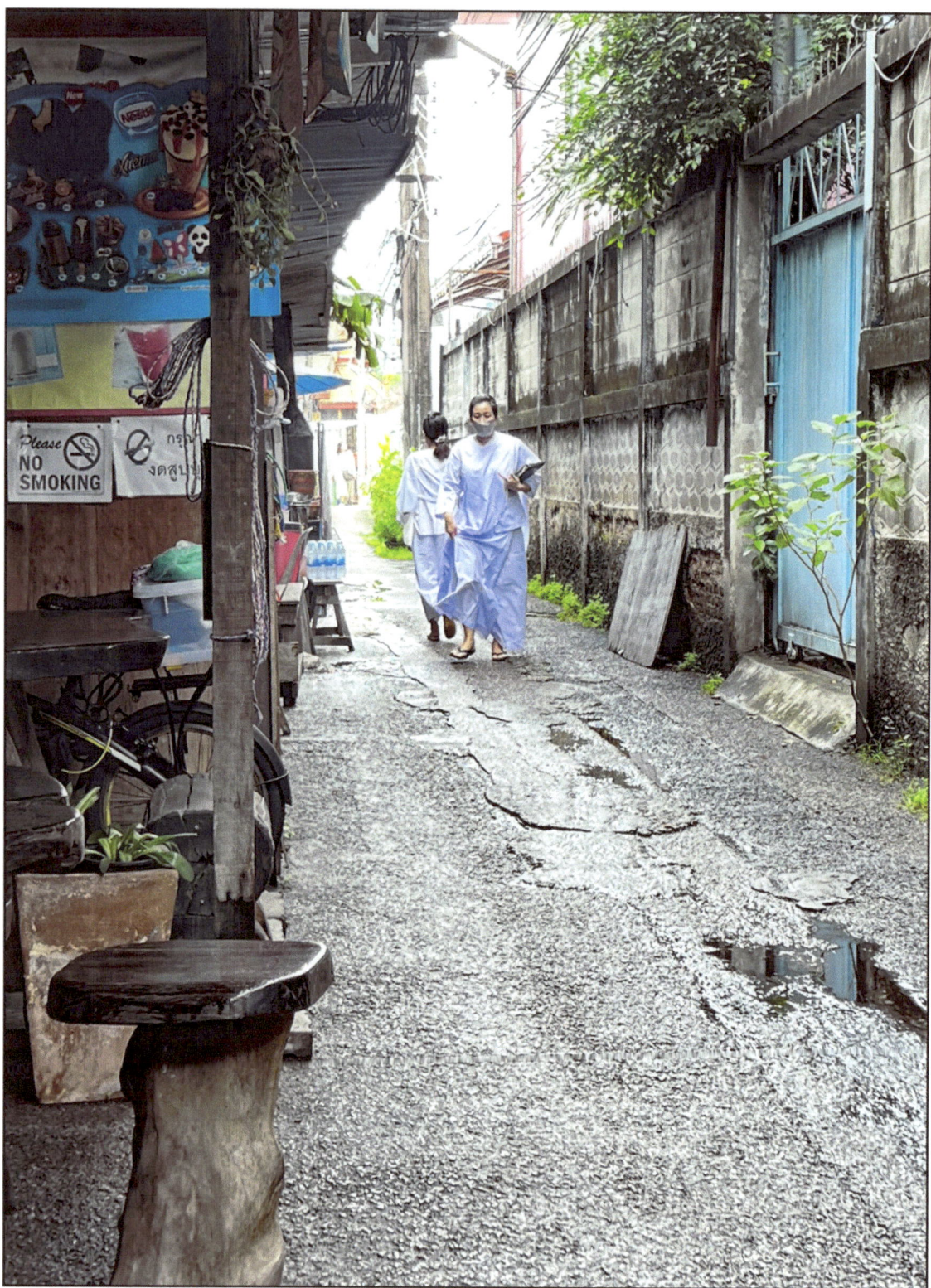

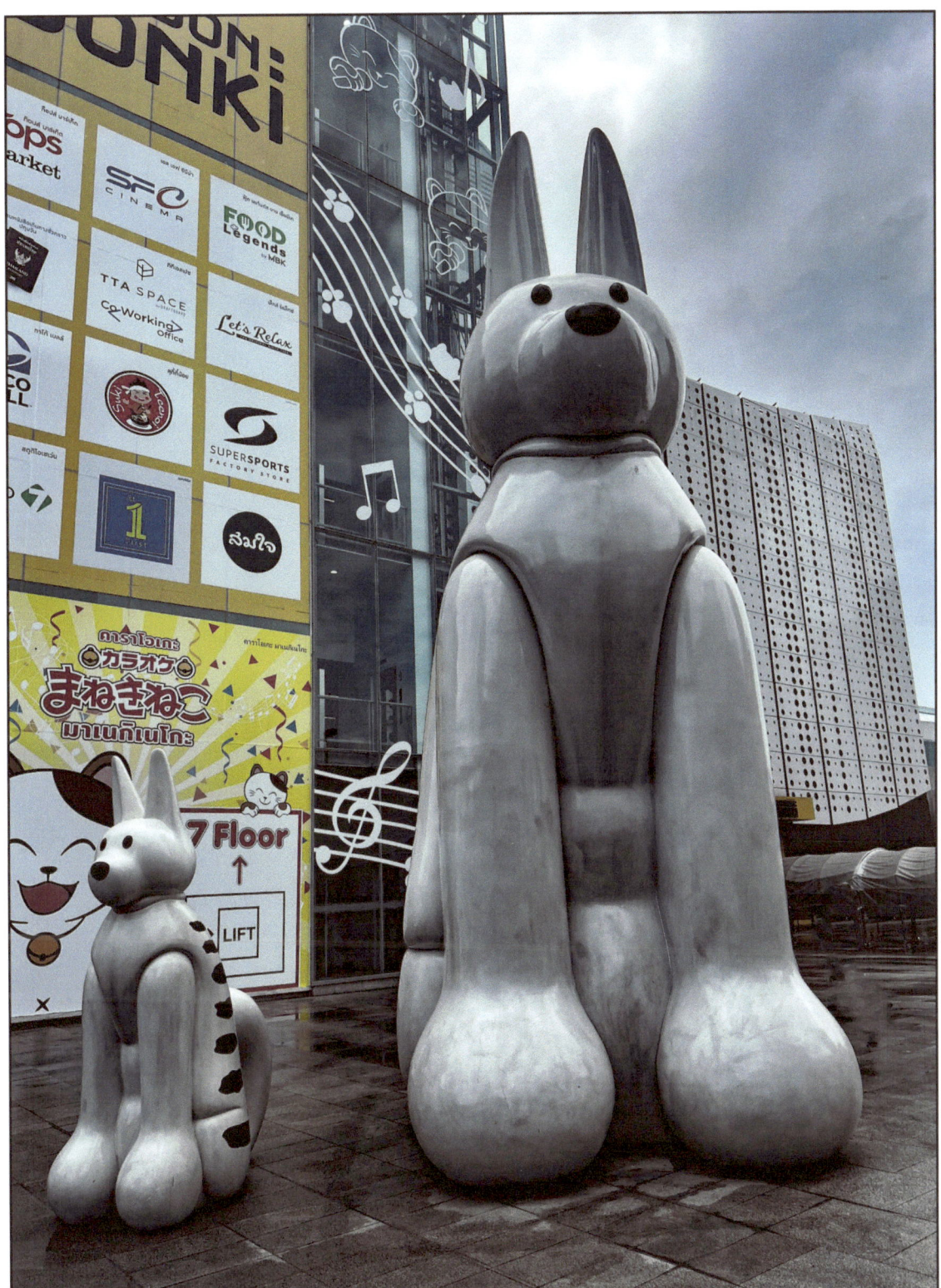

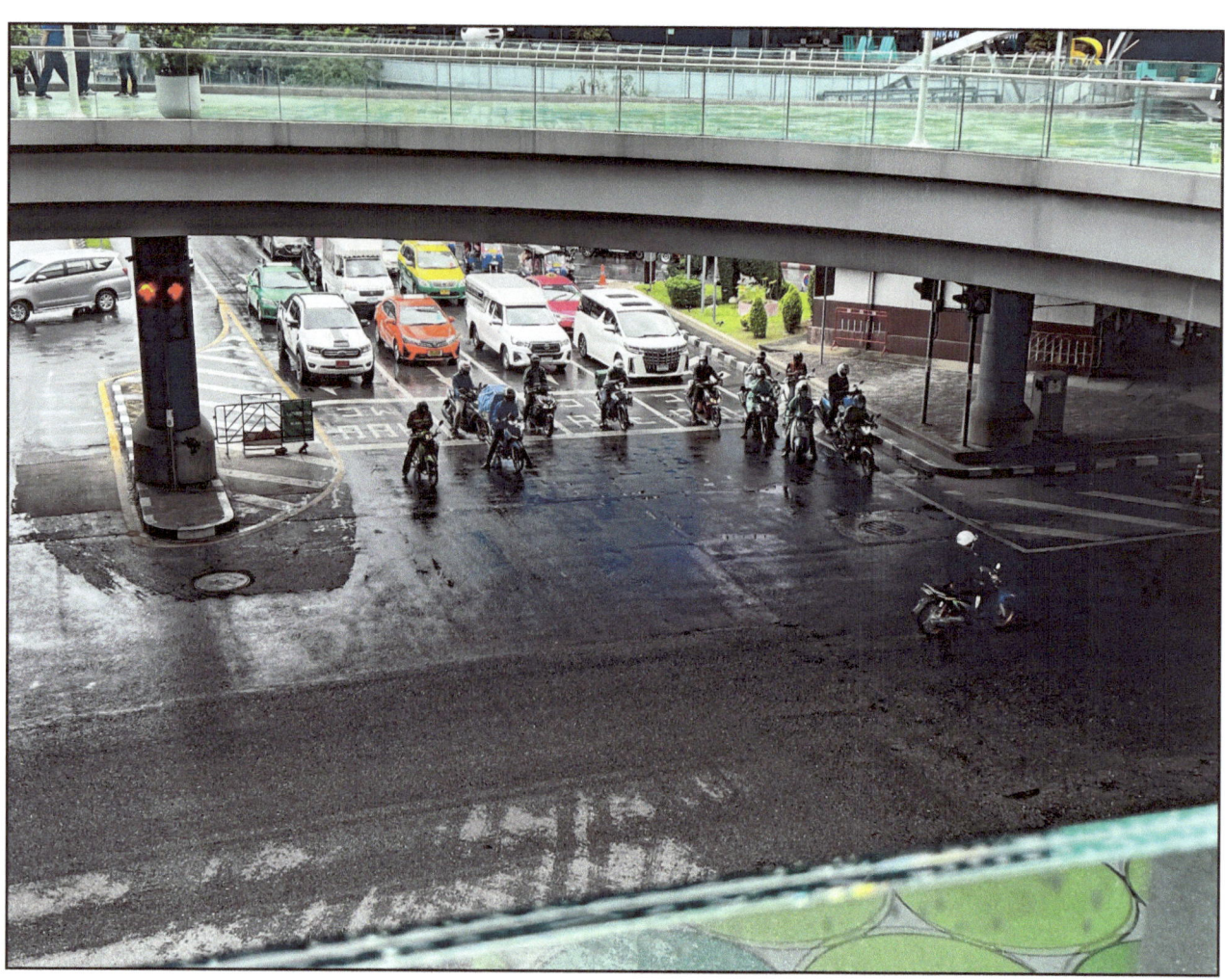

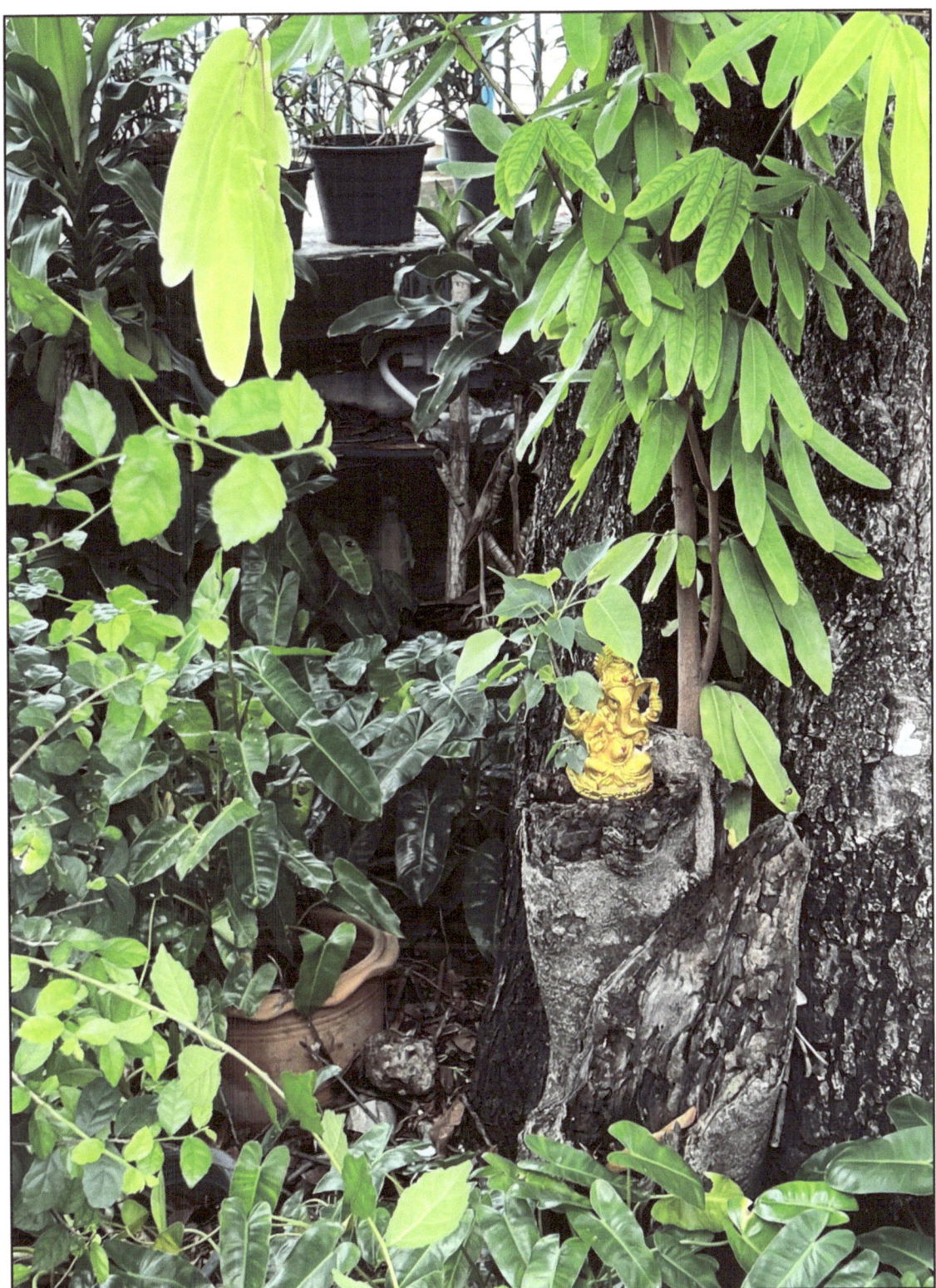

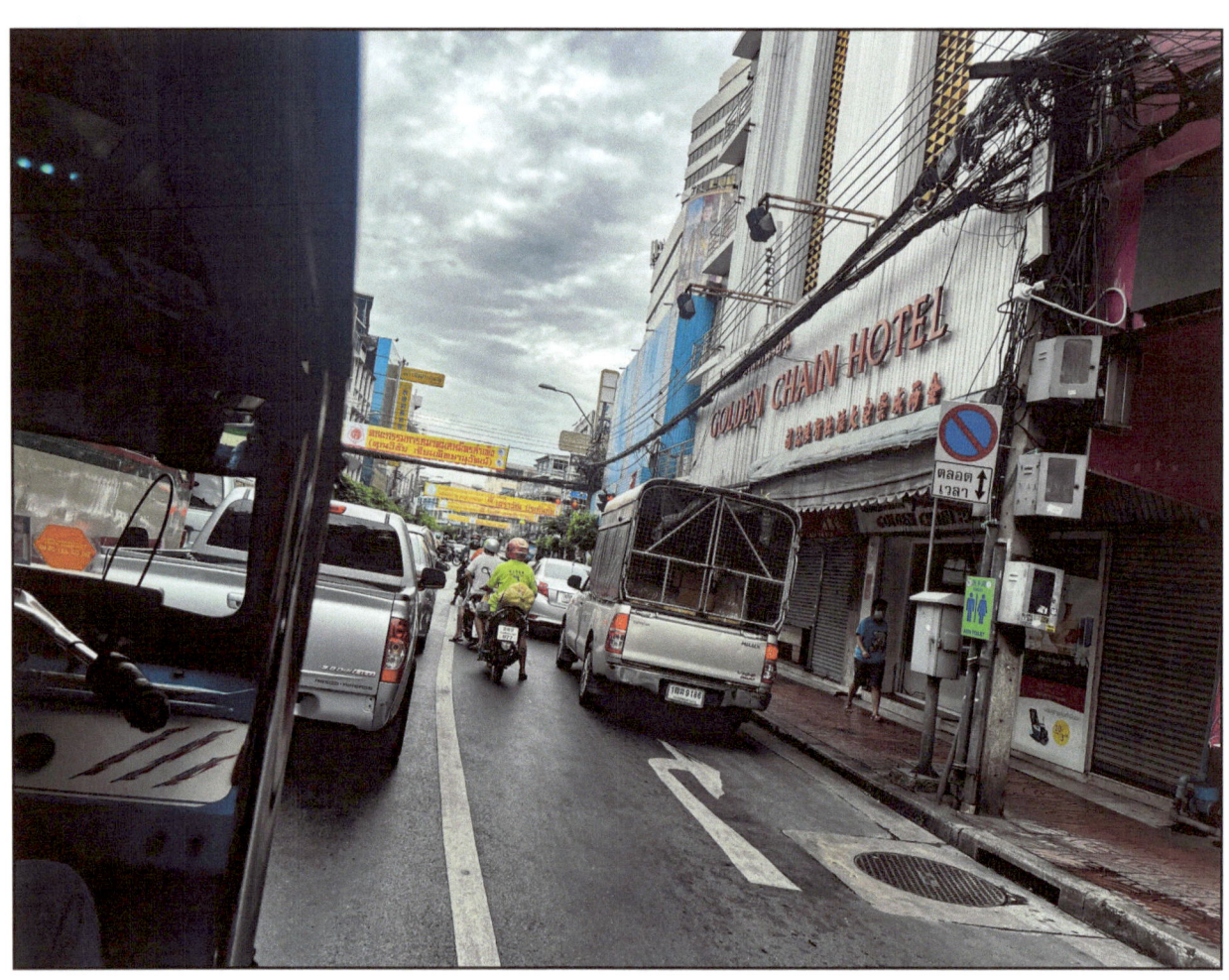

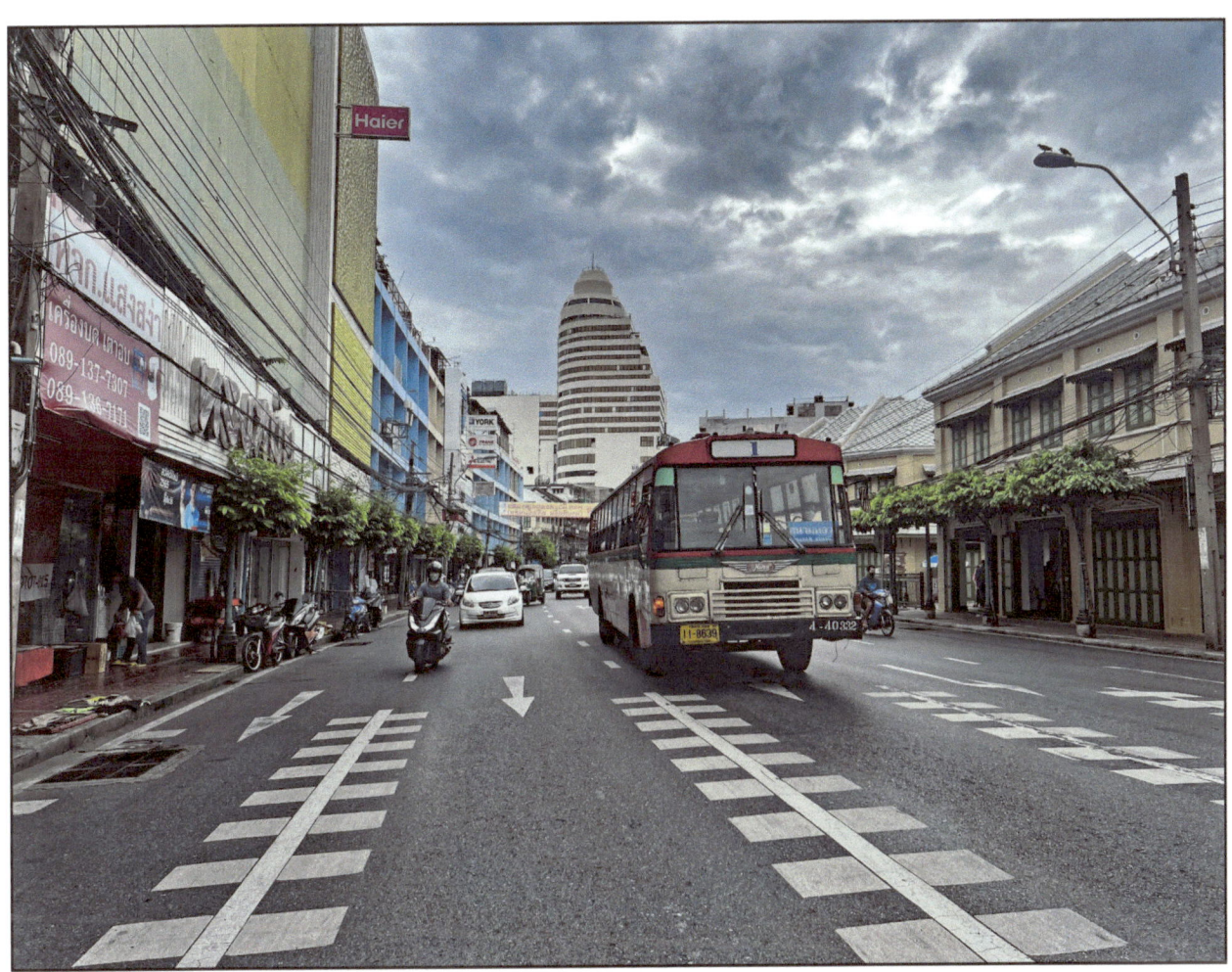

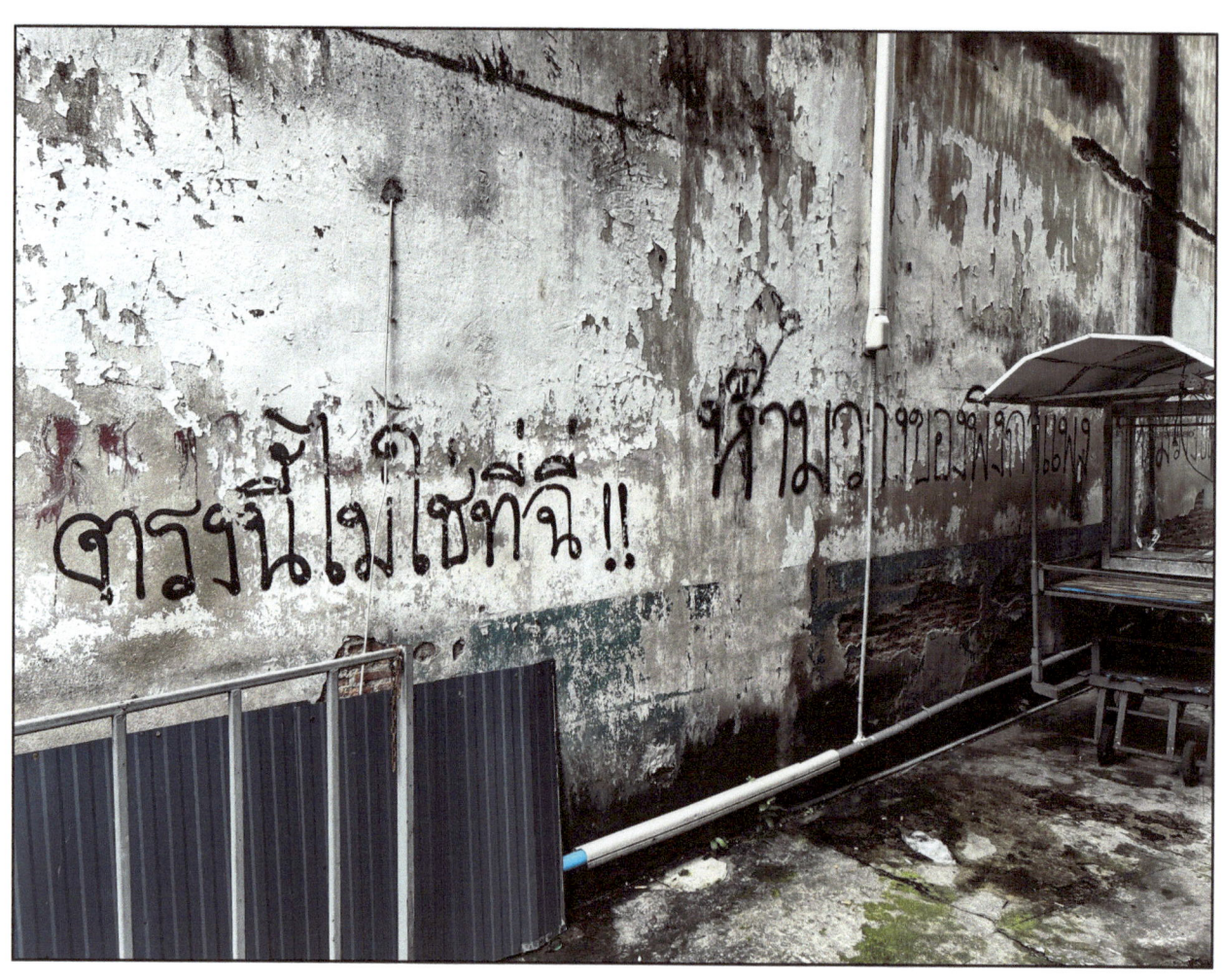

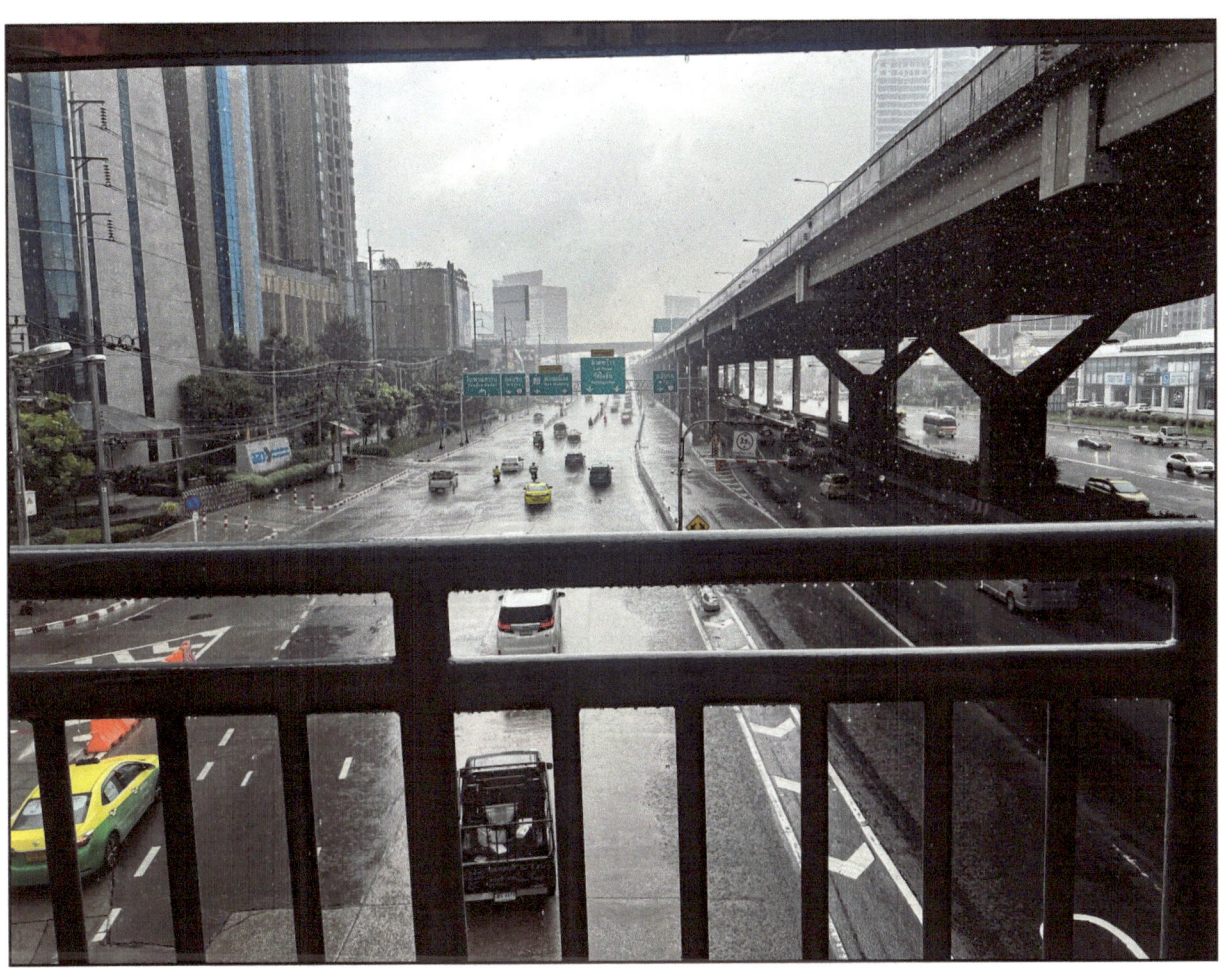

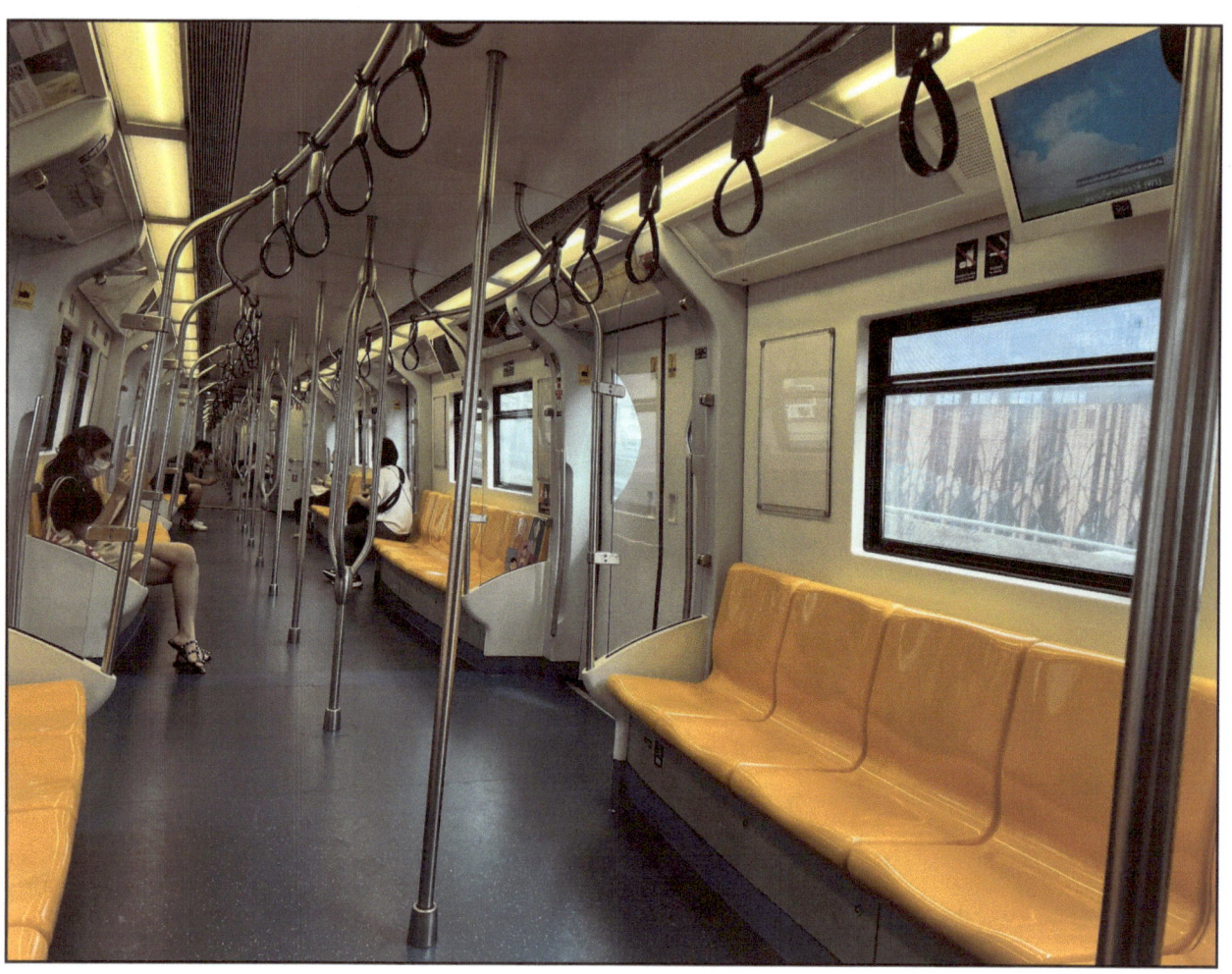

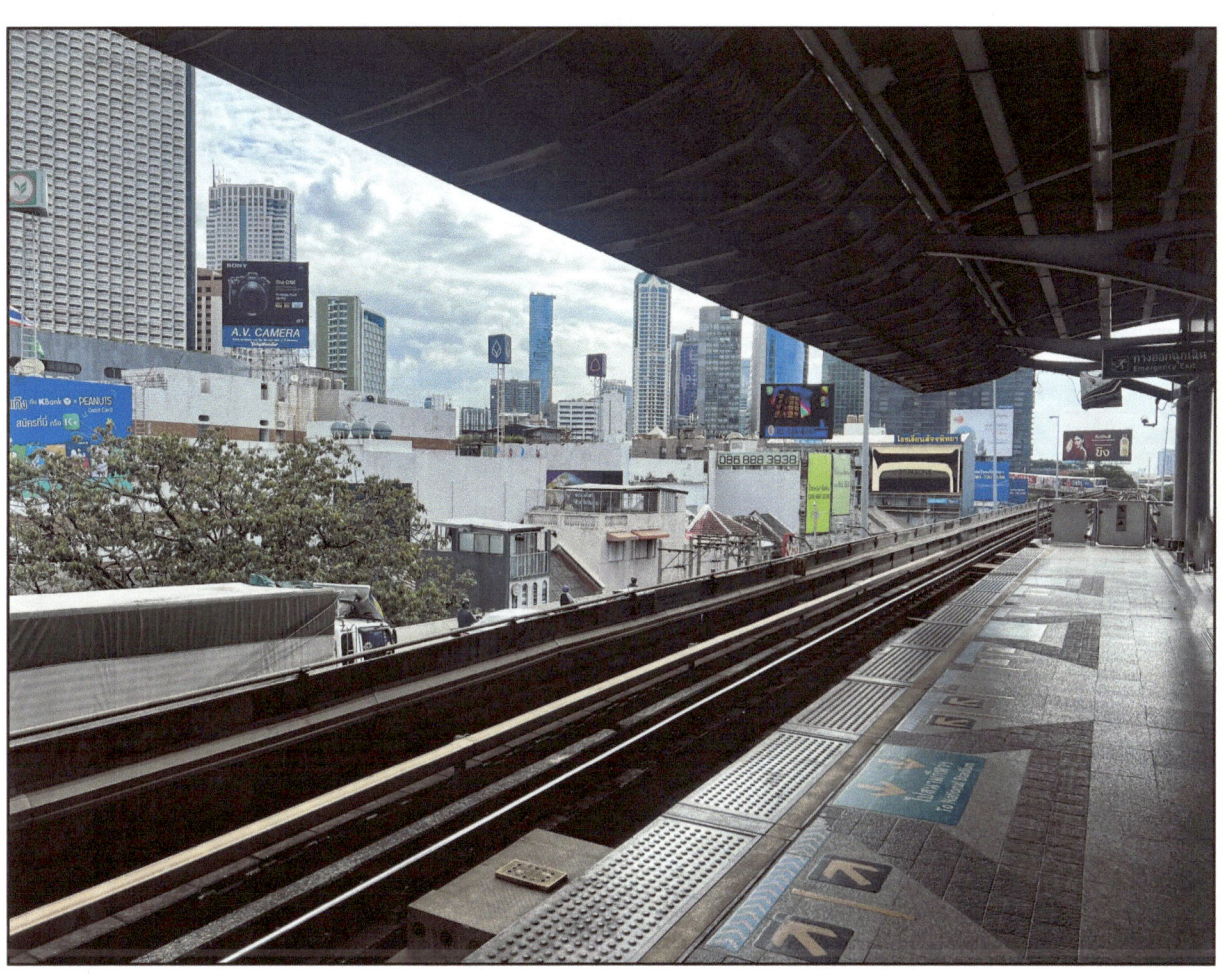

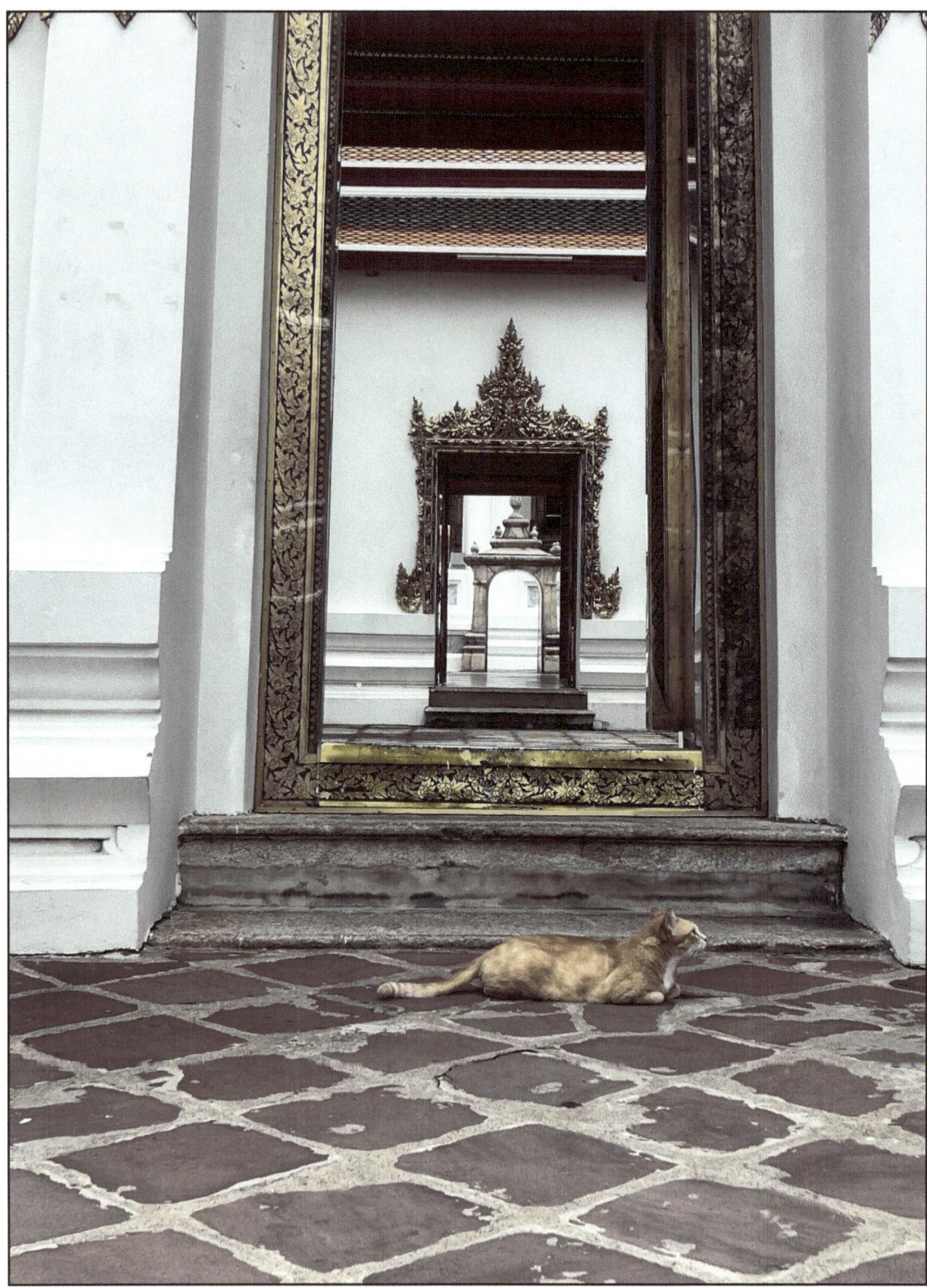

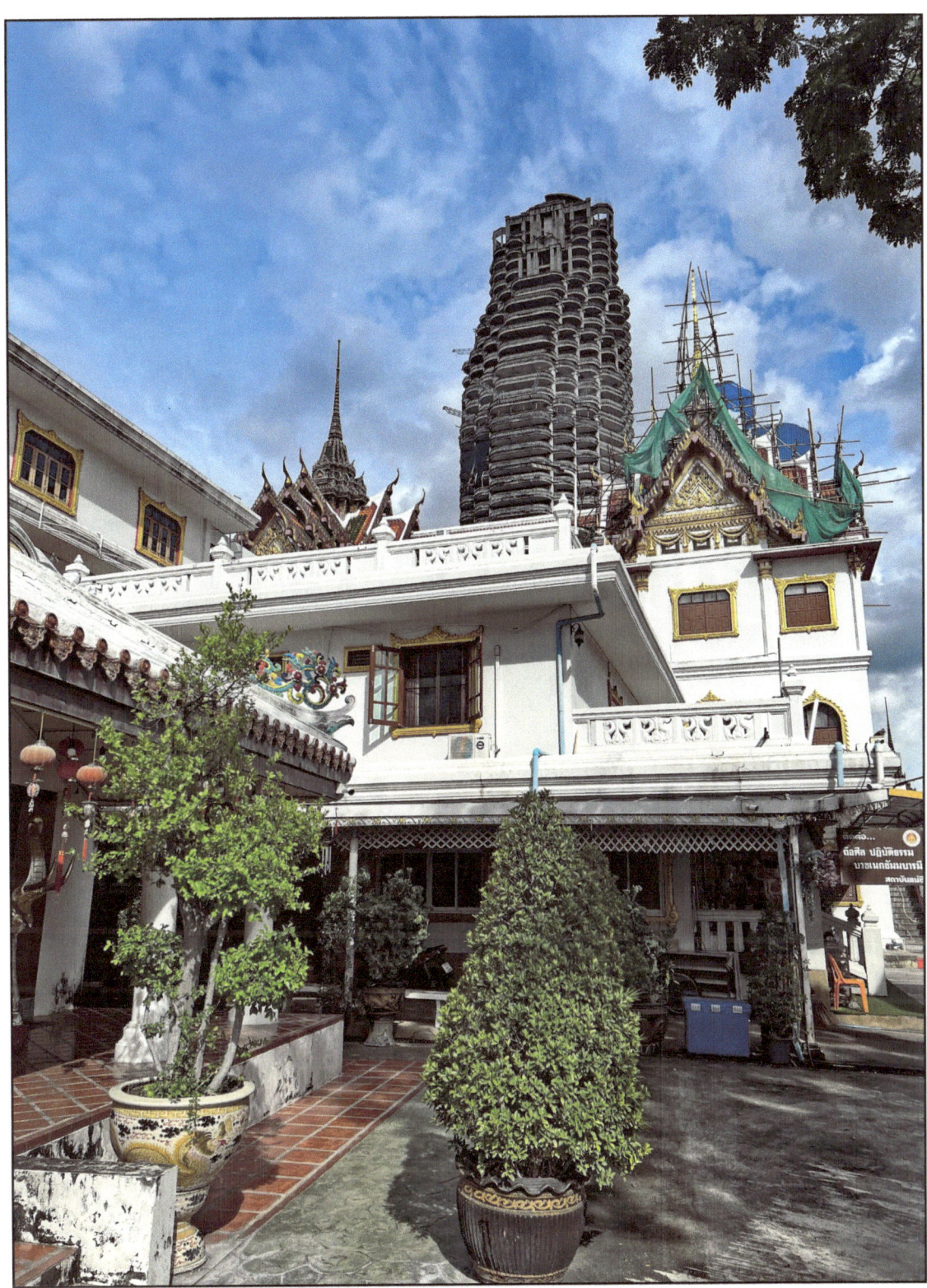

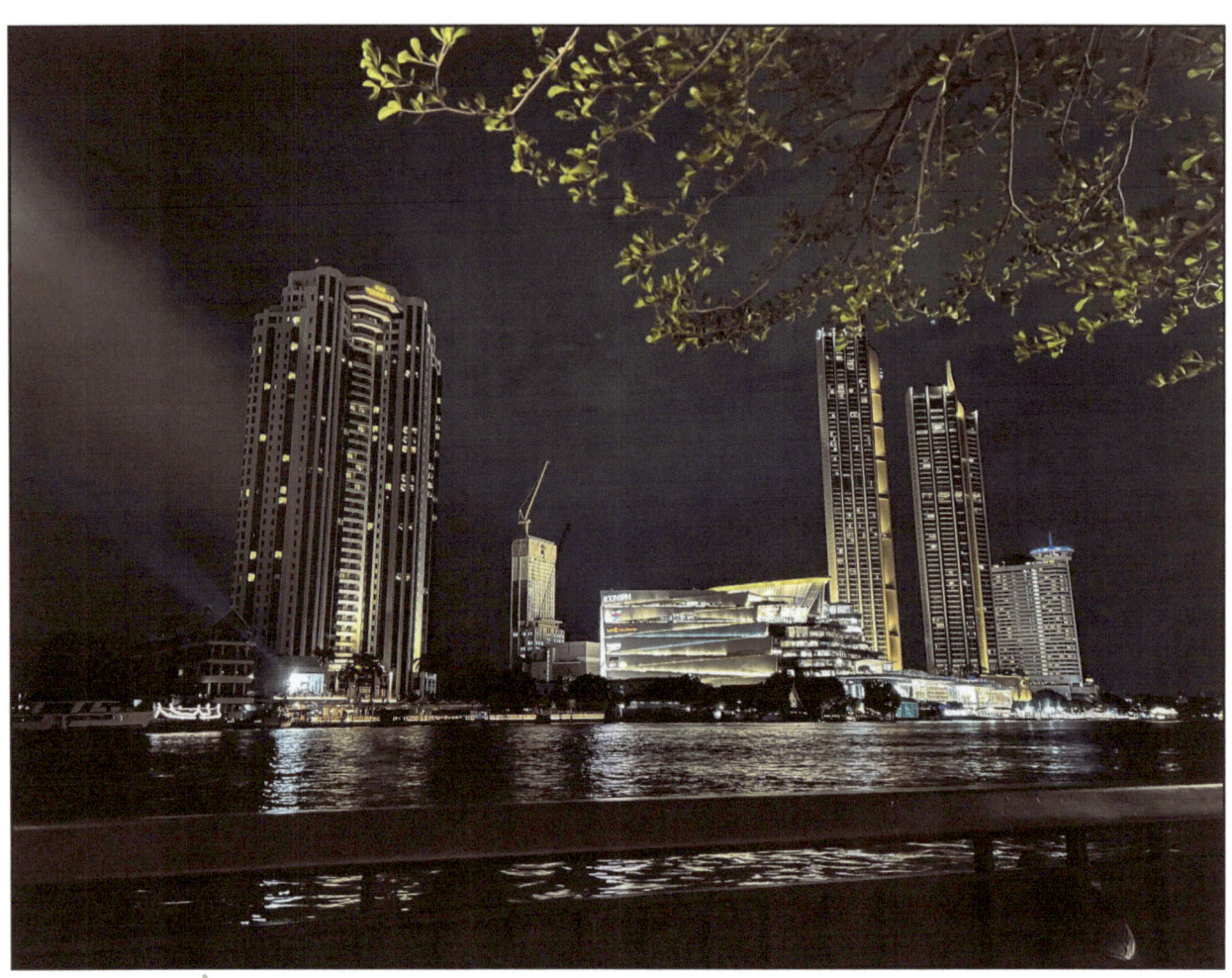

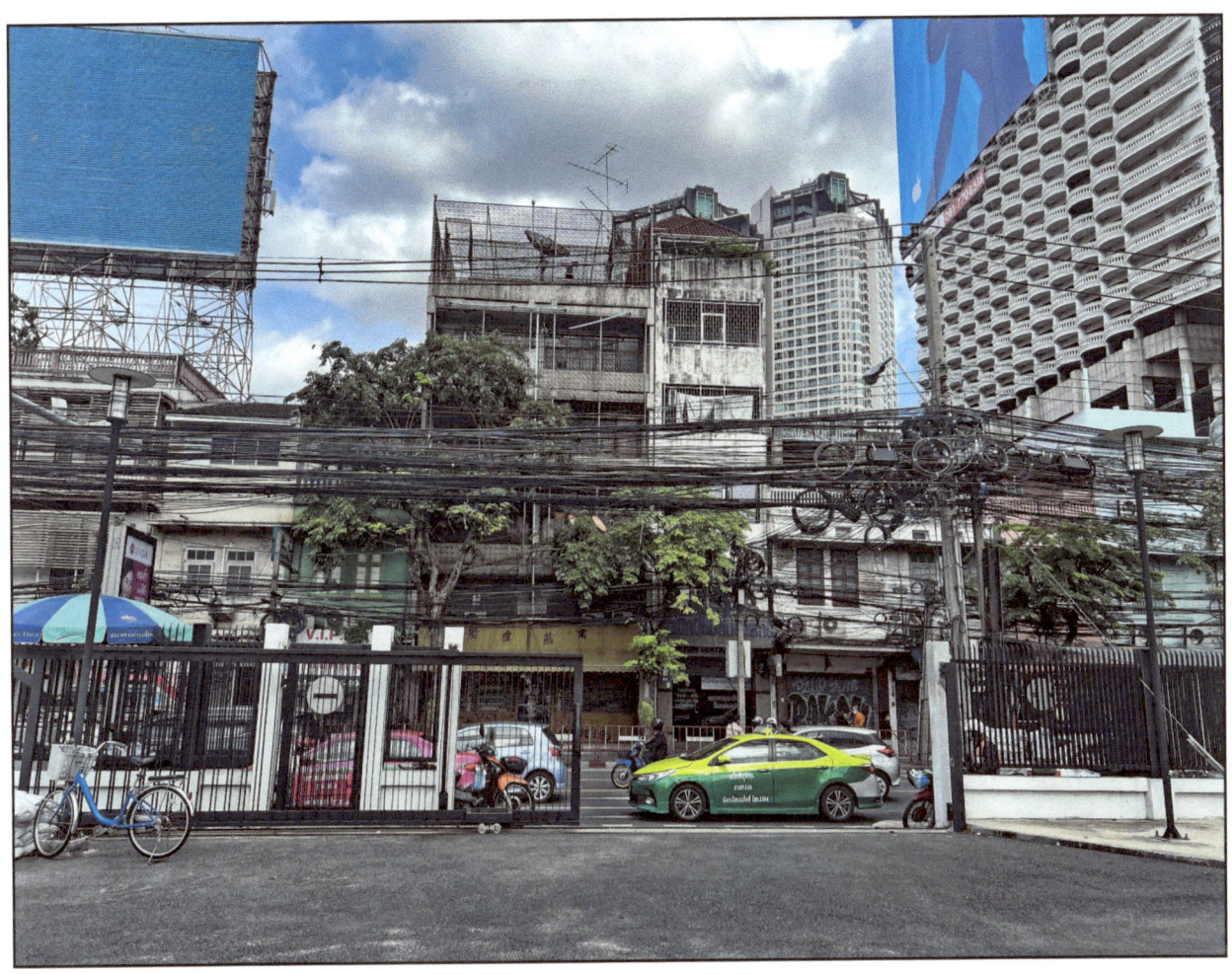

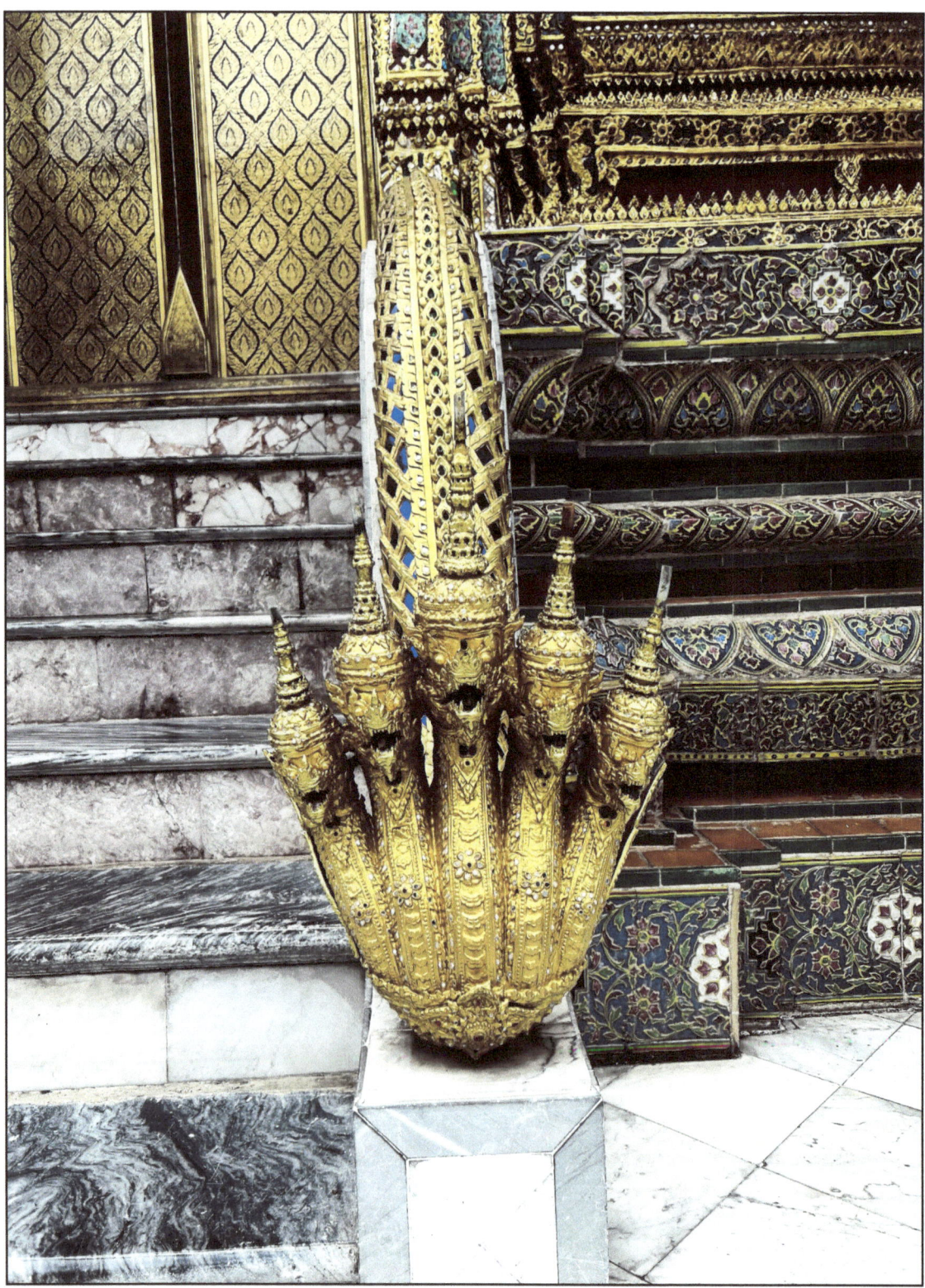

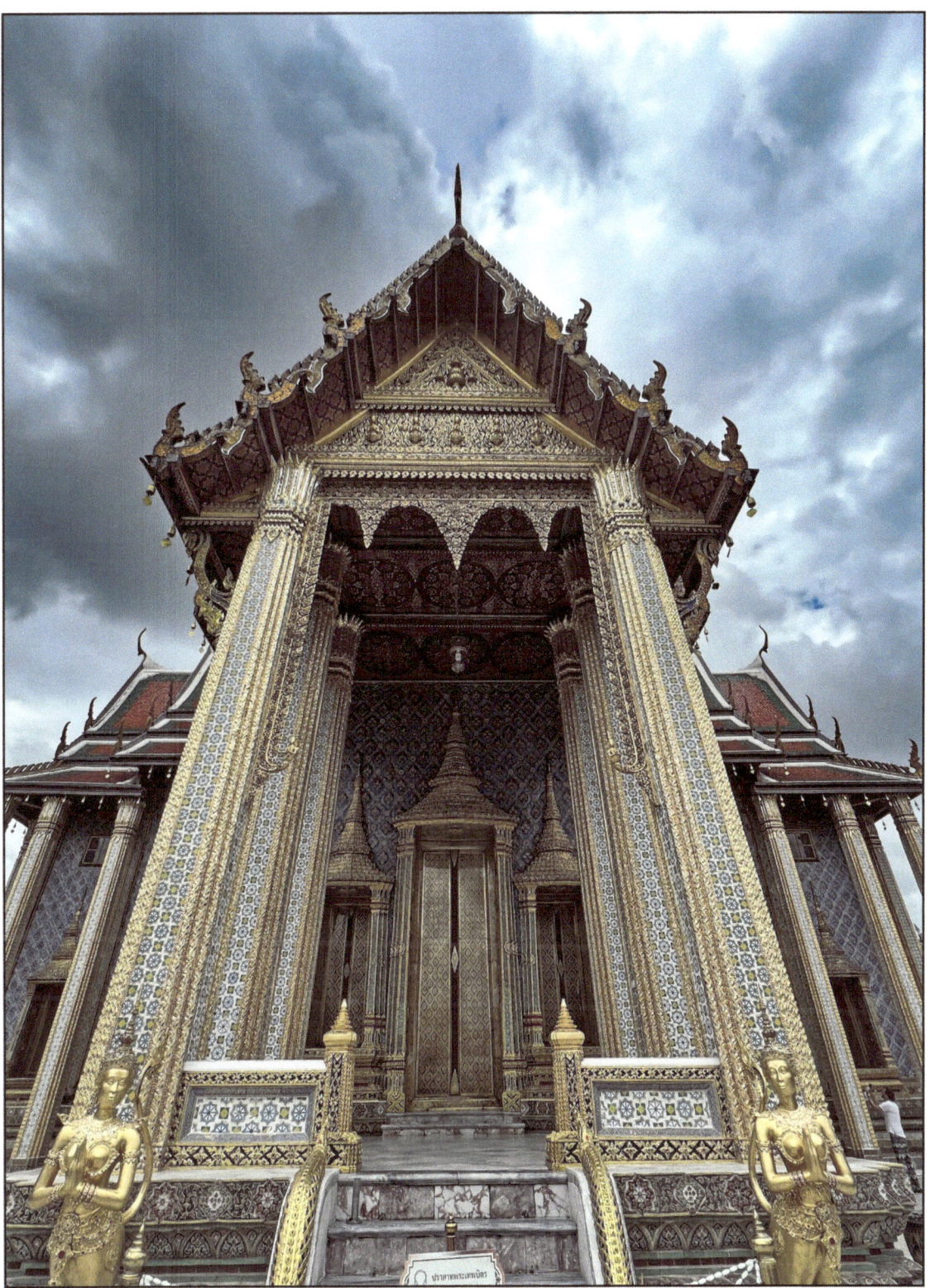

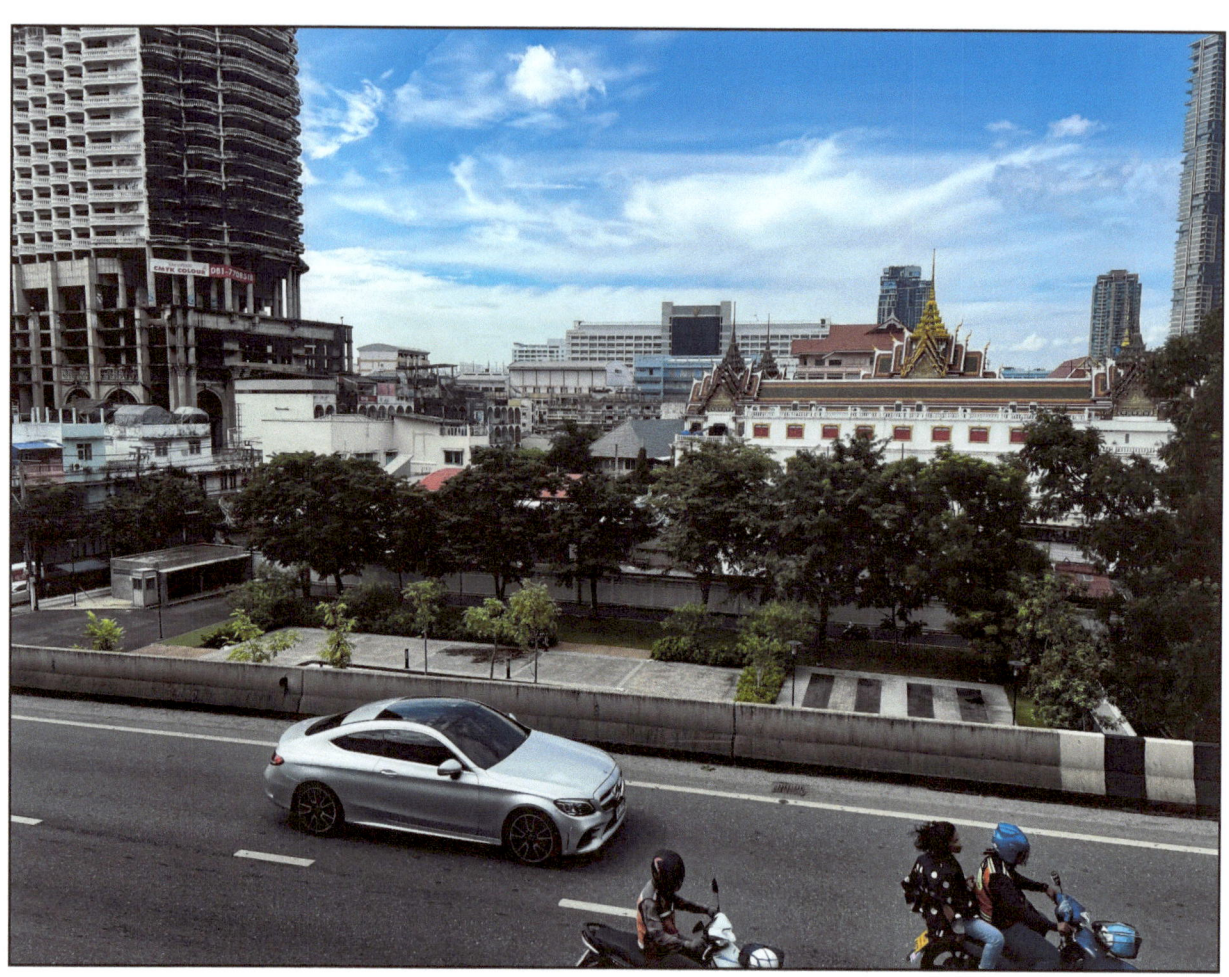

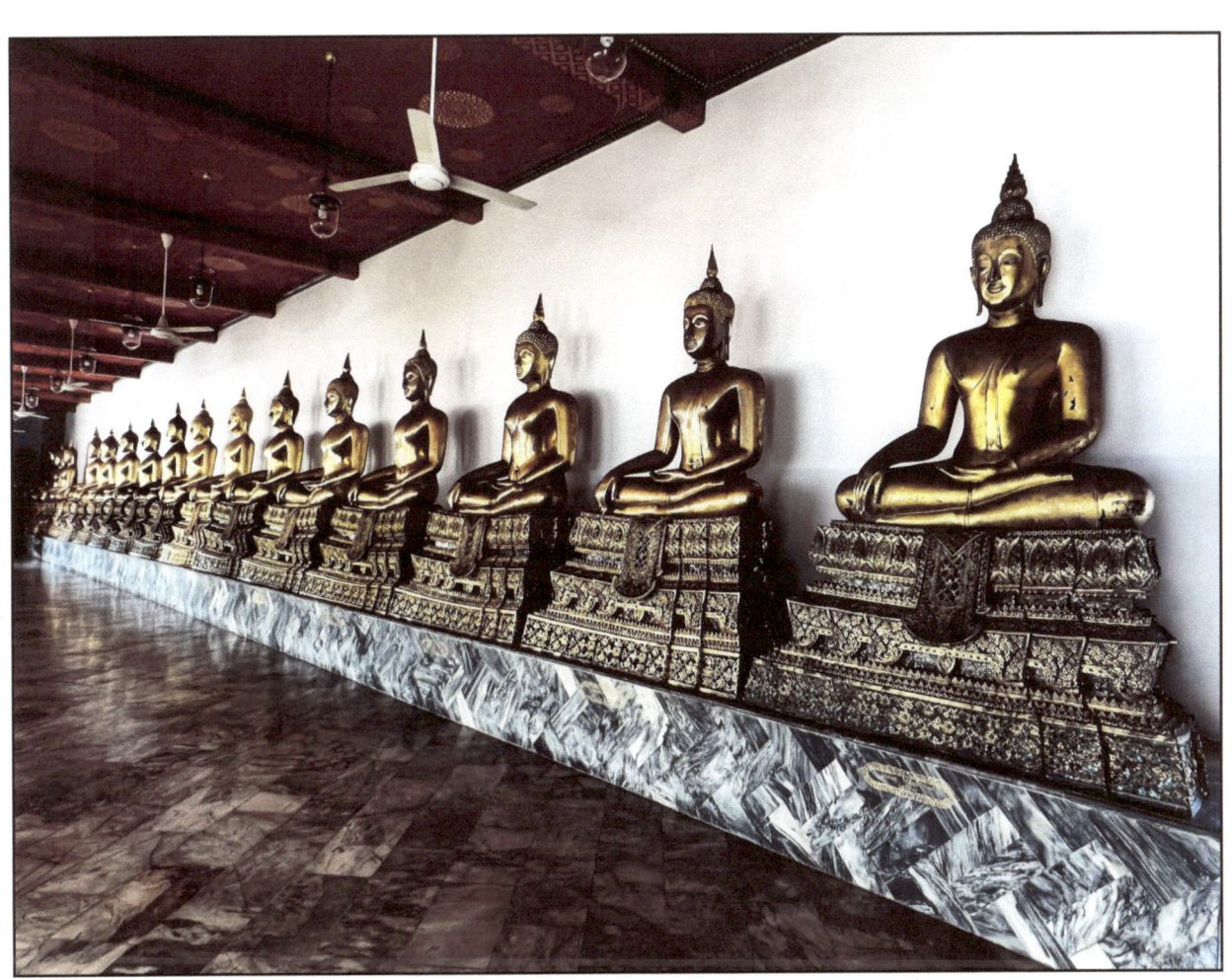

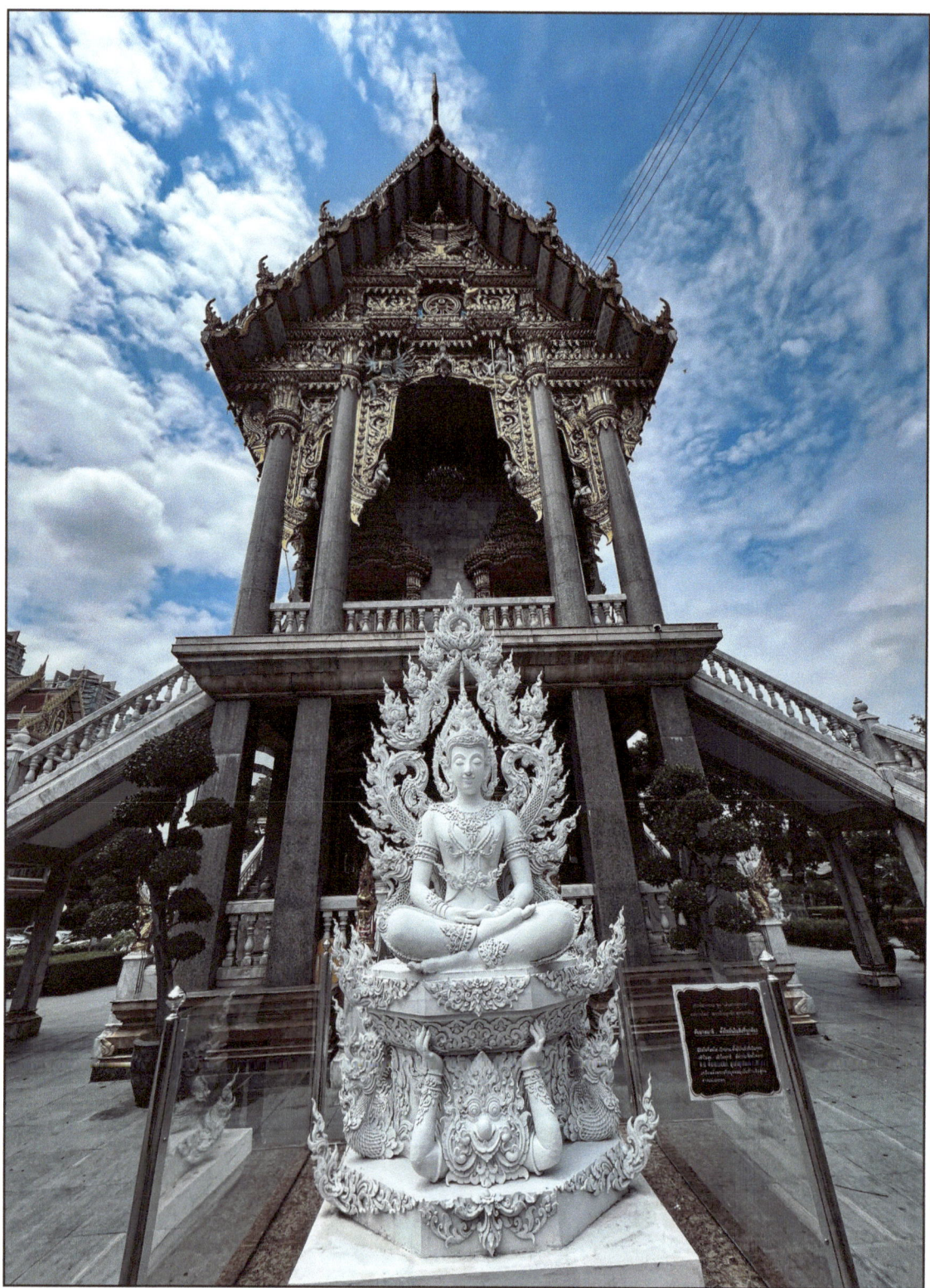

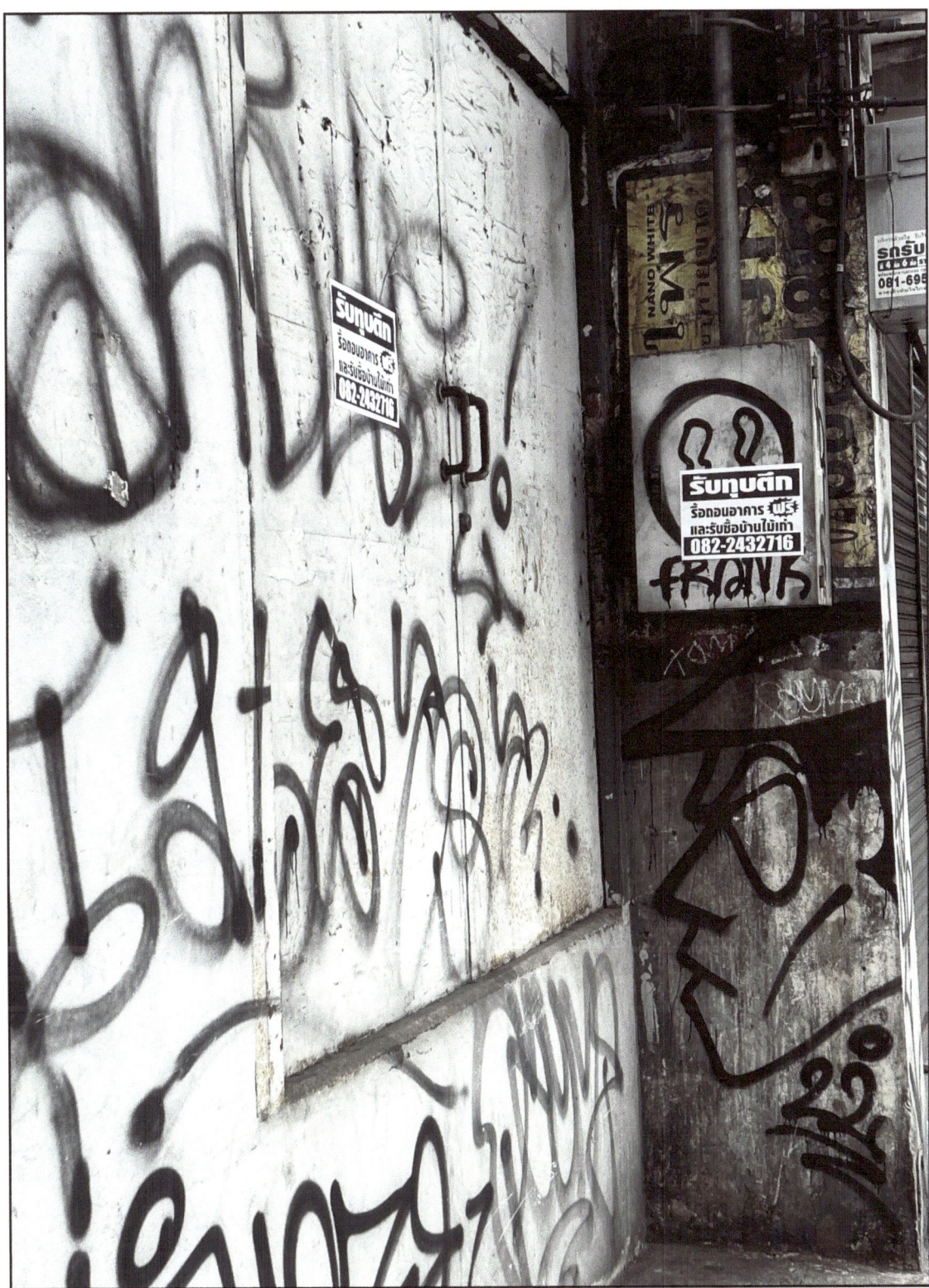

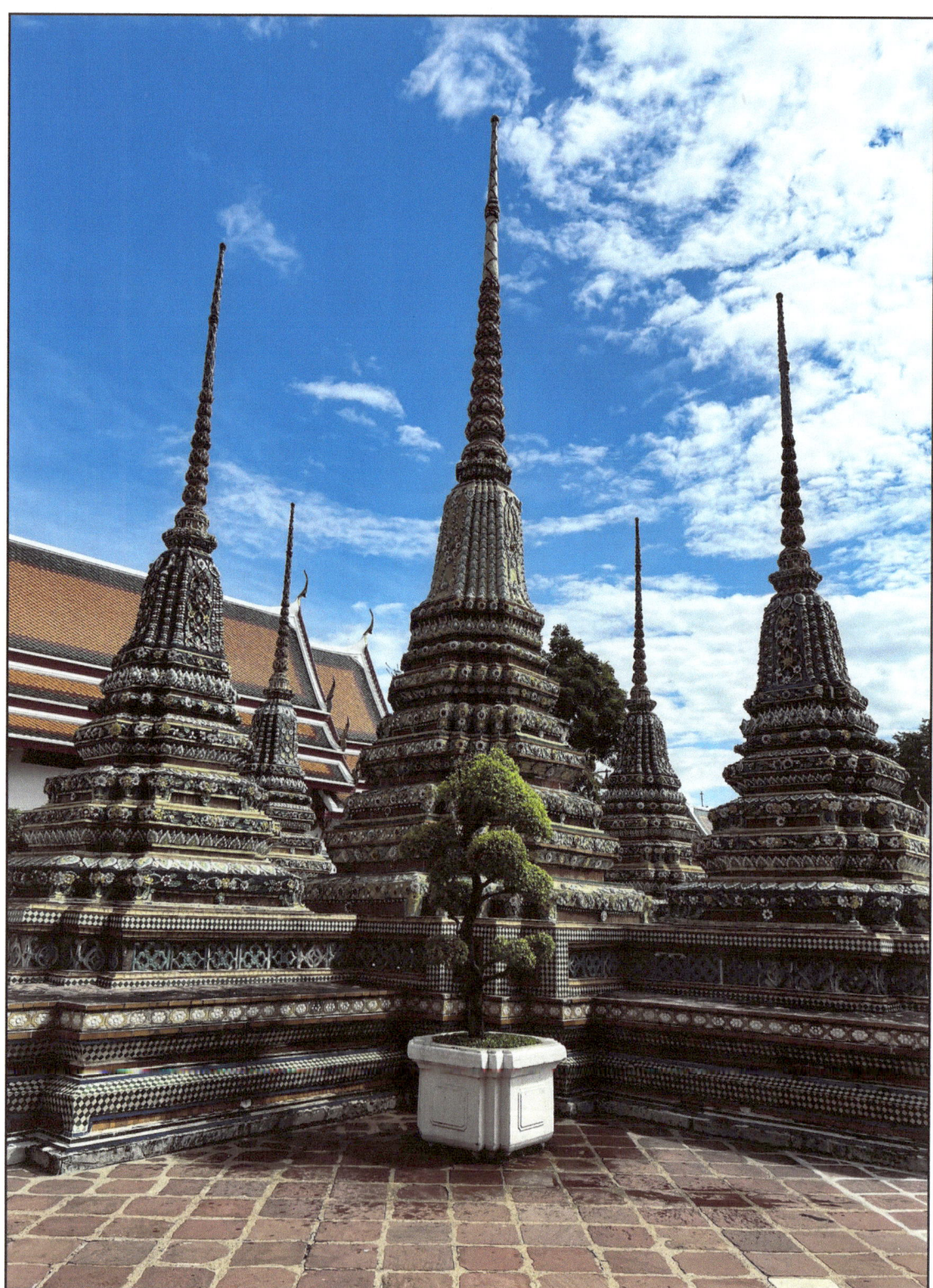

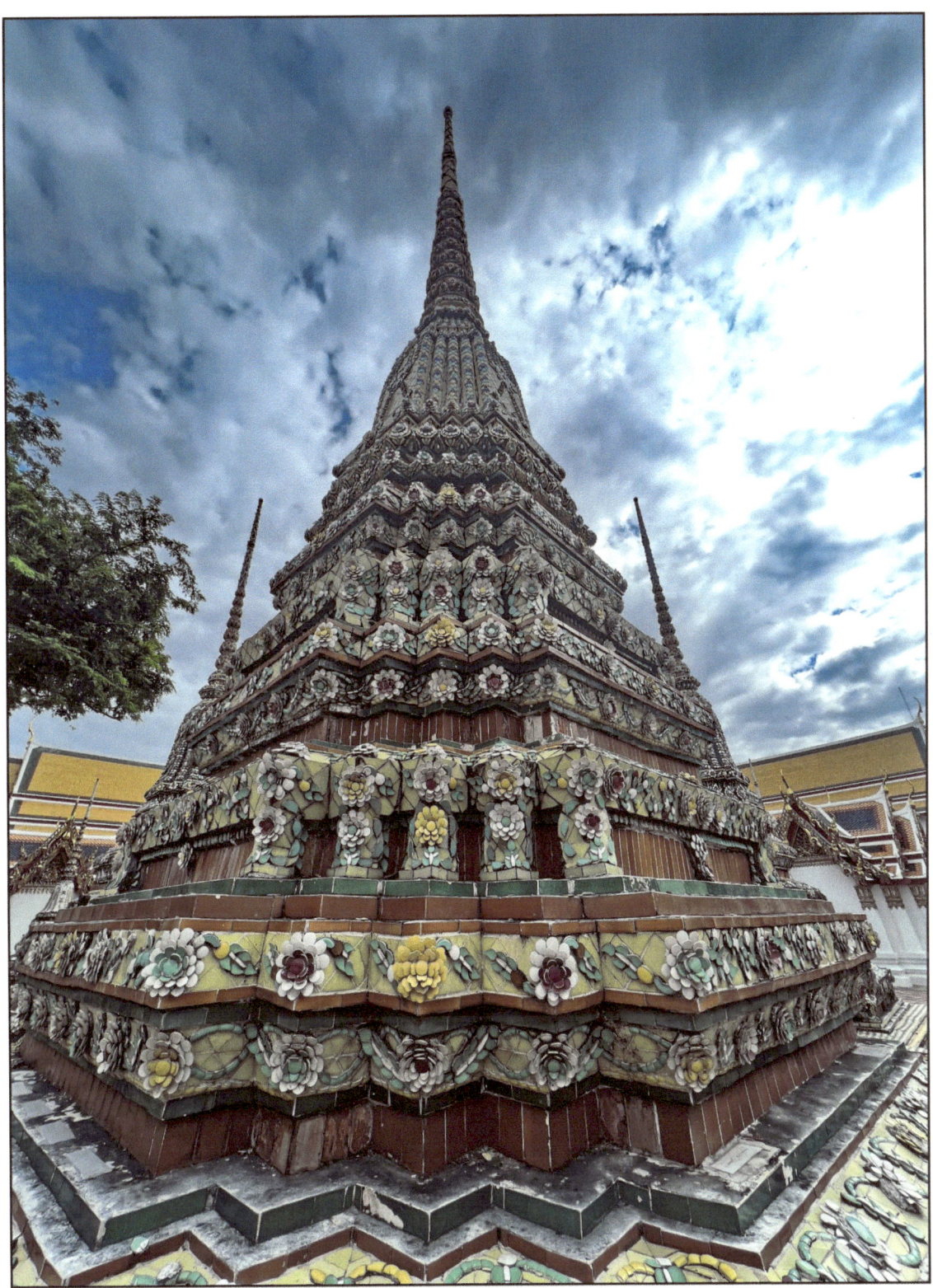

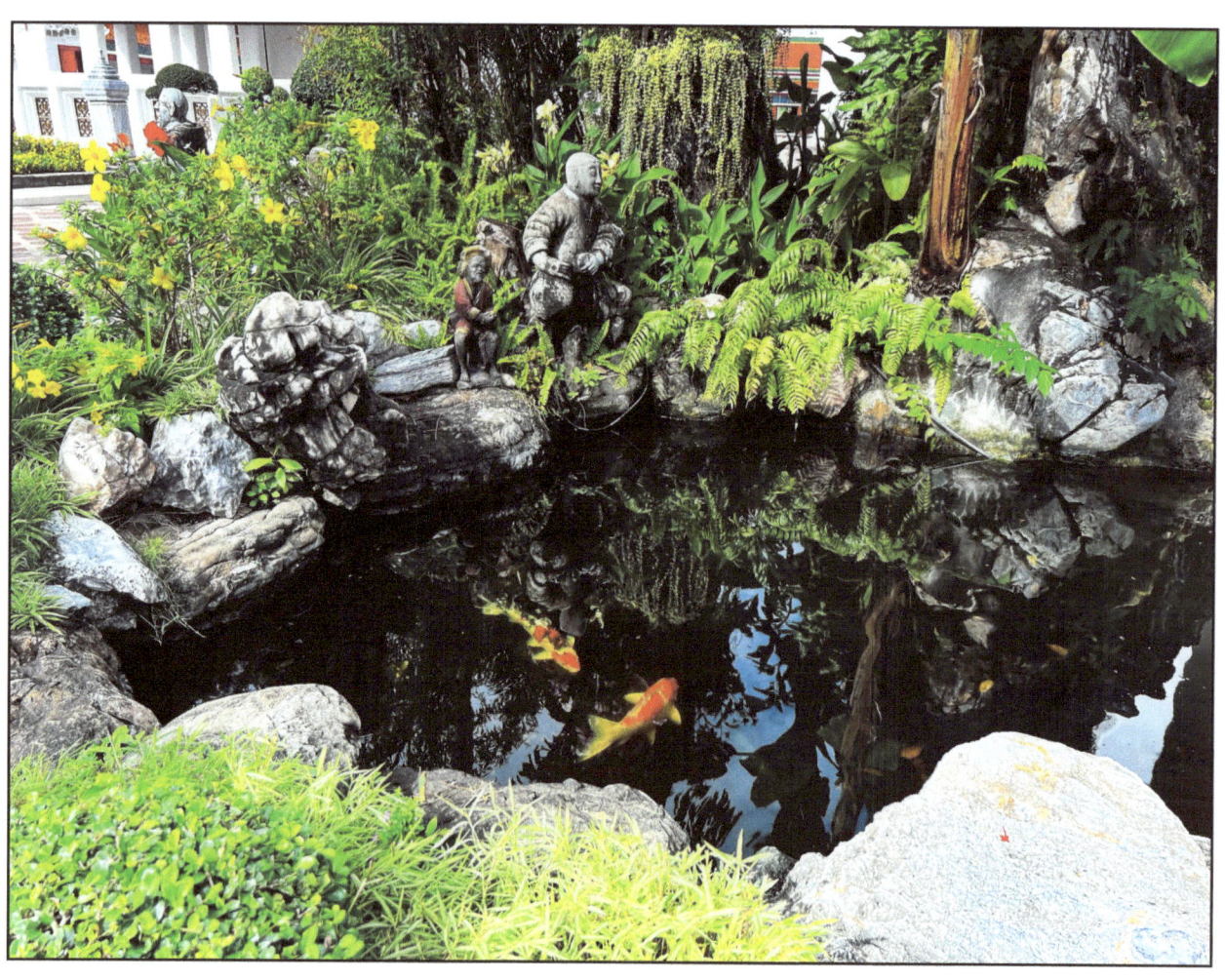

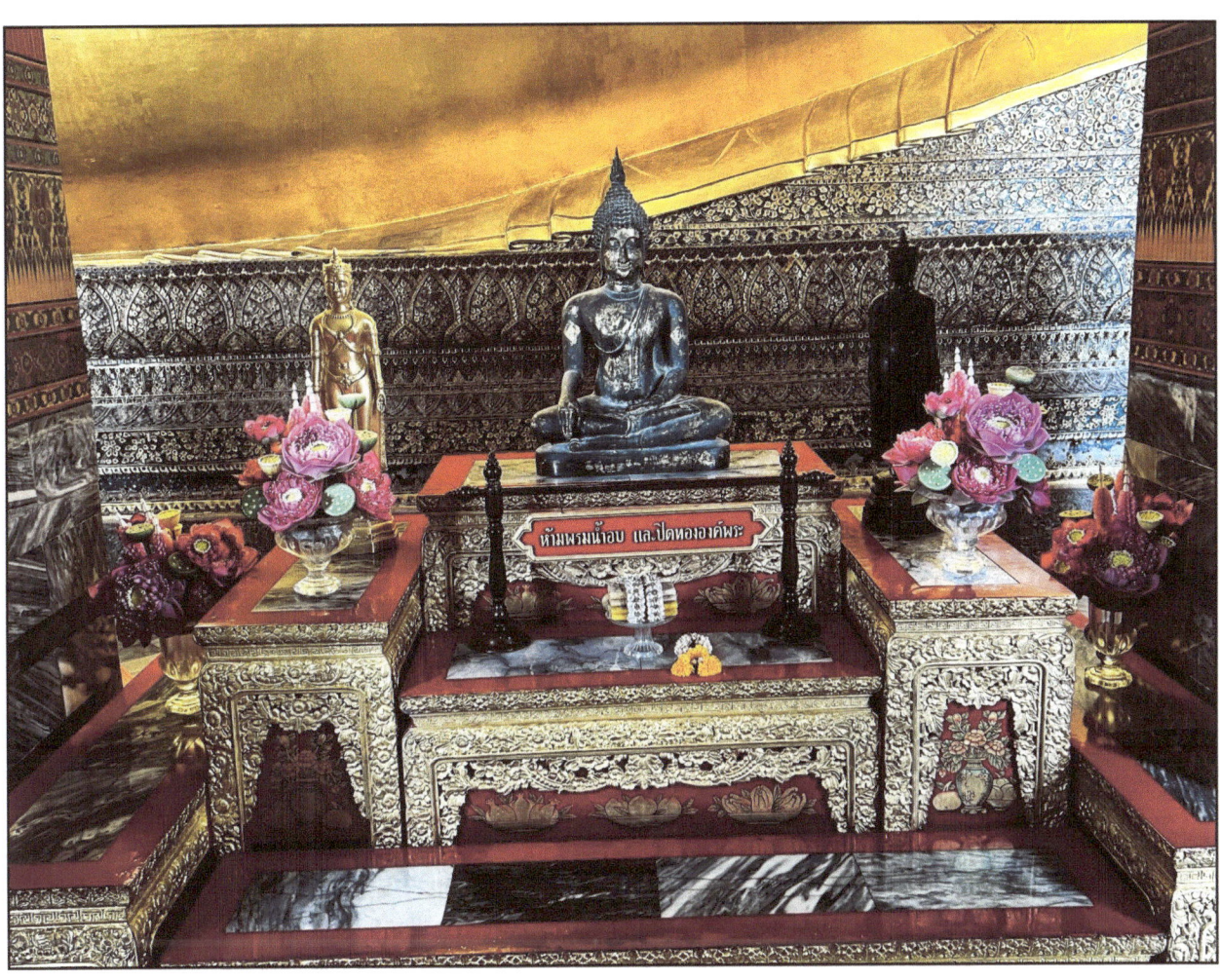

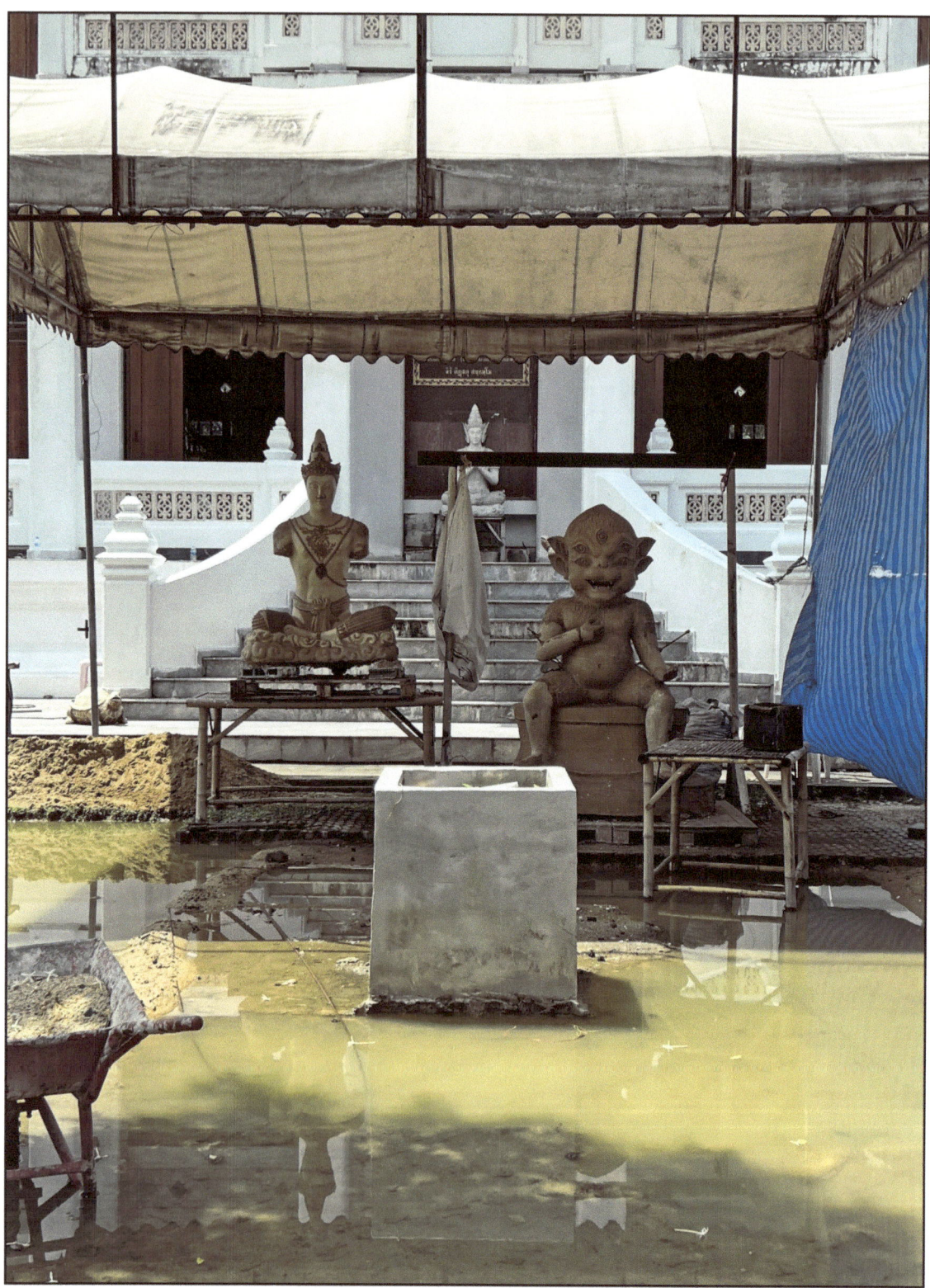

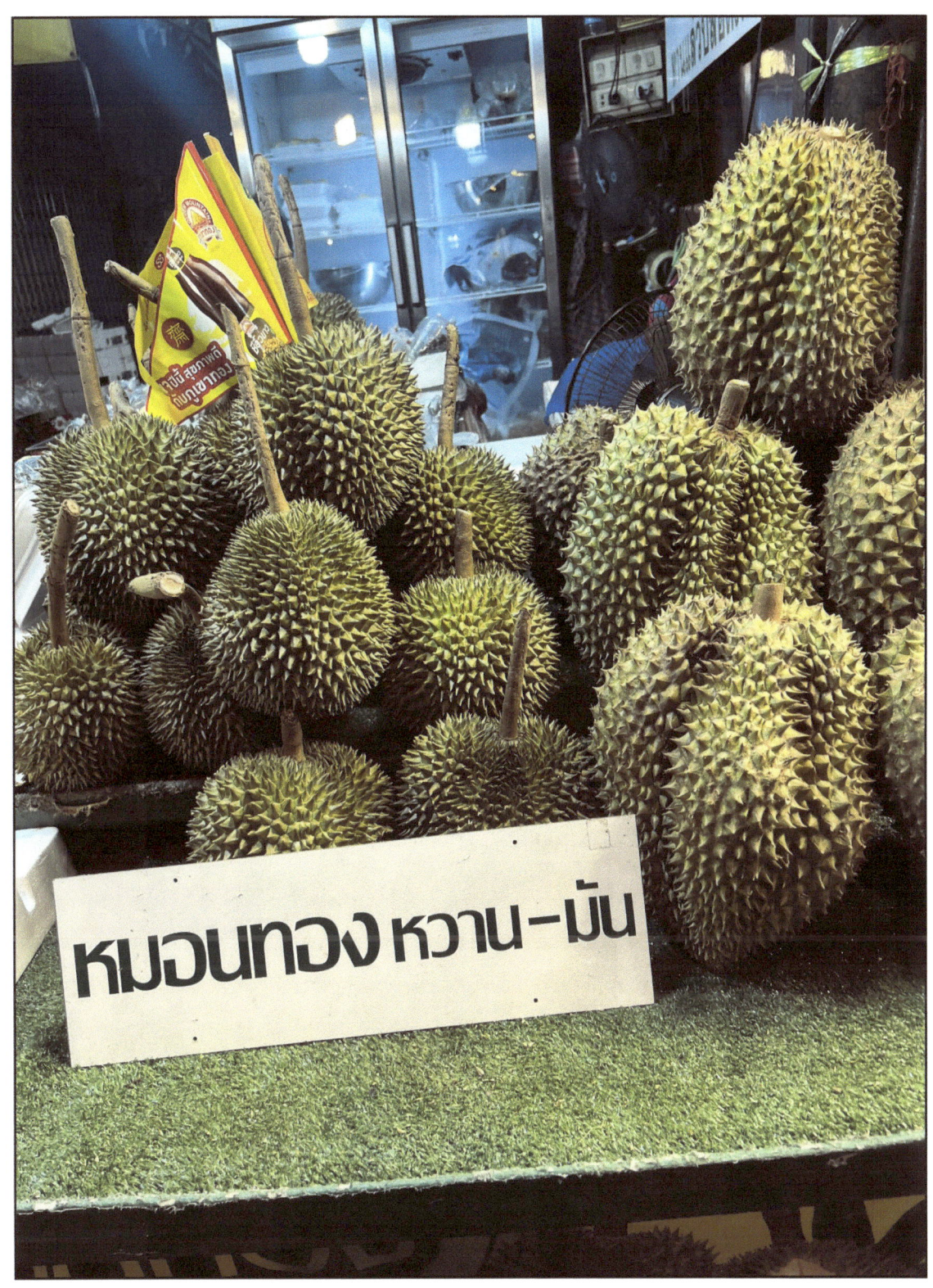

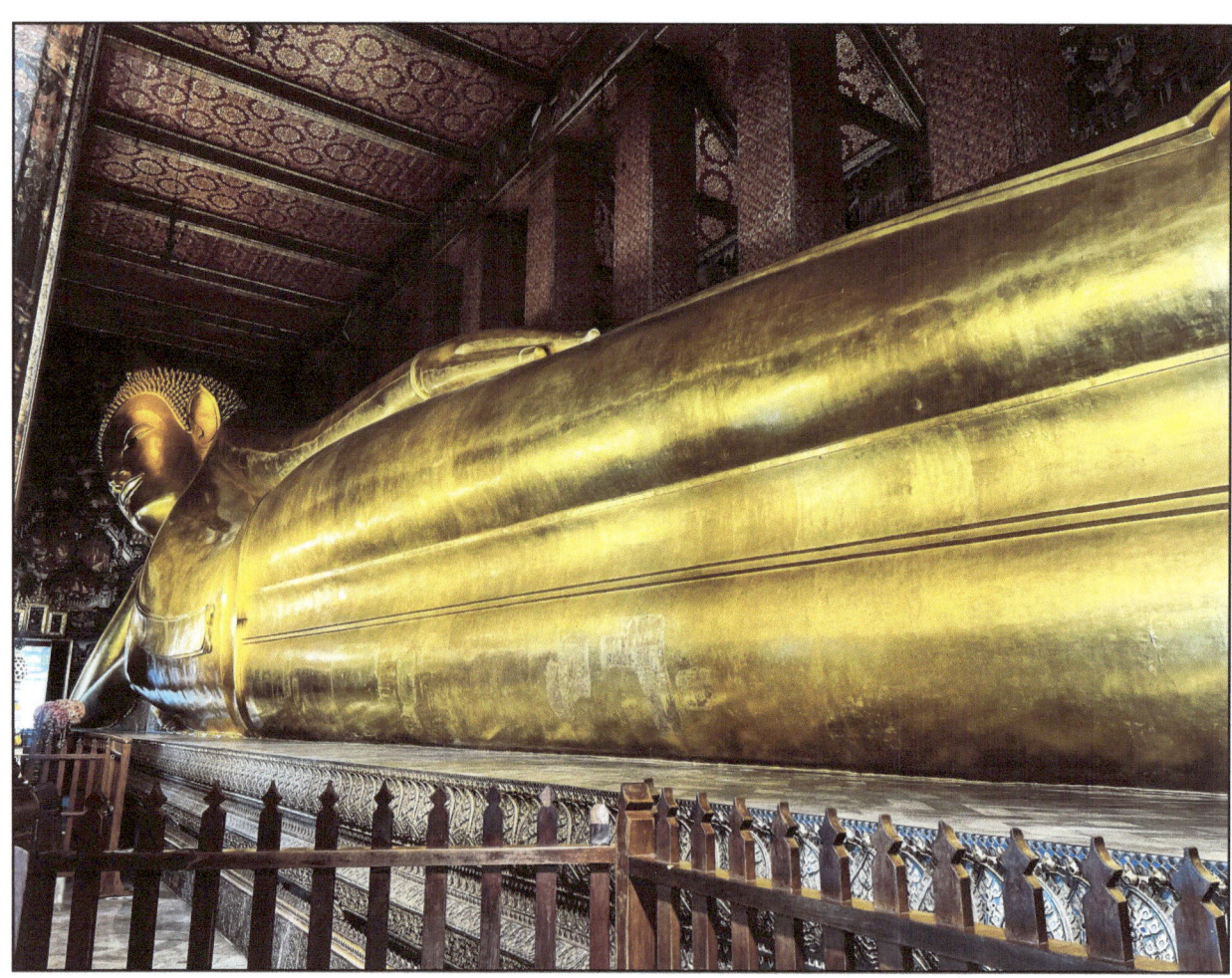

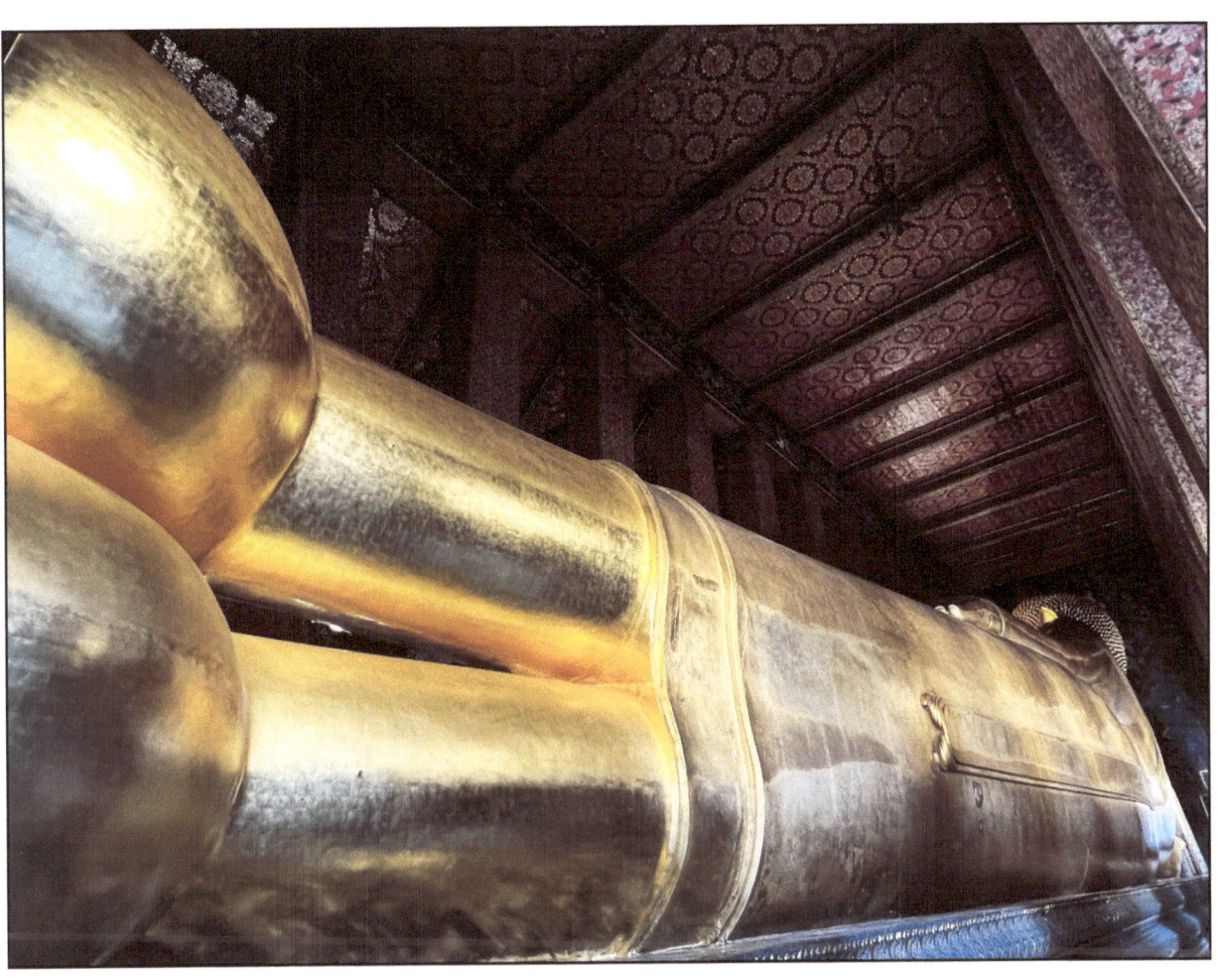

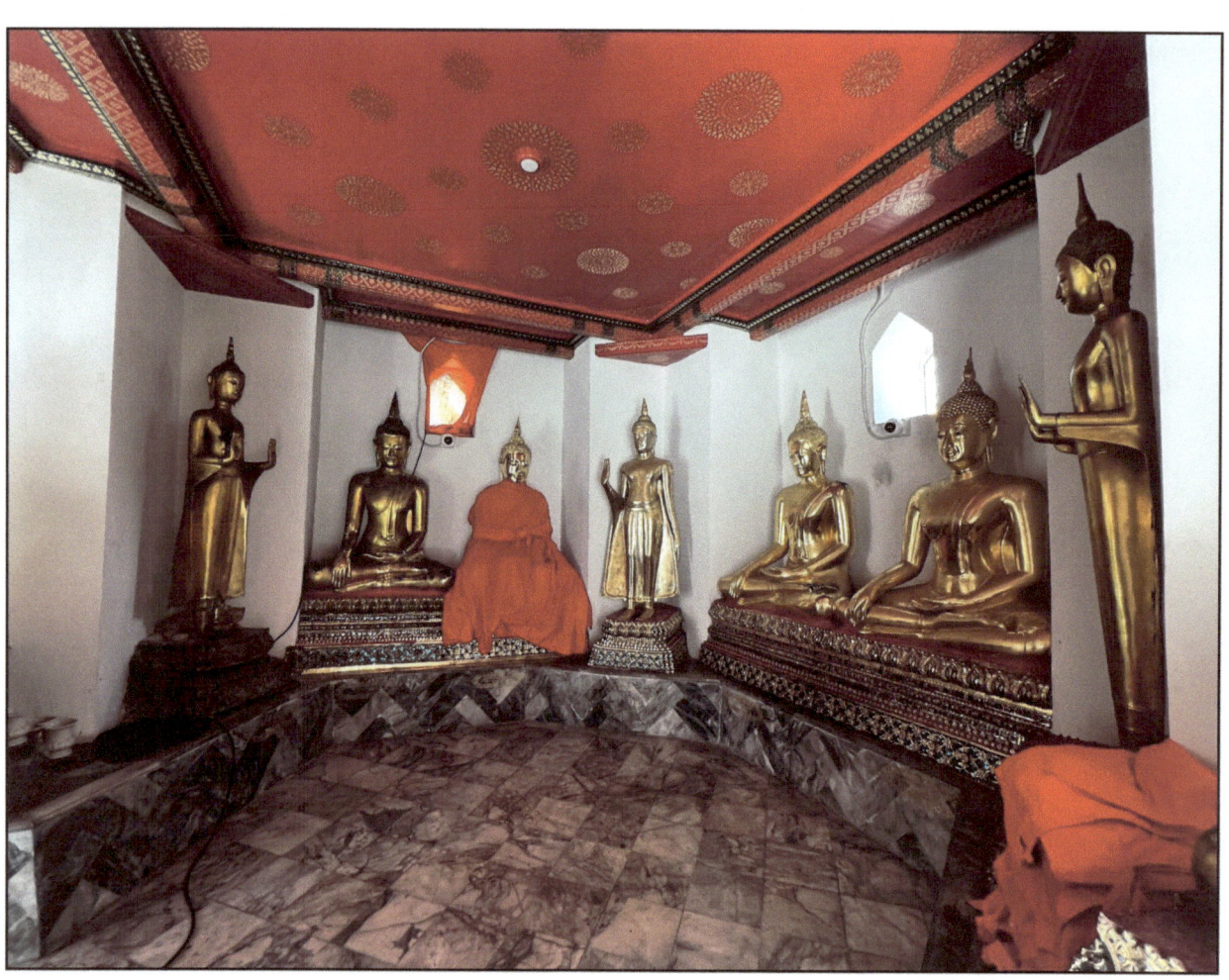

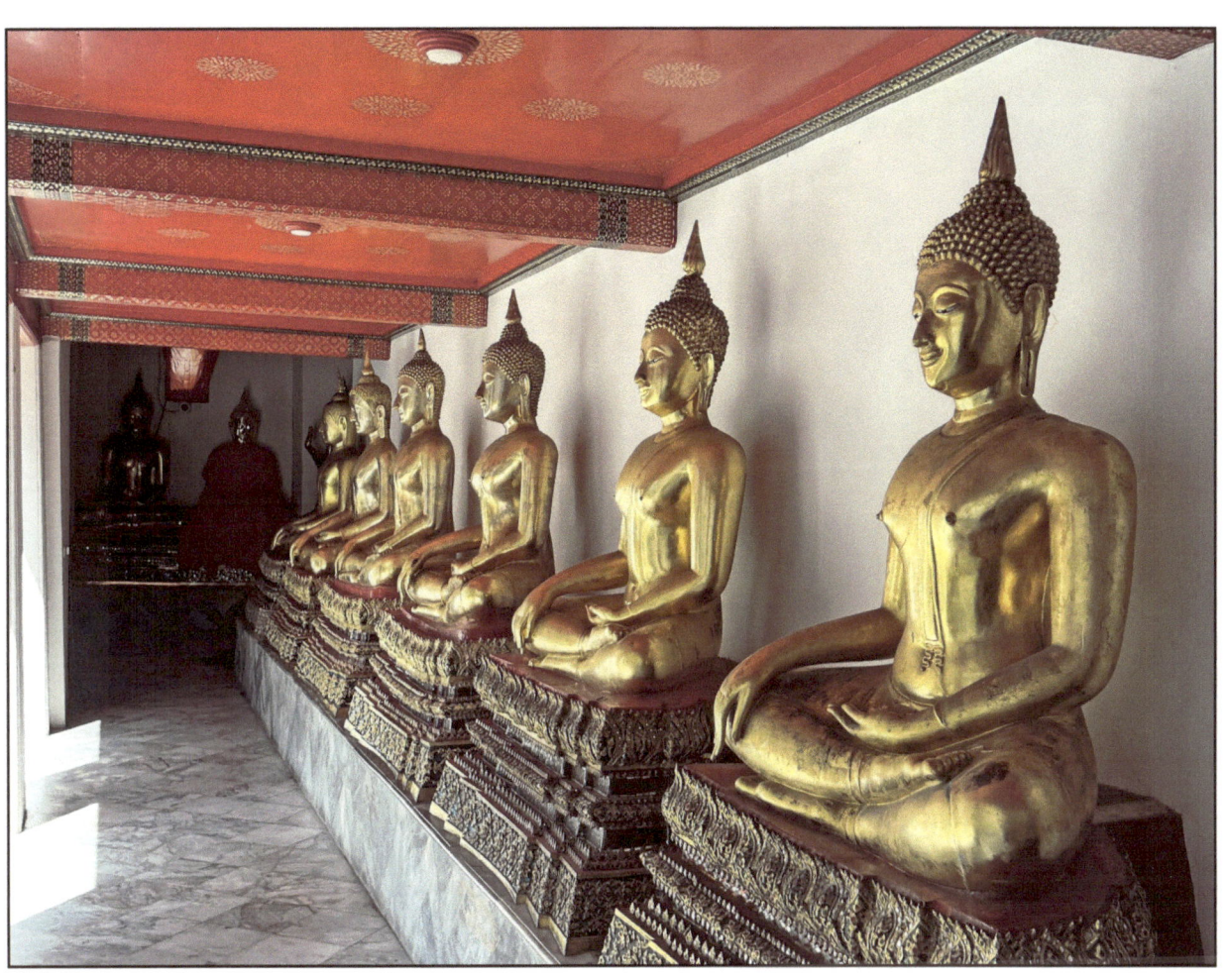

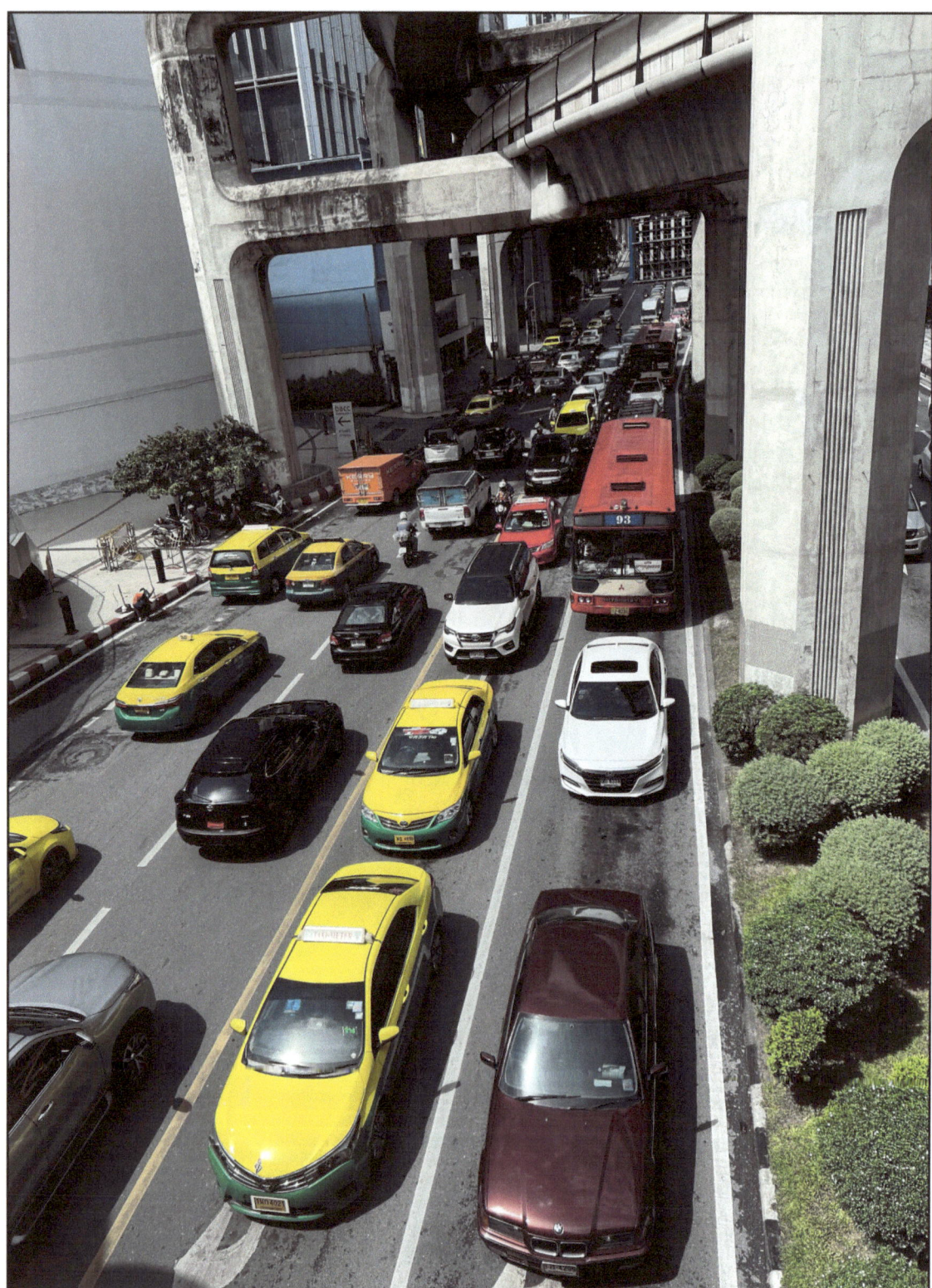

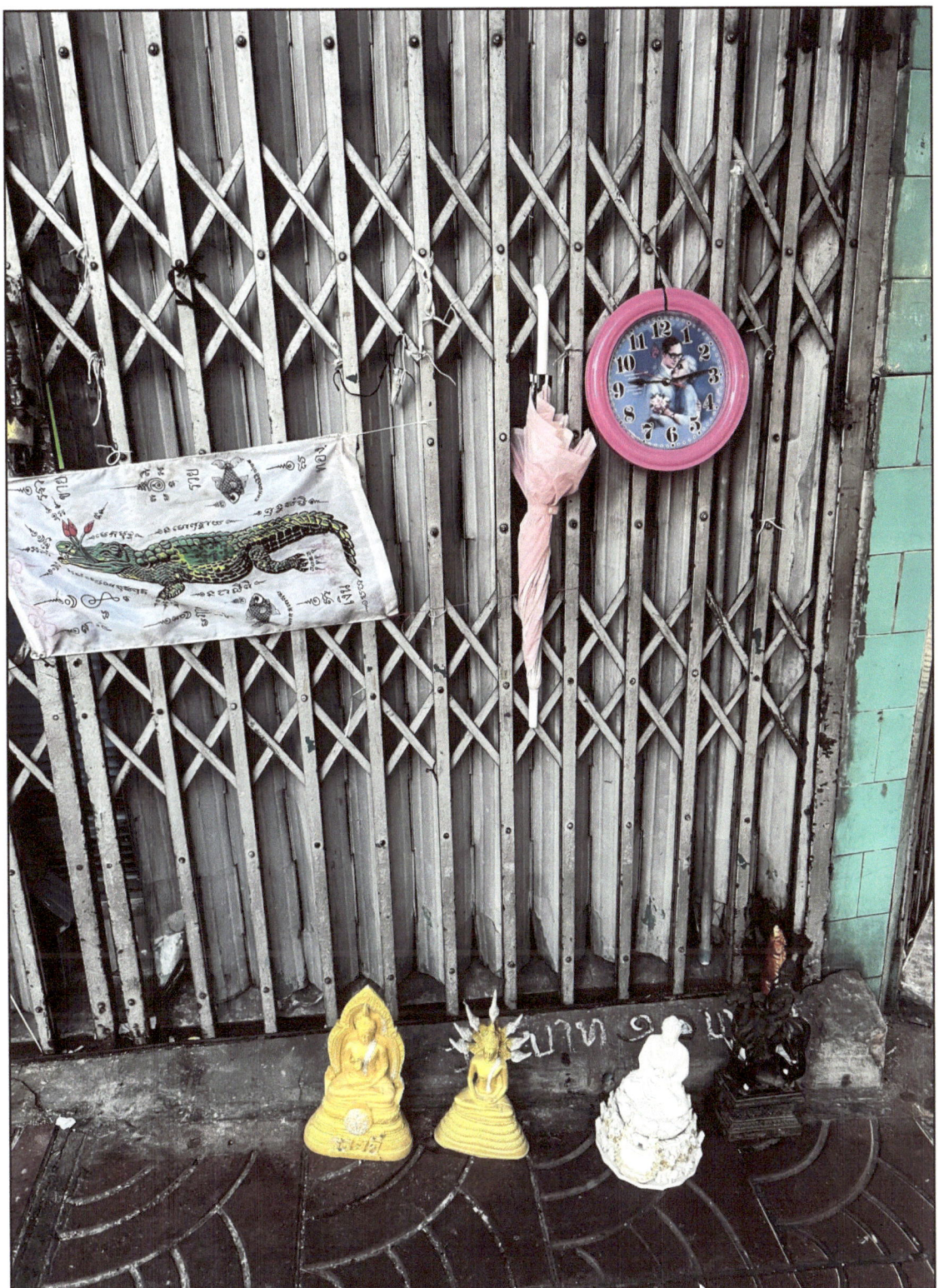

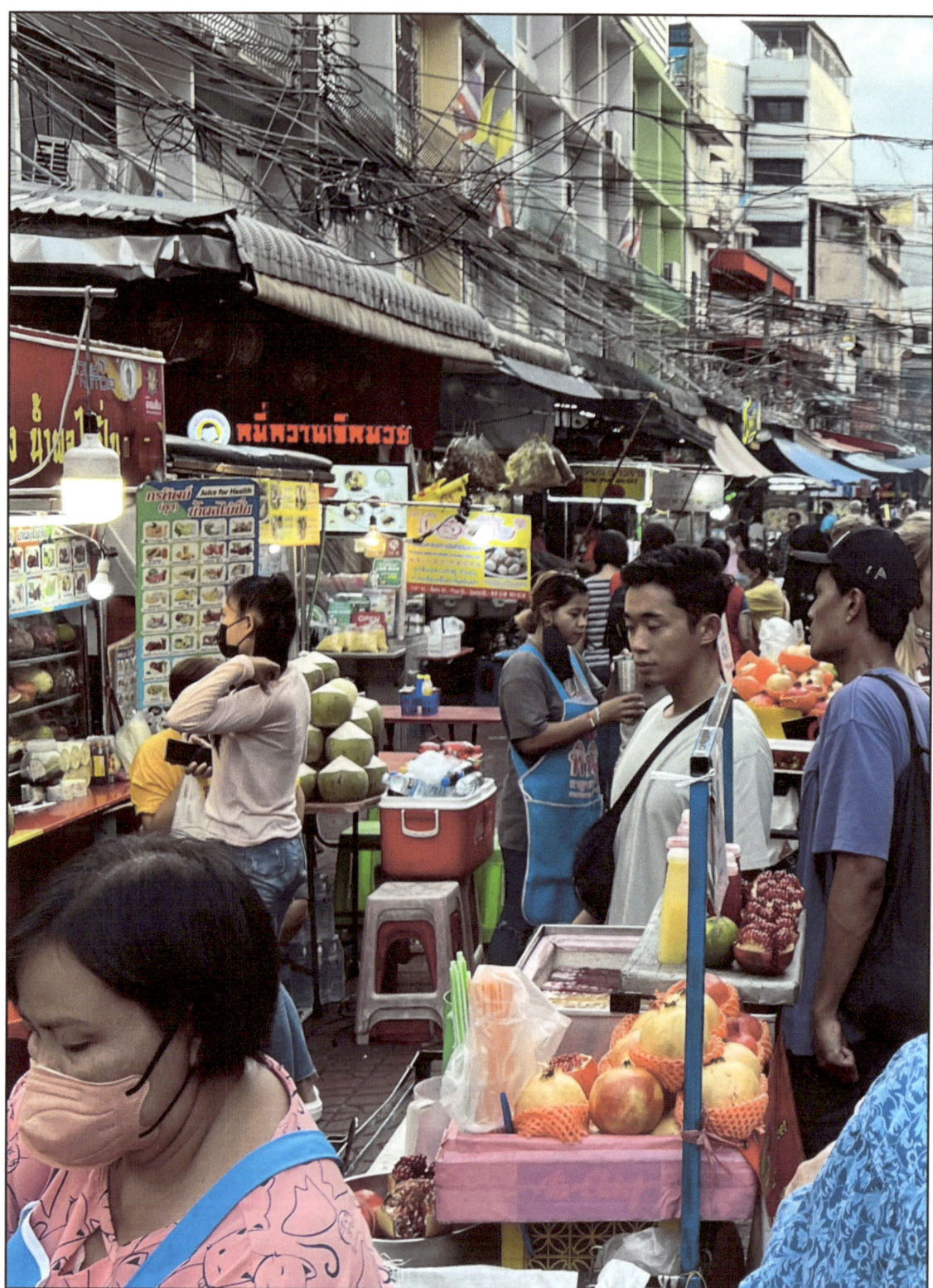

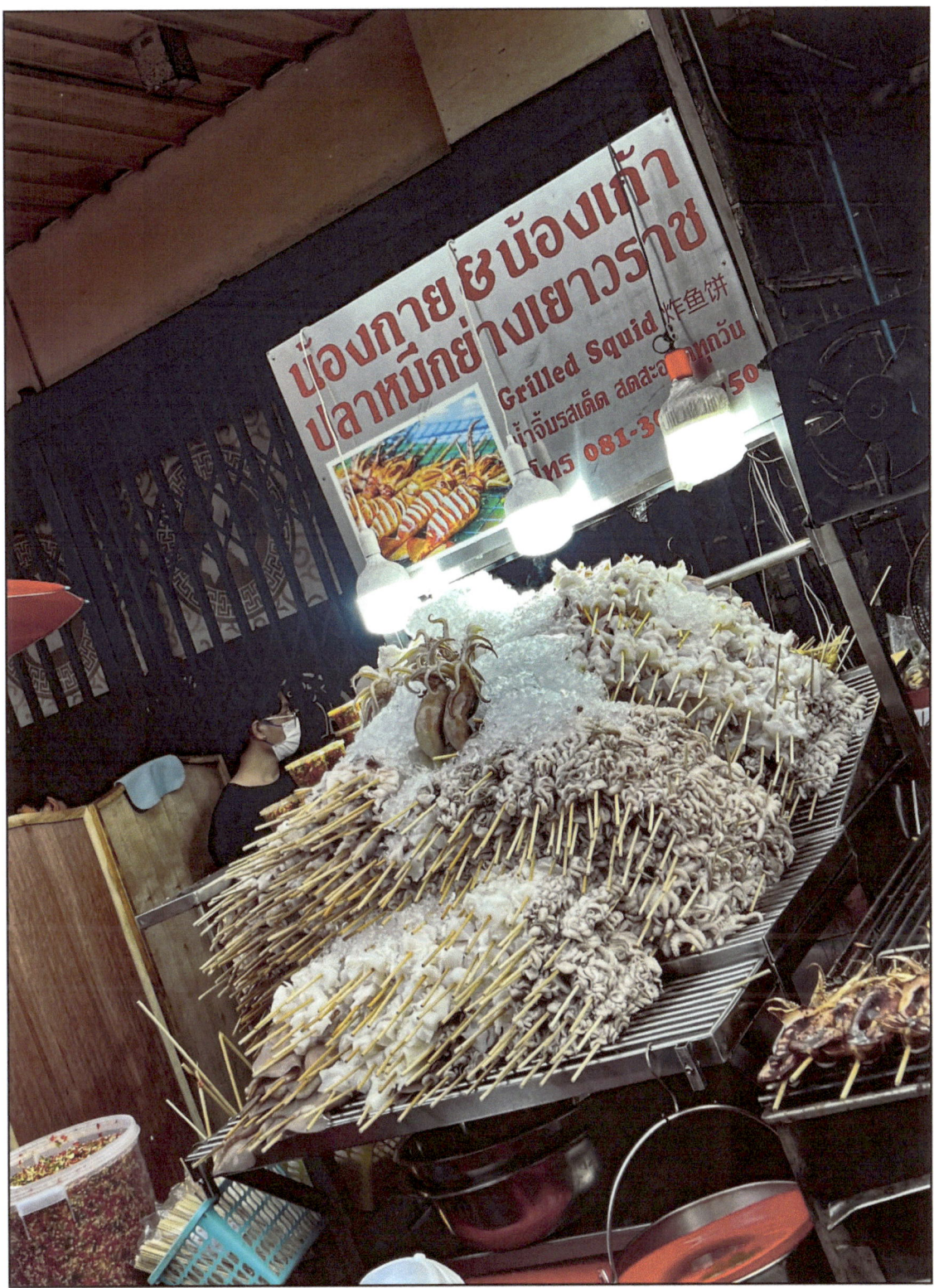

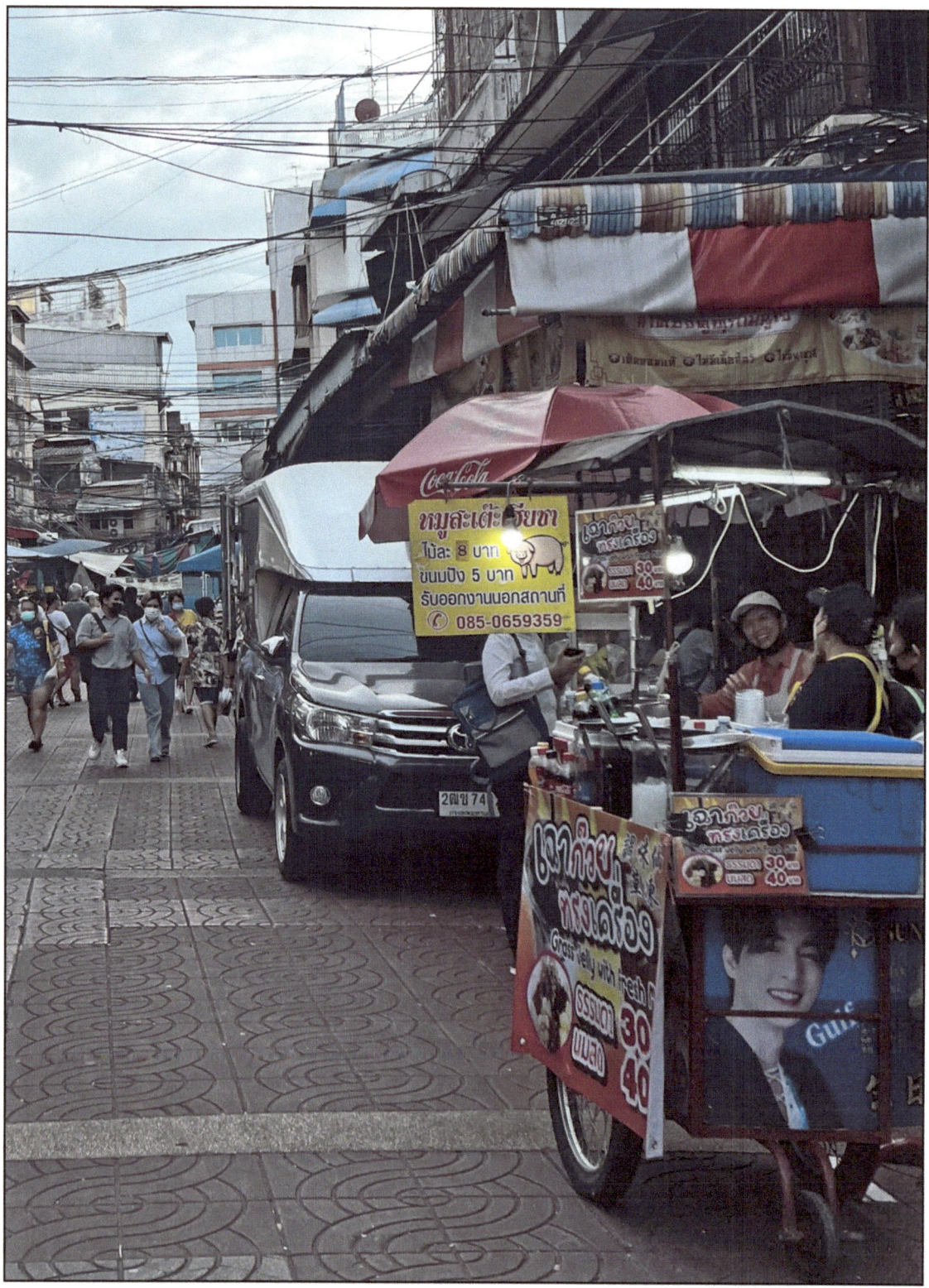

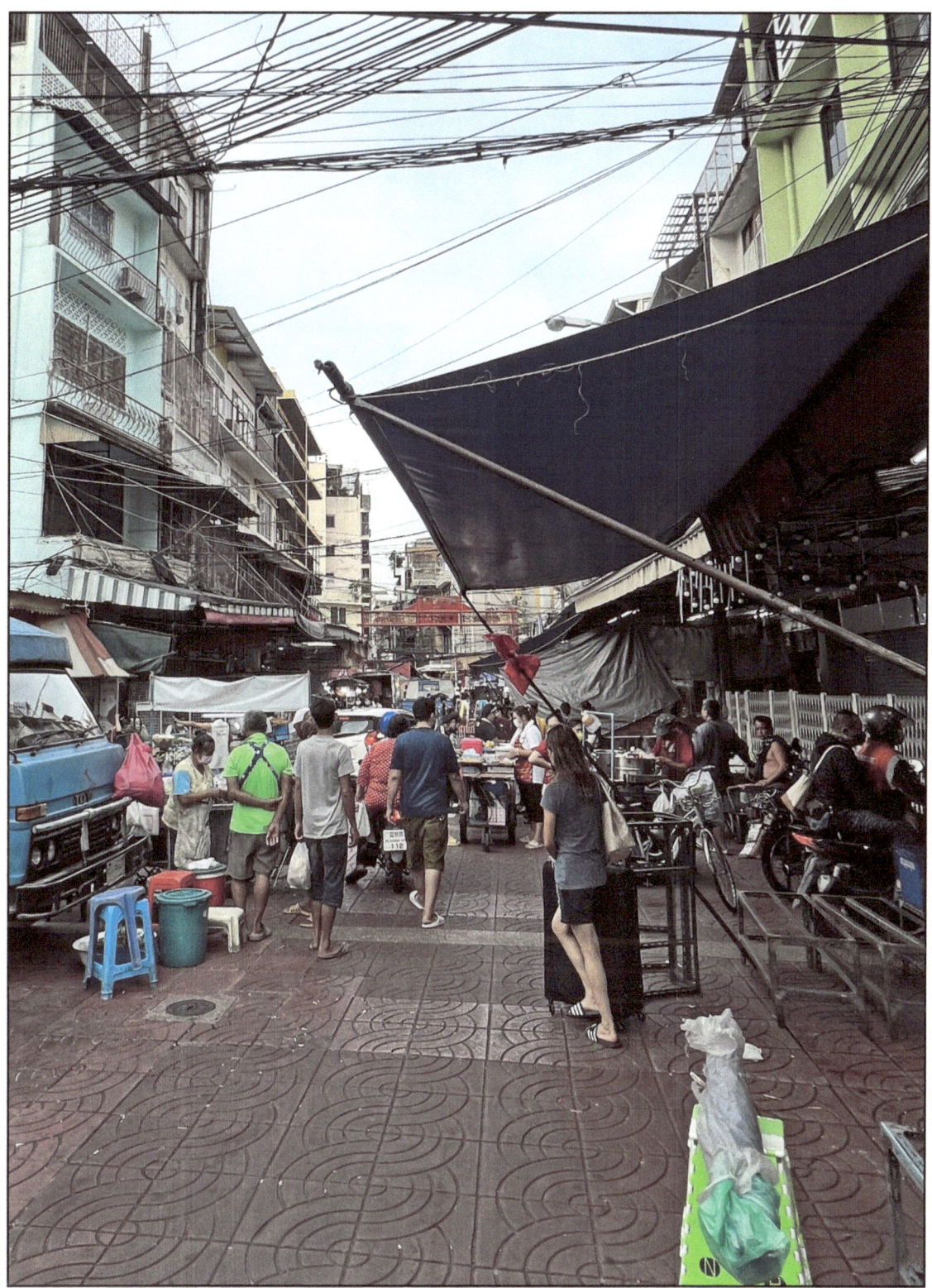

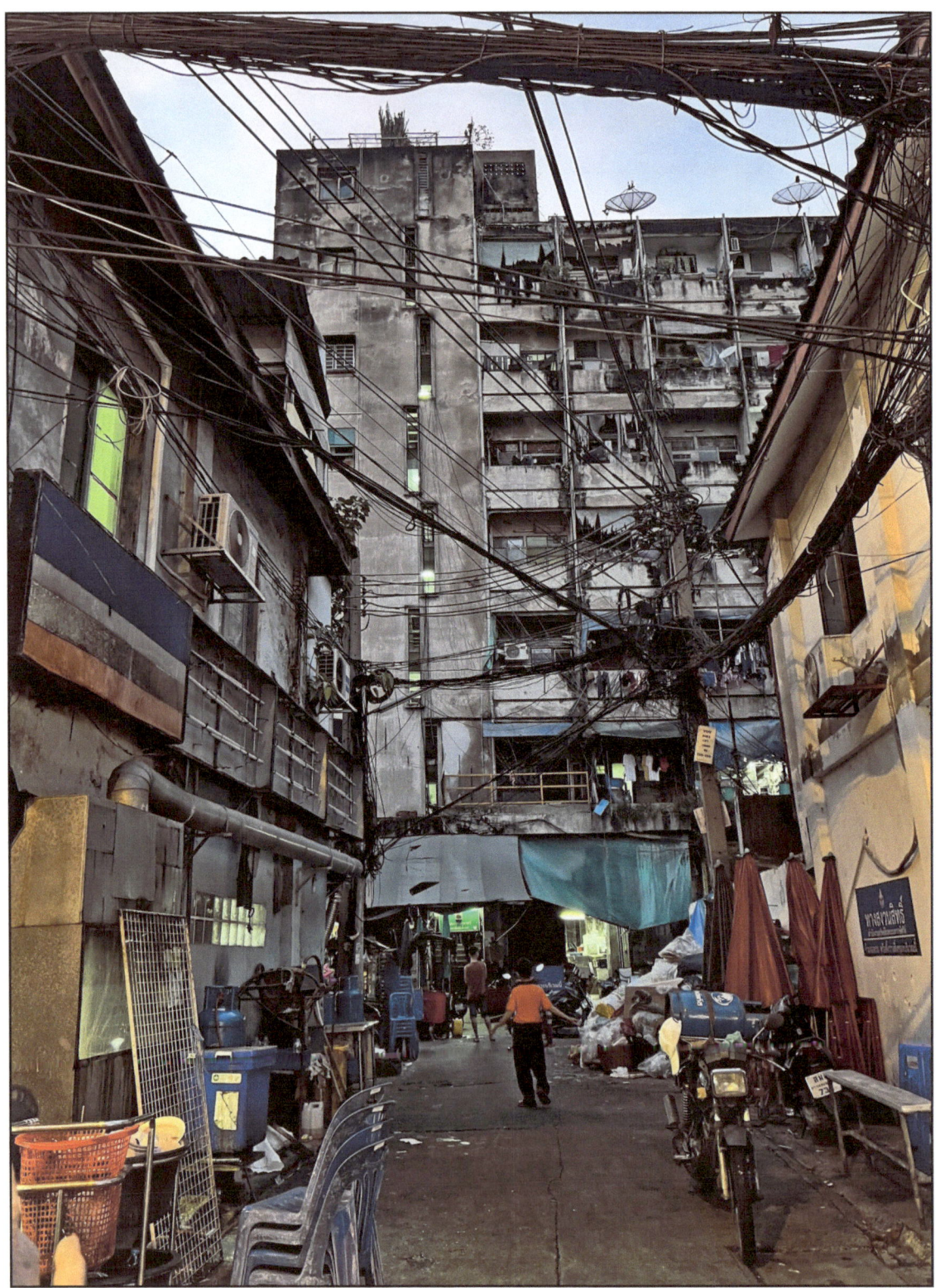

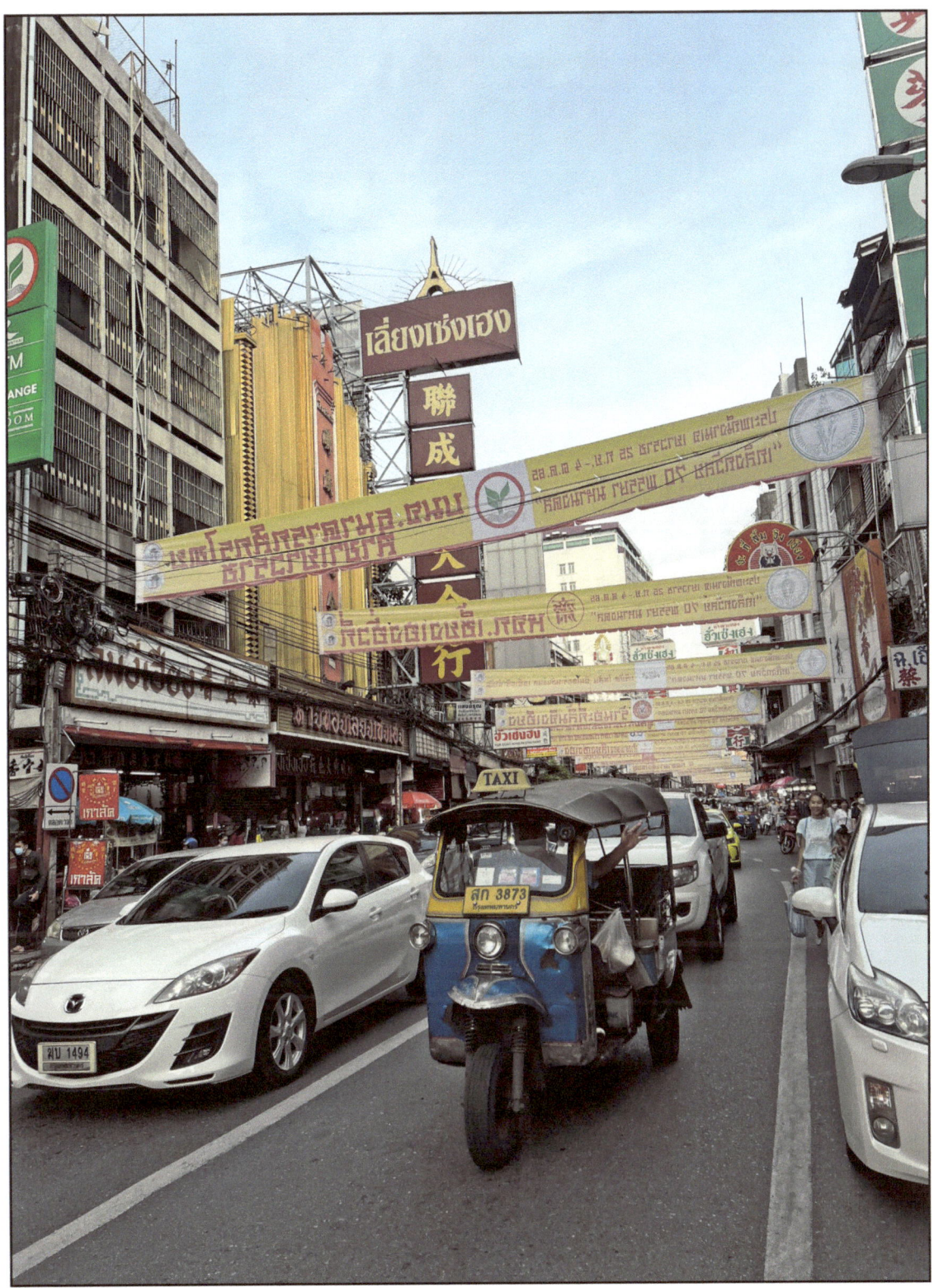

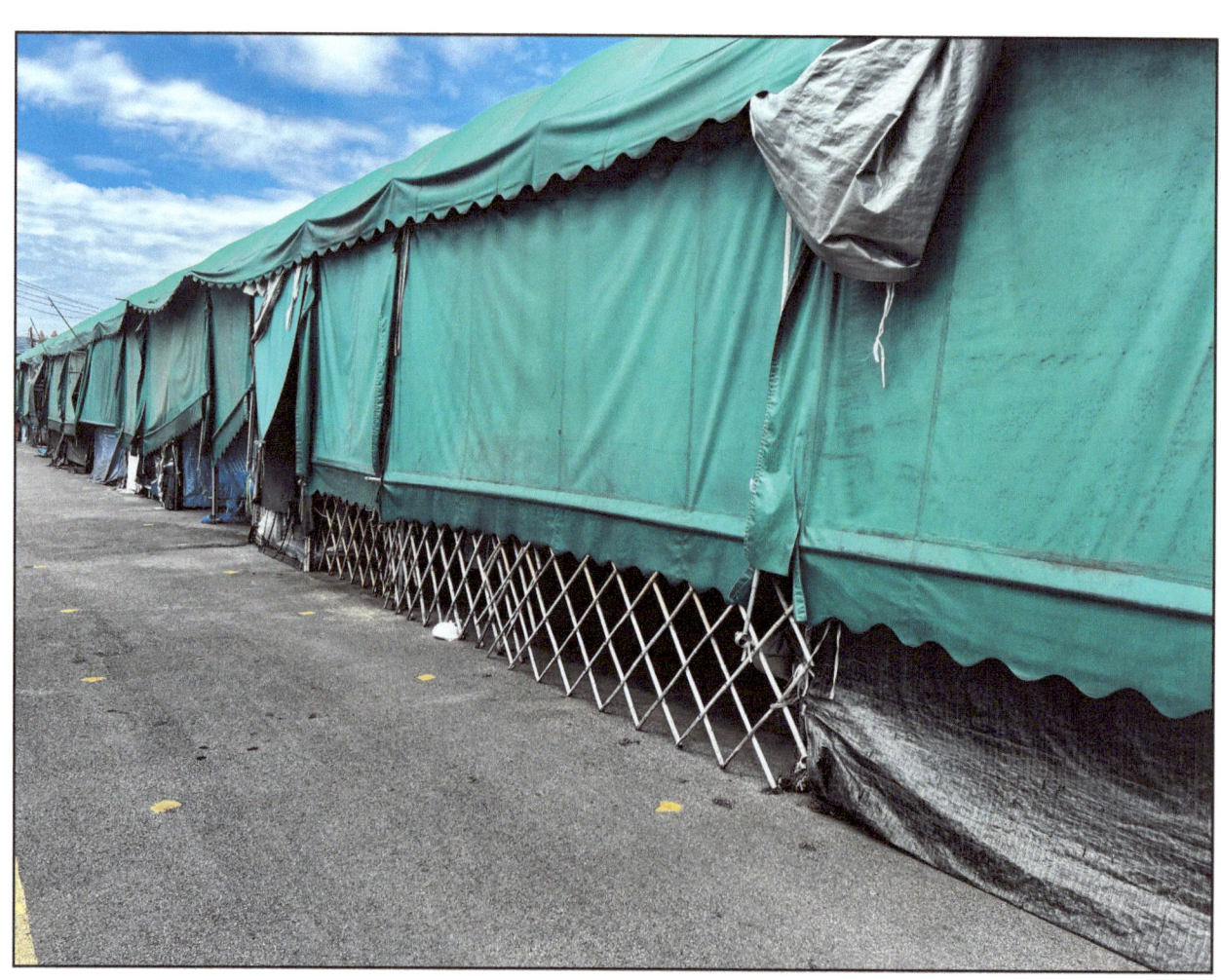

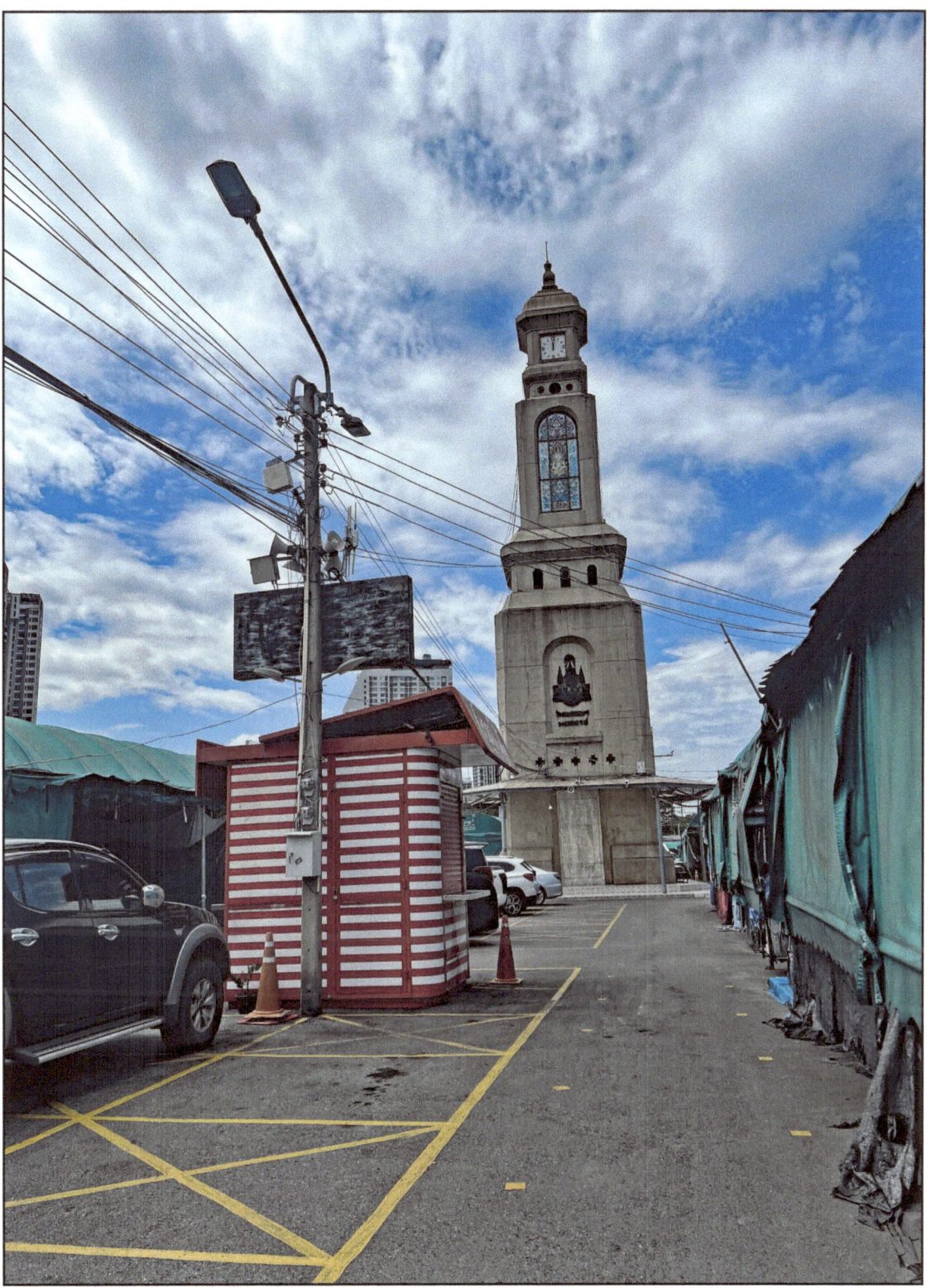

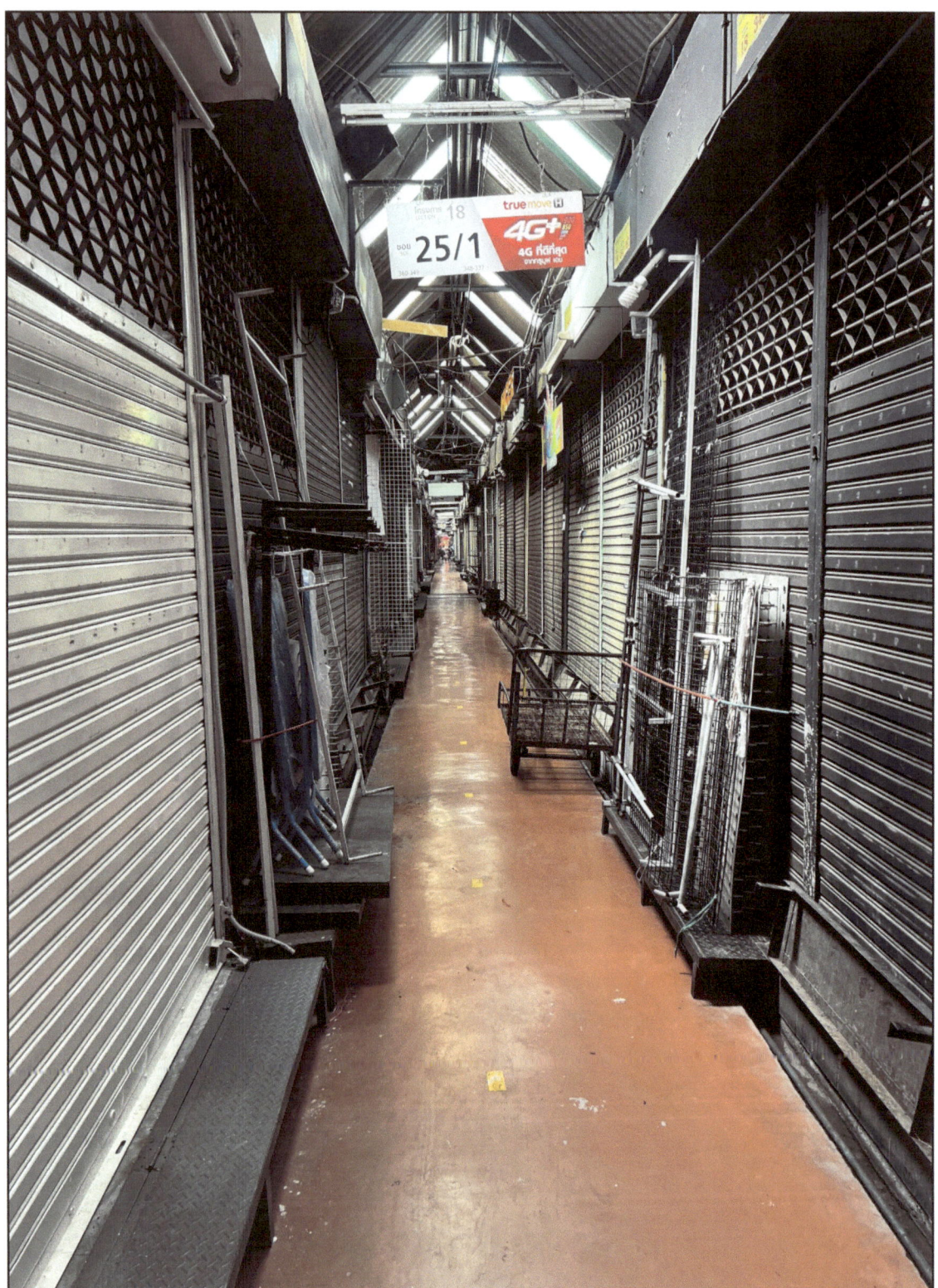

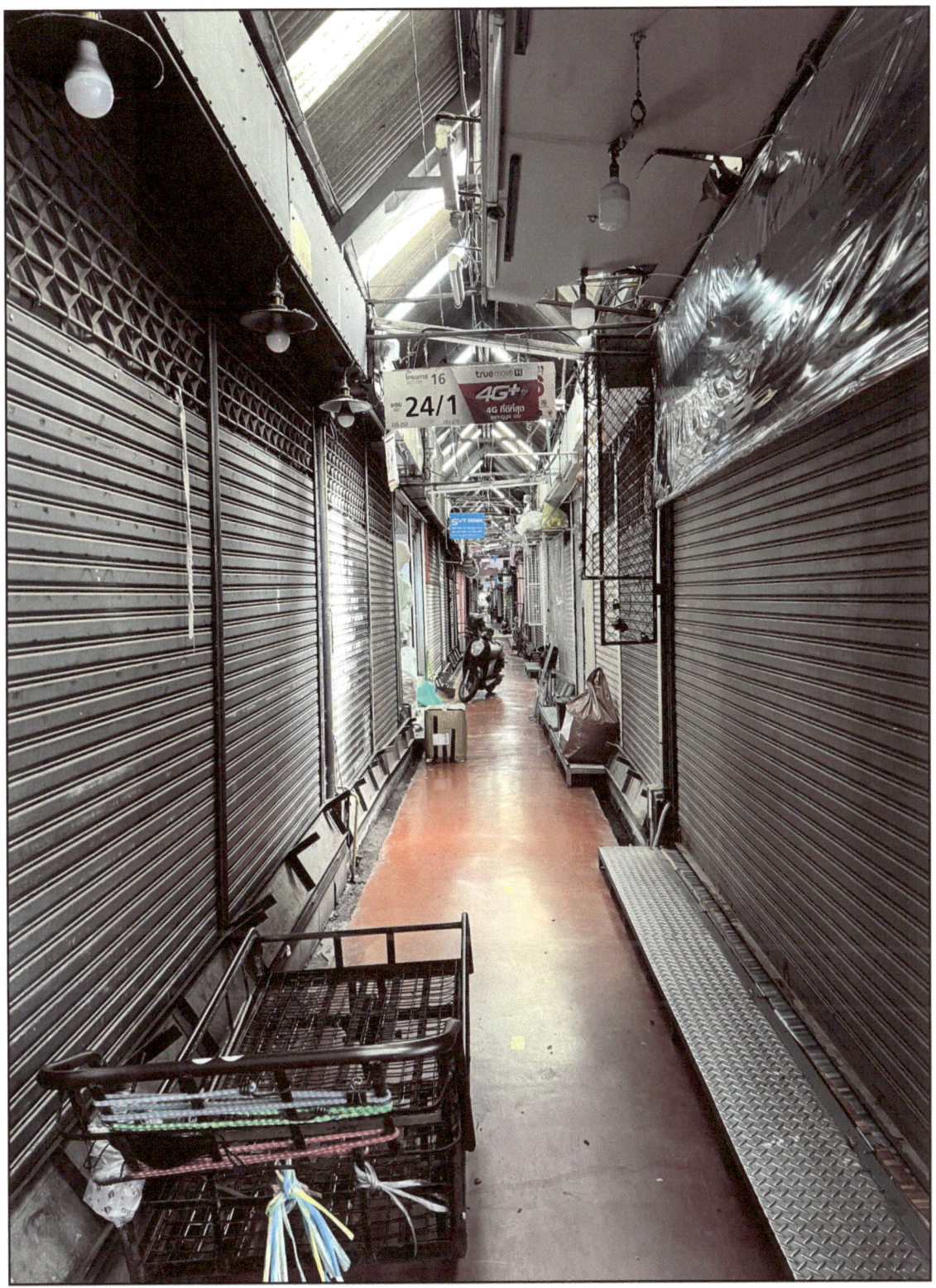

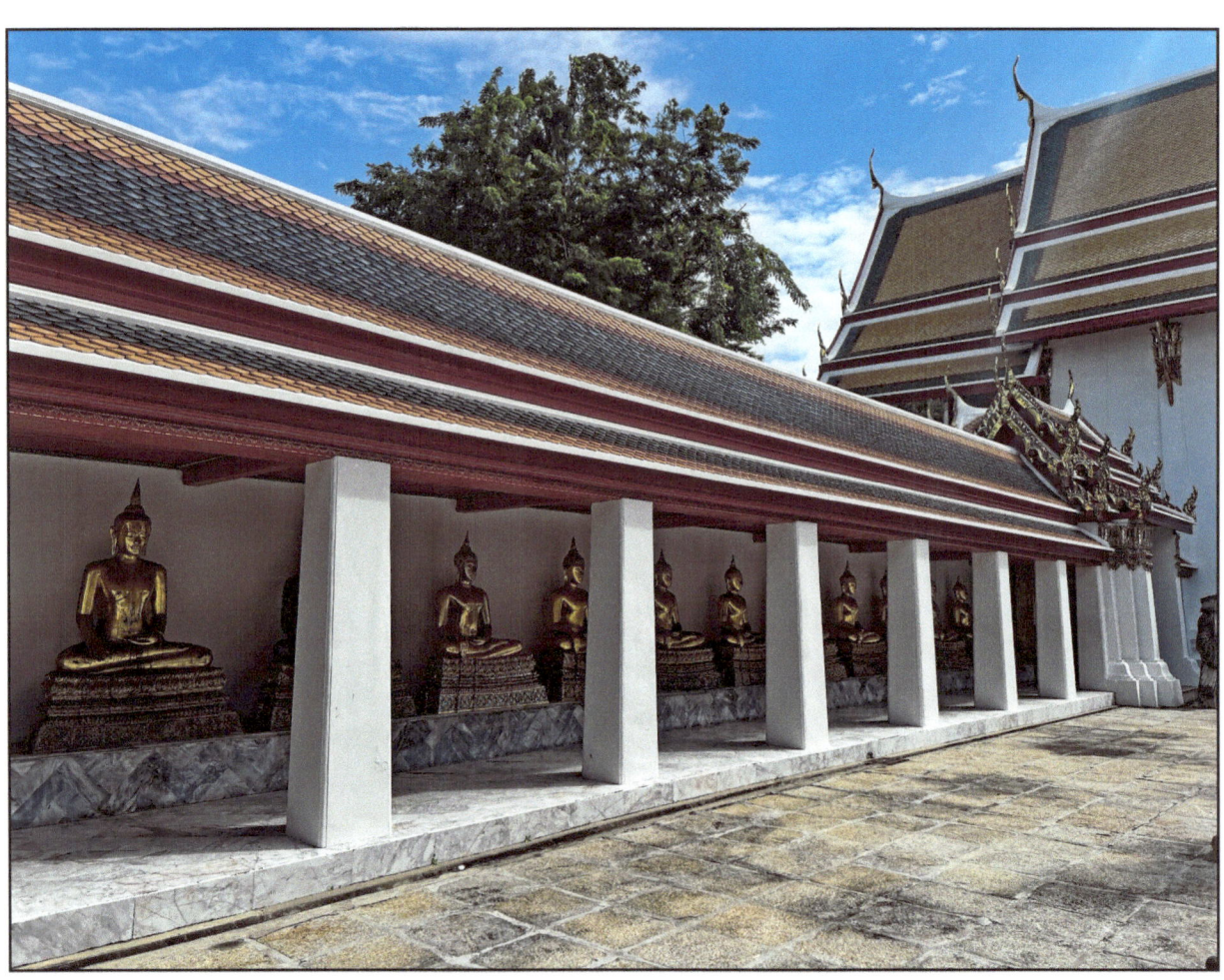

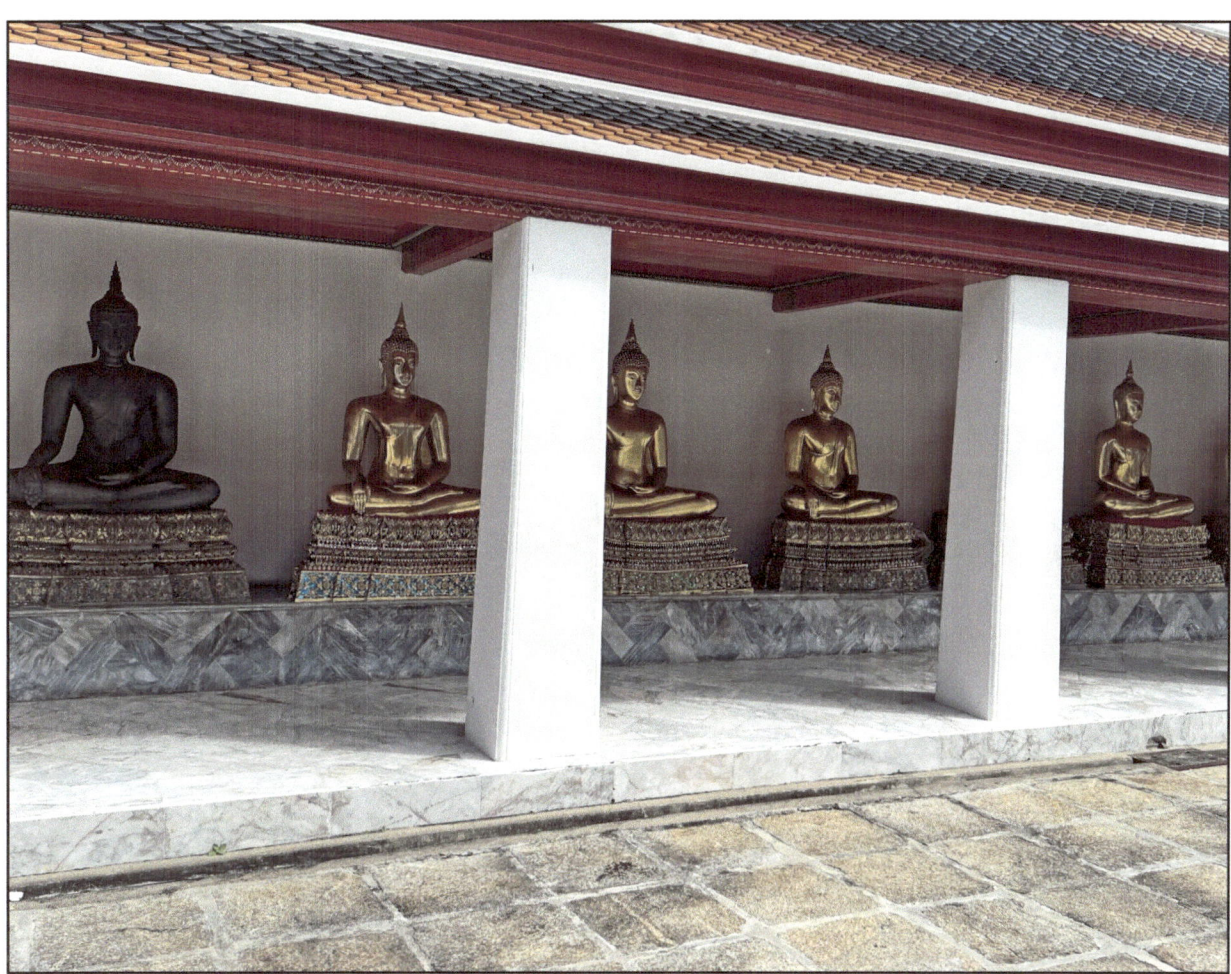

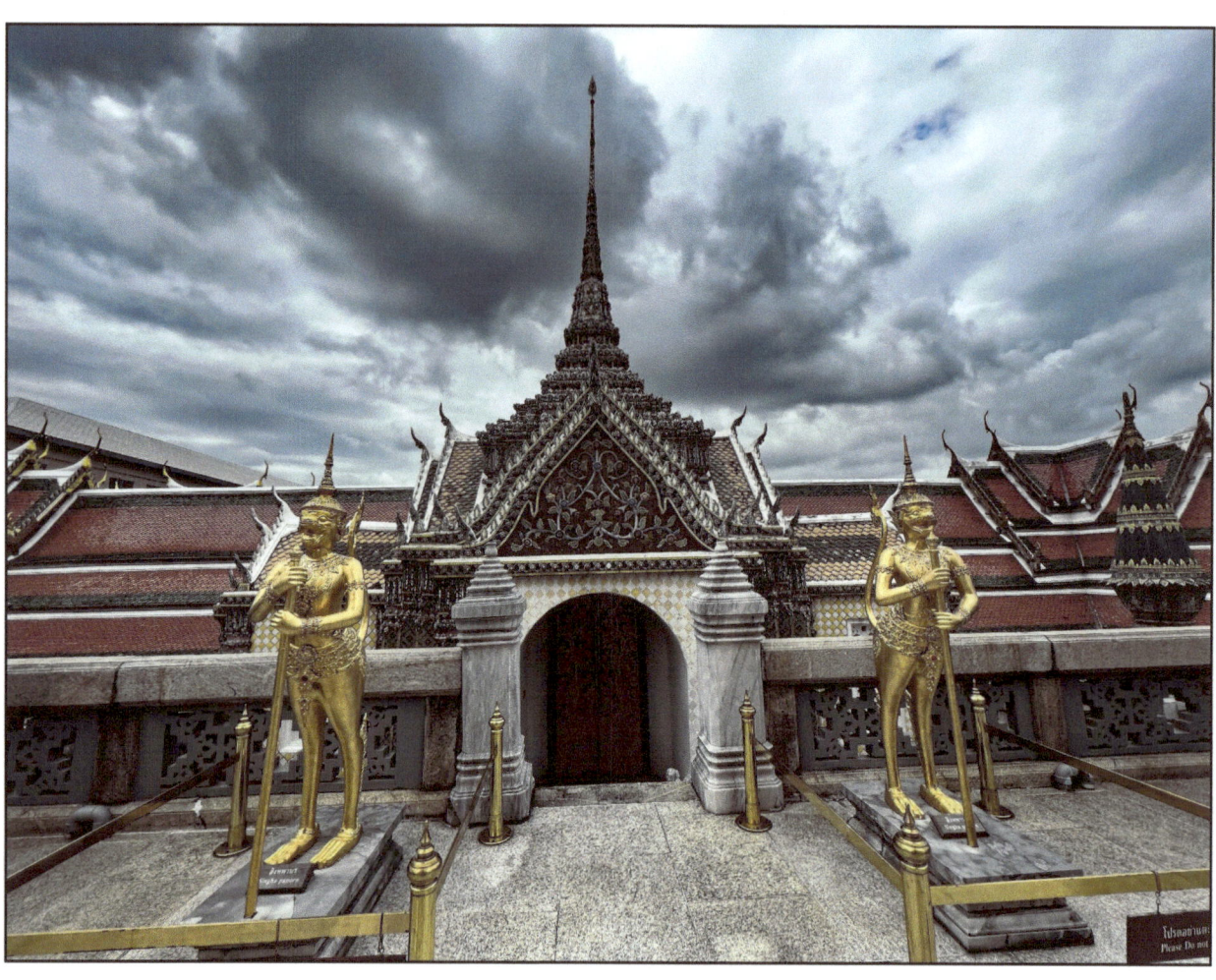

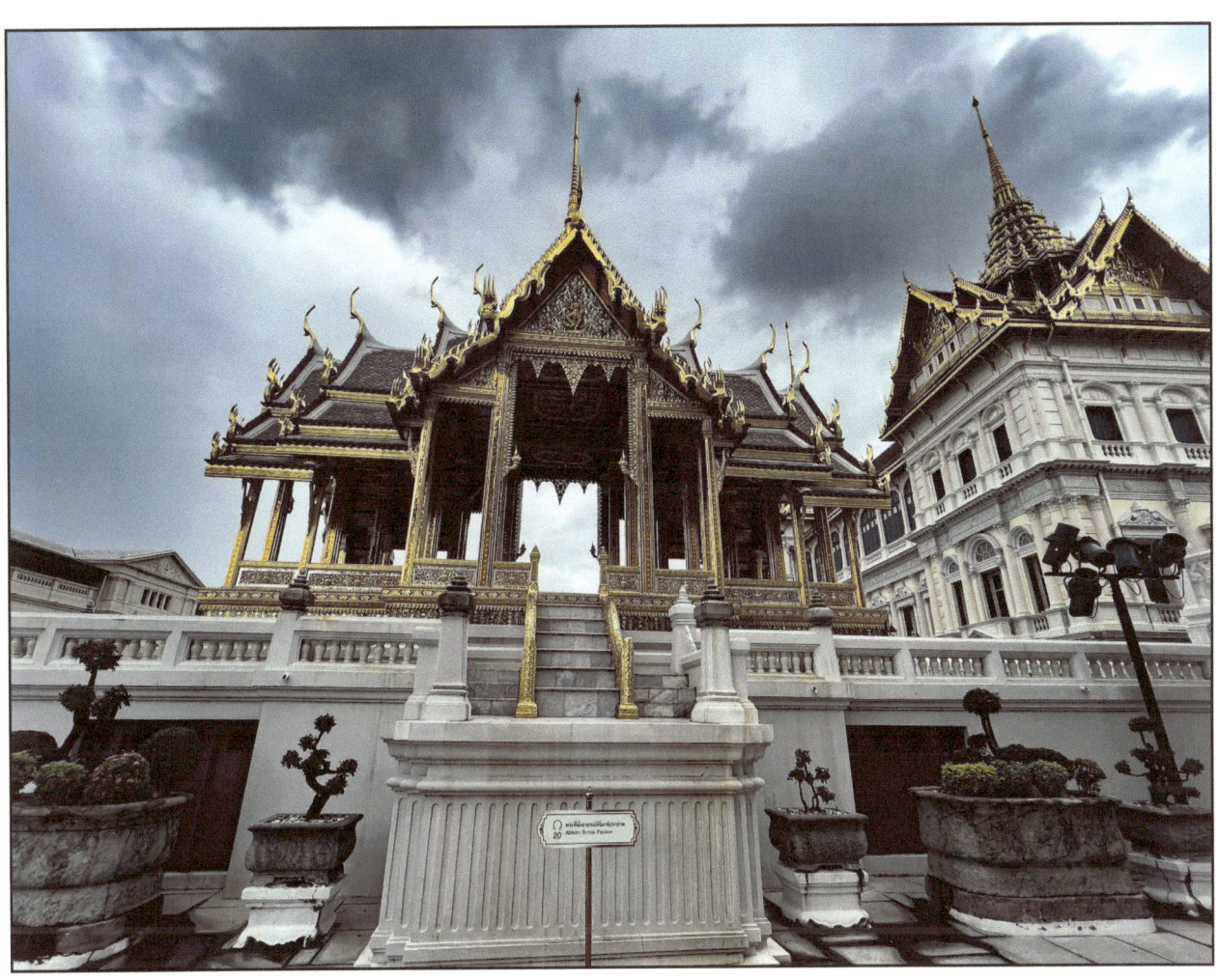

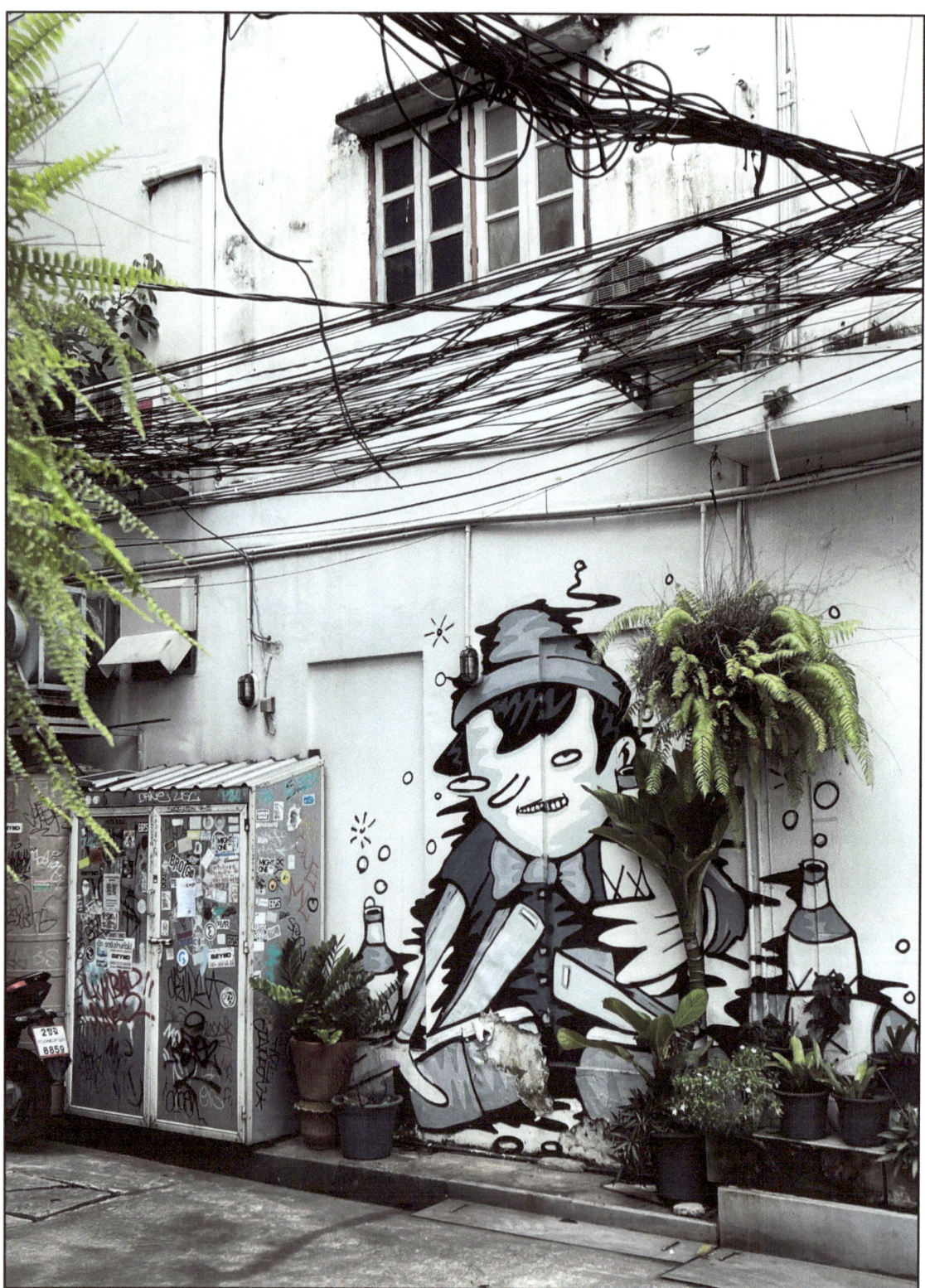

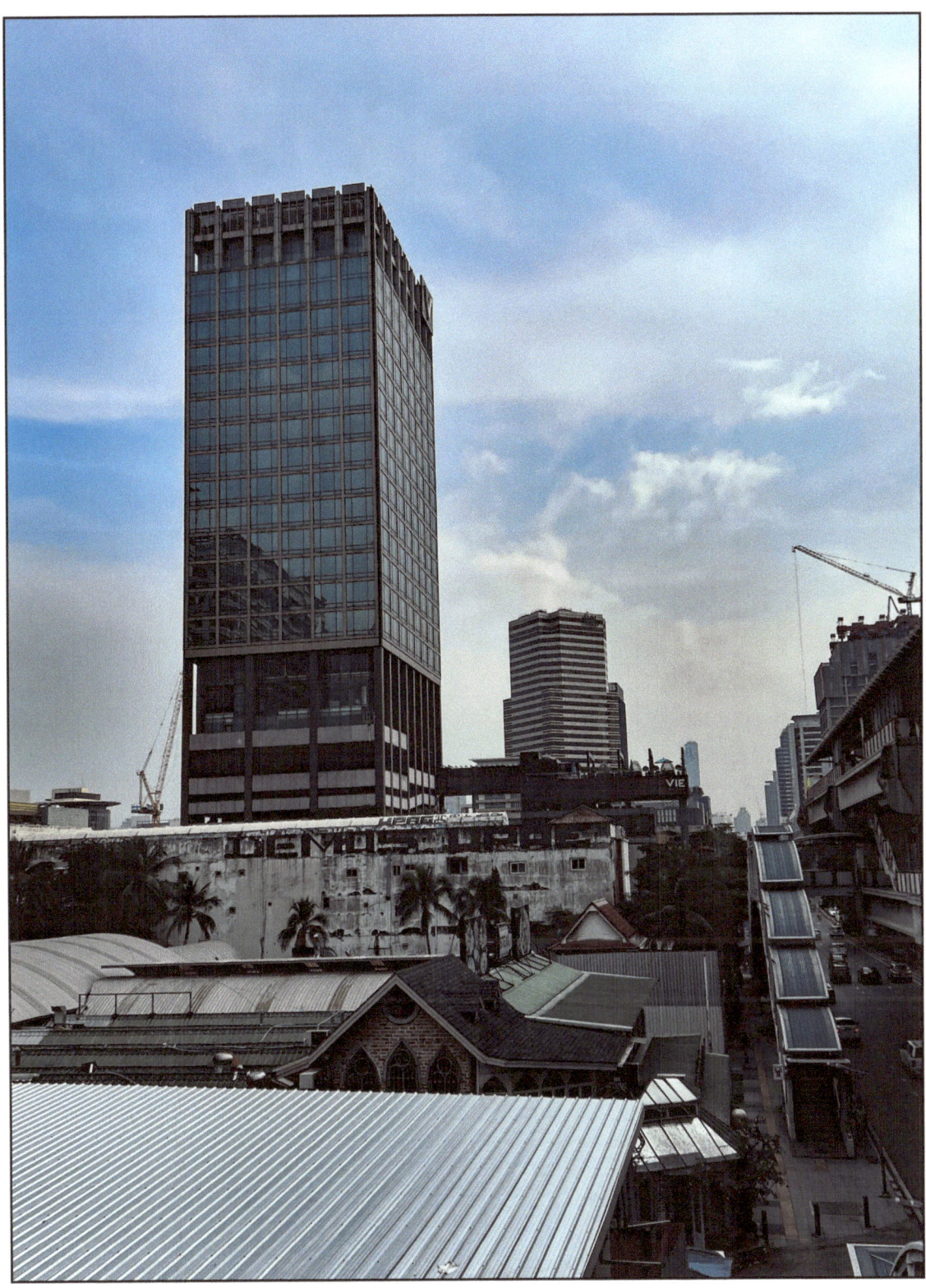

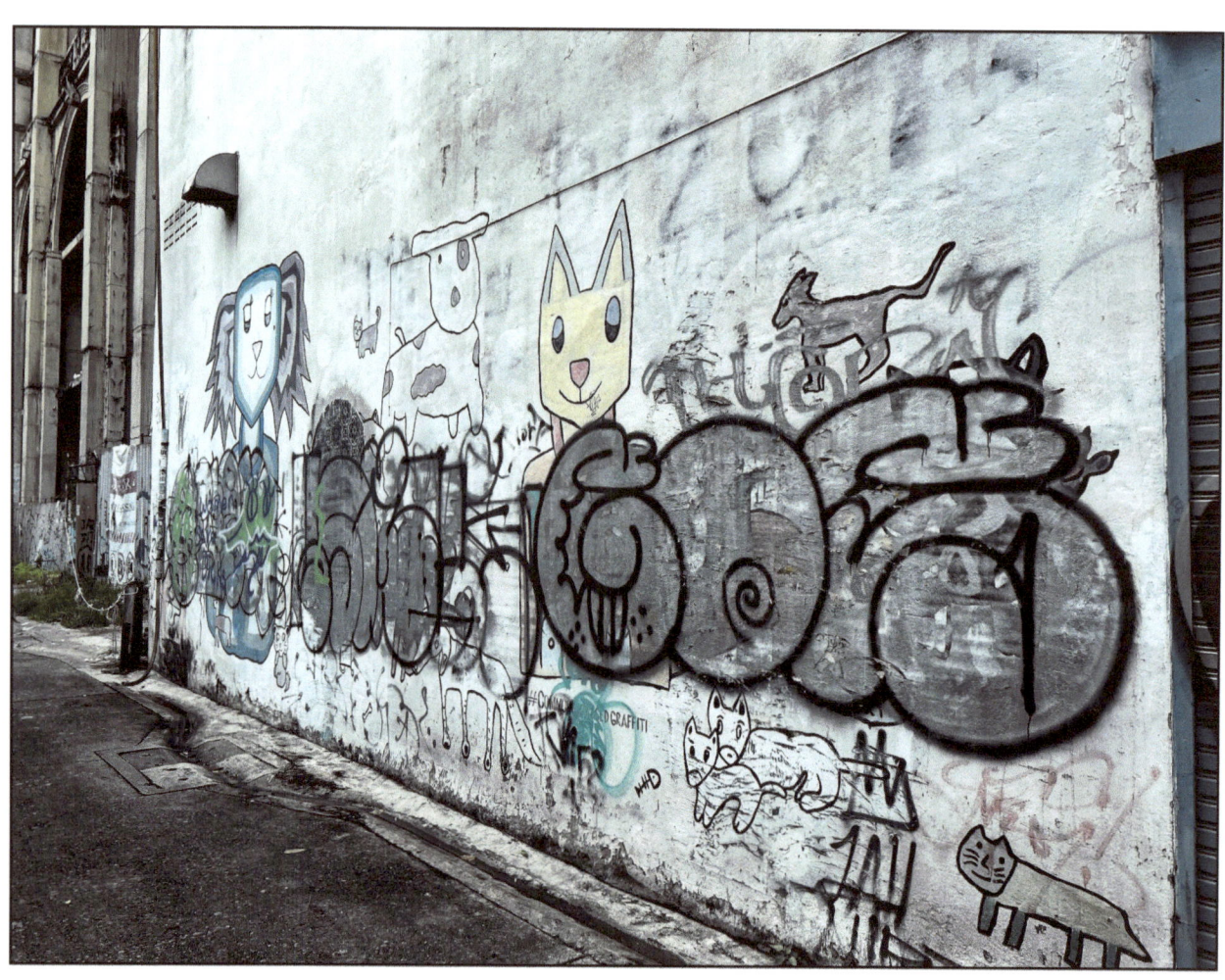

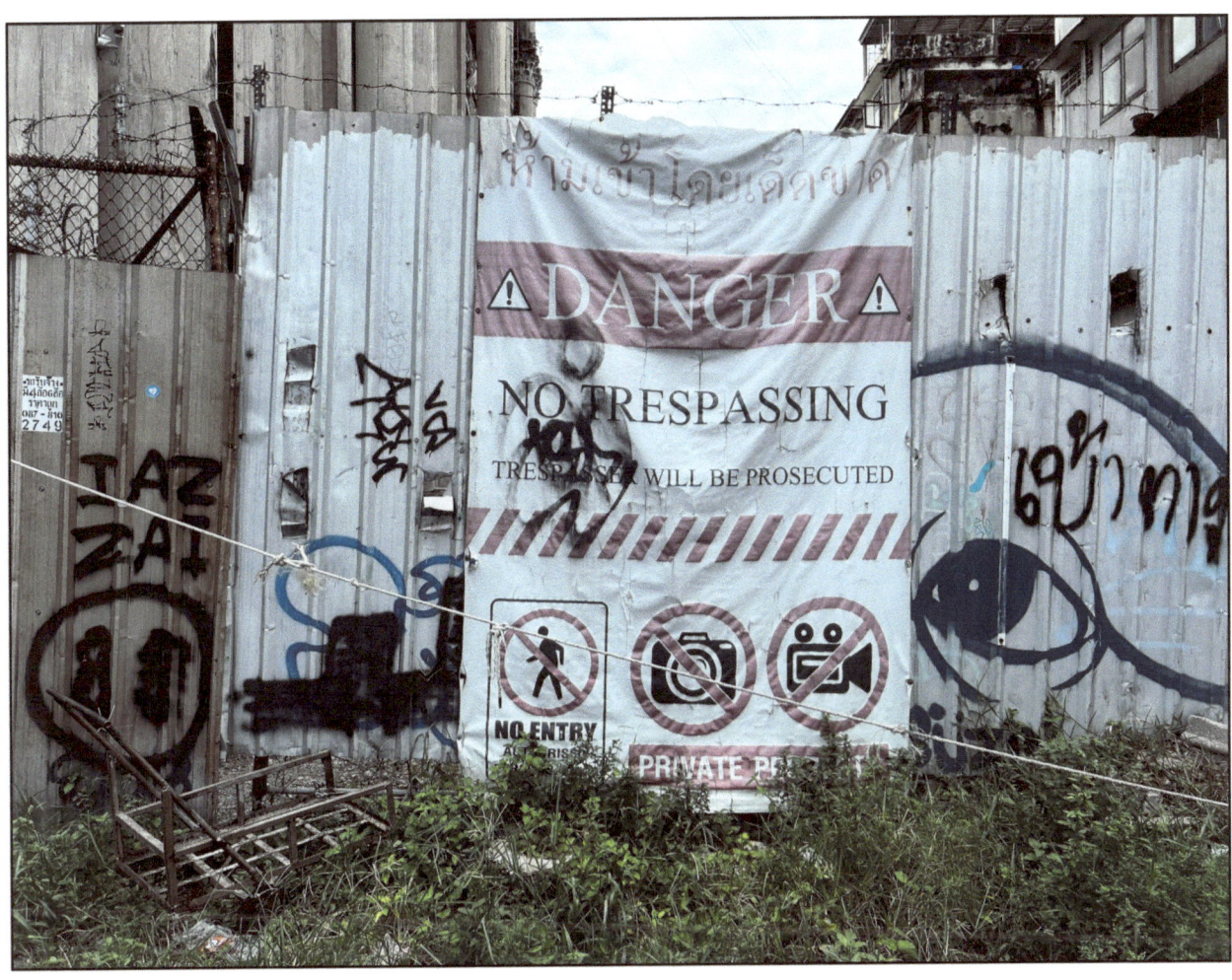

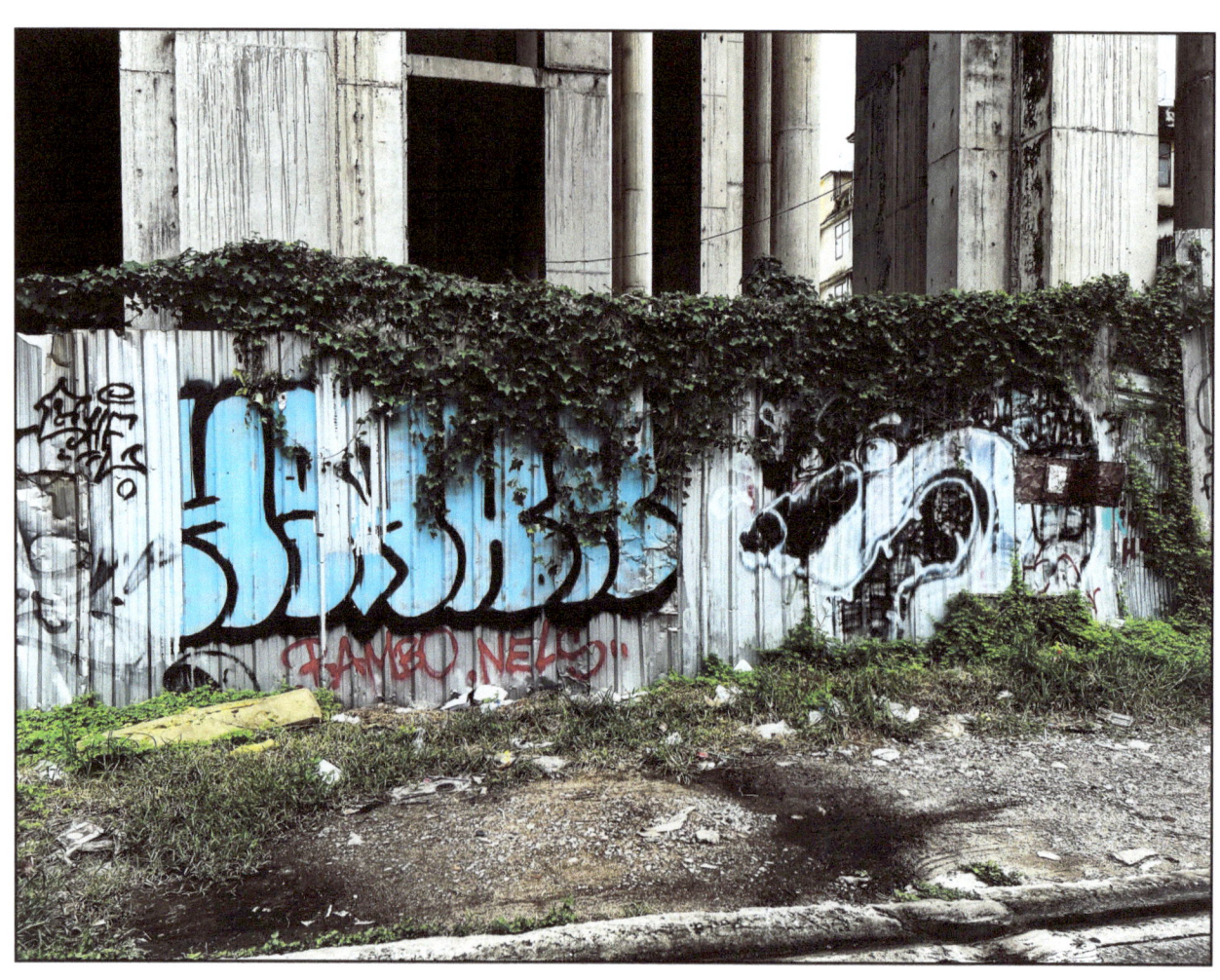

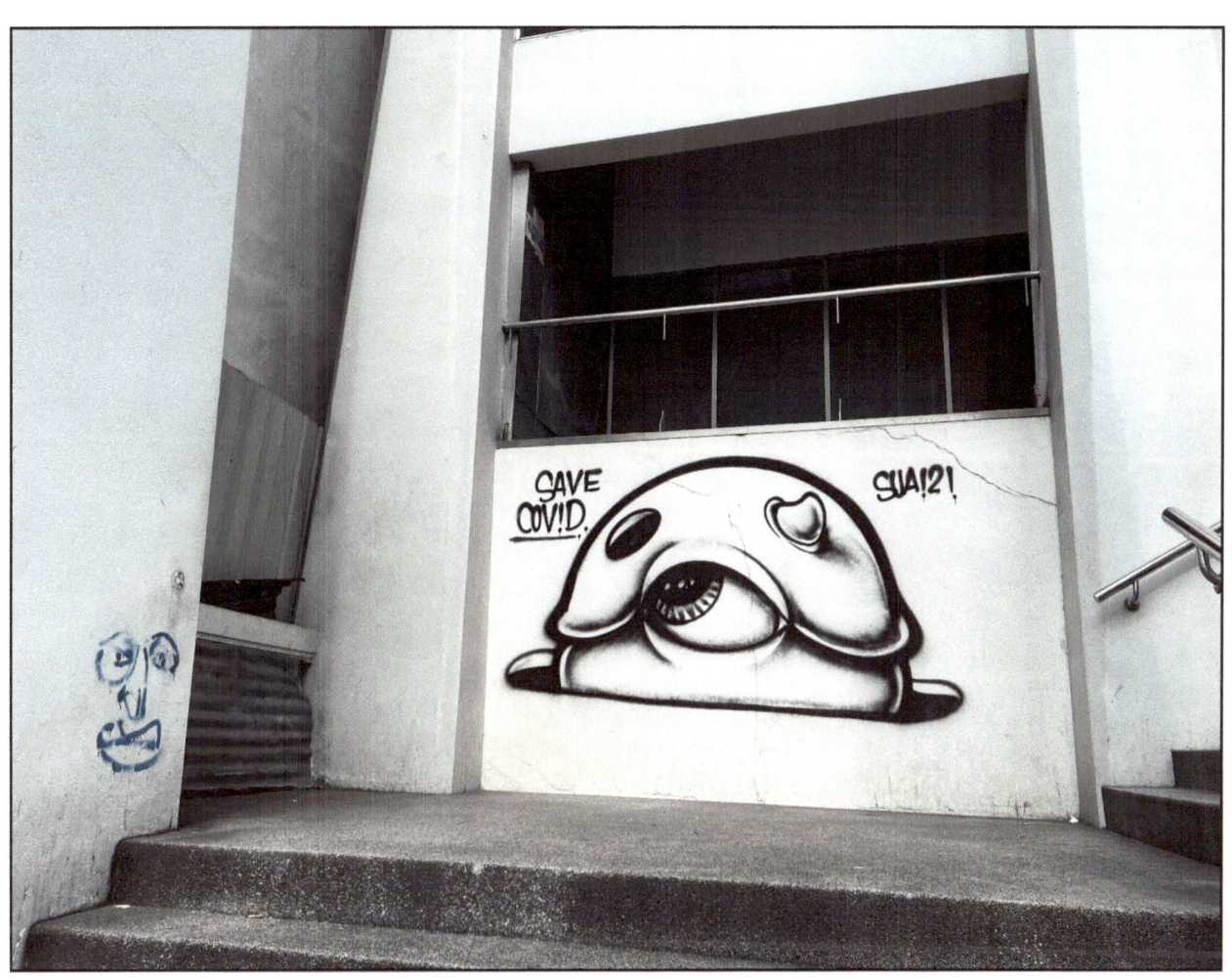

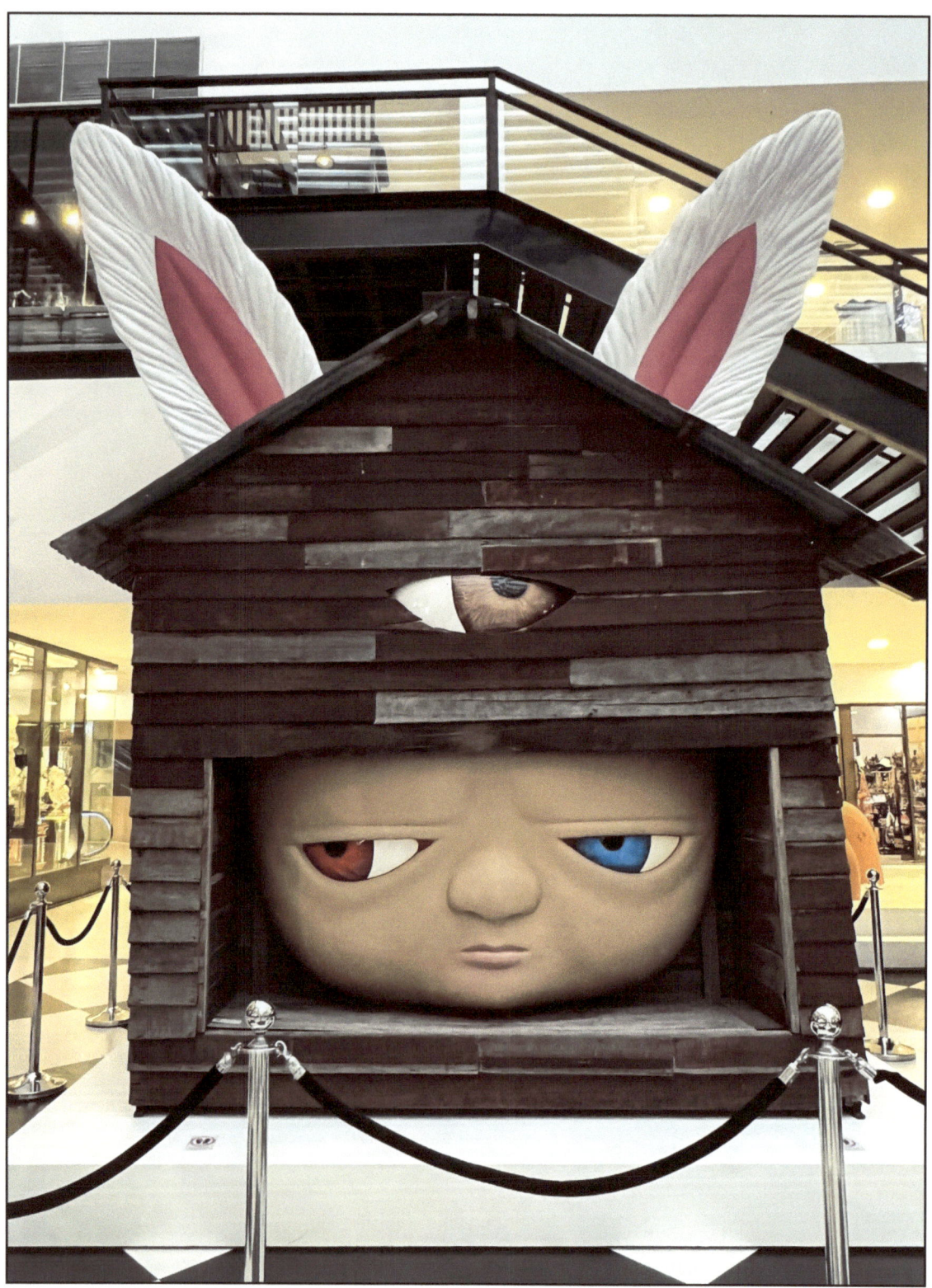

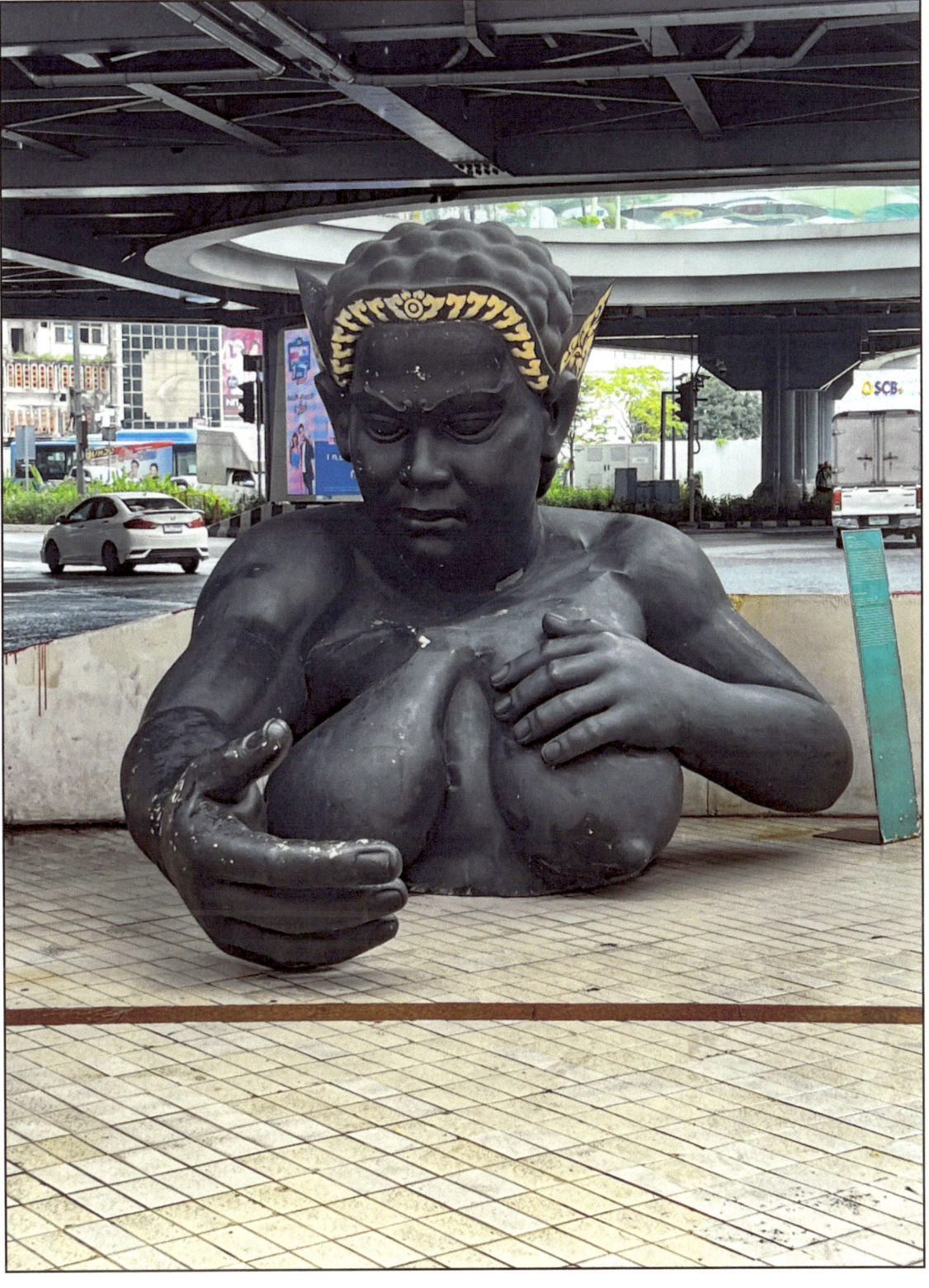

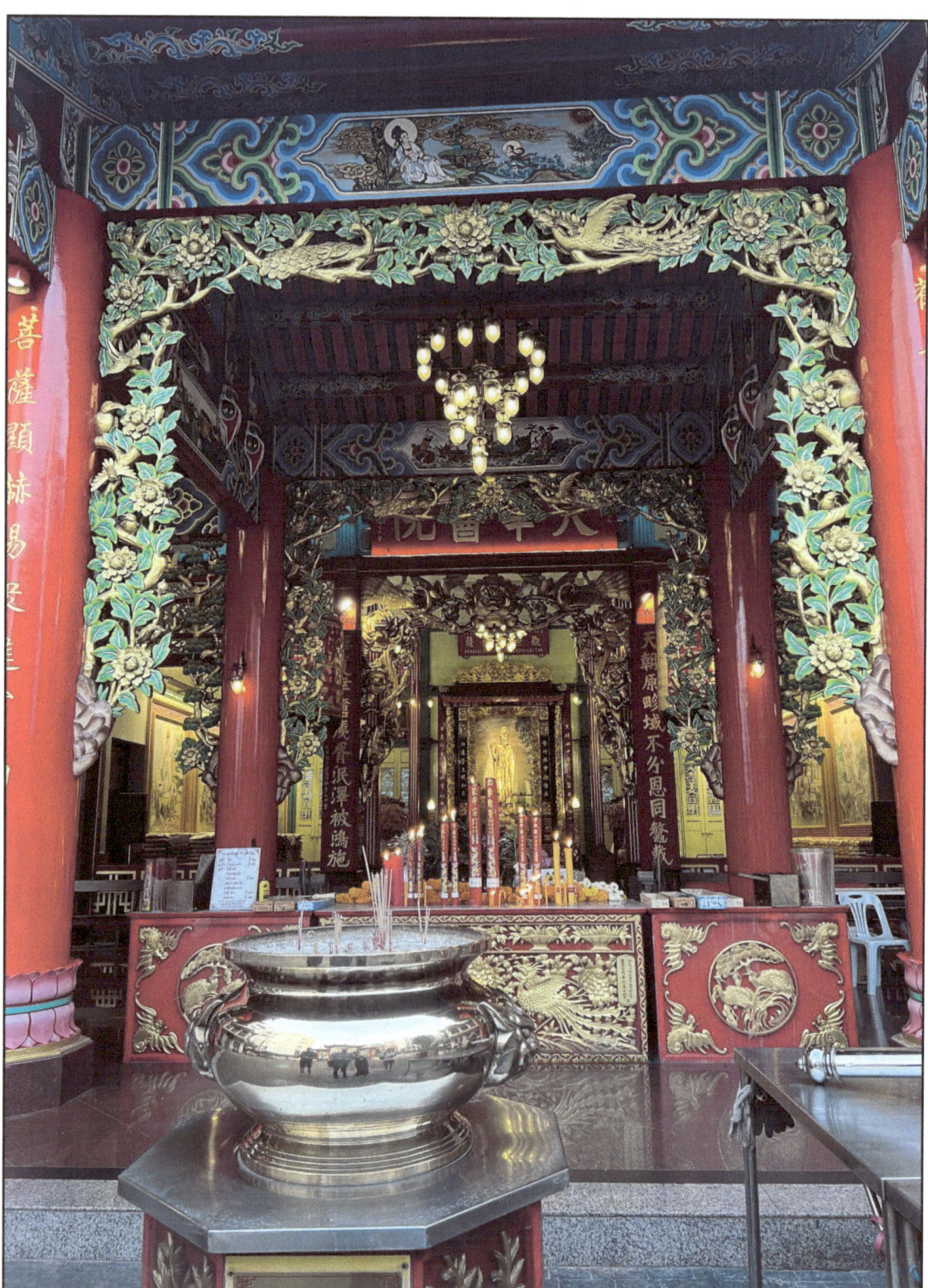

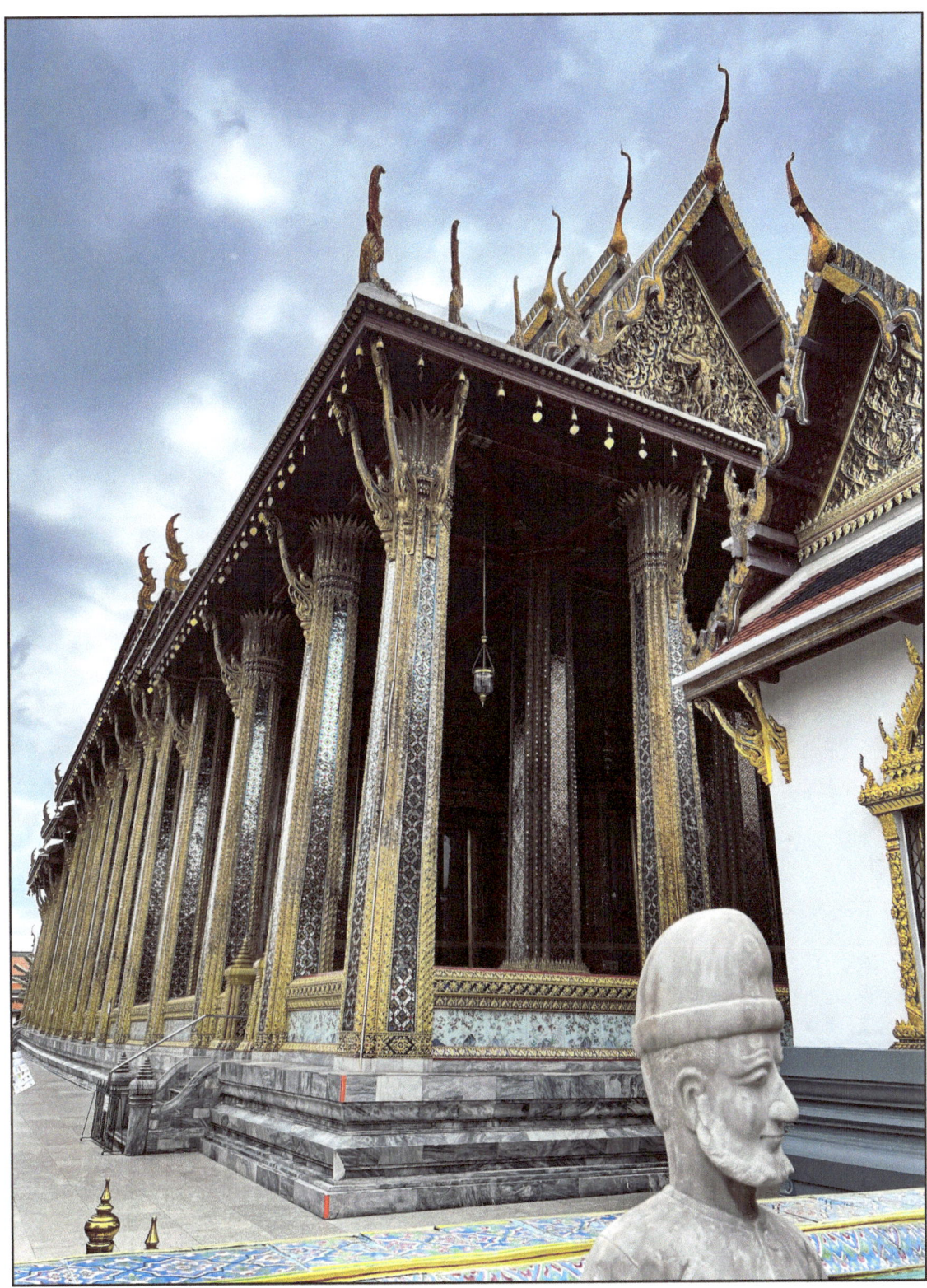

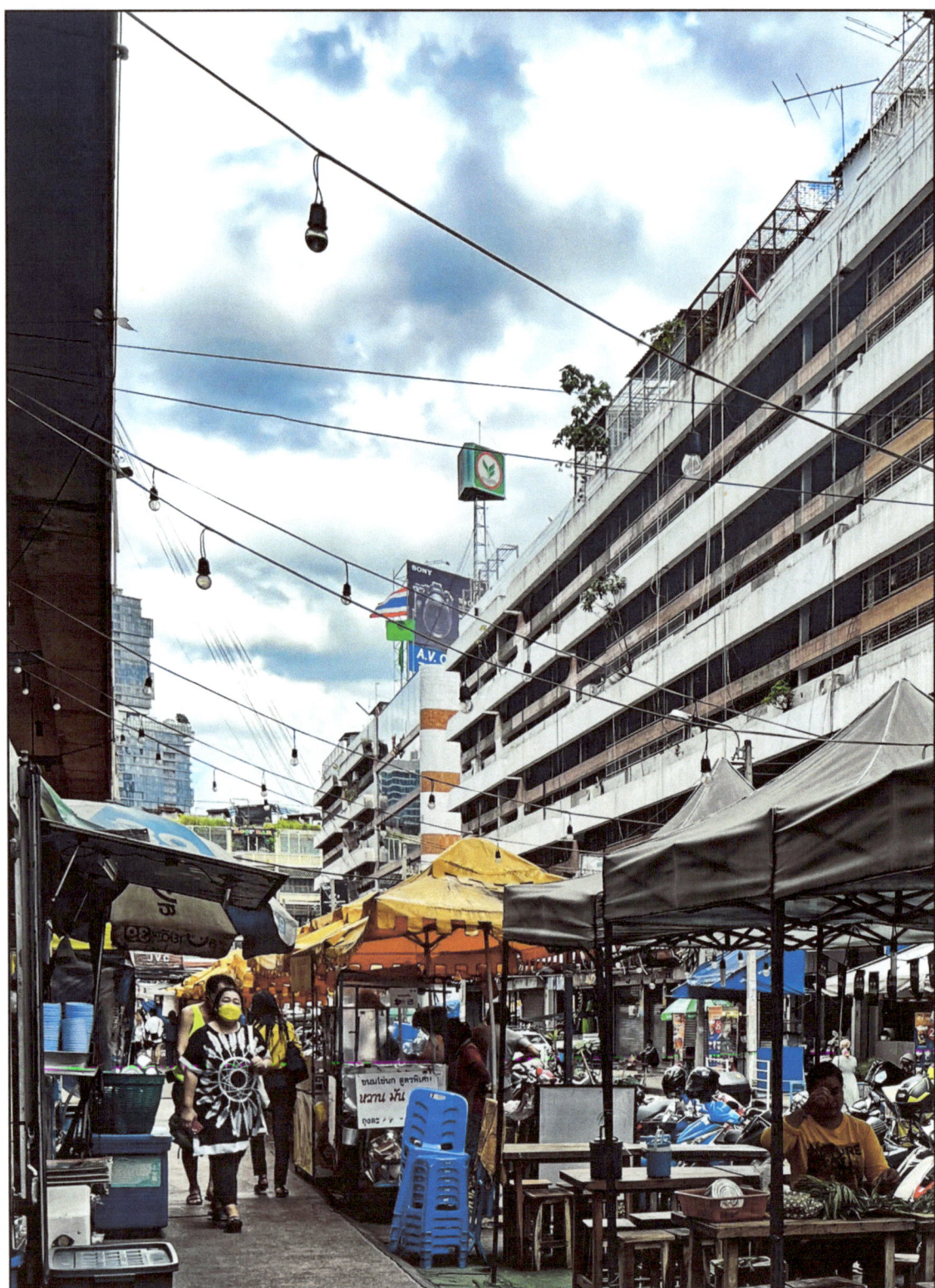

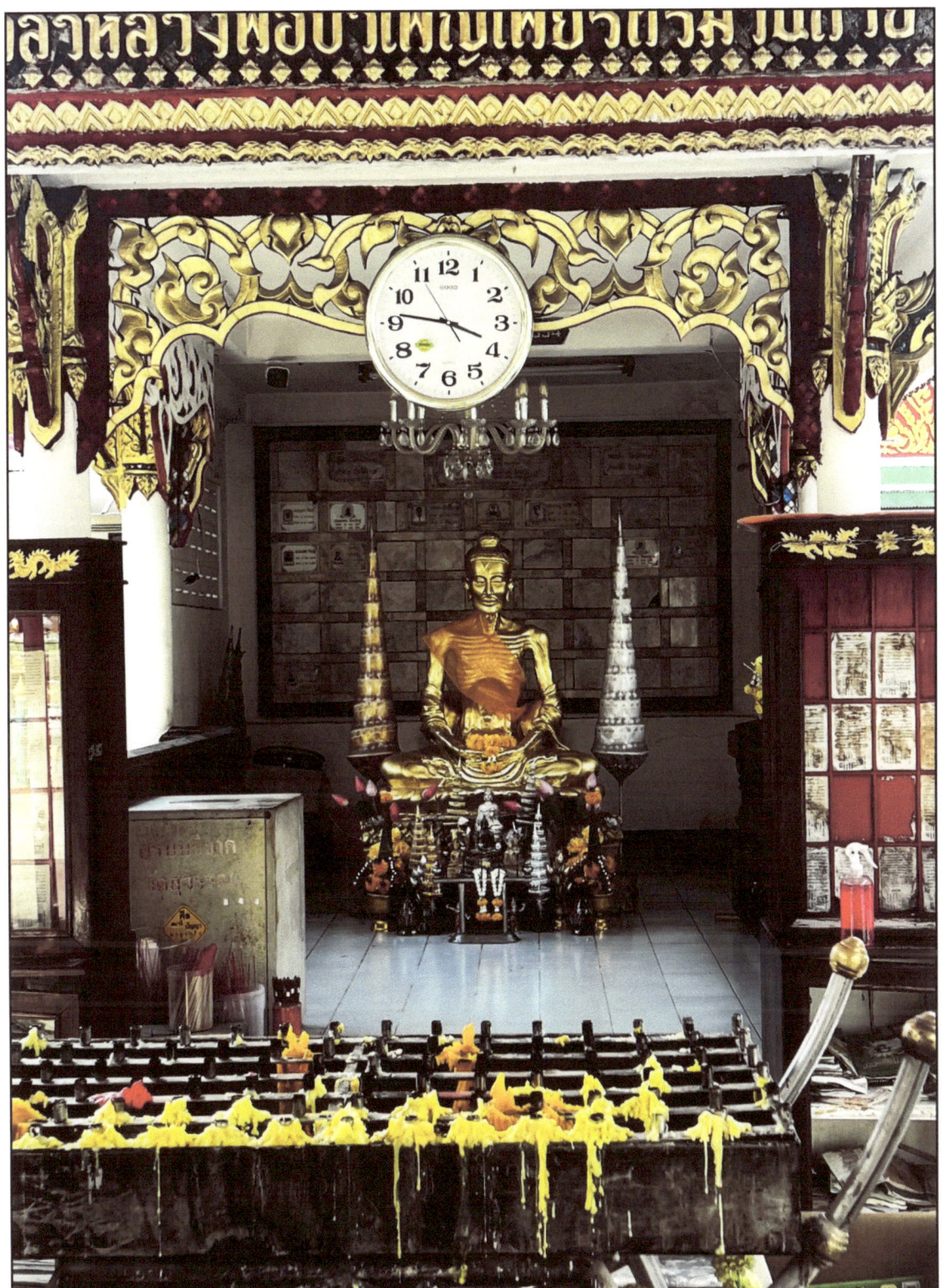

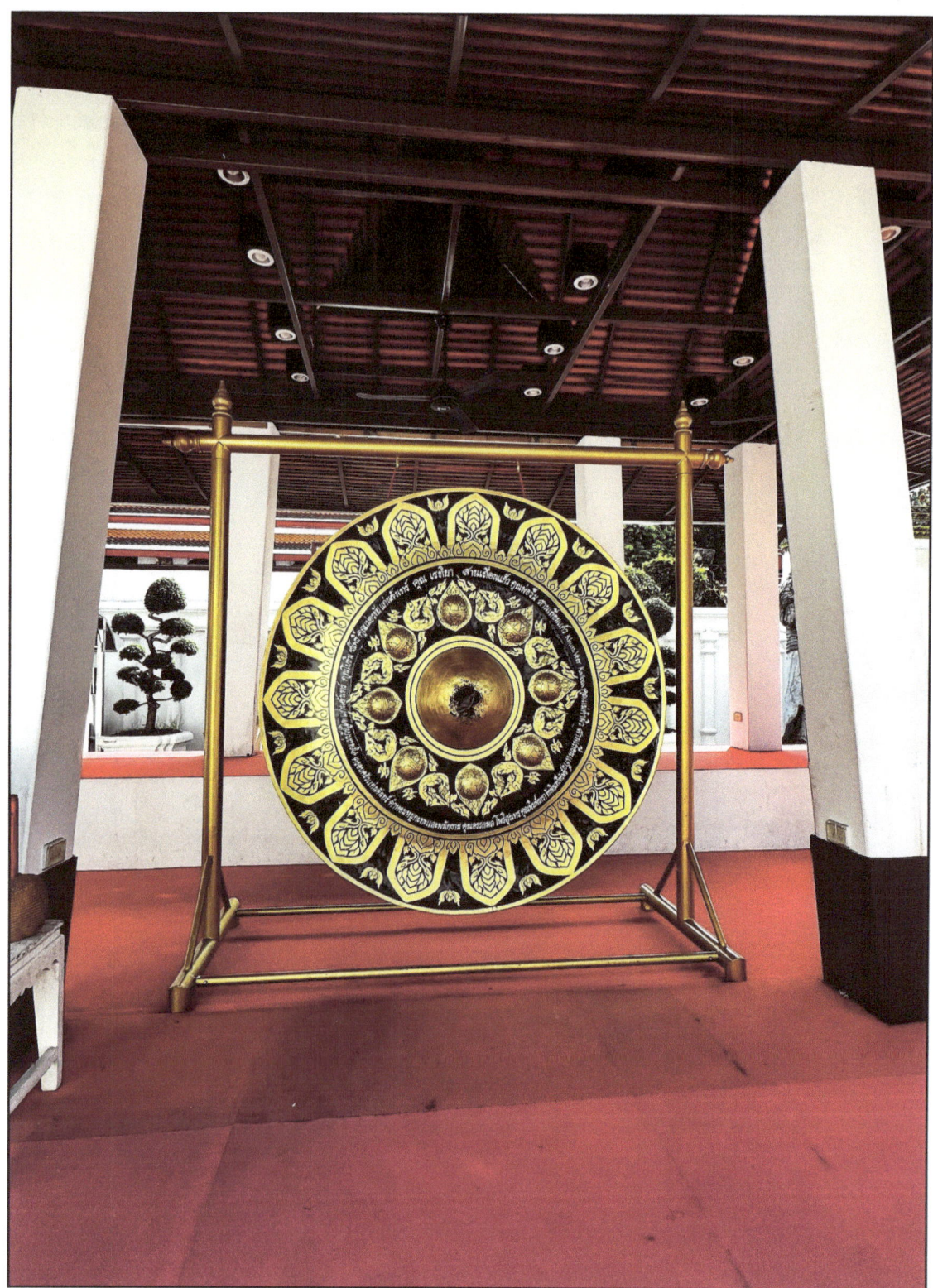

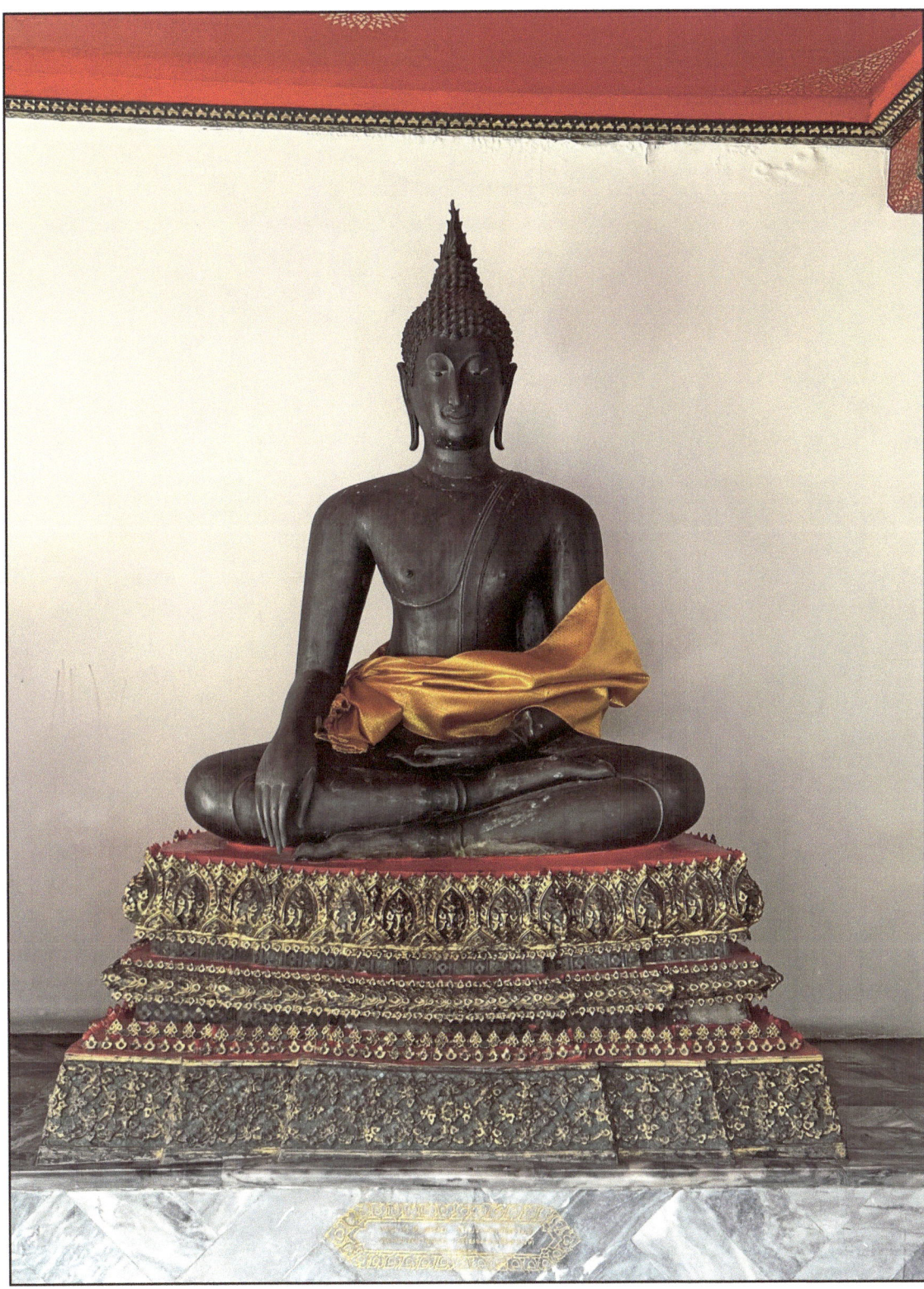

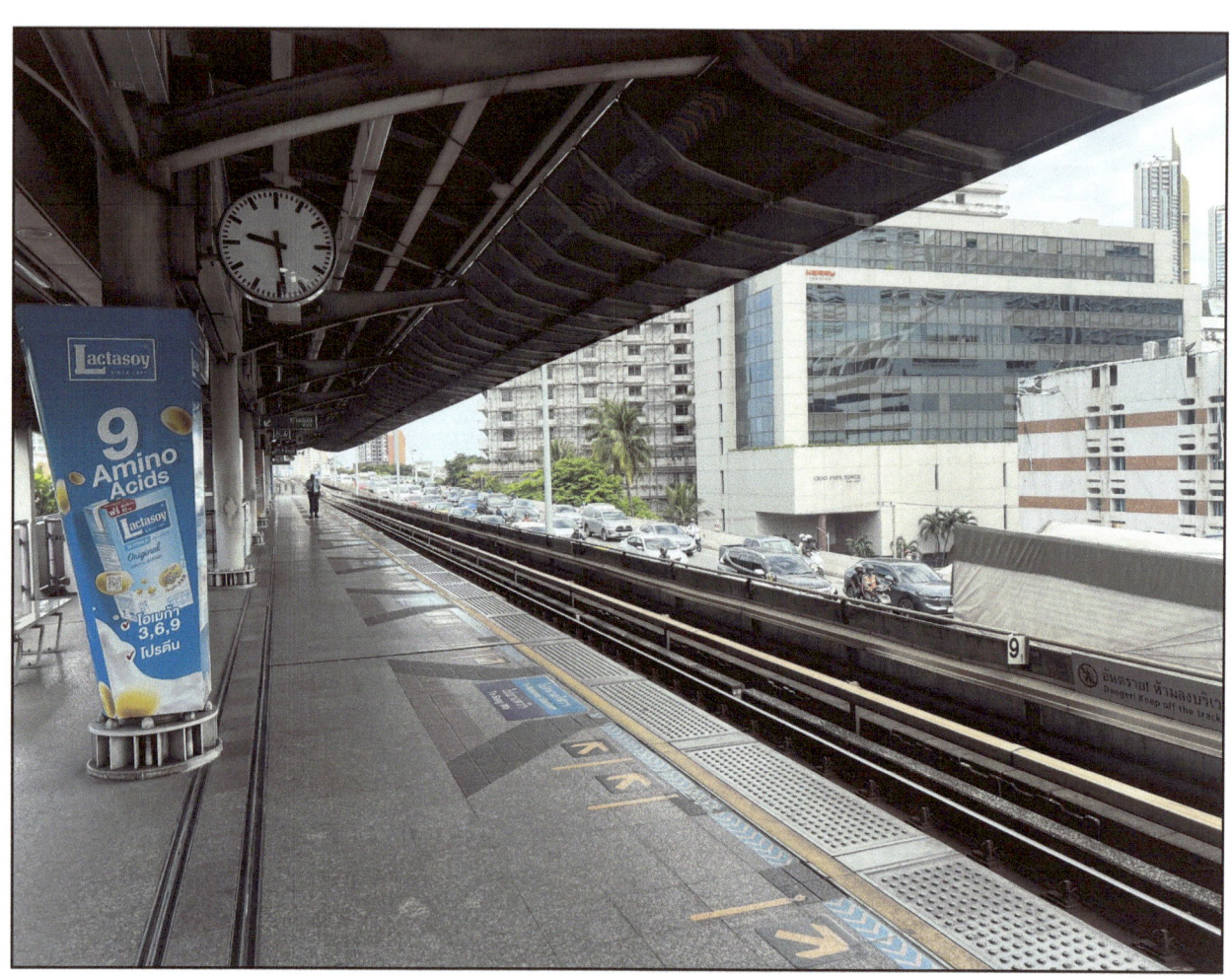

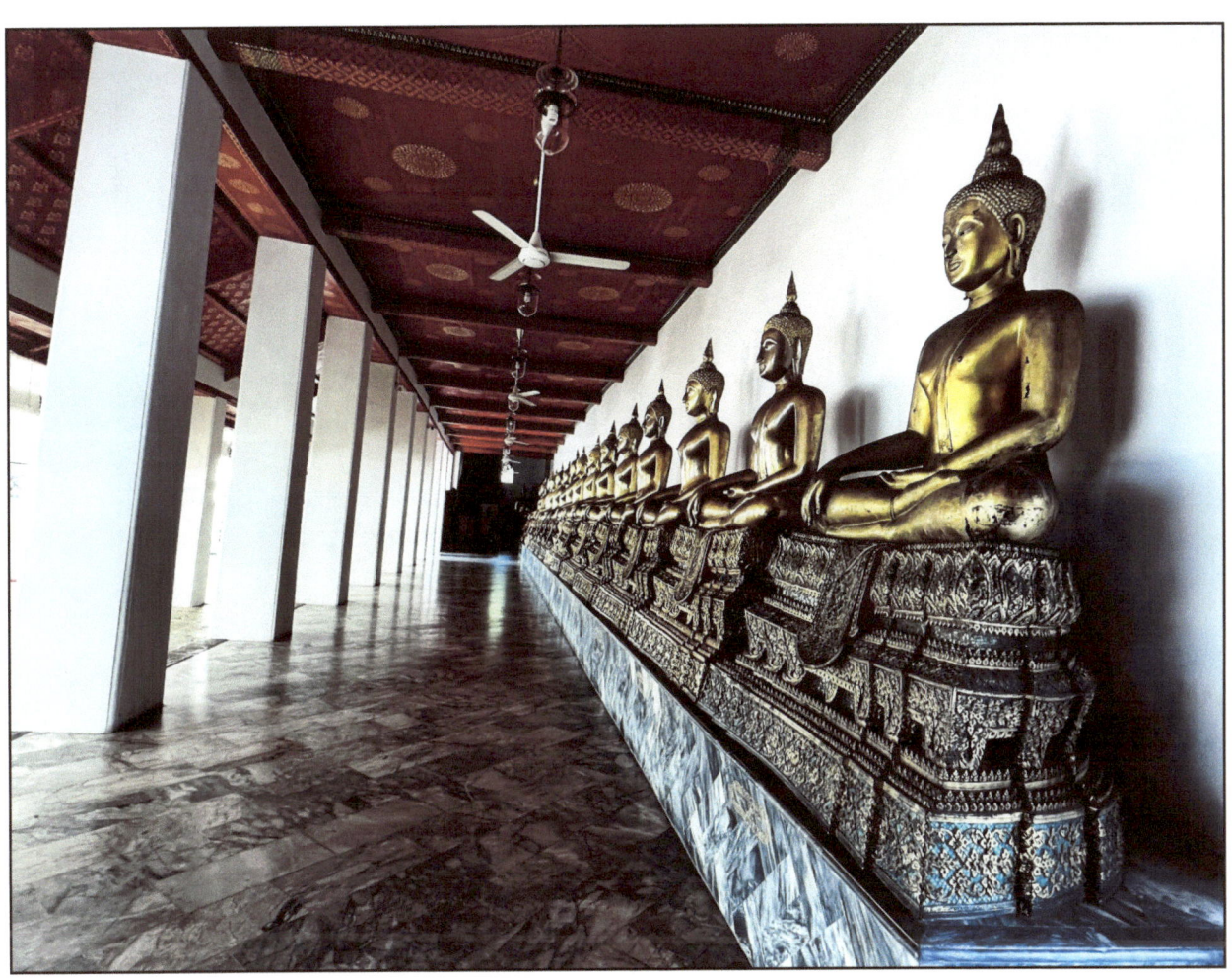

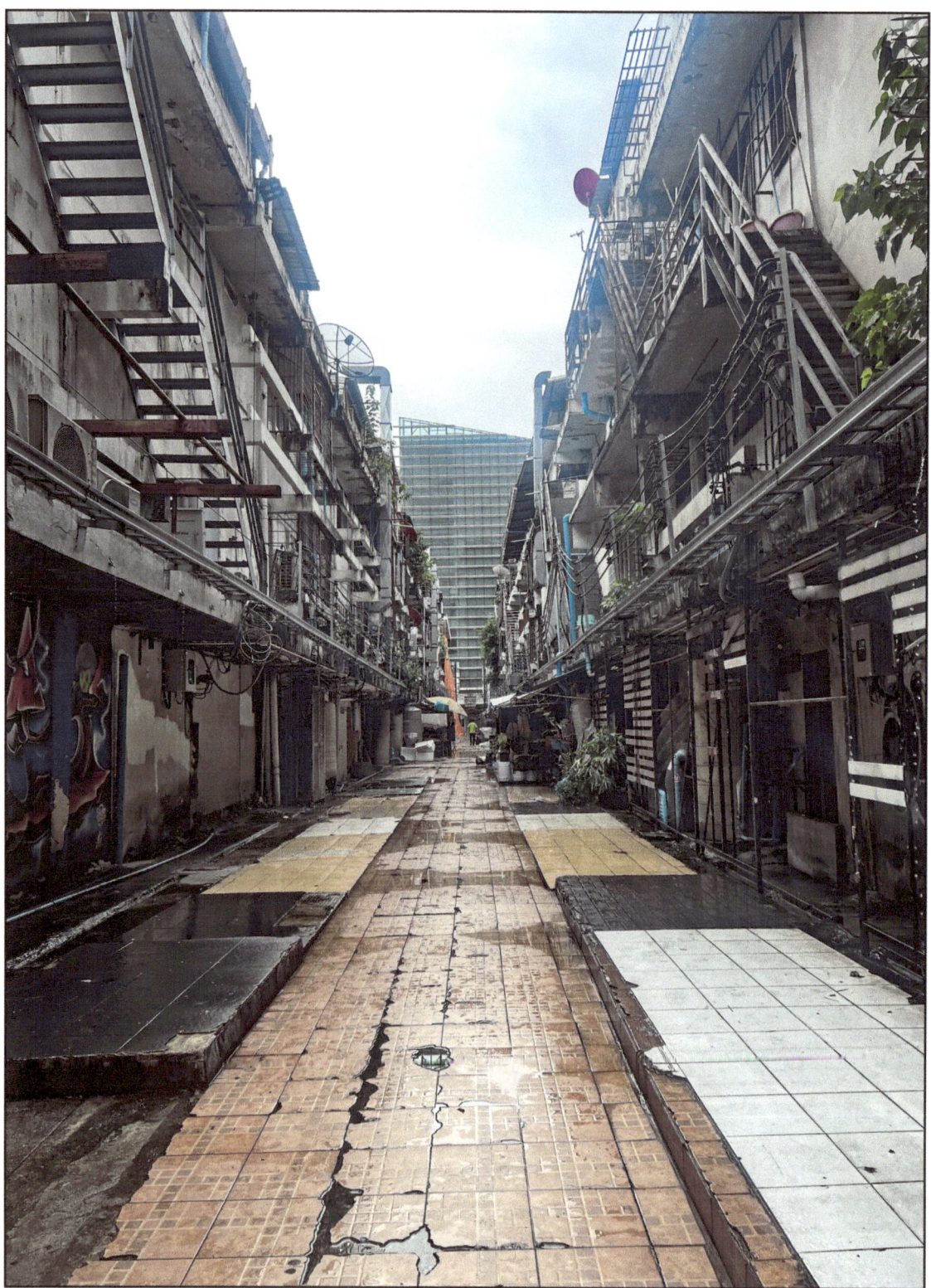

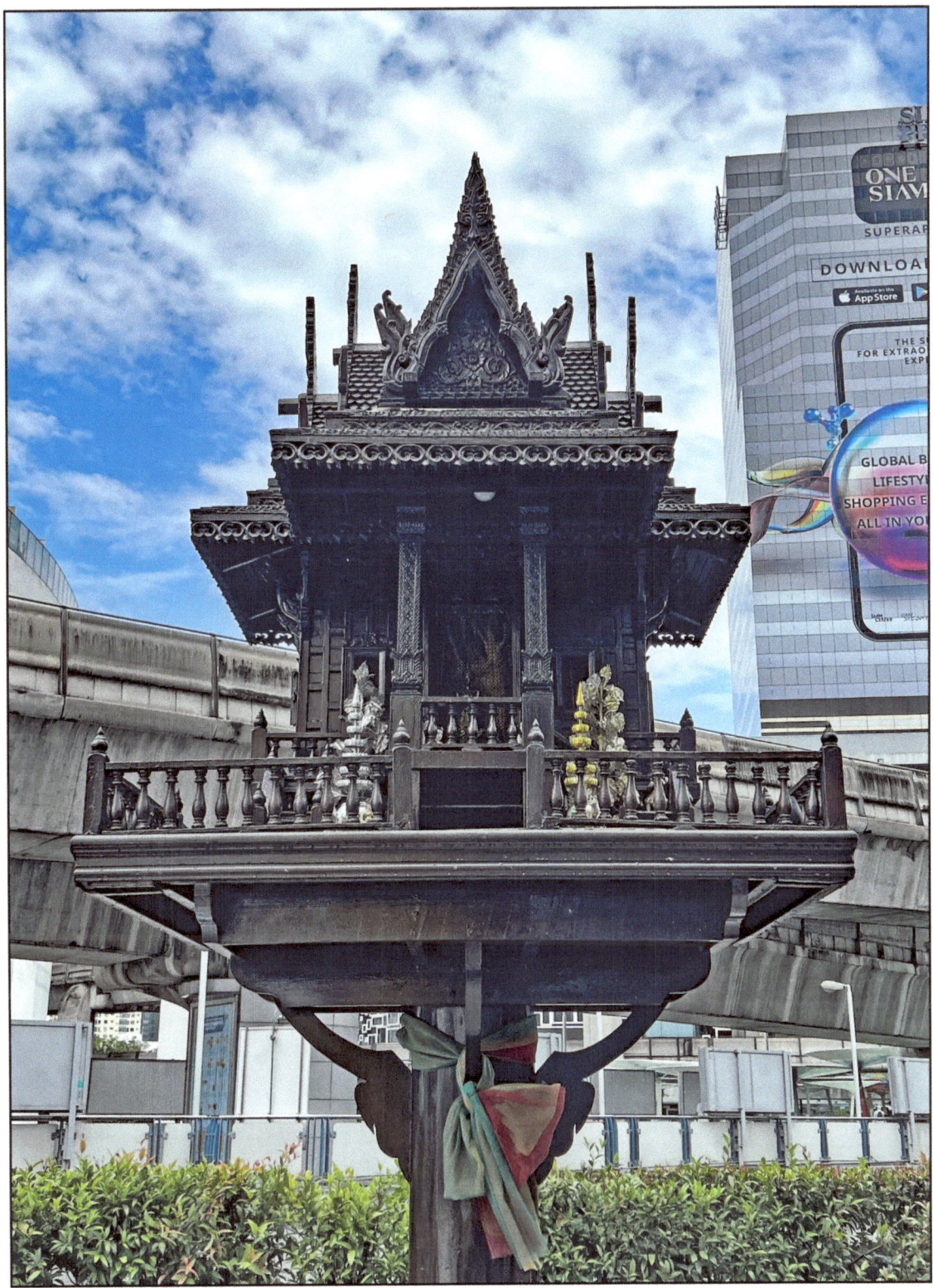

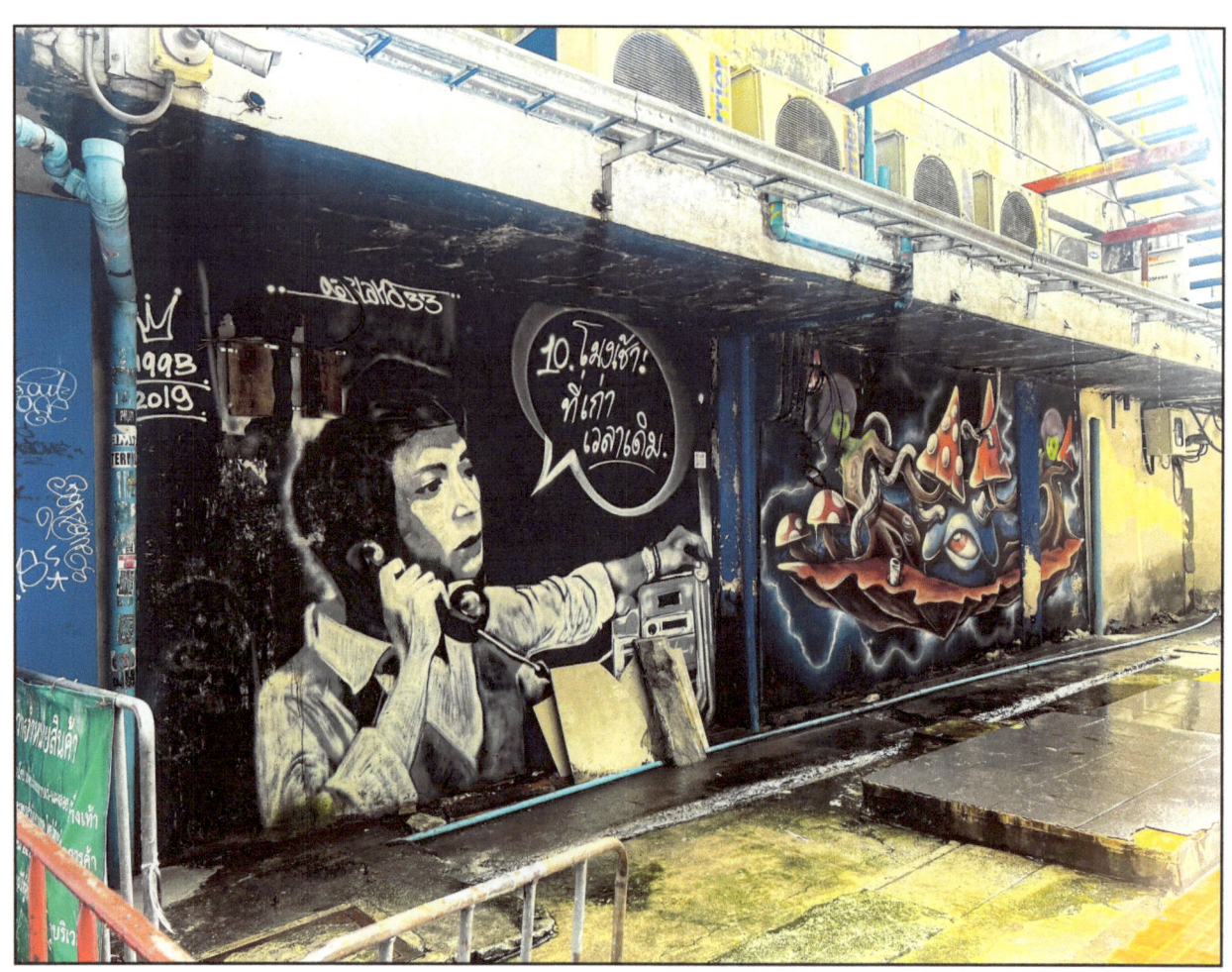

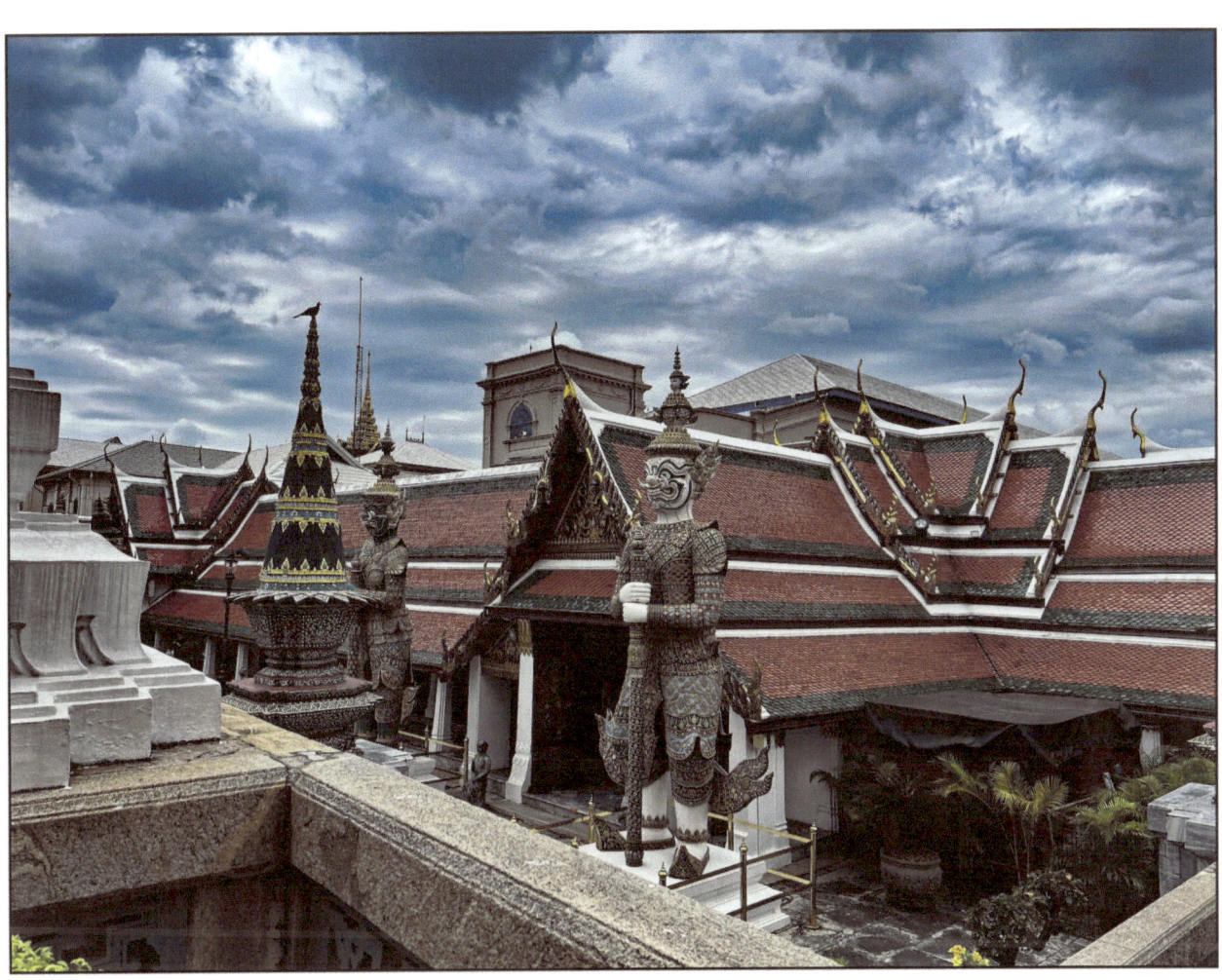

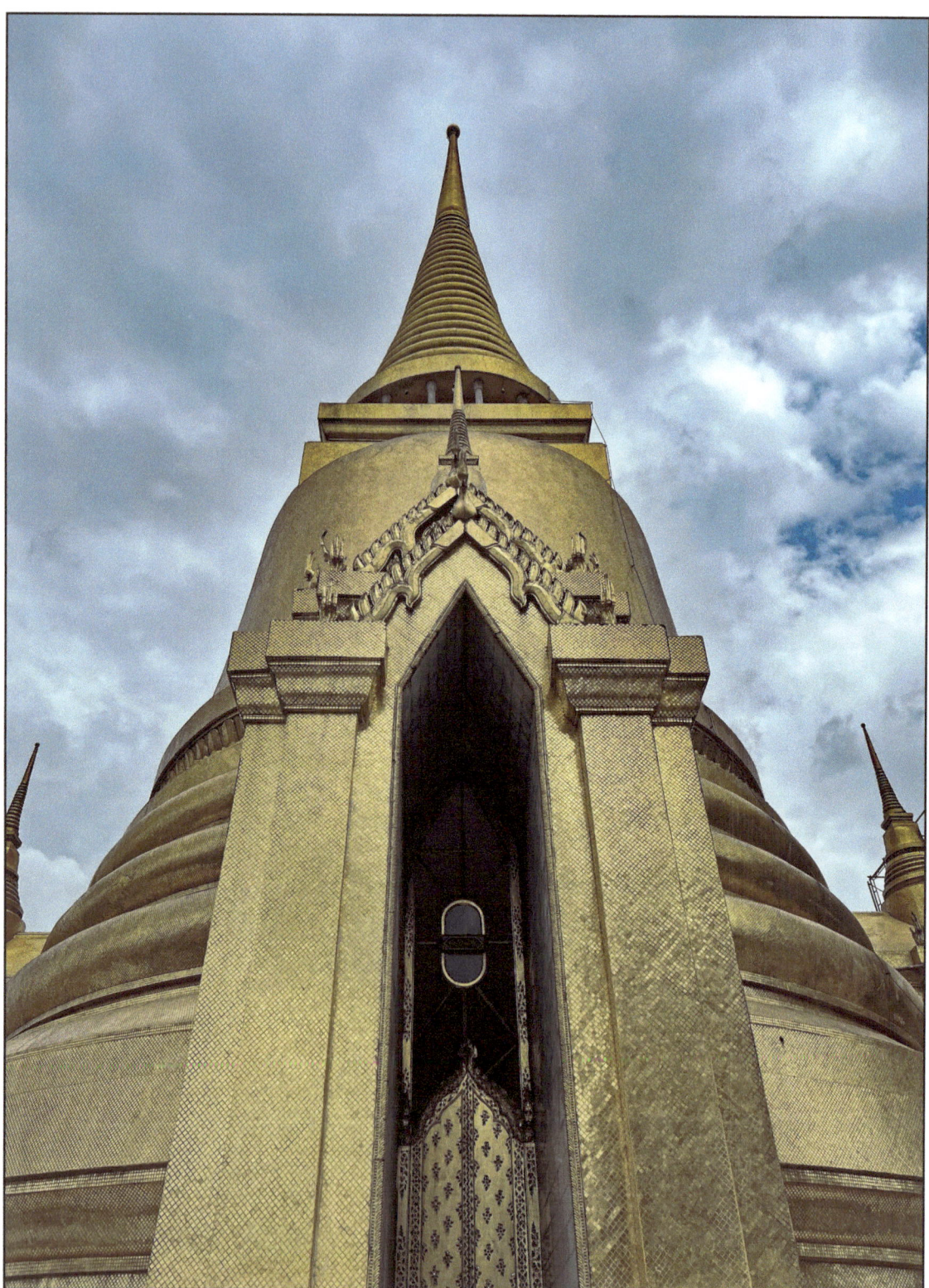

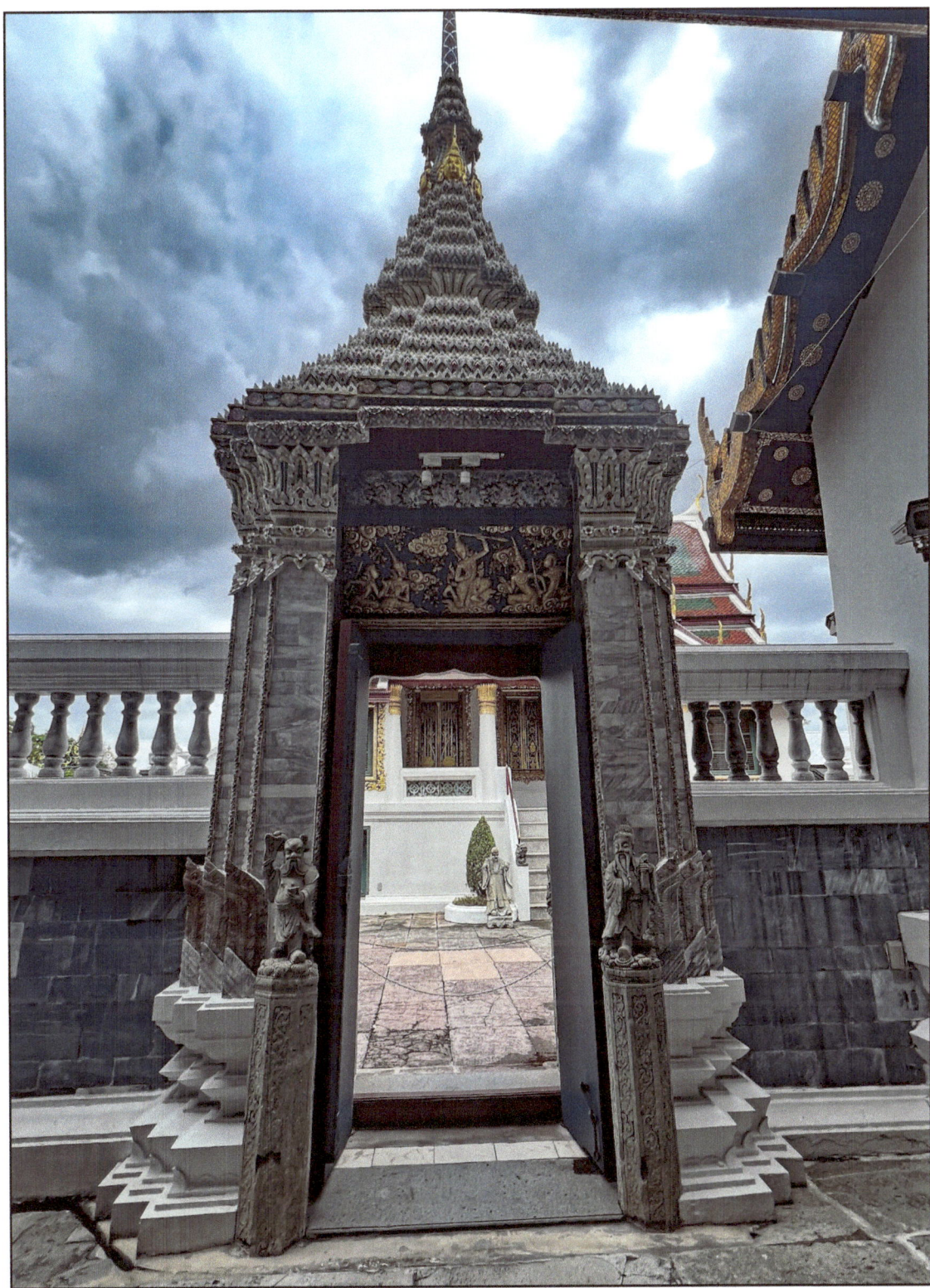

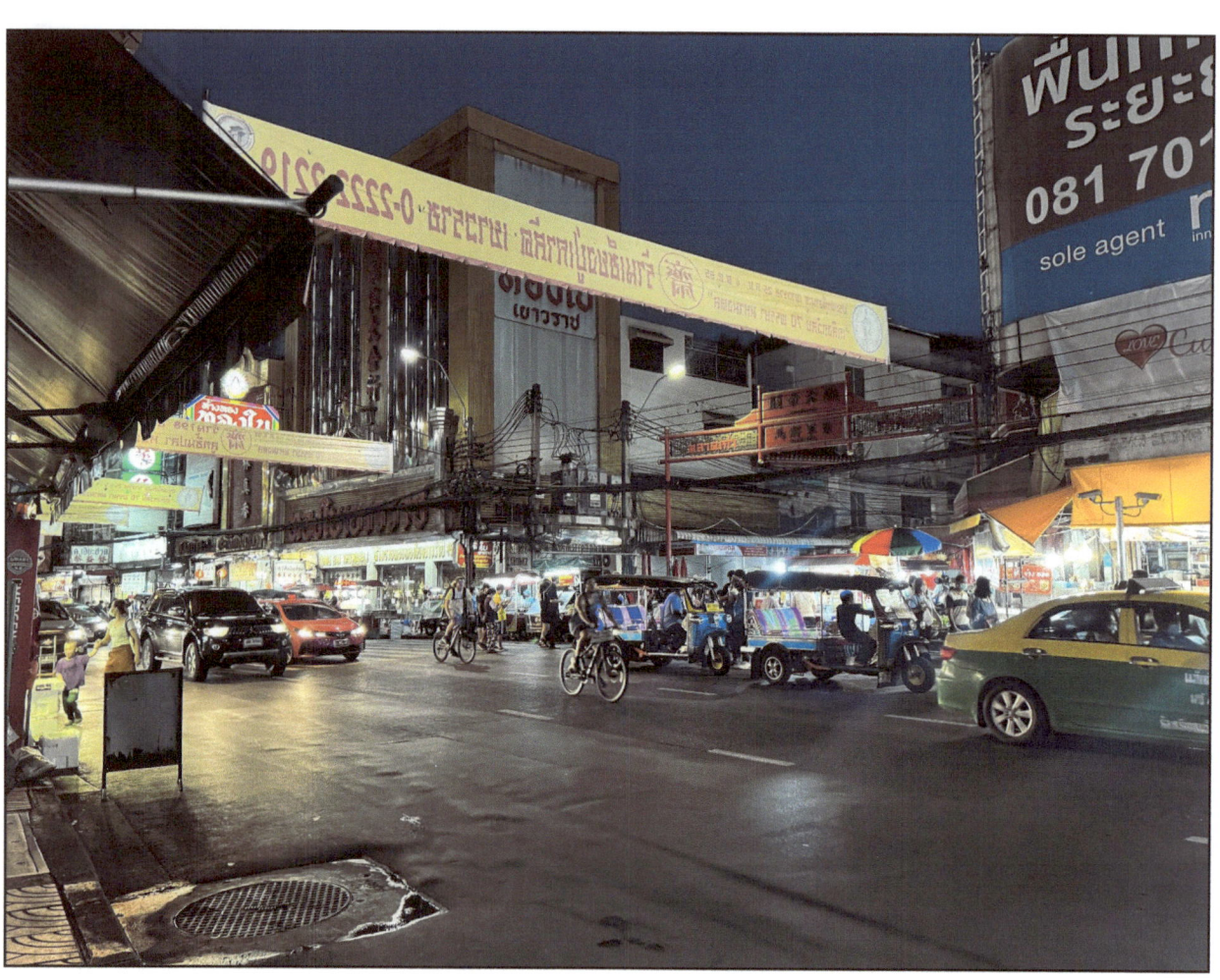

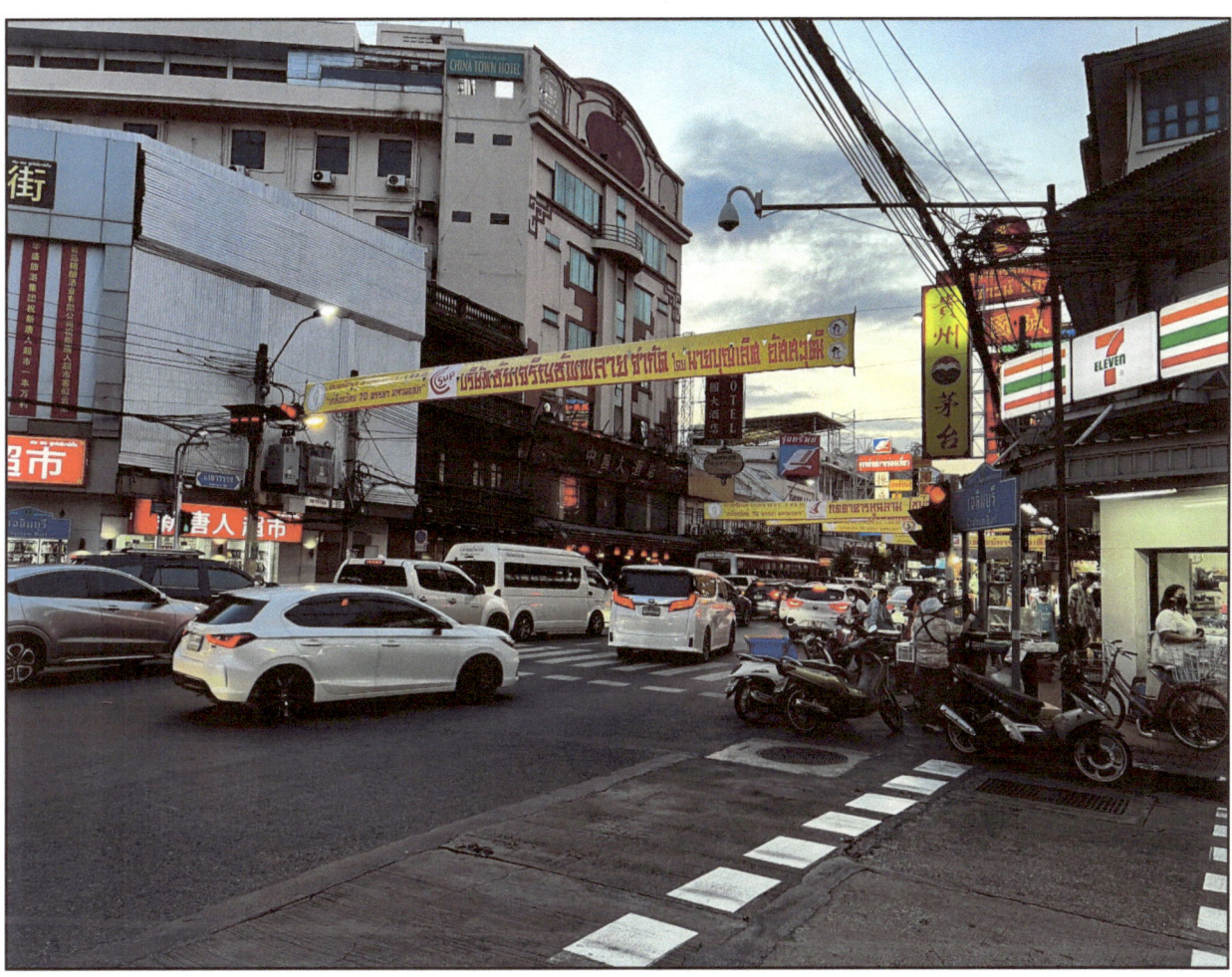

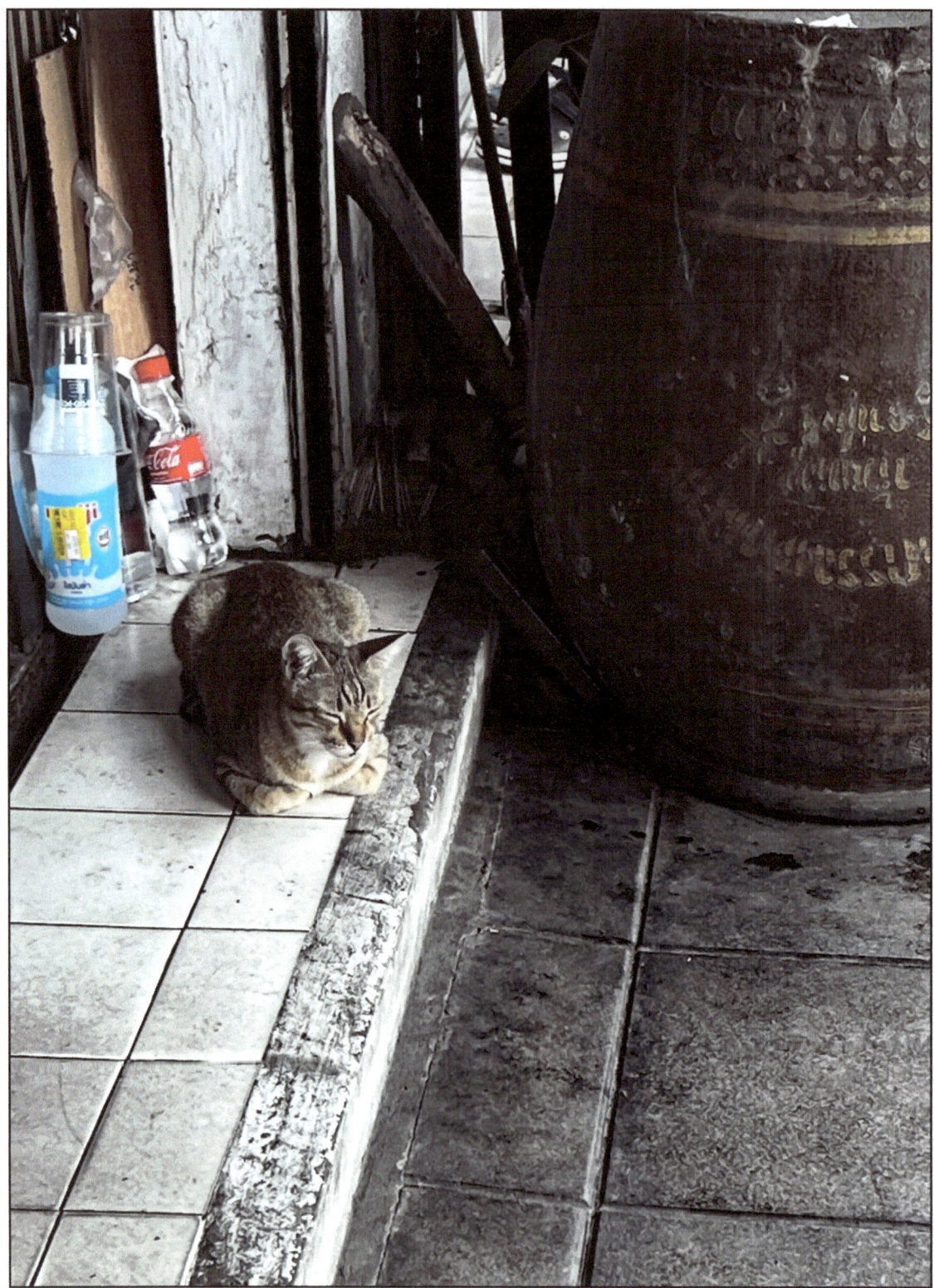

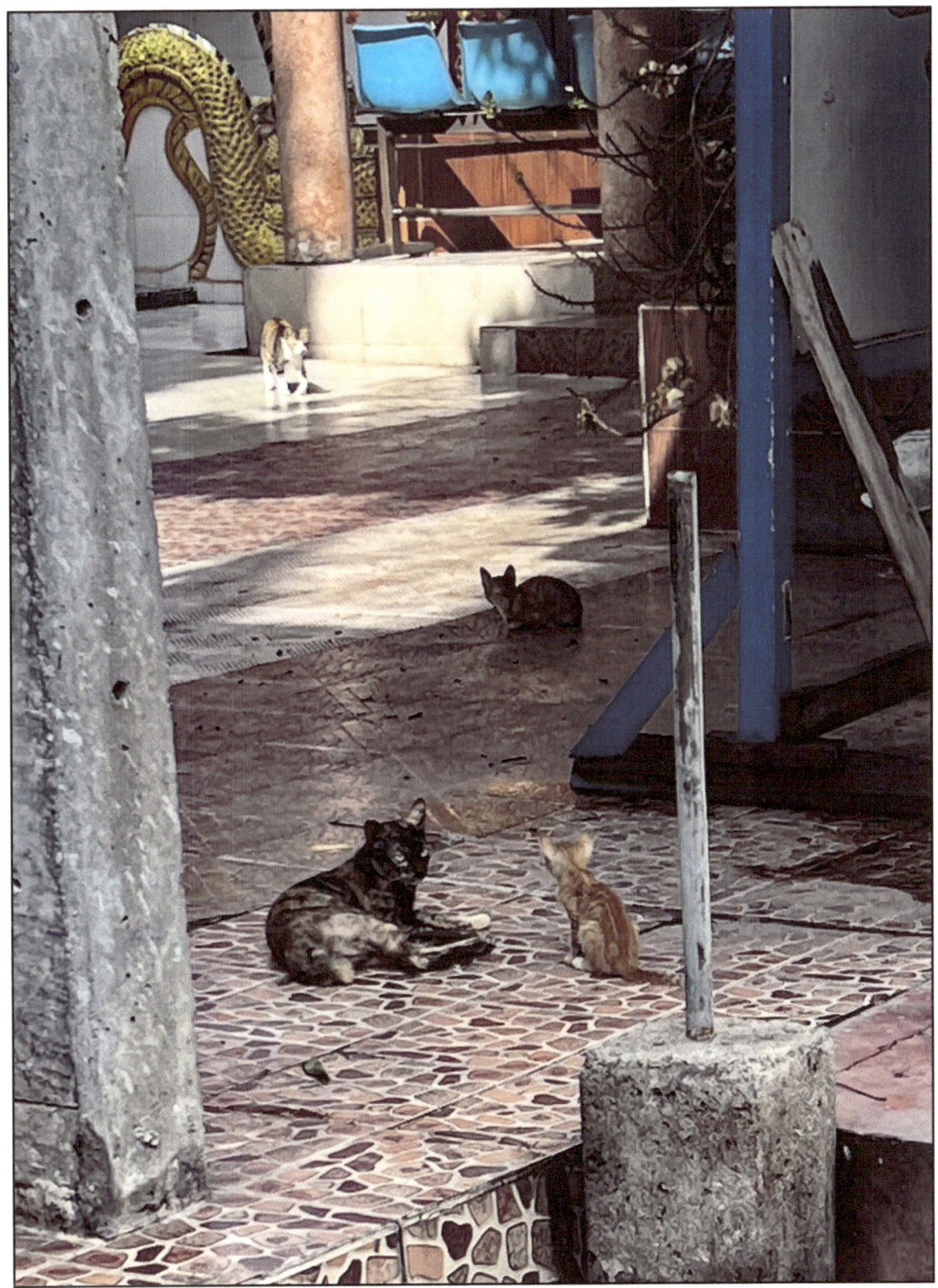

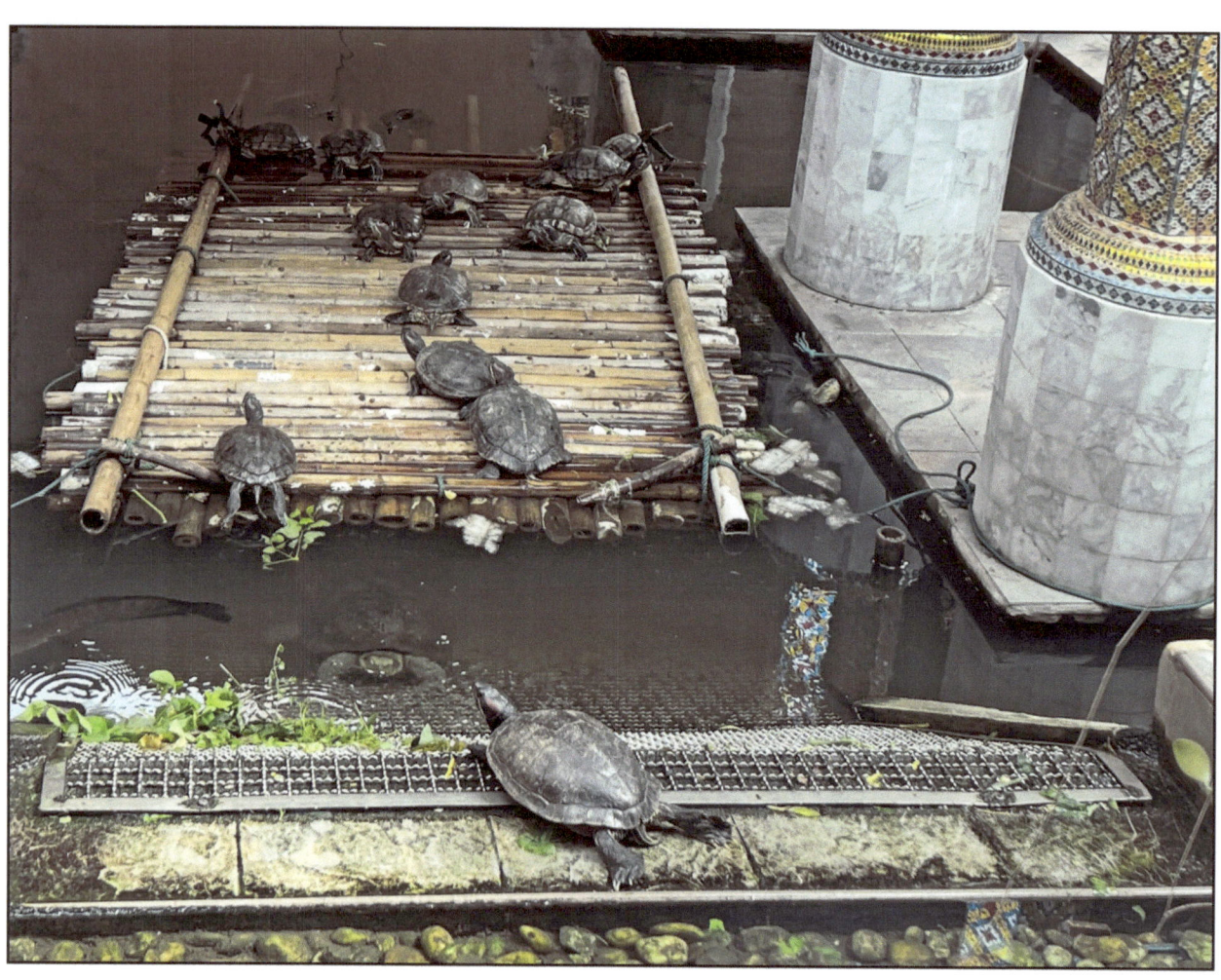

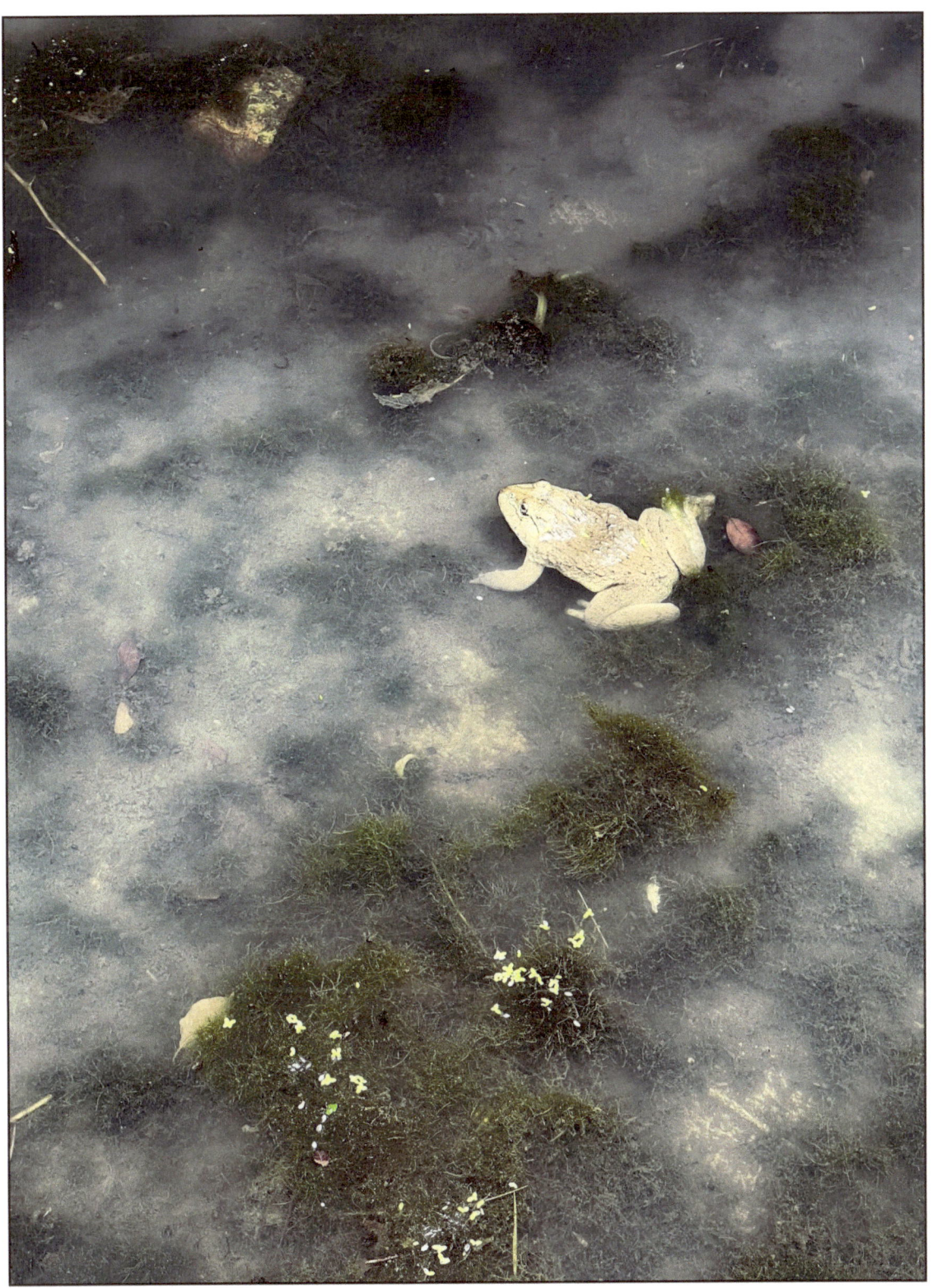

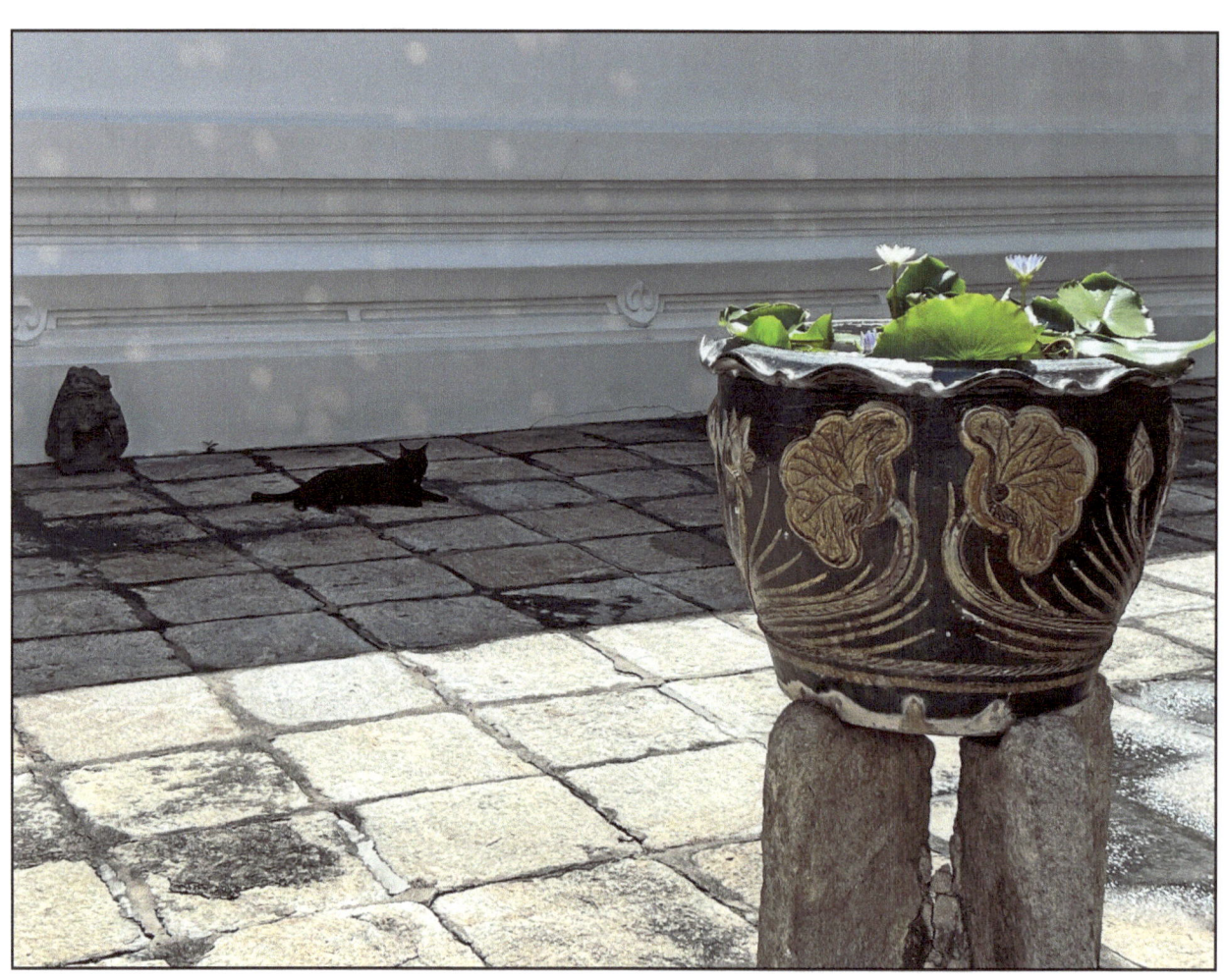

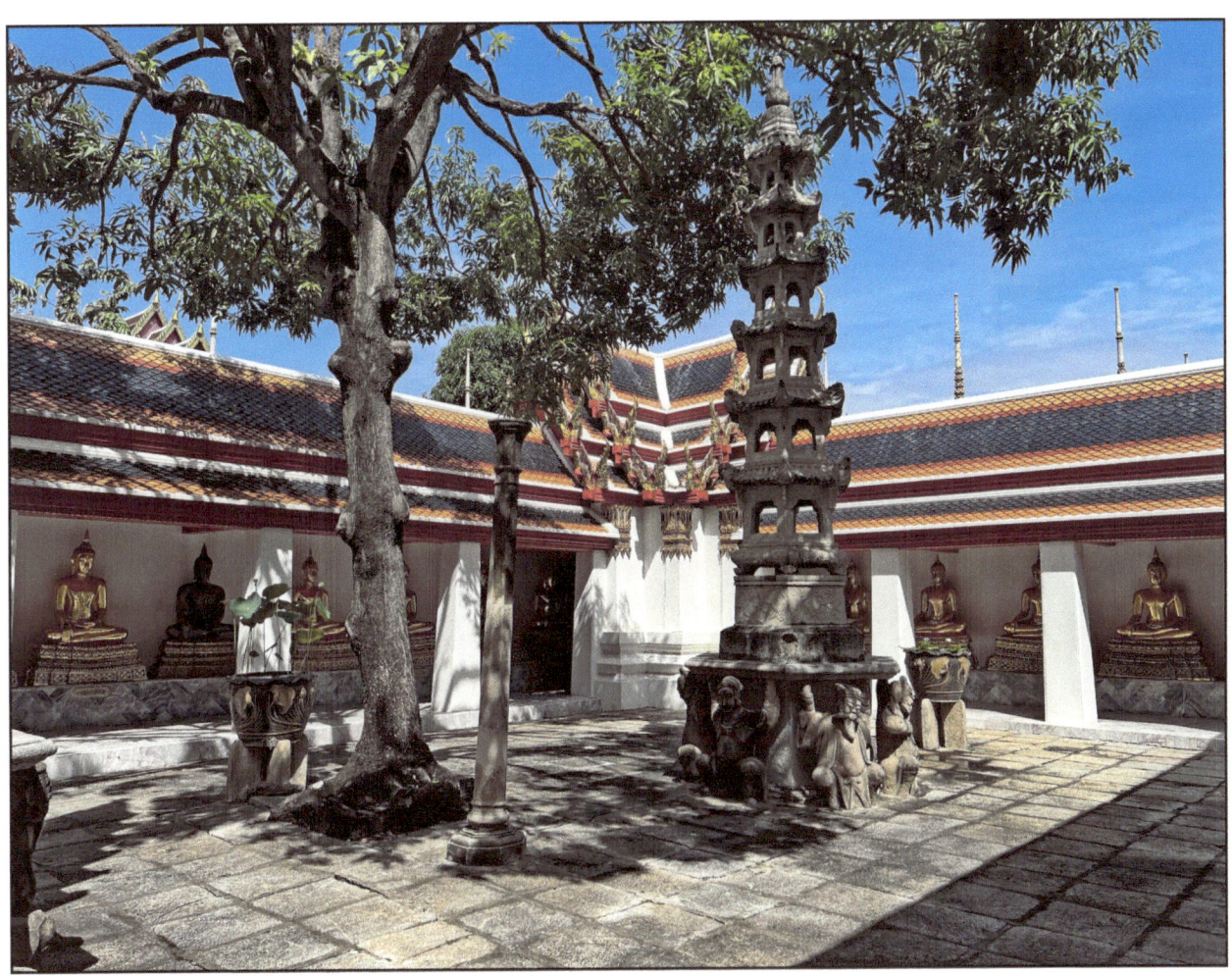

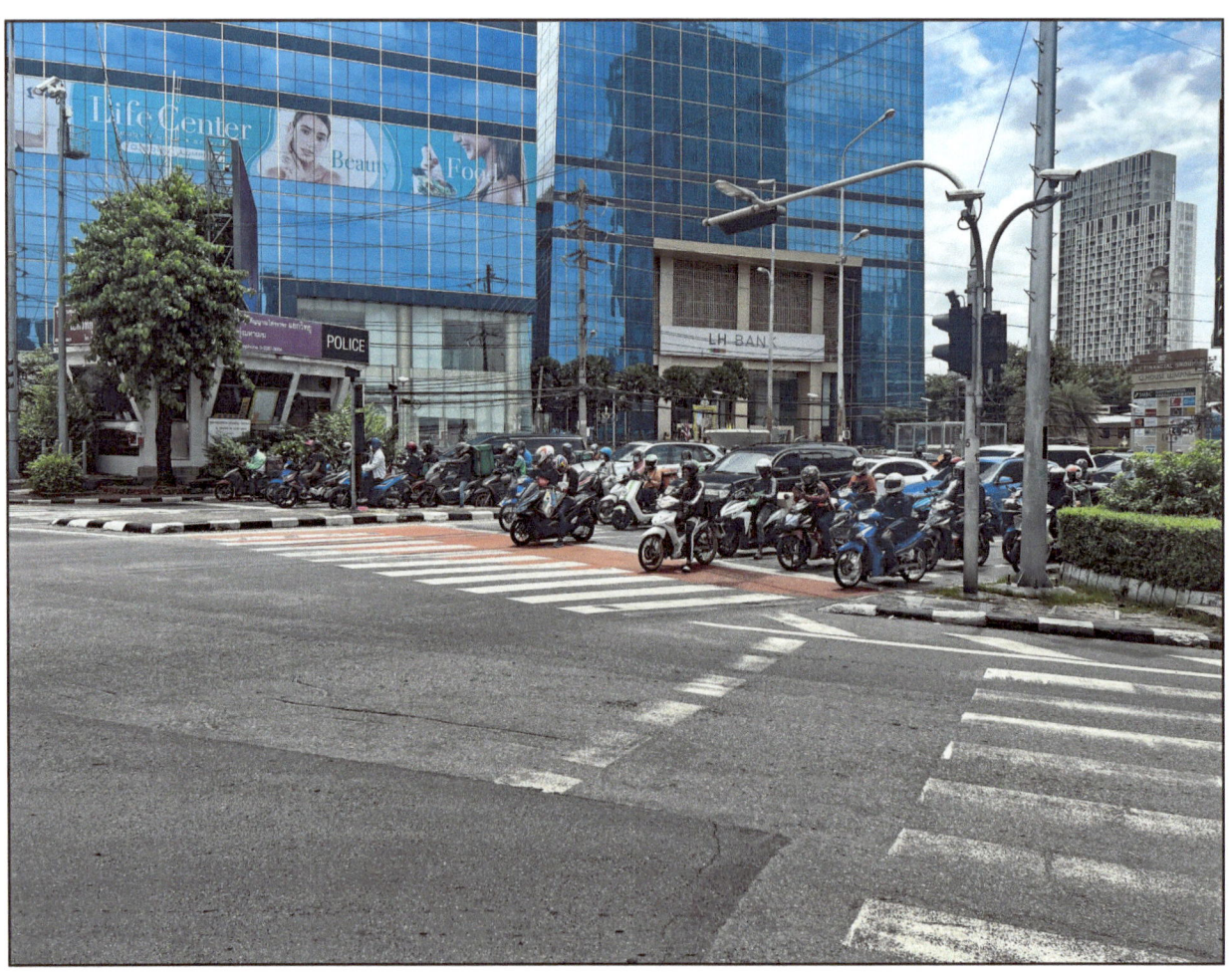

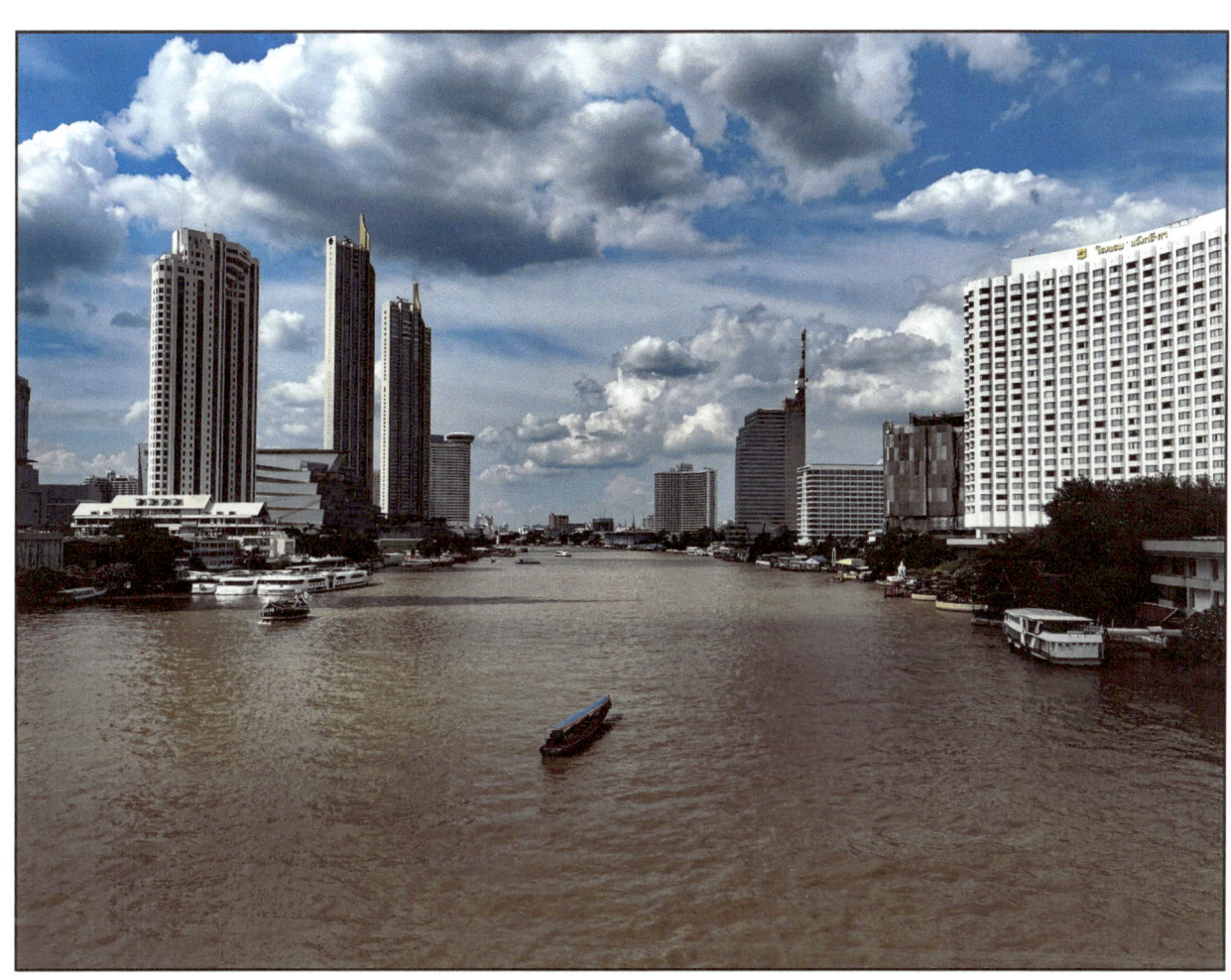

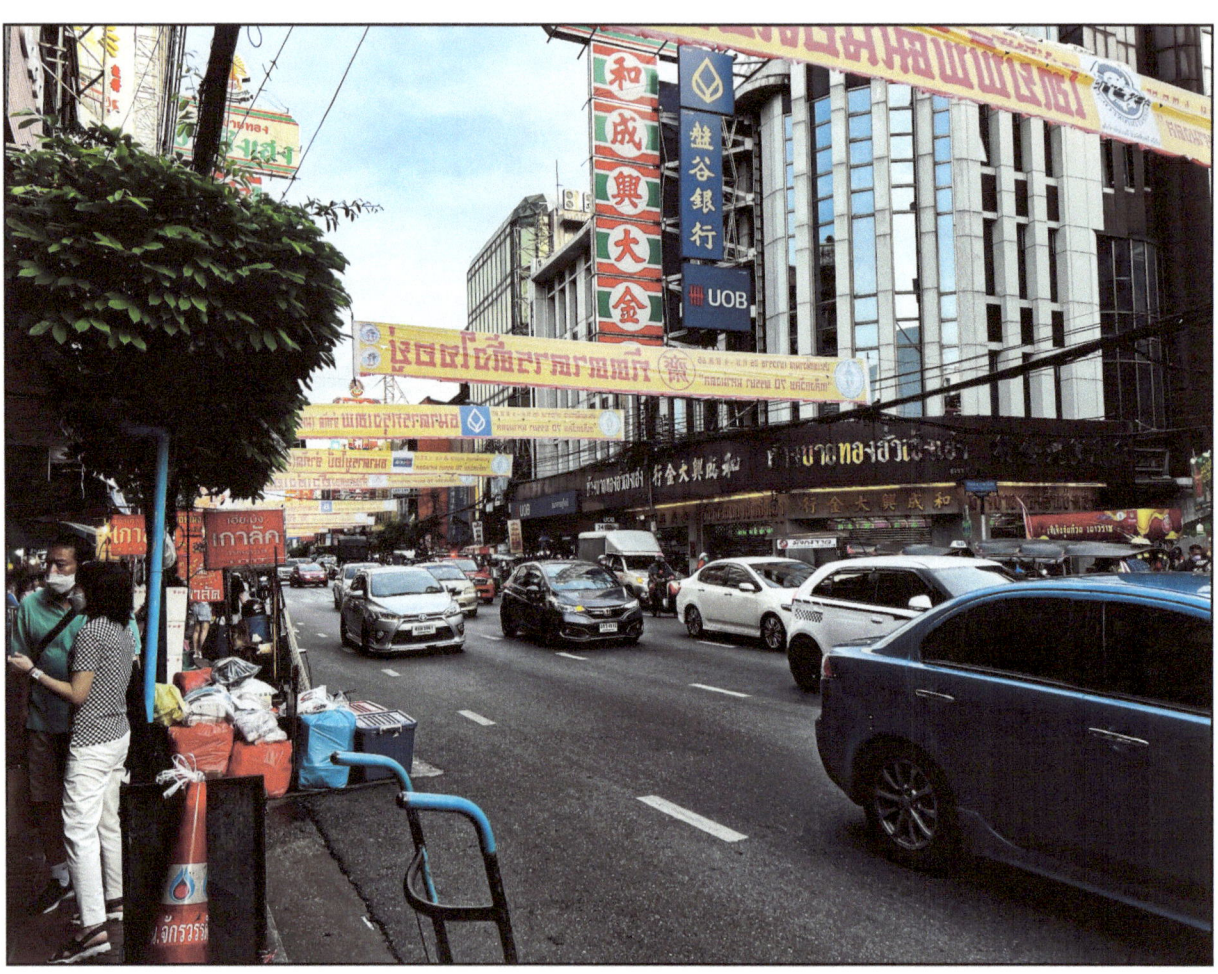

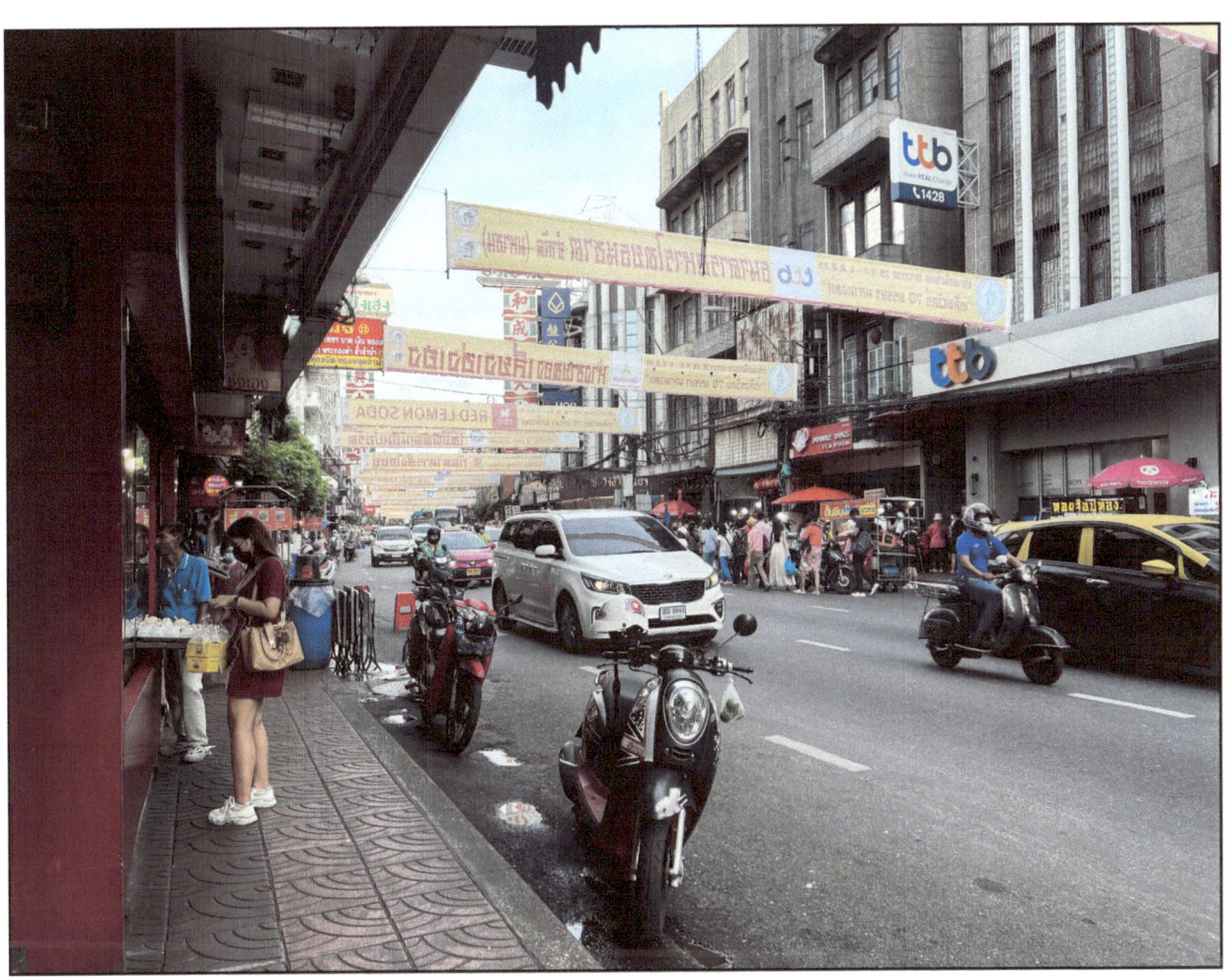

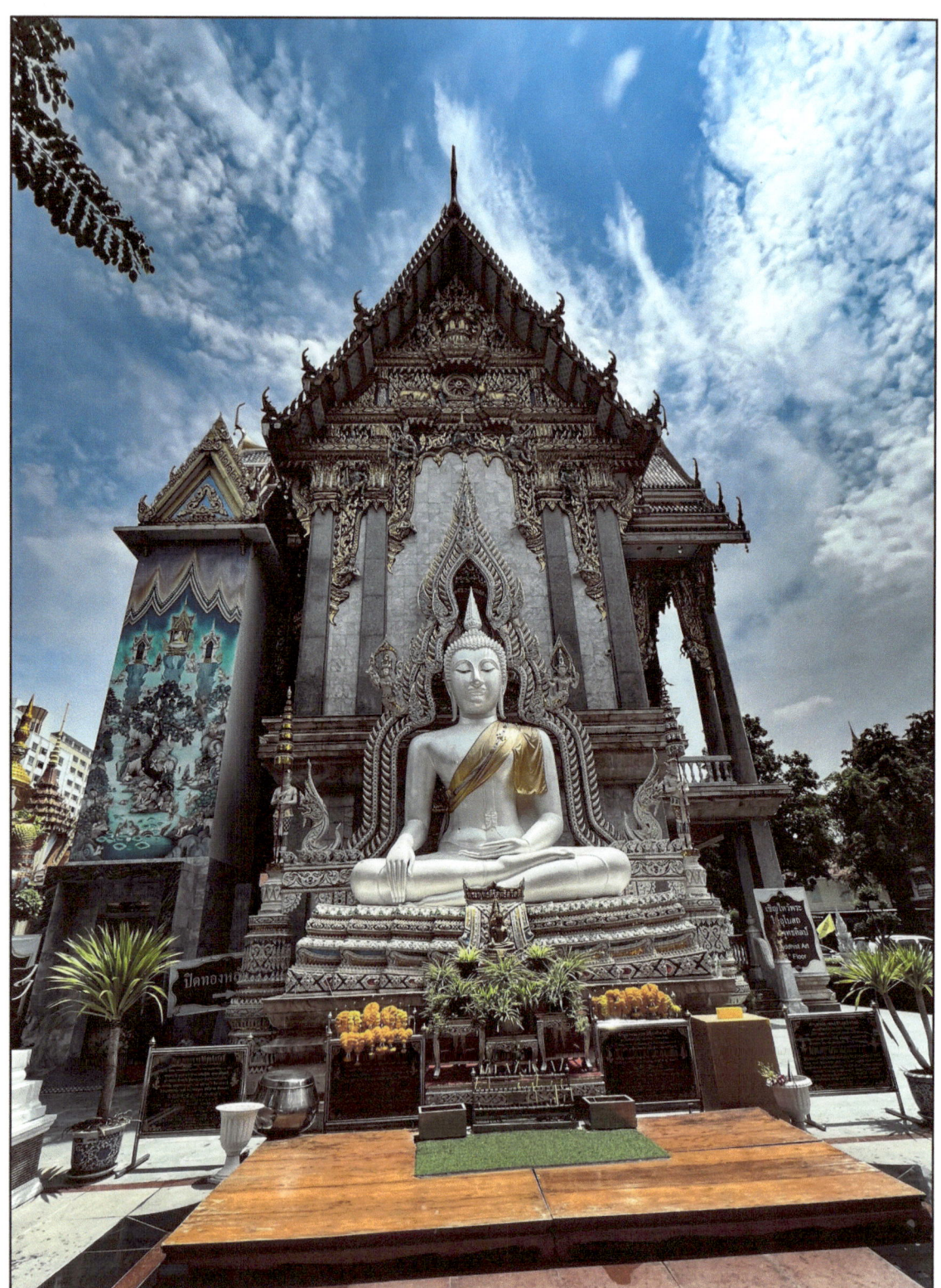

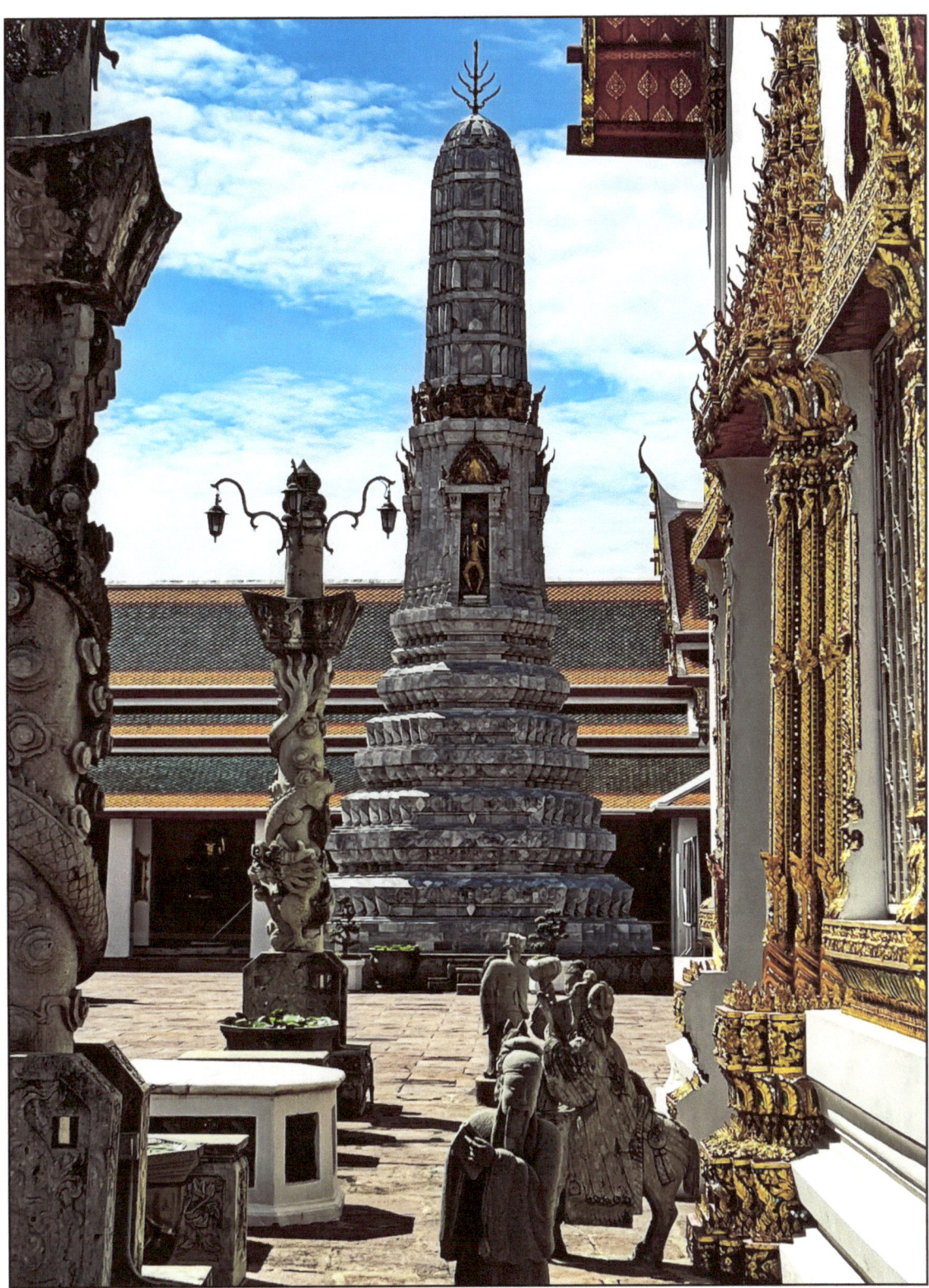

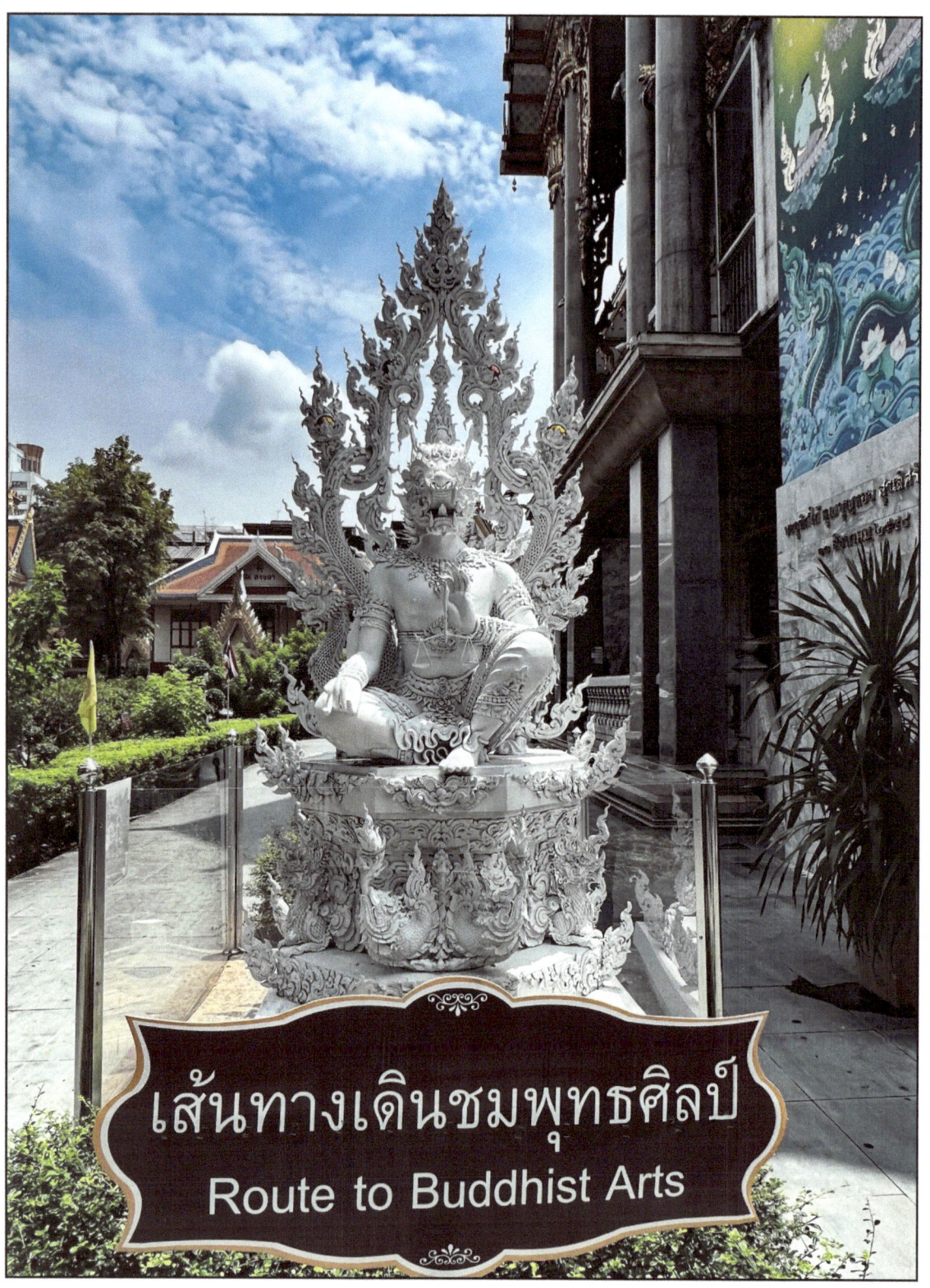

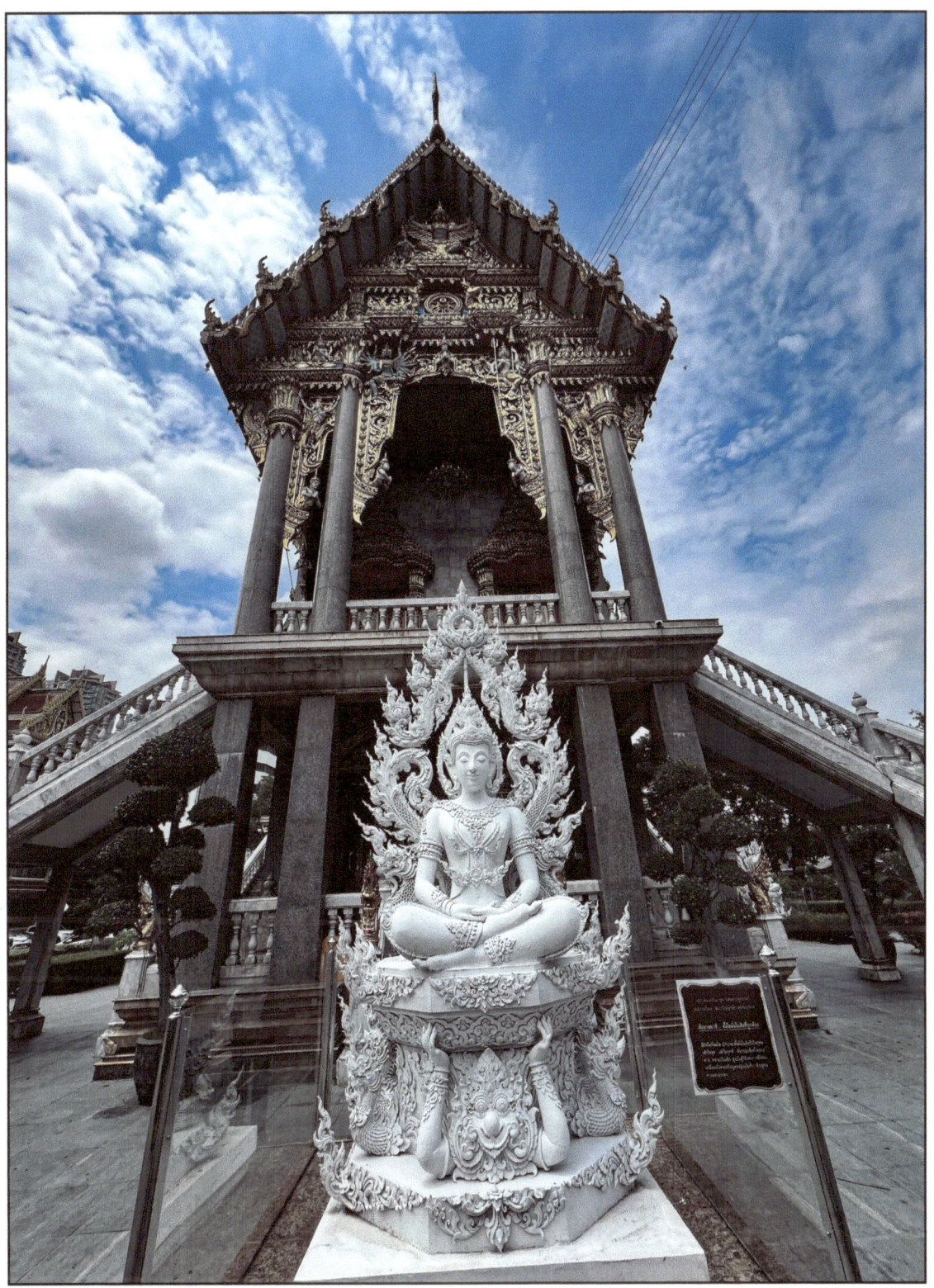

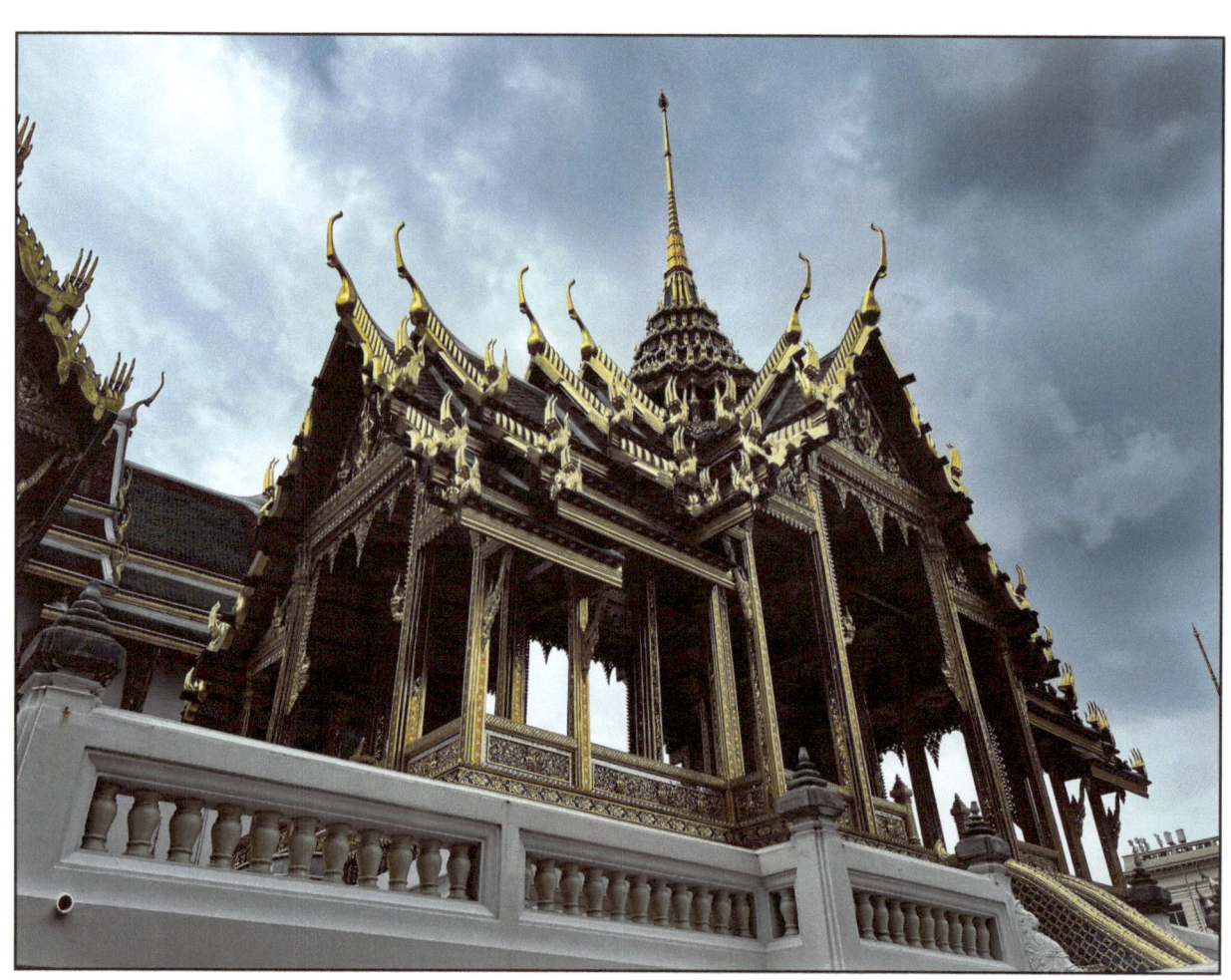

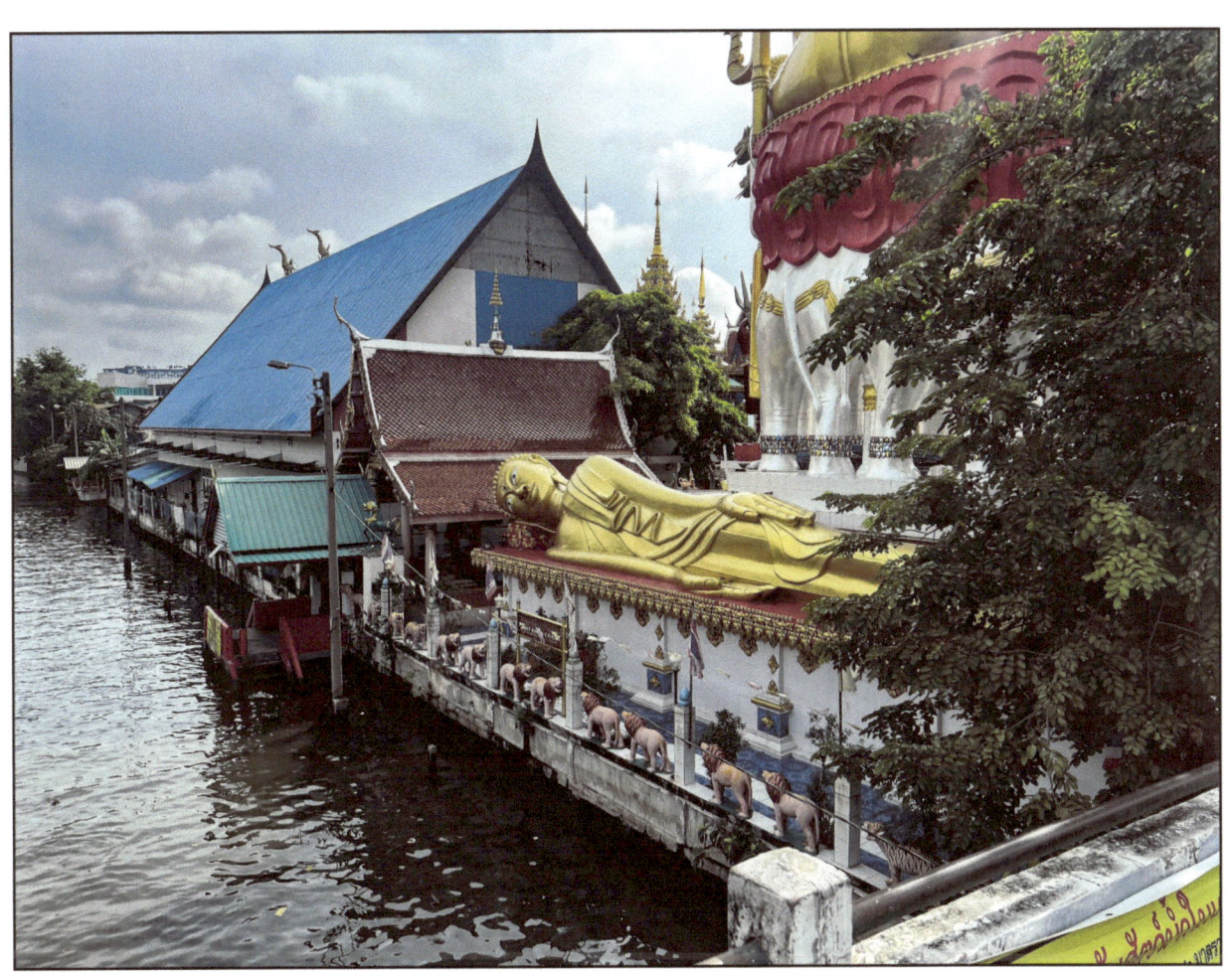

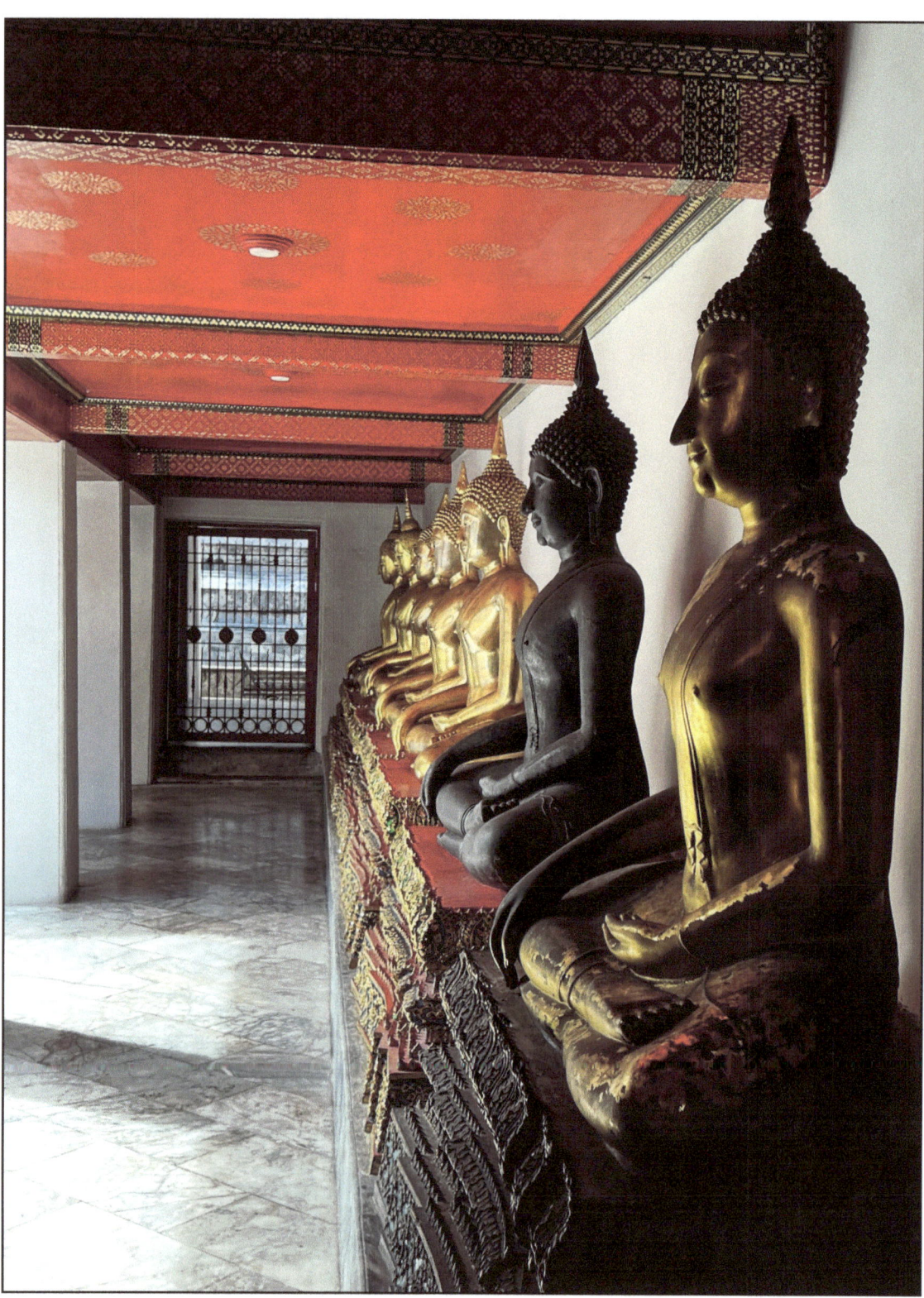

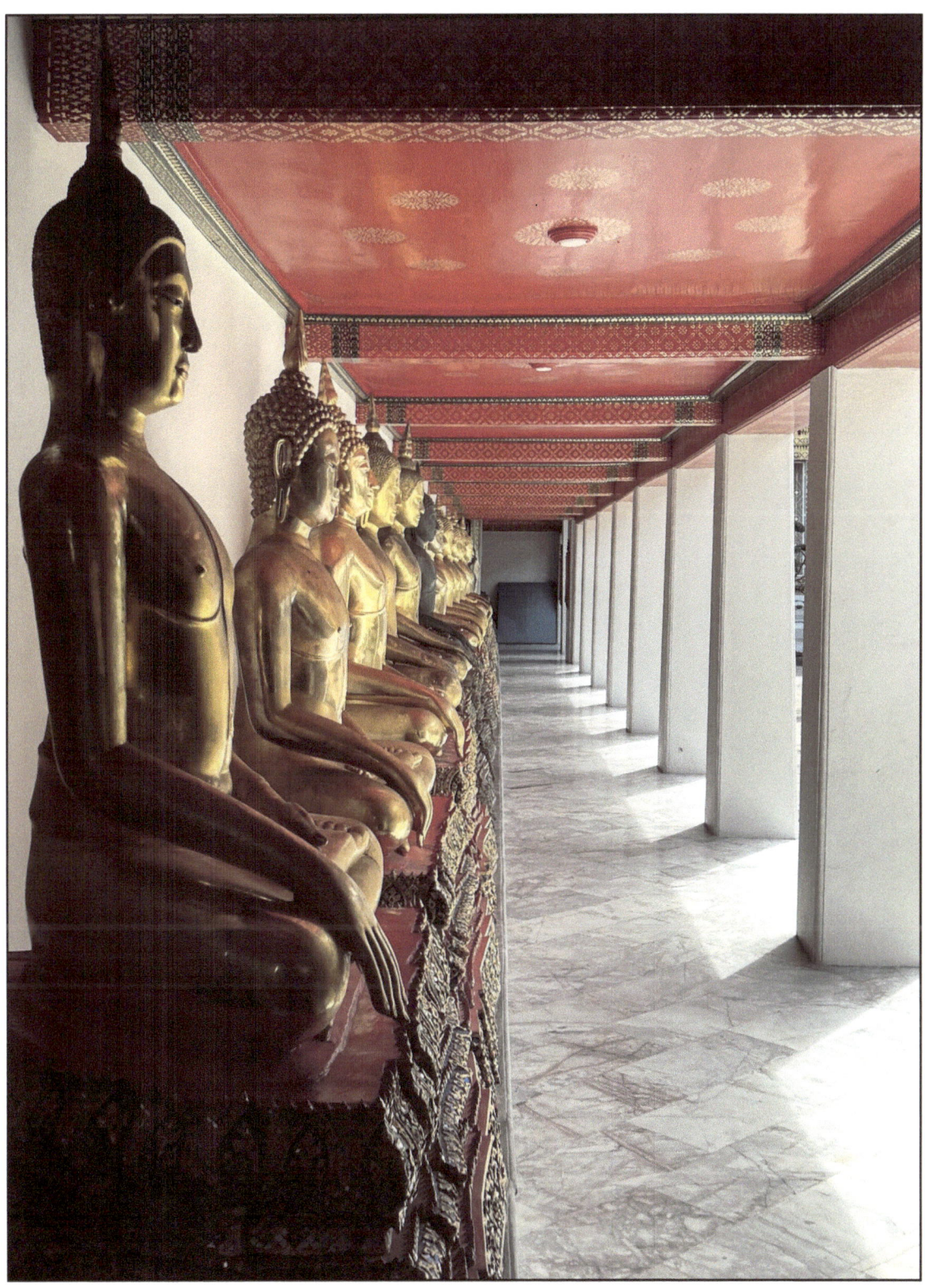

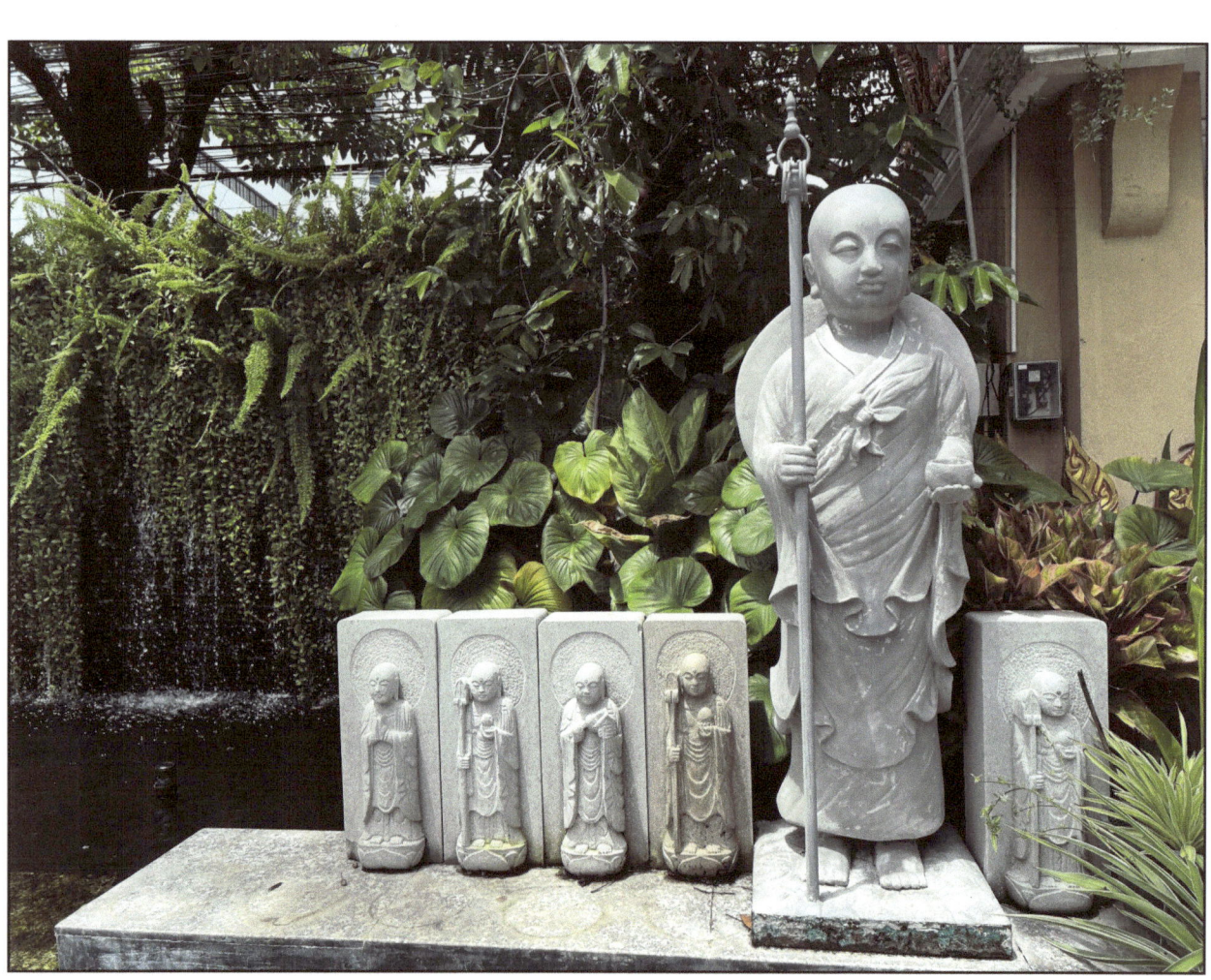

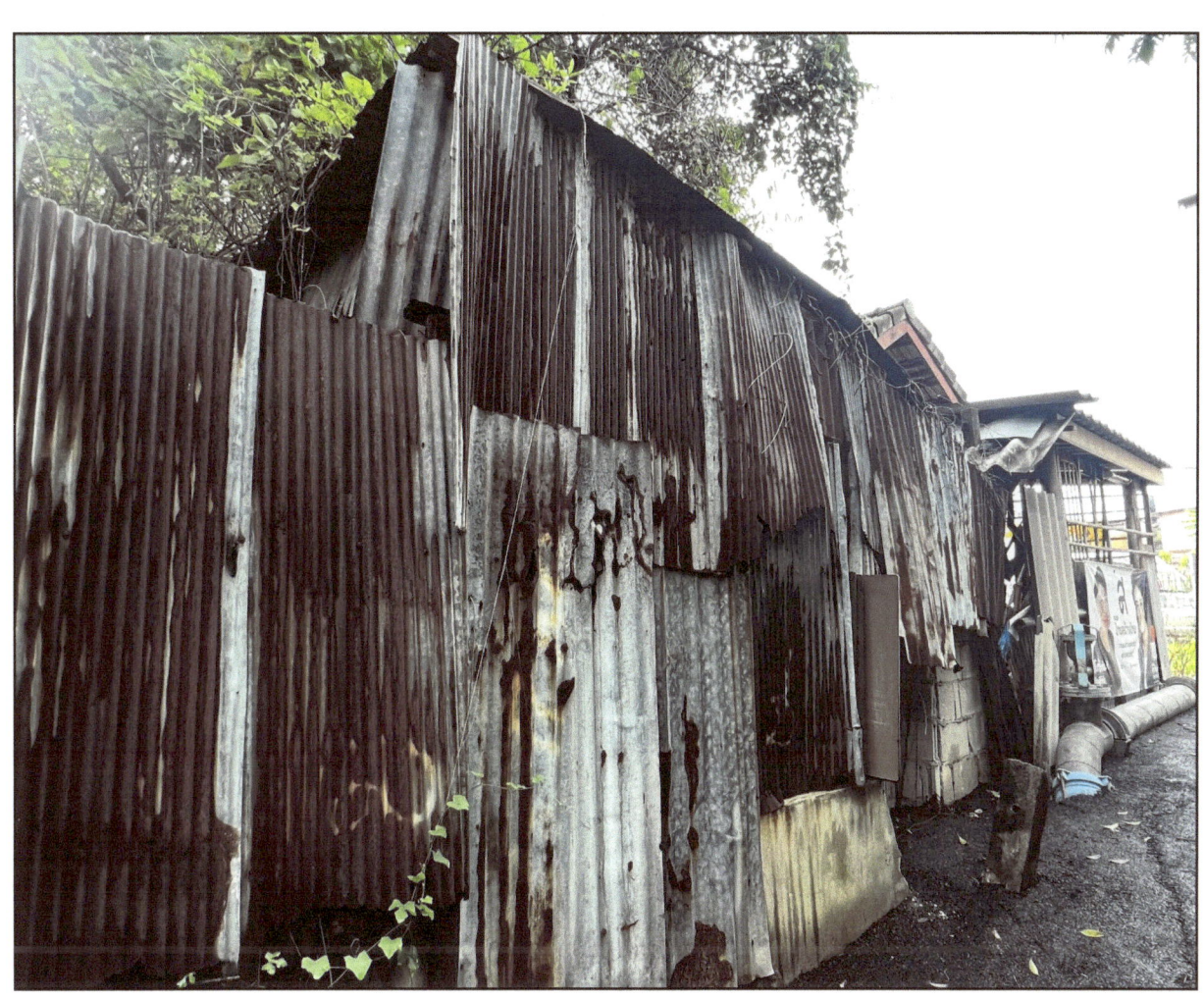

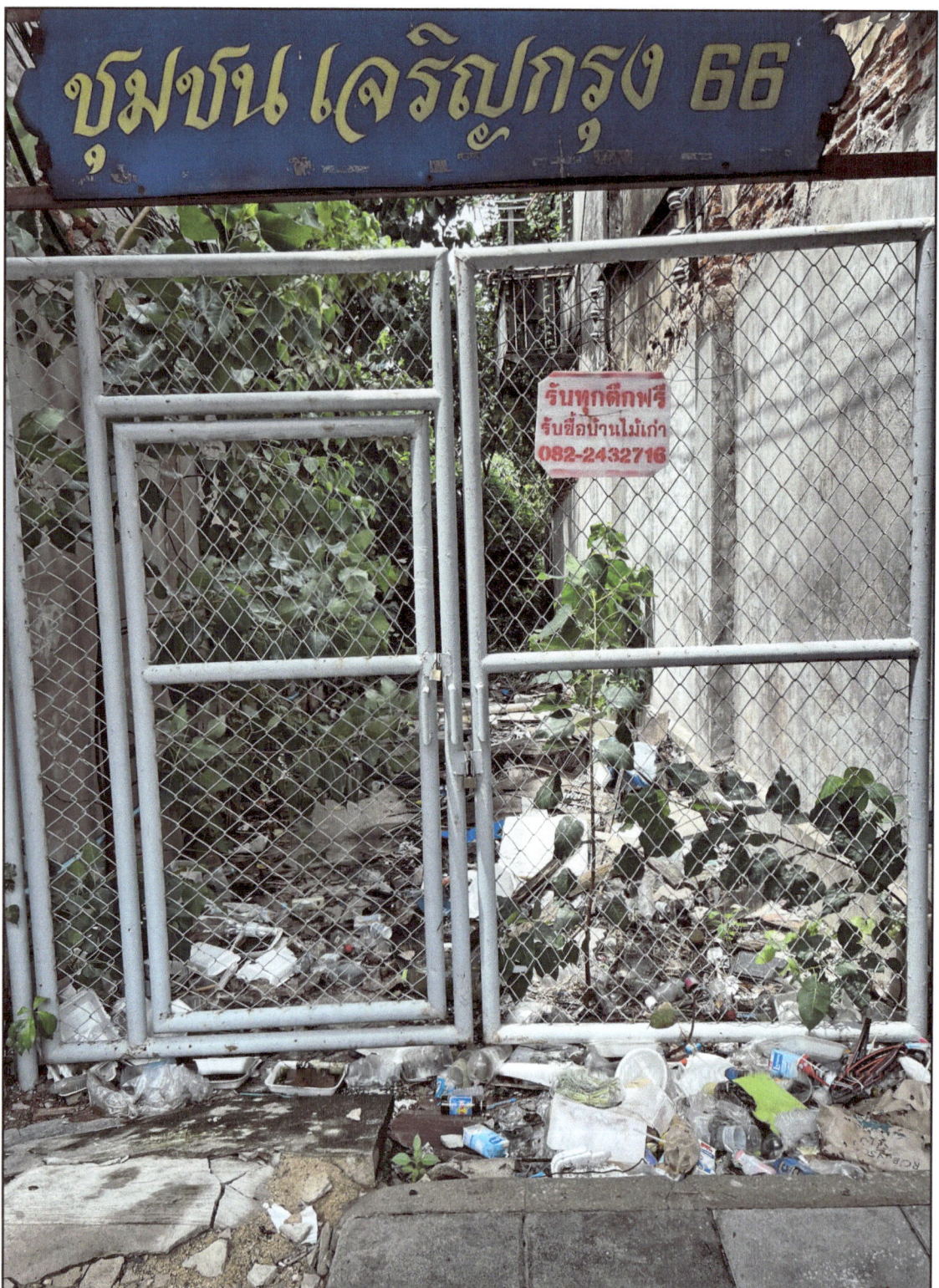

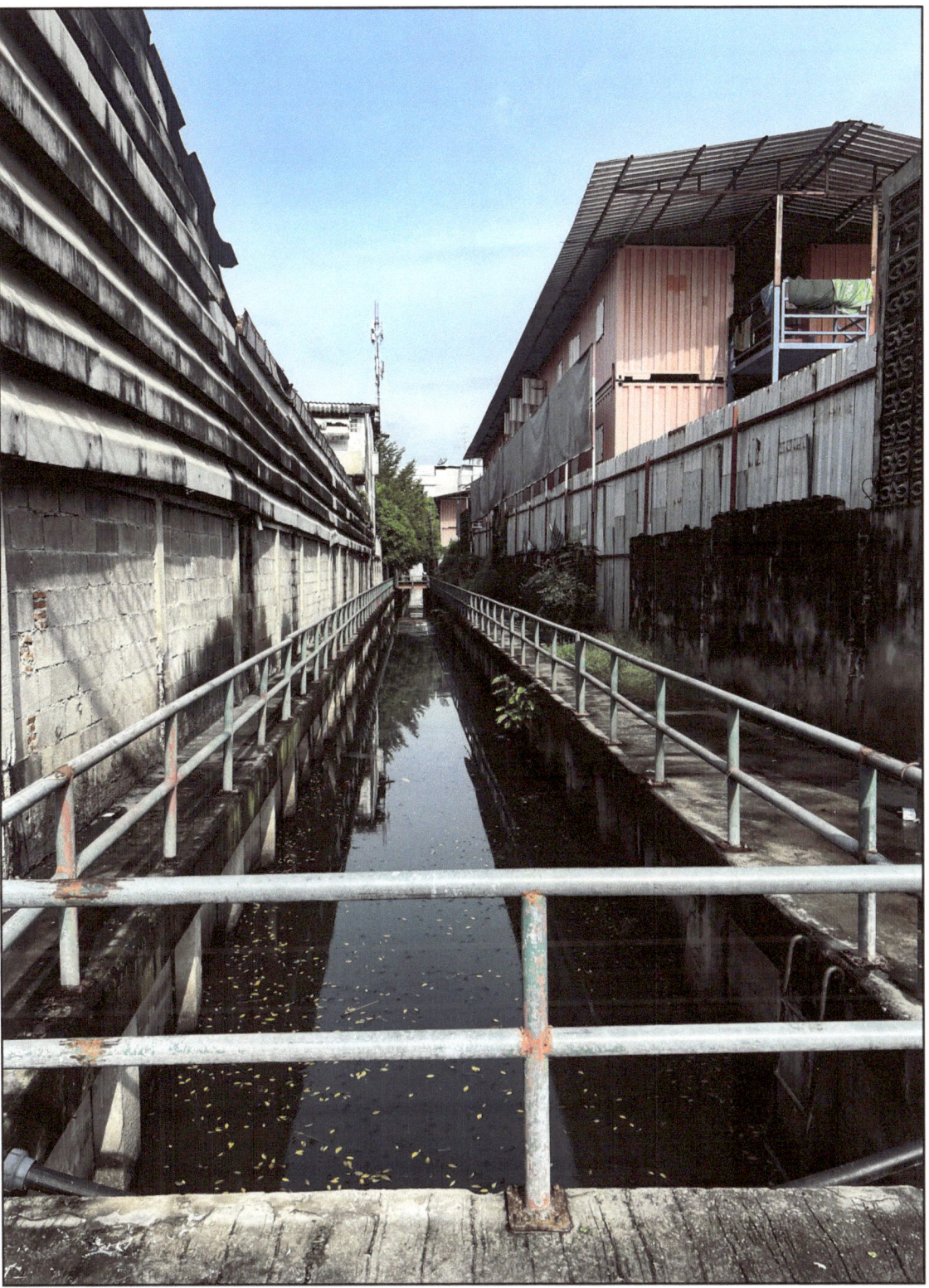

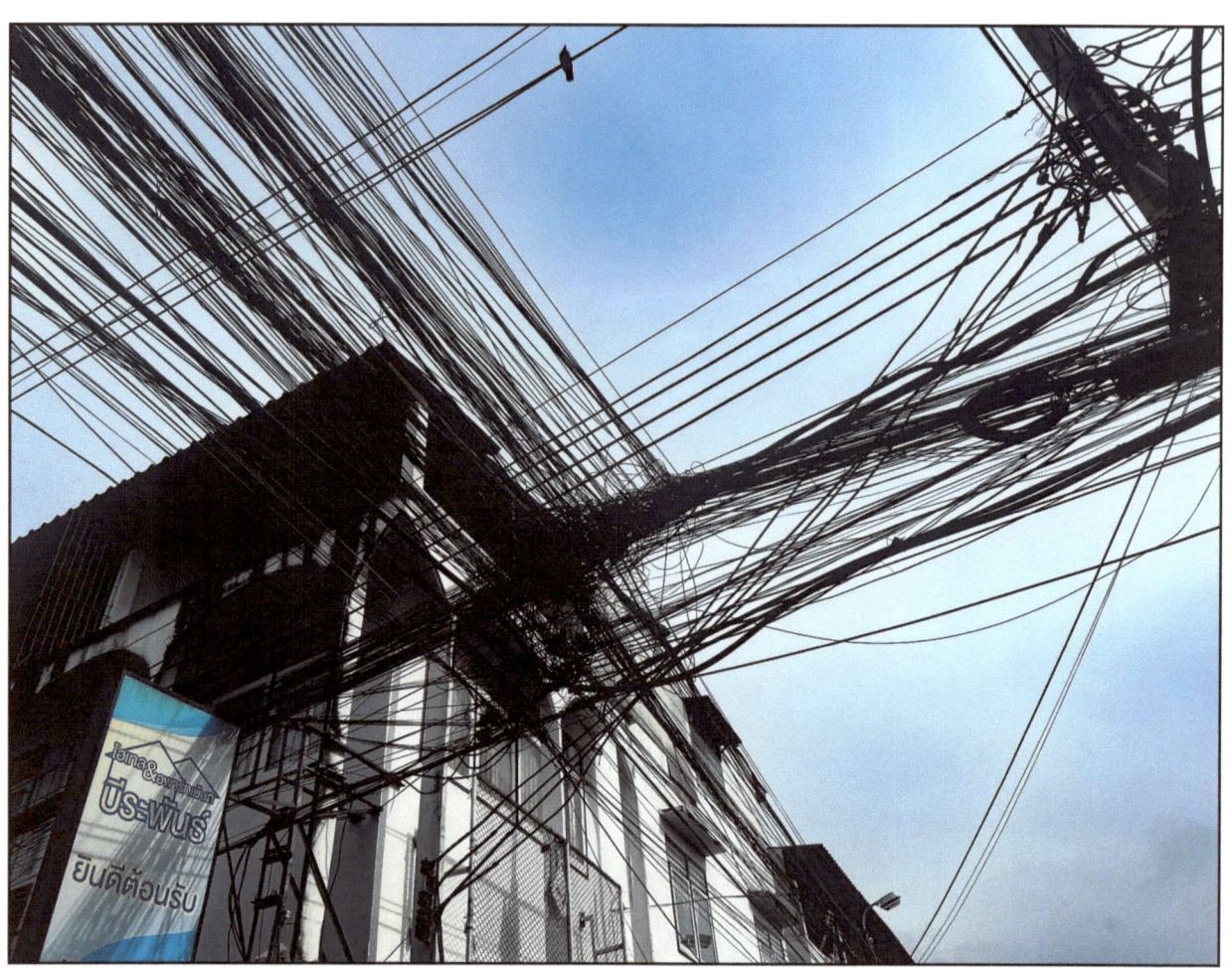

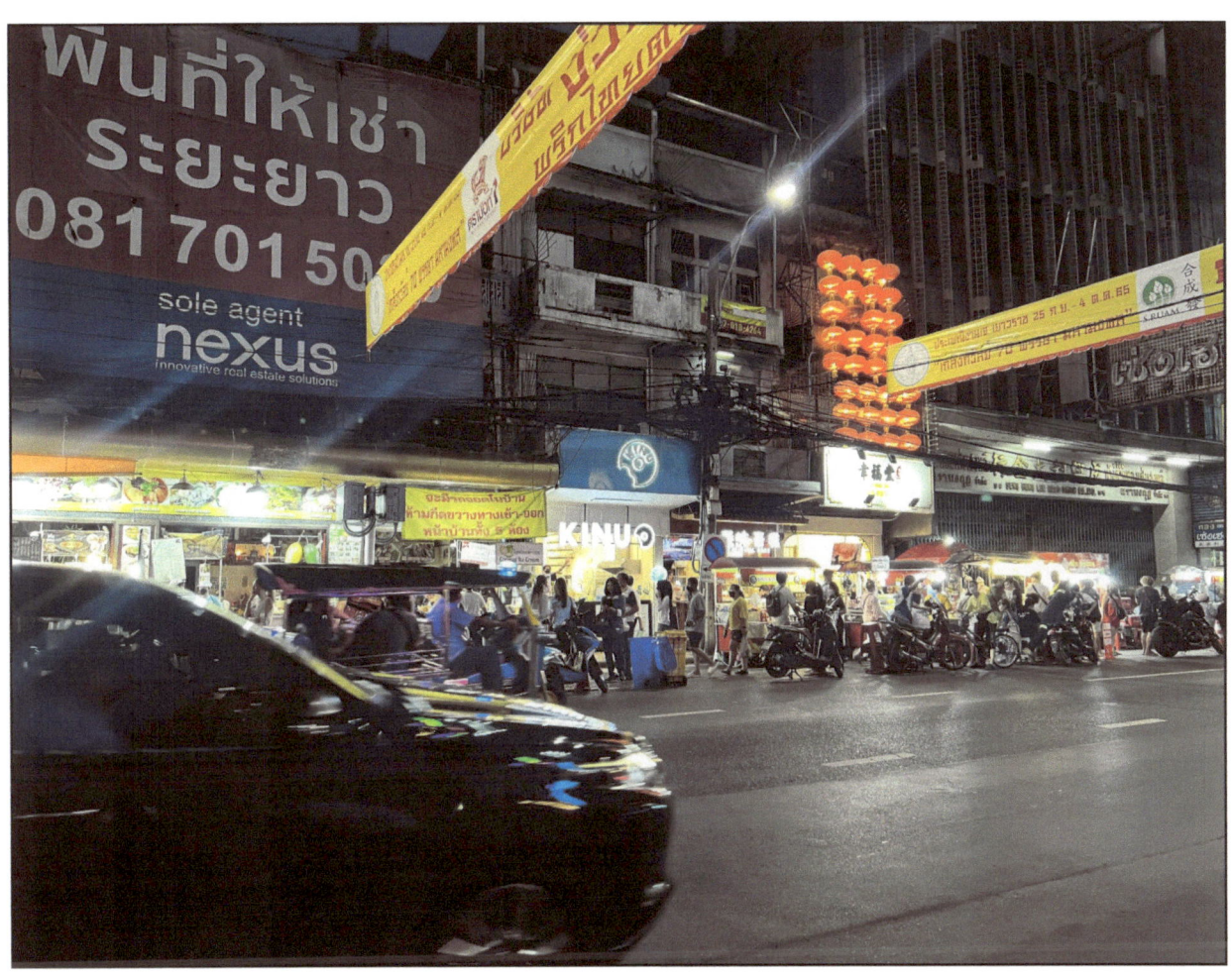

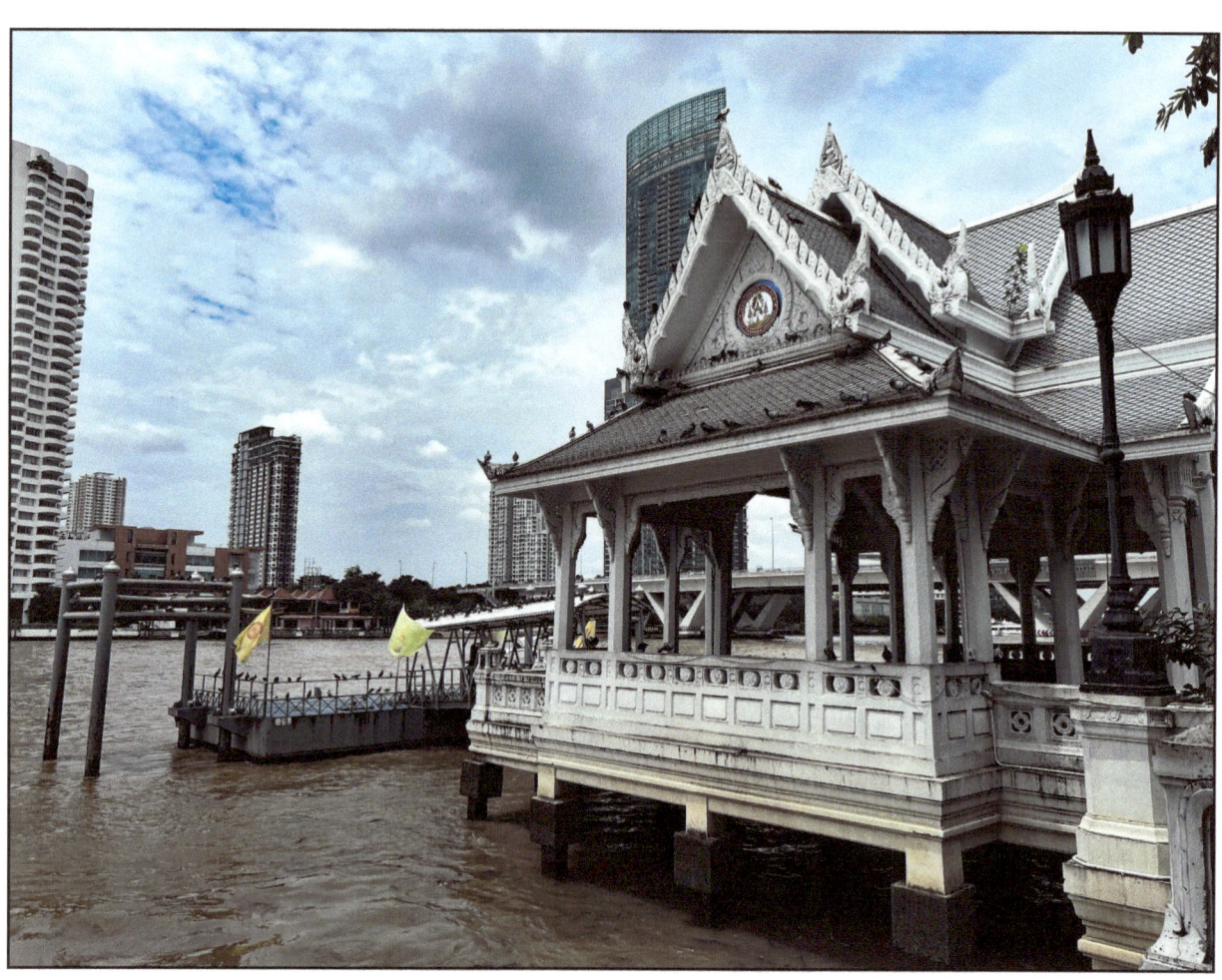

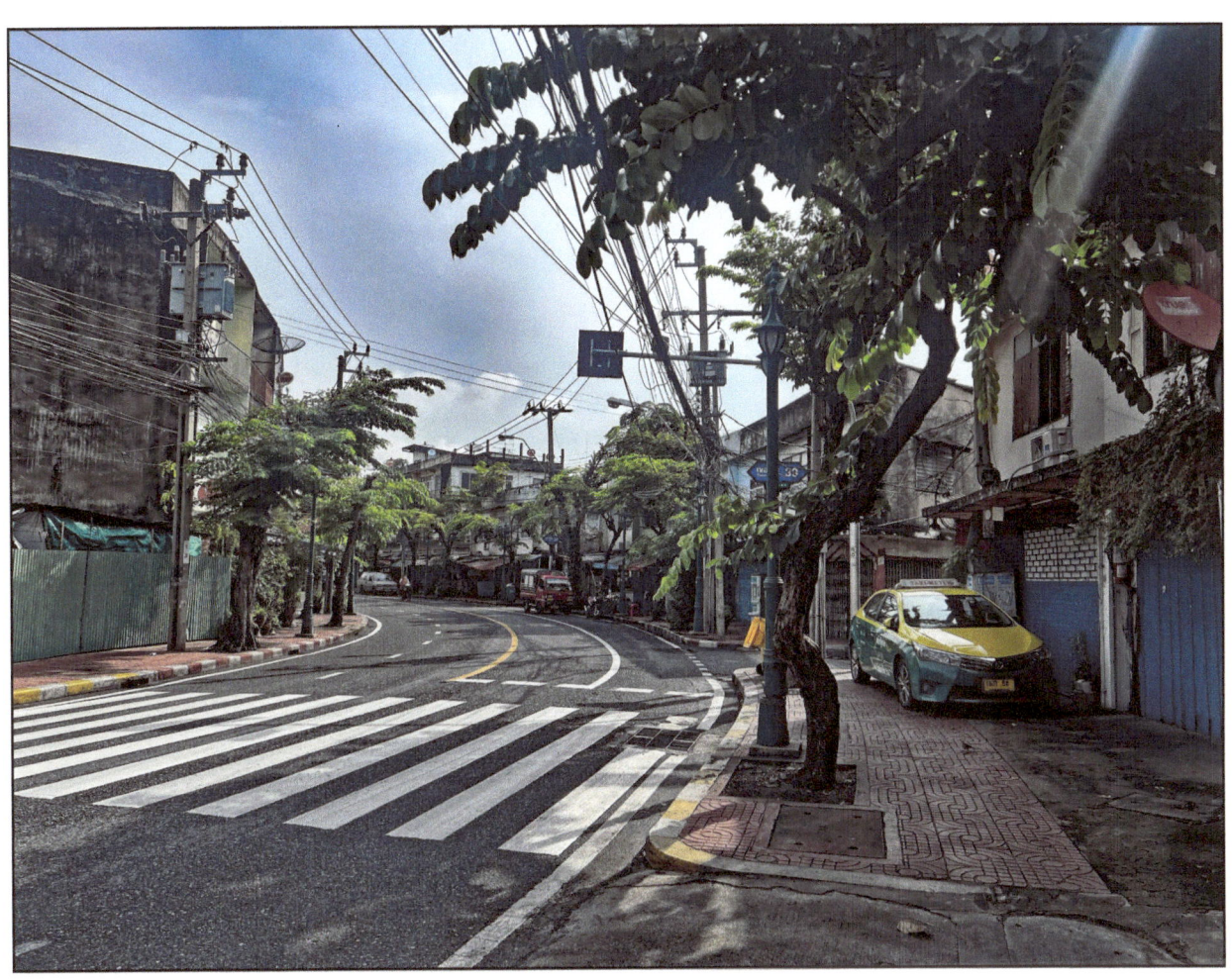

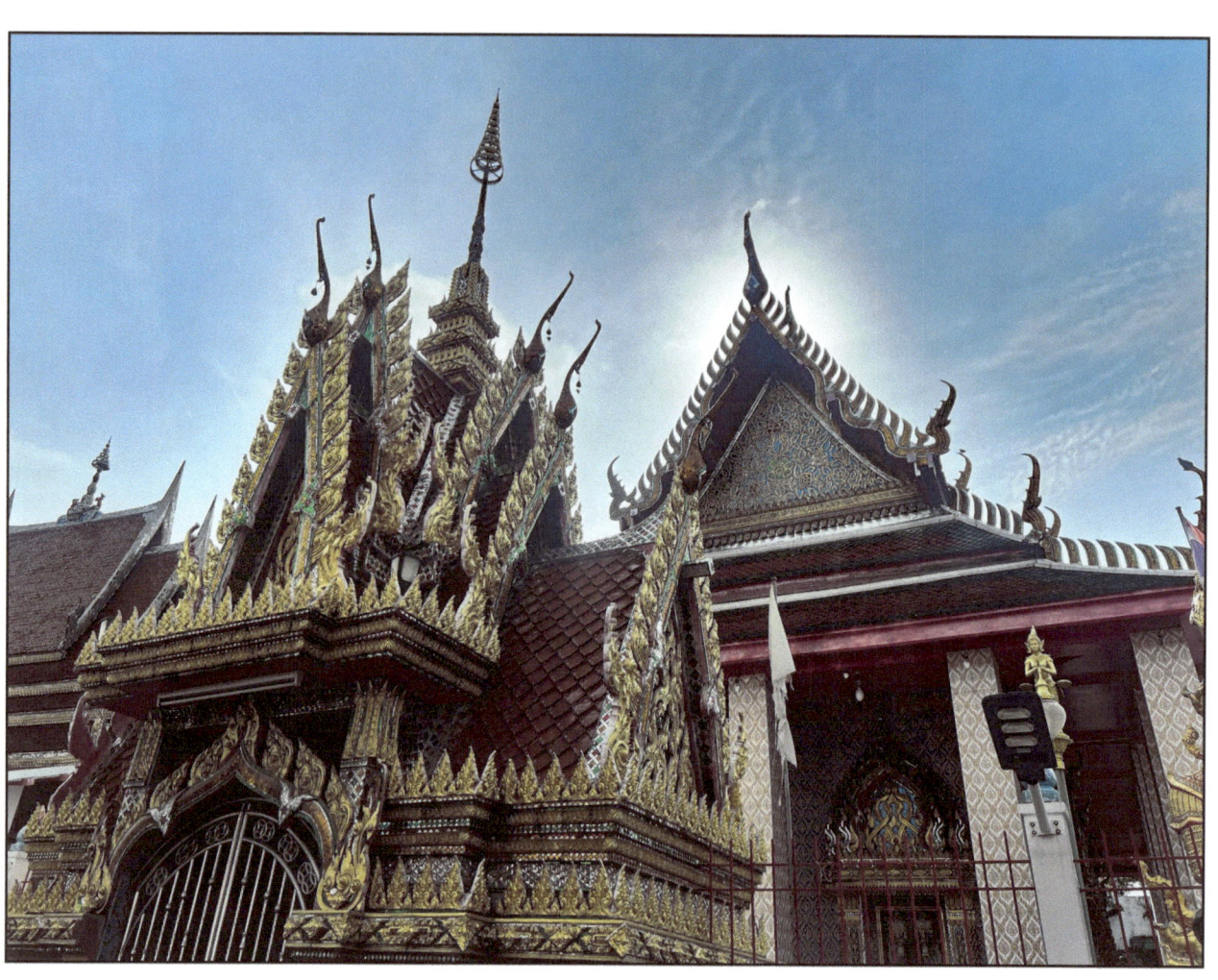

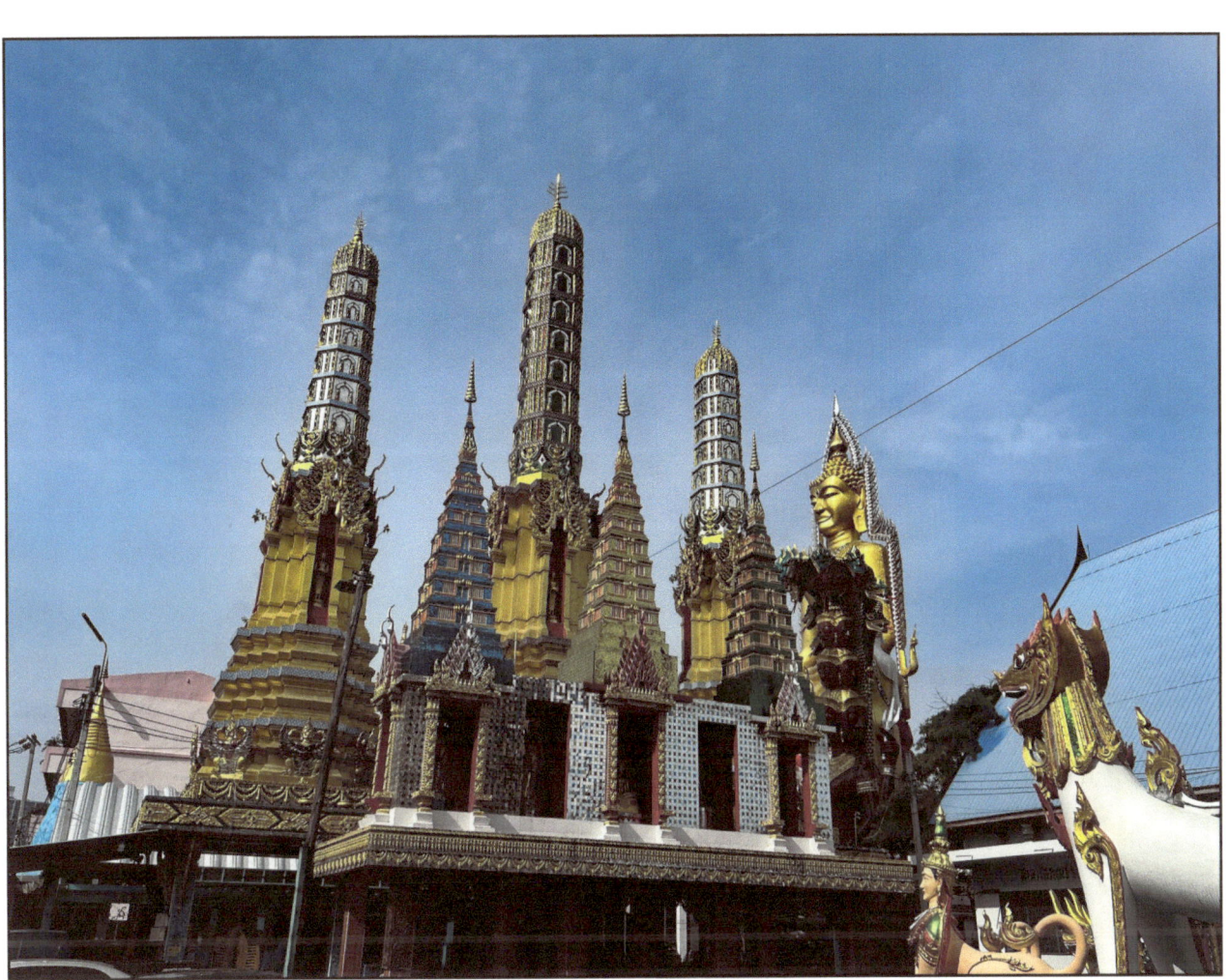

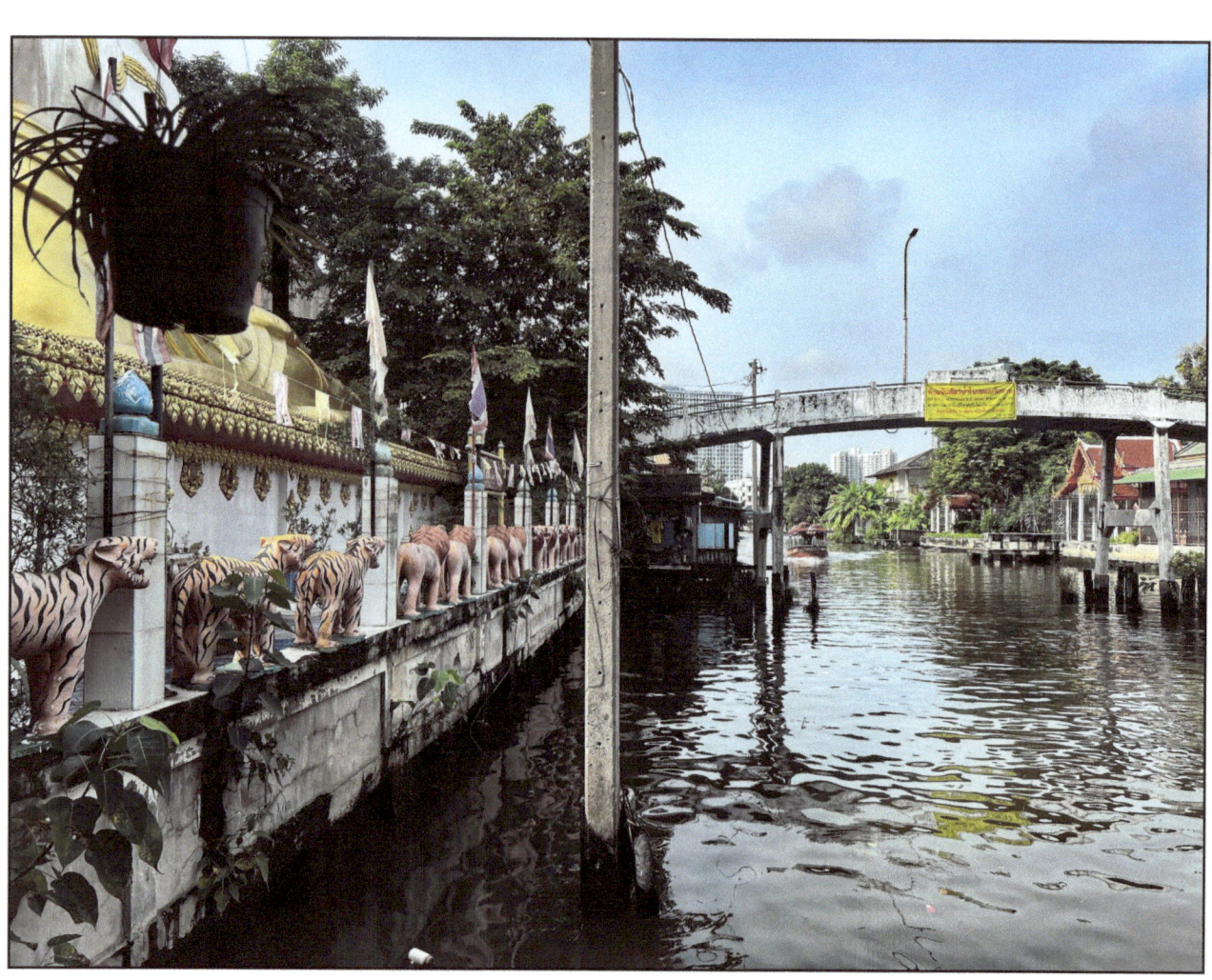

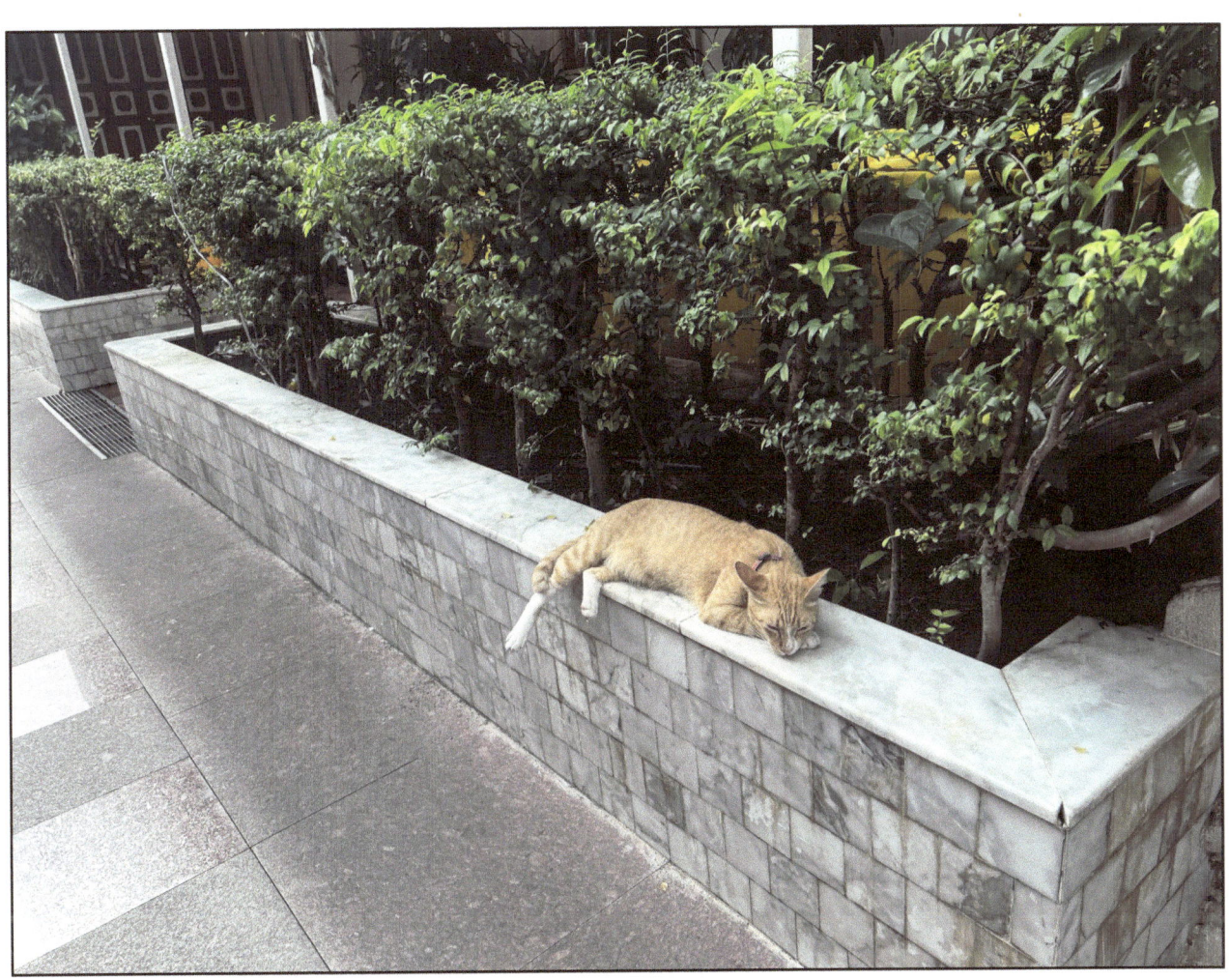

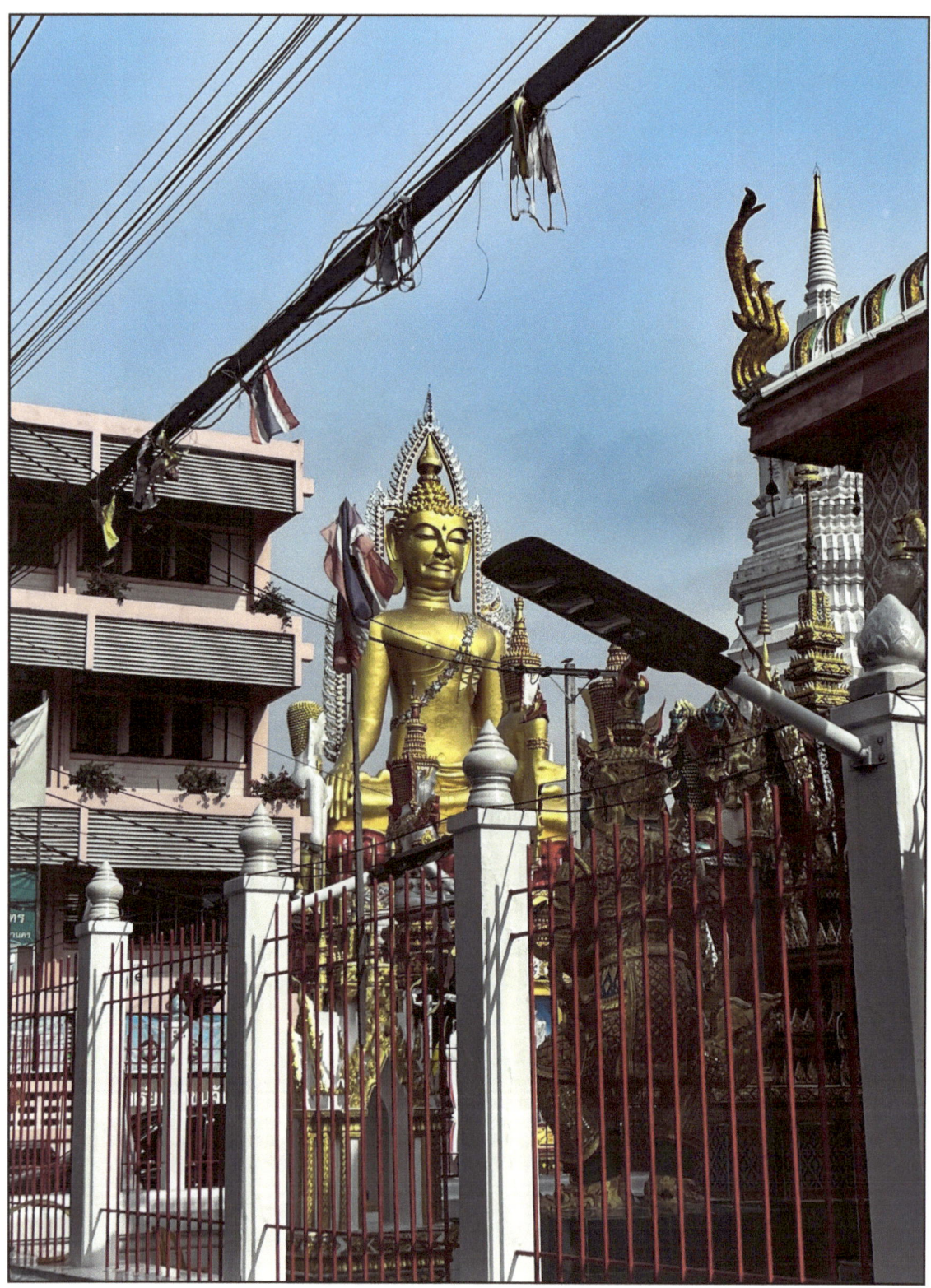

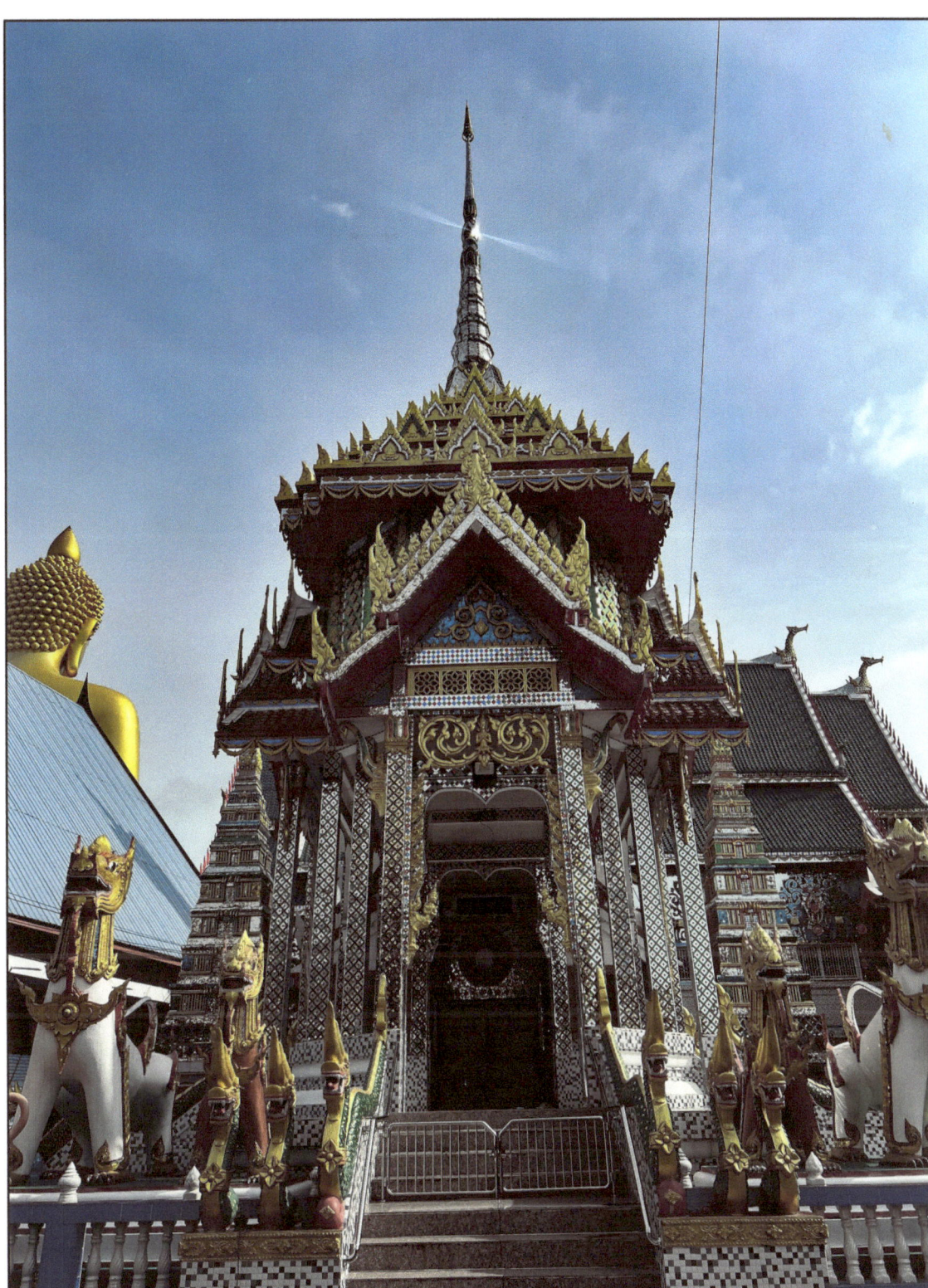

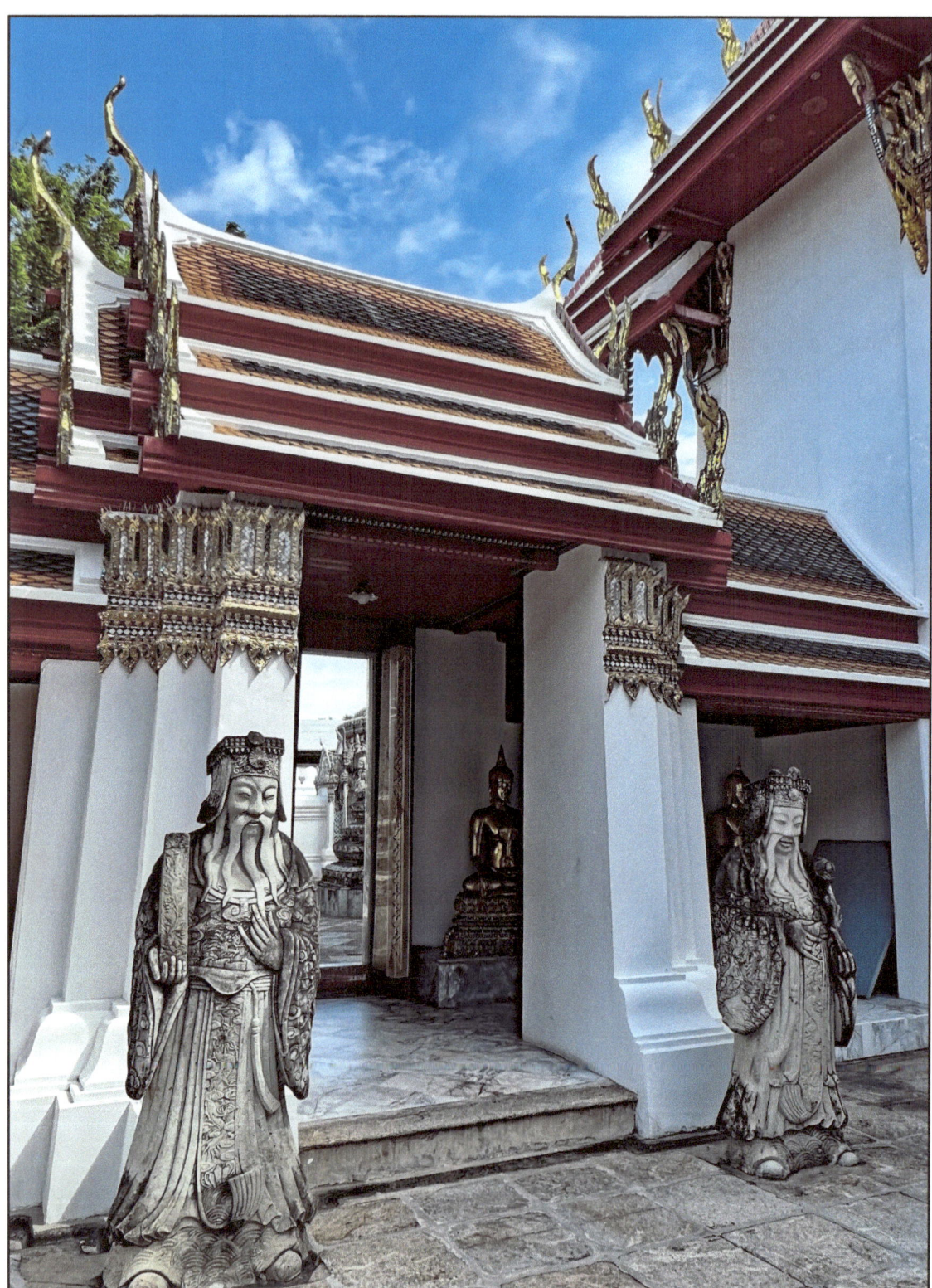

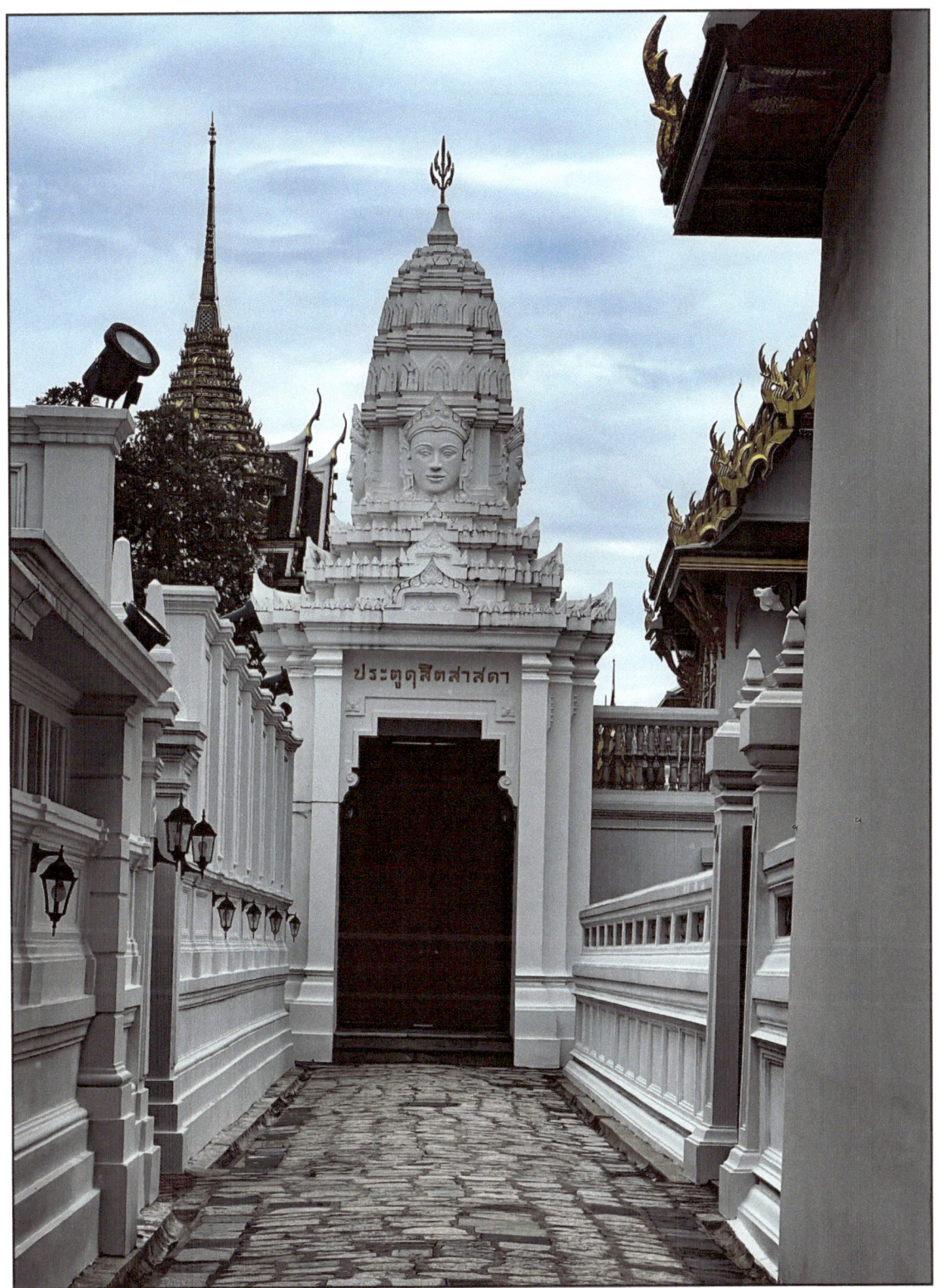

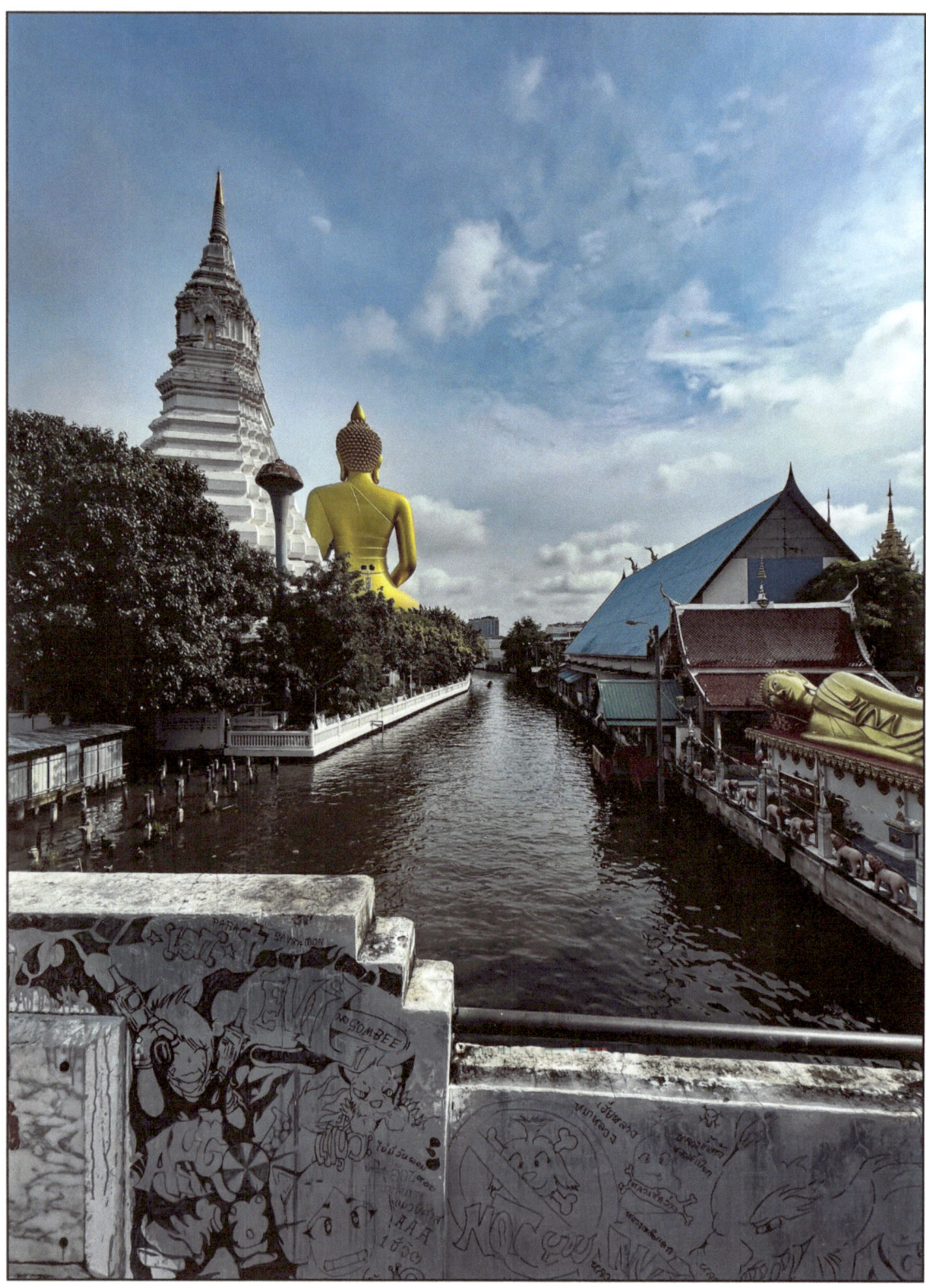

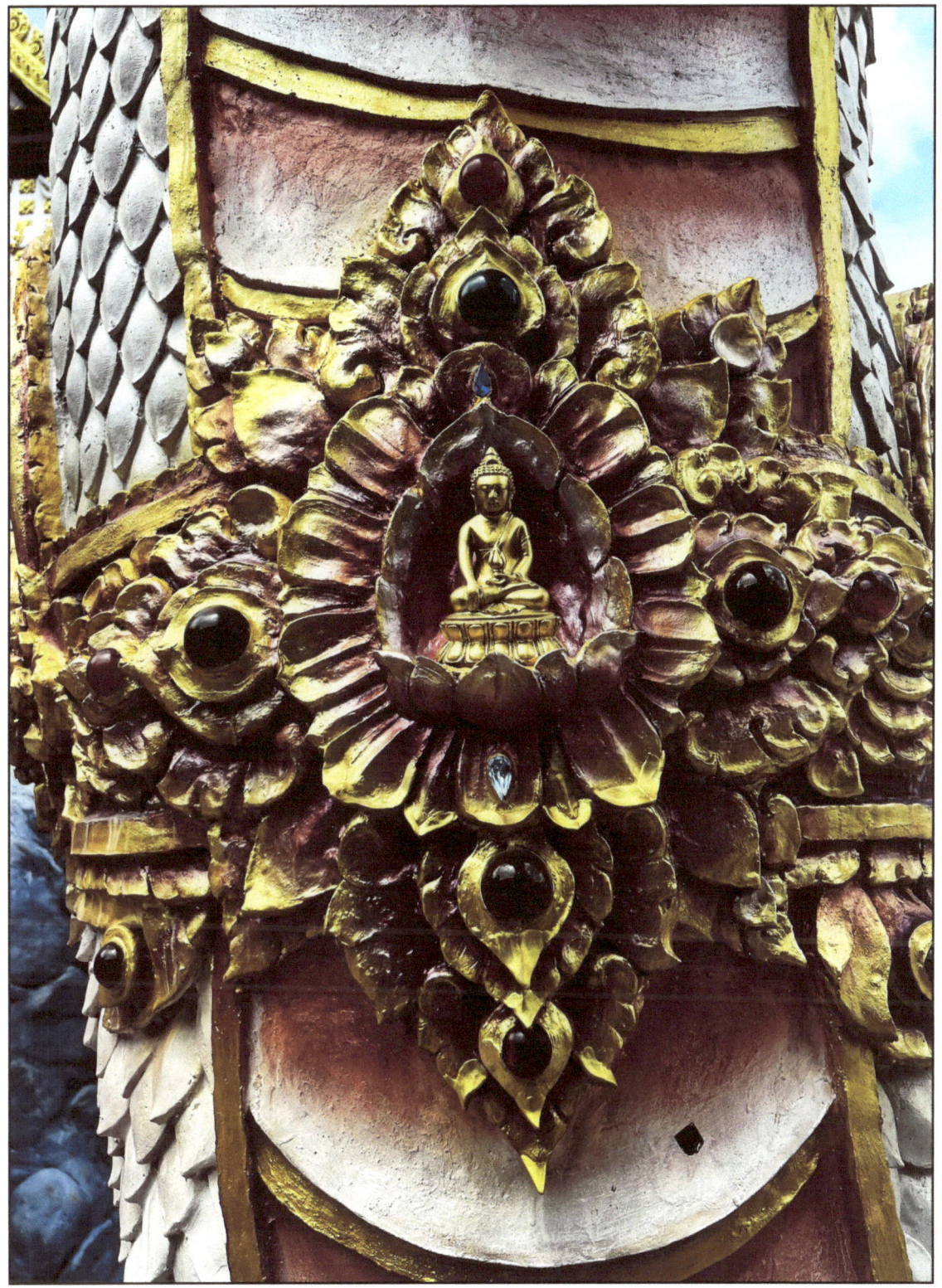

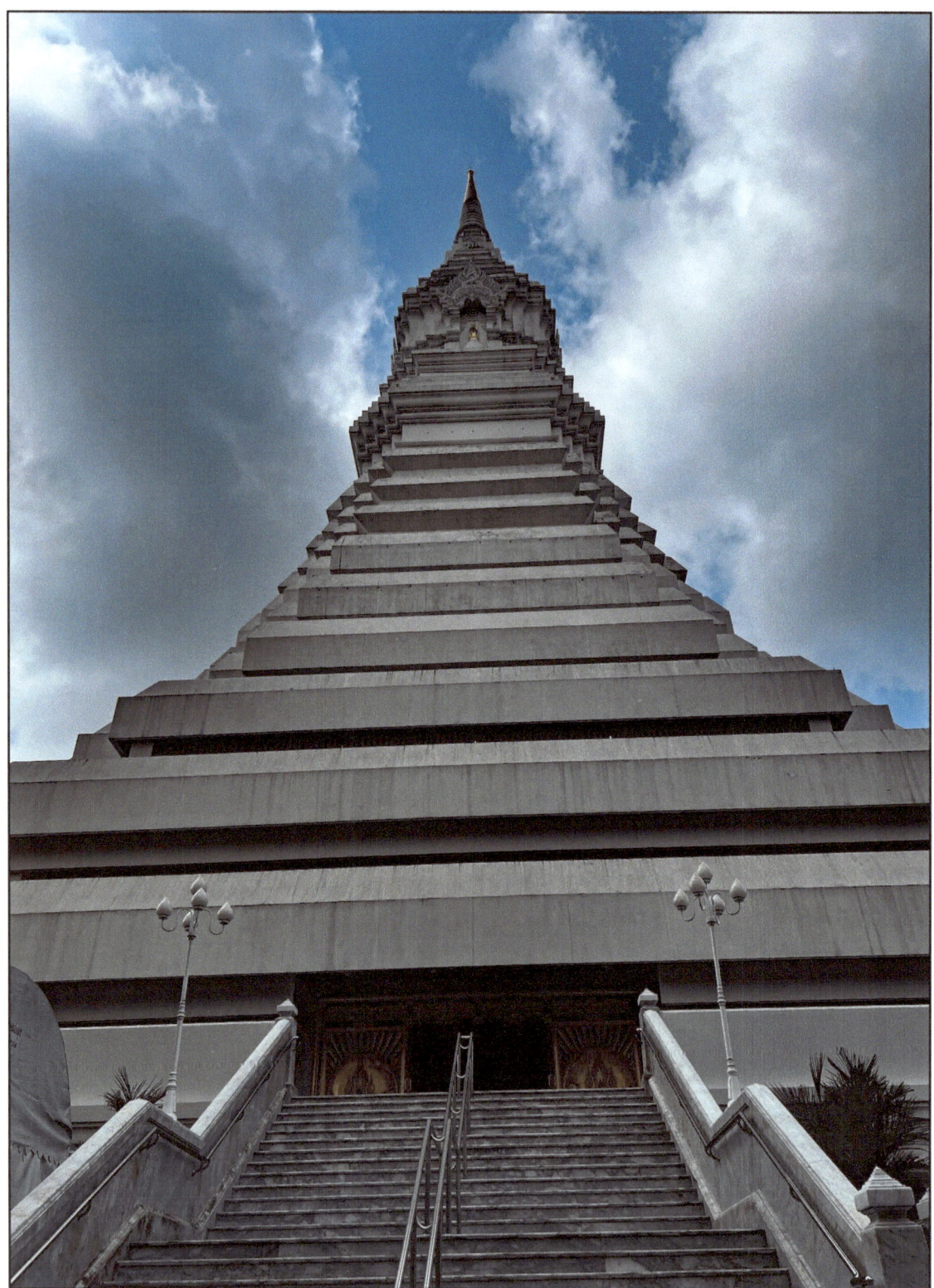

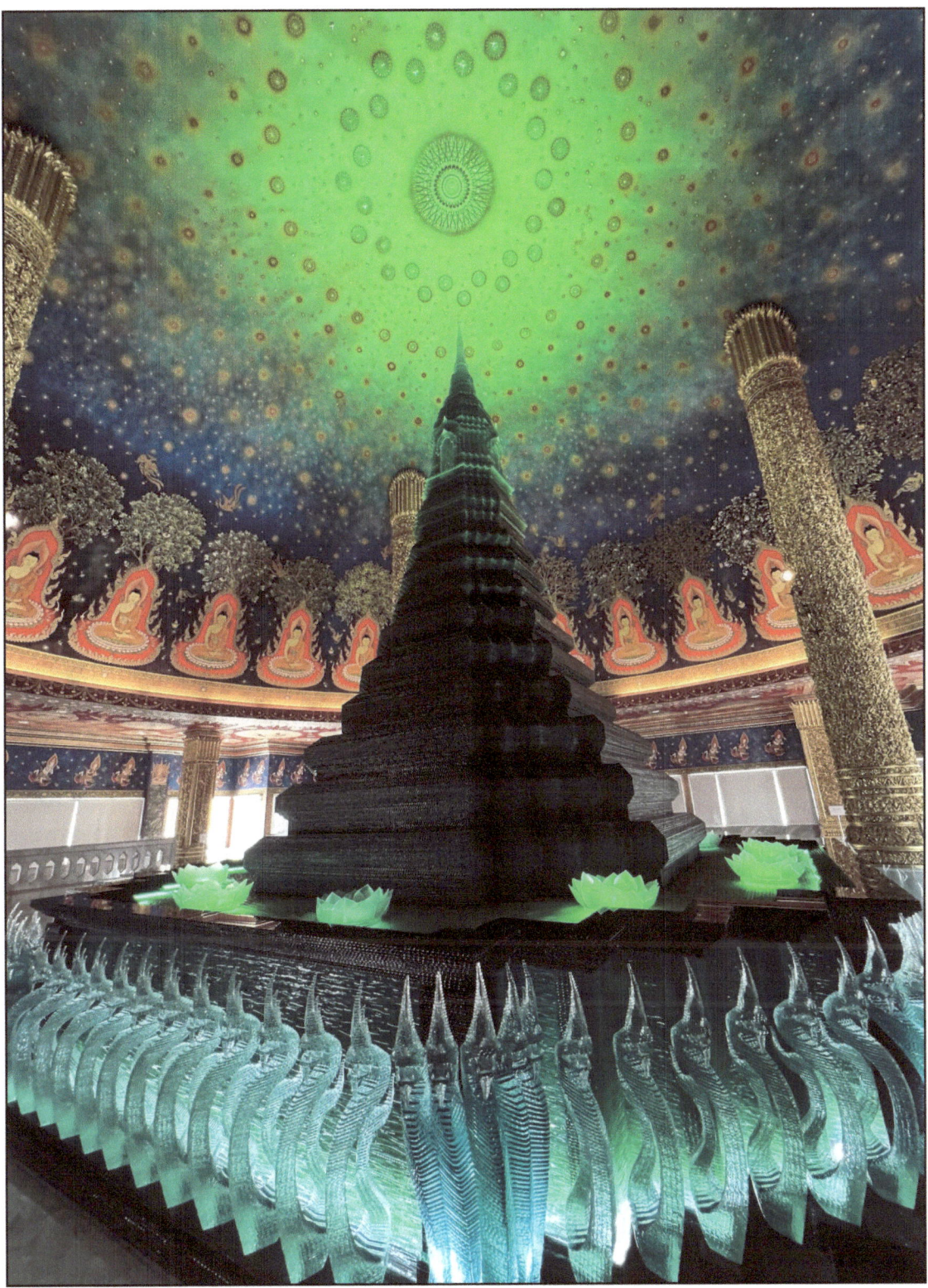

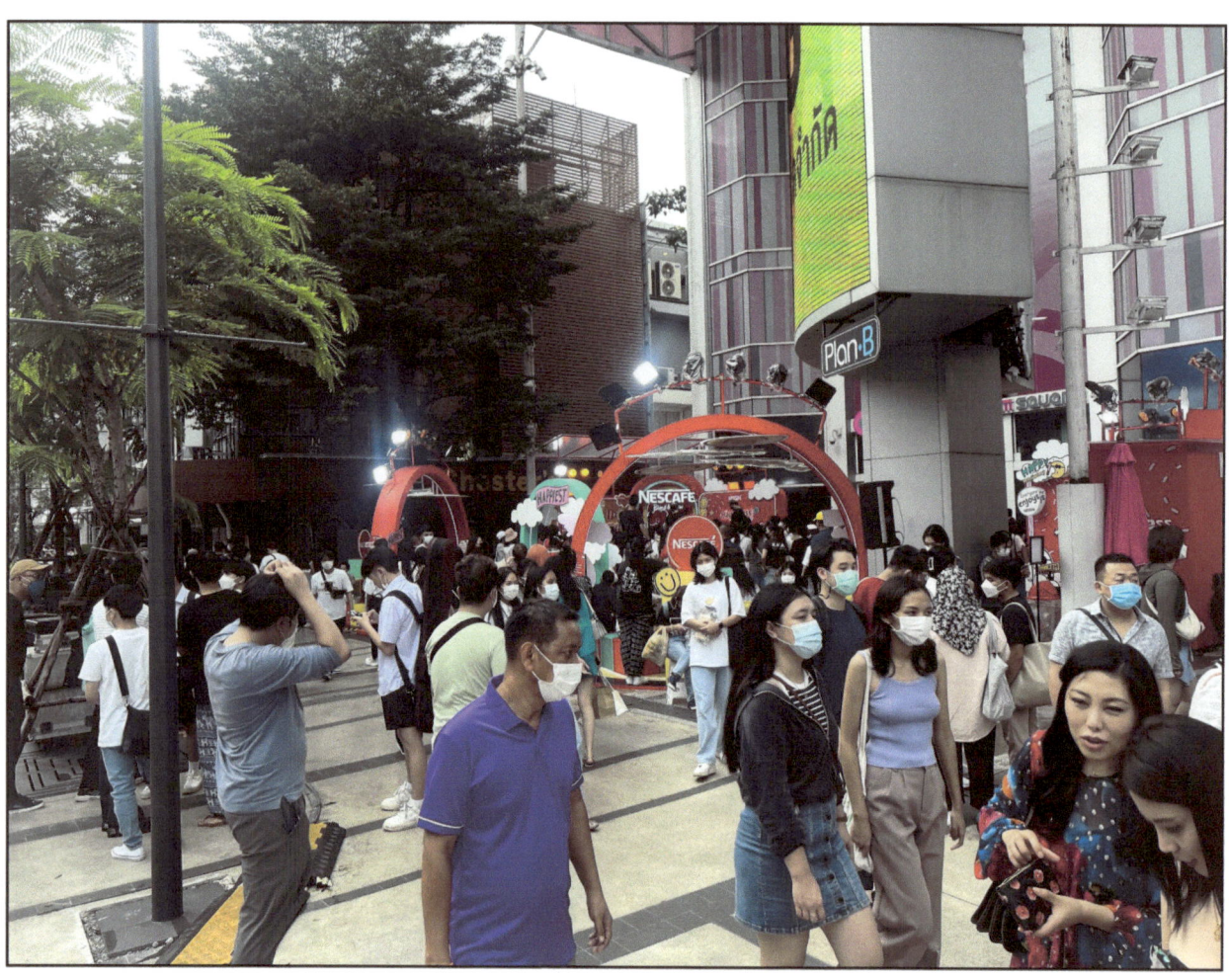

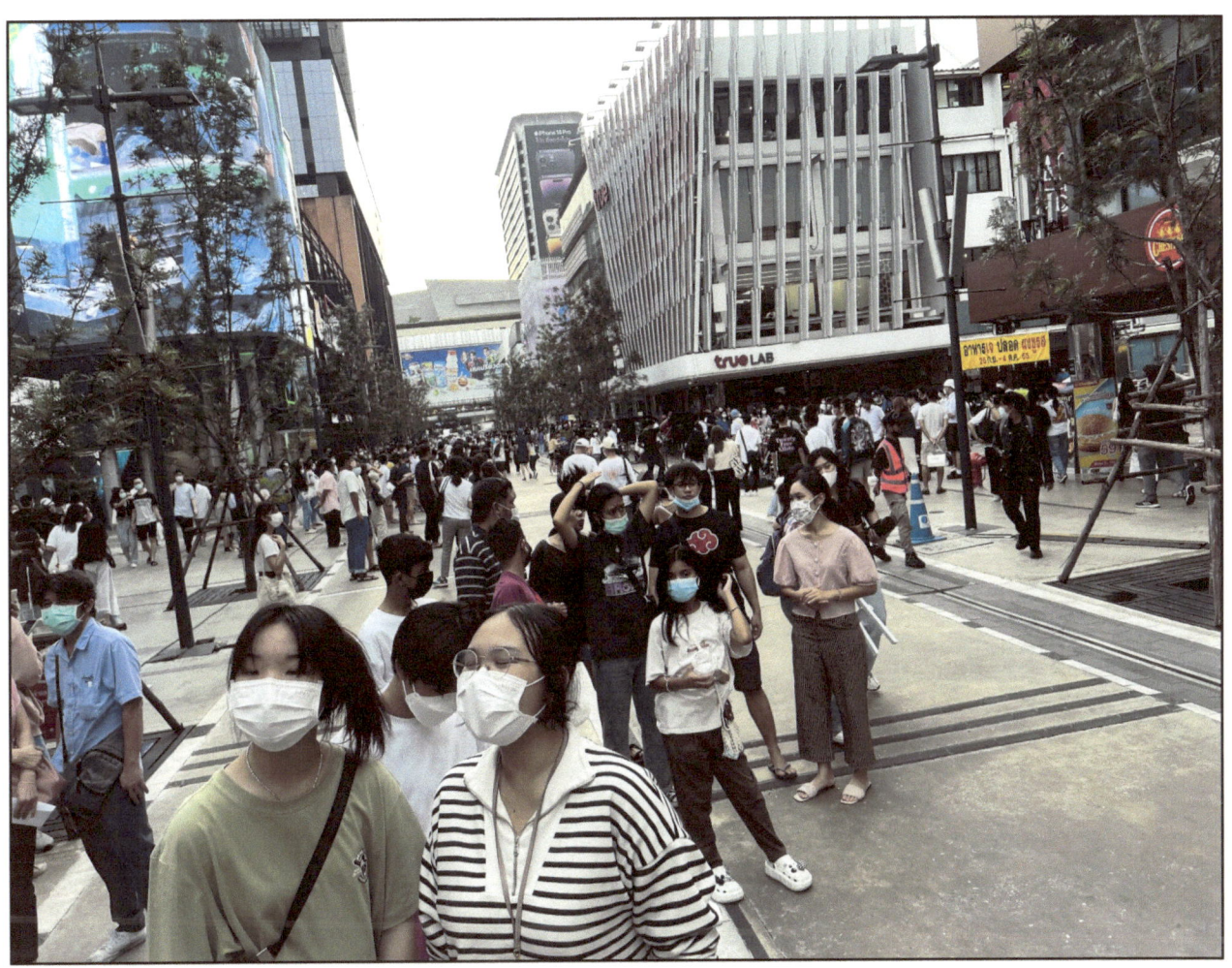

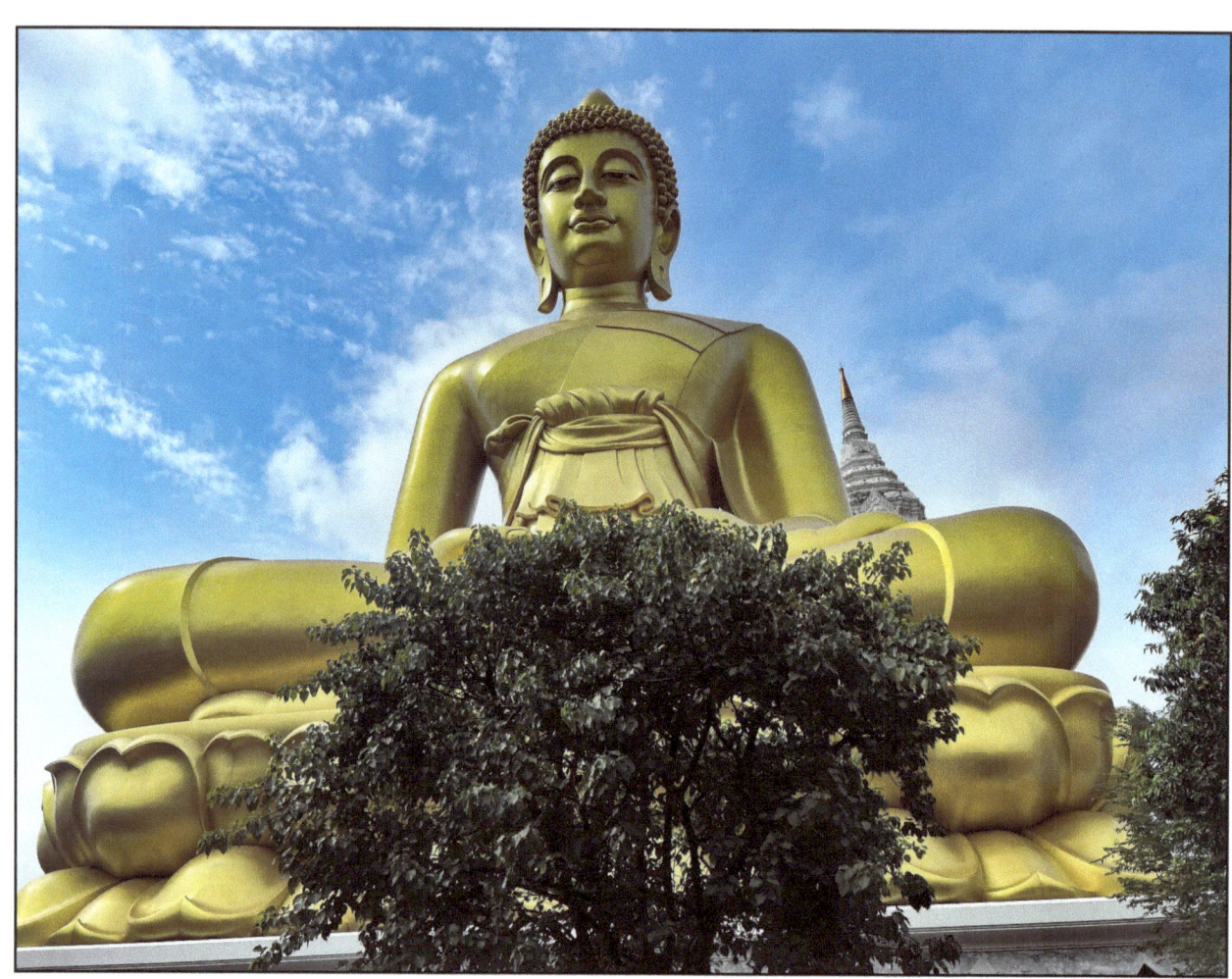

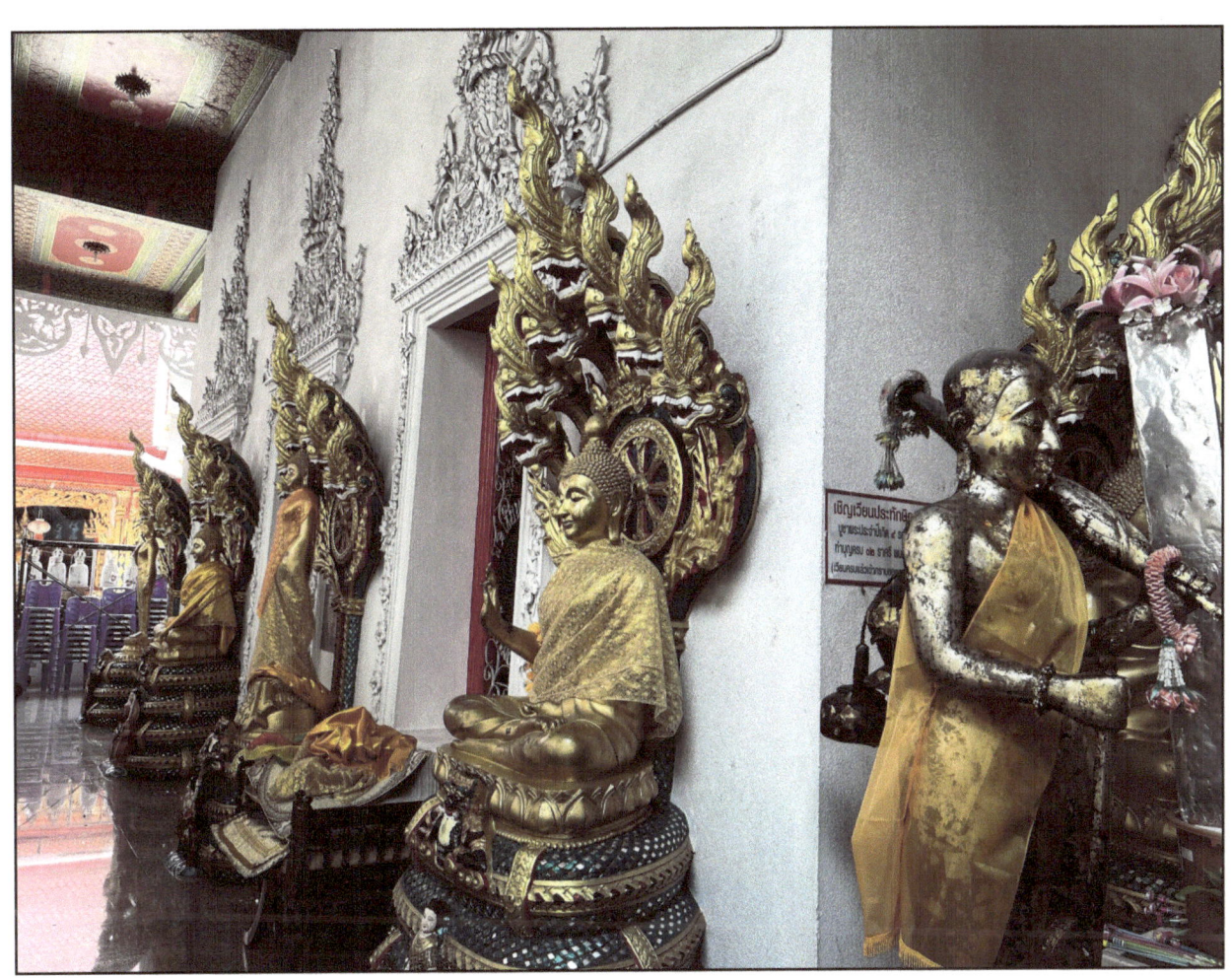

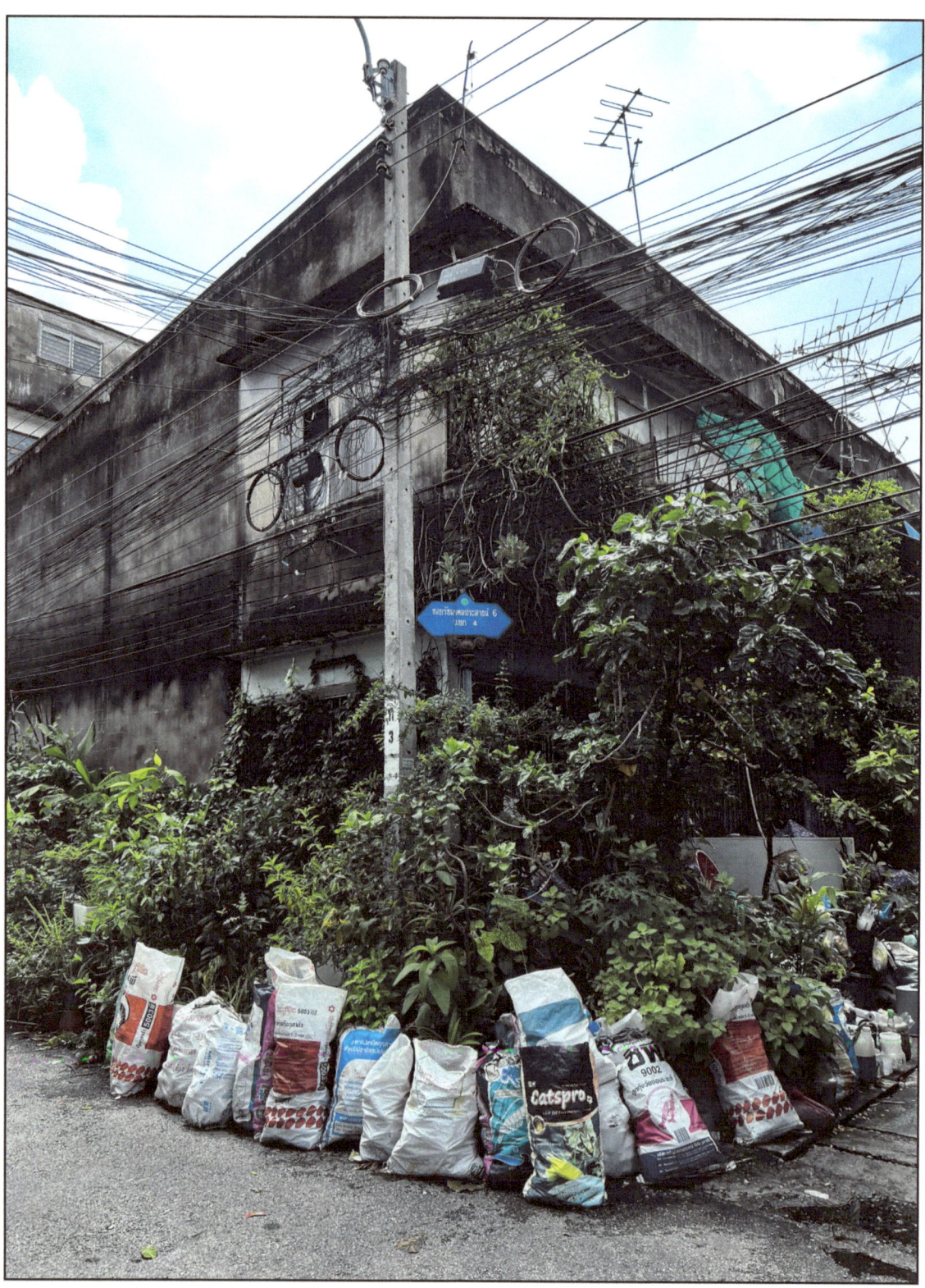

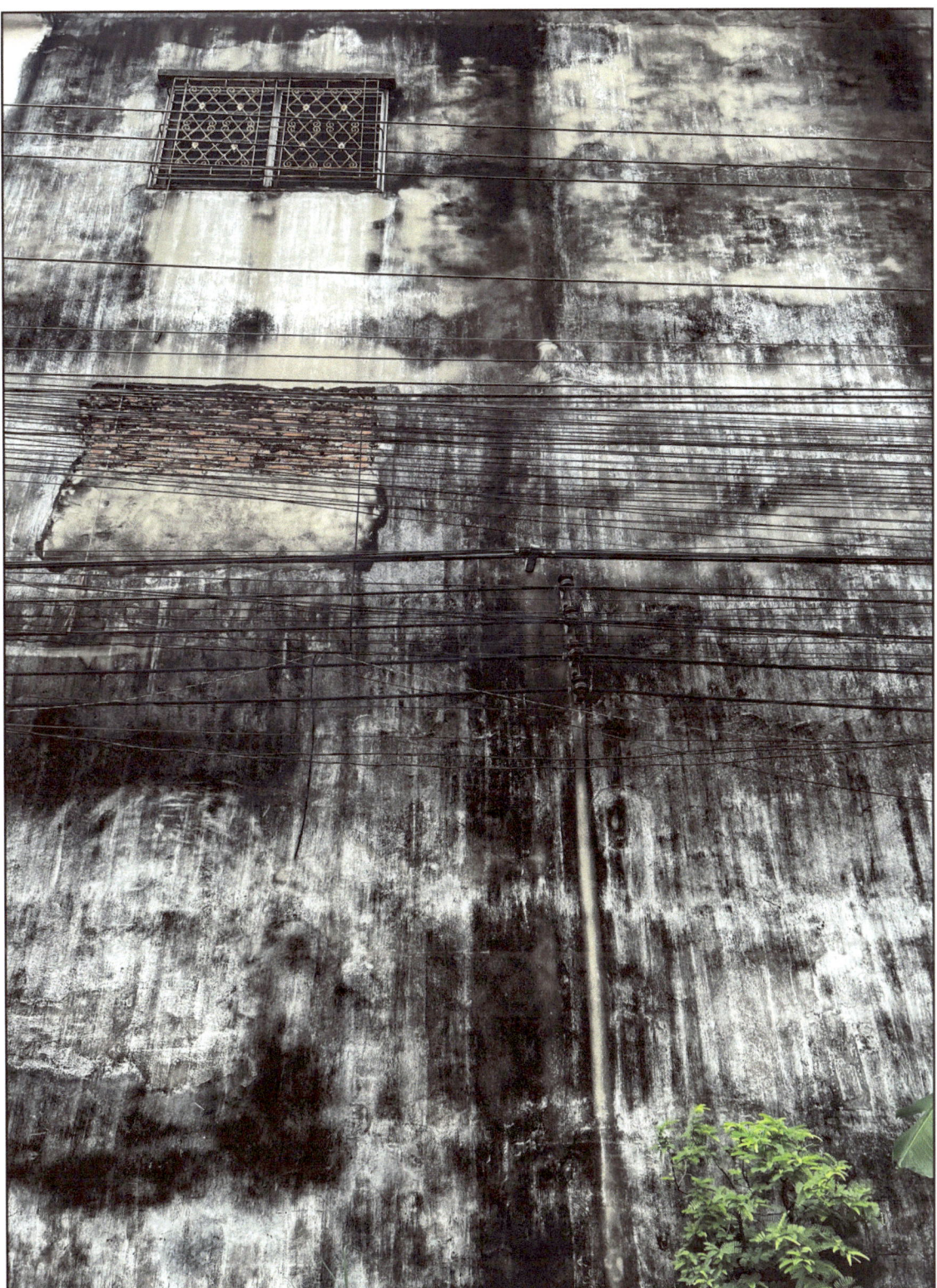

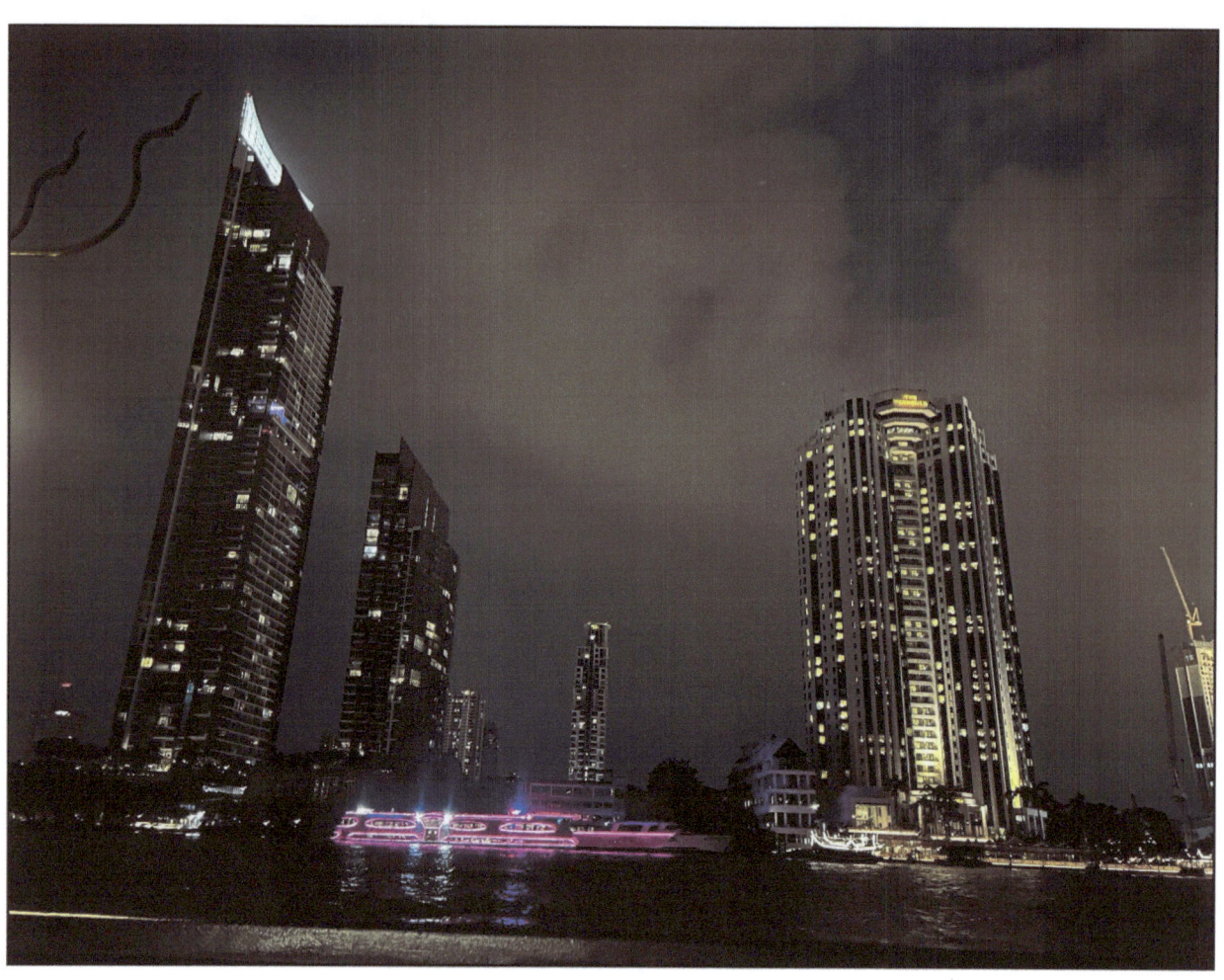

www.ingramcontent.com/pod-product-compliance
Lightning Source LLC
Chambersburg PA
CBHW051145220526
45473CB00003B/660